The law of copyright in works of literature and art and in the application of designs : with the statutes relating thereto.

Charles Palmer Phillips

The Making of Modern Law collection of legal archives constitutes a genuine revolution in historical legal research because it opens up a wealth of rare and previously inaccessible sources in legal, constitutional, administrative, political, cultural, intellectual, and social history. This unique collection consists of three extensive archives that provide insight into more than 300 years of American and British history. These collections include:

Legal Treatises, 1800-1926: over 20,000 legal treatises provide a comprehensive collection in legal history, business and economics, politics and government.

Trials, 1600-1926: nearly 10,000 titles reveal the drama of famous, infamous, and obscure courtroom cases in America and the British Empire across three centuries.

Primary Sources, 1620-1926: includes reports, statutes and regulations in American history, including early state codes, municipal ordinances, constitutional conventions and compilations, and law dictionaries.

These archives provide a unique research tool for tracking the development of our modern legal system and how it has affected our culture, government, business – nearly every aspect of our everyday life. For the first time, these high-quality digital scans of original works are available via print-on-demand, making them readily accessible to libraries, students, independent scholars, and readers of all ages.

The BiblioLife Network

This project was made possible in part by the BiblioLife Network (BLN), a project aimed at addressing some of the huge challenges facing book preservationists around the world. The BLN includes libraries, library networks, archives, subject matter experts, online communities and library service providers. We believe every book ever published should be available as a high-quality print reproduction; printed on-demand anywhere in the world. This insures the ongoing accessibility of the content and helps generate sustainable revenue for the libraries and organizations that work to preserve these important materials.

The following book is in the "public domain" and represents an authentic reproduction of the text as printed by the original publisher. While we have attempted to accurately maintain the integrity of the original work, there are sometimes problems with the original work or the micro-film from which the books were digitized. This can result in minor errors in reproduction. Possible imperfections include missing and blurred pages, poor pictures, markings and other reproduction issues beyond our control. Because this work is culturally important, we have made it available as part of our commitment to protecting, preserving, and promoting the world's literature.

GUIDE TO FOLD-OUTS MAPS and OVERSIZED IMAGES

The book you are reading was digitized from microfilm captured over the past thirty to forty years. Years after the creation of the original microfilm, the book was converted to digital files and made available in an online database.

In an online database, page images do not need to conform to the size restrictions found in a printed book. When converting these images back into a printed bound book, the page sizes are standardized in ways that maintain the detail of the original. For large images, such as fold-out maps, the original page image is split into two or more pages

Guidelines used to determine how to split the page image follows:

• Some images are split vertically; large images require vertical and horizontal splits.
• For horizontal splits, the content is split left to right.
• For vertical splits, the content is split from top to bottom.
• For both vertical and horizontal splits, the image is processed from top left to bottom right.

Addison on Wrongs and their Remedies; being a Treatise
on the Law of Torts *Fourth Edition* By L. F. WOLFERSTAN, Esq., Barrister
at Law *Medium 8vo* 1870. *Price 1l 18s cloth*

Roscoe's Digest of the Law of Evidence on the Trial of
Actions at Nisi Prius *Twelfth Edition* By JOHN DAY and MAURICE POWELL,
Esqrs, Barristers at Law *In royal 12mo* 1870. *Price 1l 15s cloth.*

Smith's Real and Personal Property.—A Compendium of
the Law of Real and Personal Property Primarily Connected with Conveyancing.
Designed as a Second Book for Students, and as a Digest of the Most Useful Learning
for Practitioners By JOSIAH W SMITH, B C L, Q C, Judge of County Courts.
Fourth Edition In 2 vols demy 8vo 1870. *Price 1l 18s cloth*

Tudor's Mercantile Cases.—A Selection of Leading Cases
on Mercantile and Maritime Law With Notes By OWEN DAVIES TUDOR,
of the Middle Temple, Esq, Barrister at Law *Second Edition Royal 8vo* 1868
Price 1l 18s cloth

Morgan's Statutes, General Orders, and Regulations Re-
lating to the Practice, Pleading, and Jurisdiction of the Court of Chancery, with
copious Notes *Fourth Edition*, carefully revised and considerably enlarged. By
GEORGE OSBORNE MORGAN, M.A, of Lincoln's Inn, Barrister at Law, late
Stowell Fellow of University College, and Eldon Law Scholar in the University of
Oxford, and CHALONER W CHUTE, M.A, of the Middle Temple, Barrister-at-
Law, Fellow of Magdalen College, Oxford *In 8vo.* 1868 *Price 30s cloth.*

Chancery Court and Chamber Forms.—Forms and Prece-
dents of Pleadings and Proceedings in the High Court of Chancery, with practical
Notes and Observations, and References to the Fourth Edition of Daniell's Chancery
Practice, and incorporating the Forms in Braithwaite's Record and Writ Practice
By LEONARD FIELD and EDWARD CLENNELL DUNN, Barristers-at-Law,
and JOHN BIDDLE, of the Master of the Rolls' Chambers *In 8vo.* 1868. *Price
32s cloth*

Roscoe's Digest of the Law of Evidence in Criminal
Cases *Seventh Edition* By JAMES FITZJAMES STEPHEN, Esq, one of Her
Majesty's Counsel, and Recorder of Newark on-Trent *In royal 12mo* 1868. *Price
1l 11s 6d cloth*

Brooke's Treatise on the Office and Practice of a Notary.
A Treatise on the Office and Practice of a Notary of England With a full collec-
tion of Precedents *Third Edition* By LEONE LEVI, Esq, F S A, of Lincoln's
Inn, Barrister-at-Law, Professor of the Principles and Practice of Commerce in
King's College, London, &c, &c *In 8vo* 1867. *Price 21s cloth*

Archbold's Pleading and Evidence in Criminal Cases.
With the Statutes, Precedents of Indictments, &c, and the Evidence necessary to
support them. By JOHN JERVIS, Esq (late Lord Chief Justice of the Court of
Common Pleas) *The Sixteenth Edition*, including the Practice in Criminal Proceedings
by Indictment. By WILLIAM BRUCE, of the Middle Temple, Esq, Barrister at-
Law *In royal 12mo* 1867 *Price 1l 11s 6d cloth*

Russell on Crimes.—A Treatise on Crimes and Mis-
demeanors. By SIR WILLIAM OLDNALL RUSSELL, Knt, late Chief Justice
of Bengal *Fourth Edition* By CHARLES SPRENGEL GREAVES, Esq, one of
Her Majesty's Counsel *In 3 vols royal 8vo* 1865 *Price 5l 15s 6d cloth*

Wharton's Articled Clerk's Manual.—A Manual for
Articled Clerks By J J. S WHARTON, M A, Oxon, Barrister-at-Law,
Author of "The Law Lexicon," &c. *Ninth Edition*, greatly enlarged, and with
the addition of Book-keeping, by Single and Double Entry By CHARLES
HENRY ANDERSON, Editor of the "Legal Examiner," &c *In royal 12mo*
1864 *Price 18s cloth*

Biddle's Table of References to Unrepealed Public General
Acts, Arranged in the Alphabetical Order of their Short or Popular Titles By JOHN
BIDDLE, of the Master of the Rolls' Chambers Second Edition, much Enlarged,
and Corrected to the end of the Session 32 & 33 Vict. 1869, including References to
all the Acts in Chitty's Collection of Statutes *[Royal 8vo* 1869 *Price 7s 6d cloth*

THE

LAW OF COPYRIGHT

IN WORKS OF

LITERATURE AND ART.

LONDON
PRINTED BY SPOTTISWOODE AND CO.
NEW STREET SQUARE

THE
LAW OF COPYRIGHT

IN WORKS OF

LITERATURE AND ART

AND

IN THE APPLICATION OF DESIGNS.

WITH THE STATUTES RELATING THERETO.

BY CHARLES PALMER PHILLIPS,

OF LINCOLN'S INN, ESQ., BARRISTER-AT-LAW

AUTHOR OF 'THE LAW OF LUNACY'

LONDON.

V & R. STEVENS, SONS, & HAYNES,

Law Booksellers and Publishers,

26 BELL YARD, LINCOLN'S INN.

1863

p558cof

Rec June 29, 1880

TO

THE RIGHT HONOURABLE

FREDERICK

BARON CHELMSFORD OF CHELMSFORD

IN THE COUNTY OF ESSEX,

LATE LORD HIGH CHANCELLOR OF GREAT BRITAIN,

THIS WORK

IS

(BY PERMISSION)

RESPECTFULLY INSCRIBED

BY

THE AUTHOR

PREFACE.

THE OBJECT of the author has been to write a book of moderate bulk which should present a concise and connected statement of the whole Law of Copyright in this country.

This volume contains separate chapters on Copyright before and after publication in literary and musical works—in the representation and performance of dramas and musical compositions—on the Copyright of the Crown, and of certain Universities and Colleges—on Copyright in lectures after public delivery—in published engravings—in paintings, drawings, and photographs—in sculpture—in designs (ornamental and useful)—lastly, on international Copyright.

All the important judicial decisions and dicta at law and in equity upon the subject will, the author hopes, be found in the following pages, and in the Appendix are the statutes to which it may be necessary to refer.

16 OLD SQUARE, LINCOLN'S INN ·
October 1863.

CONTENTS.

—+—

CONTENTS.

CHAPTER VIII.

COPYRIGHT IN PUBLISHED ENGRAVINGS.

CHAPTER IX

COPYRIGHT-AFTER-PUBLICATION IN PAINTINGS, DRAWINGS, AND PHOTOGRAPHS

CHAPTER X.

COPYRIGHT-AFTER-PUBLICATION IN SCULPTURE

CHAPTER XI

COPYRIGHT IN THE APPLICATION OF DESIGNS

LIST

OF

CASES CITED.

—◆—

ERRATA AND ADDENDA.

Page   9, line 18, *for* 'Defendan' *read* 'Defendant'
  „   18, „   4, „ 'Leech' *read* 'Leech'
  „   59, „   3, „ 'right' *read* 'title'
  „   60, „ 21, „ 'Baston' *read* 'Bastow'
  „   64, note (*b*), „ 'In *Newman* v *Tegg*, 2 Rup.' *read* '*Mawman* v *Tegg*,
                                    2 Russ 385'
  „ 145, line 1, see however as to general issue 24 & 25 Vict. c. 101

THE LAW OF COPYRIGHT.

CHAPTER I.

COPYRIGHT-BEFORE-PUBLICATION.

1. *Definition and Nature of the Right —2 Early Discussion of the Right —3. Effect of Publication on the Right.—4. Early Decisions on the Right.—5. Modern Decisions on the Right.—6. Transfer of the Right —7. Disposition in Bankruptcy of the Right — 8 Abandonment of the Right —9 Non-existence of the Right in Criminal Works.—10 Protection of the Right in Equity and at Law —11. As to the Existence of the Right in Private Letters — 12. Exercise of the Right in disregard of Feelings.*

1. THE term Copyright, in its popular, if not in its legal acceptation, includes two rights, which differ widely in their origin, nature, and extent. The frequent application of the term to each of them indiscriminately seems to have tended to an occasional inaccuracy of language in reference to one or other of them, and perhaps to some misapprehension of both. They are, it must always be remembered, distinct and several rights. (a)

1 Definition and nature of the right.

(a) The right to have a particular trade mark to designate a commodity has been occasionally confounded with copyright, but it is no right at all, unless it is a right which can be said to exist only, and to be tested only by its violation See *Farina* v. *Silverlock*, 2 Jur N.S. pt. 1, p 1008, 4 Kay & Jo 650.

B

Copyright-before-publication is the more ancient of the two. It is the exclusive privilege of first publishing any original and material product of intellectual labour. Its basis is property; a violation of it is an invasion of property, and it depends entirely upon the Common Law; the privilege is simply a right of user, incidental to the property exclusively vested in the absolute and lawful possessor of the material product.

The right exists in every unpublished innocent production of art, literature, or science.

In reference to this copyright, it is right to notice thus early this marked difference between a published and an unpublished work. A work lawfully published, in the popular sense of the word, may be treated differently from a work which has never been in that situation; the former is liable to be translated, abridged, analysed, exhibited in morsels, complemented, and otherwise treated in a manner that the latter is not. (a)

The original ideas which spring up in the thoughtful brain of the author, or of the artist, and which he has not divulged, are themselves indeed beyond the reach of the common law of property in this country, because they have no physical existence, and because their incorporeal character excludes the possibility of any satisfactory proof of his sole possession of them; but when any material has embodied those ideas, then, indirectly through that material, the ideas can be and are recognised by the common law. It then protects their privacy, until the material has itself been, by its owner, given to the world.

In the forcible language of *Yates*, J. (b) 'ideas are

(a) See Sir *J. L. K. Bruce* V C,   and Sm 693
in *P. Albert* v *Strange*, 2 De G   (b) 4 Burr 2378

indeed free but while the author confines them to his study; they are like birds in a cage, which none but he can have a right to let fly, for till he thinks proper to emancipate them they are under his own dominion. It is certain every man has a right to keep his own sentiments if he pleases. He has certainly a right to judge whether he will make them public, or commit them only to the sight of his friends: in that state a manuscript is in every sense his peculiar property, and no man can take it from him, or make any use of it which he has not authorised, without being guilty of a violation of his property. And as every author or proprietor of a manuscript has a right to determine whether he will publish it or not, he has a right to the first publication, and whoever deprives him of that privilege is guilty of a manifest wrong, and the Court have a right to stop it.'

If judicial authority be sought for the statement, ' that no property can exist in incorporeal ideas until embodied,' it may be well to look at *Abernethy* v. *Hutchinson.* (a) In that case Mr. Abernethy, the eminent surgeon, had filed a bill to restrain the publication in the ' Lancet' newspaper of certain lectures delivered by him, orally, to medical students at St. Bartholomew's Hospital. Upon the first argument, Lord *Eldon*, C. refused to grant the injunction, on the ground of copyright, and why? Because the plaintiff was unable to swear that his whole lecture had been reduced to writing at the date of its delivery. In other words, because the invisible ideas of the lecturer could not be treated as property in the legal sense of that word, no invasion of property could be proved. The difficulty there in the way

(a) 1 H & T 39, S C. in 3 Law J ch. 209, 213, 219, and see Sir *Geo Turner*, V C., in *Morison* v *Moat*, 9 Hare, 257

of relief, upon the ground of copyright, was pointed out by Lord *Eldon* plainly enough. He observed: 'Where the lecture is orally delivered, it is difficult to say that an injunction can be granted, upon the same principle upon which literary composition is protected, because the Court must be satisfied that the publication complained of is an invasion of the work, and this can only be done by comparing the composition with the piracy.' It is true that the same judge, afterwards, and on a second argument, granted the relief prayed, but he then granted it on another and very different ground, viz. that of breach of an implied contract between the lecturer and his audience, that the latter would do nothing more than listen to the lecture for their own instruction.

2 Early discussion of the right.

2. Copyright-before-publication was, very many years ago, incidentally discussed in *Millar* v. *Taylor*; and more recently in *Jeffreys* v. *Boosey* it is clearly not referable to any consideration peculiarly literary. (*a*)

Millar v. *Taylor* and *Jeffreys* v. *Boosey* were decided upon published works, and will therefore find a more fitting place for consideration in a later chapter of this work.

3 Effect of publication on the right.

3. It may, however, here be remarked that the language of the majority of the law lords in *Jeffreys* v. *Boosey*, and of some of the judges in *Millar* v. *Taylor*, point to a conclusion that the intent of the publisher of a work of art, literature, or science, cannot limit the extent of its actual publication by him ; if any such work be once given by him to the public eye, the ideas embodied therein cease ipso facto to be in his breast only,

(*a*) See Sir *J. L. K. Bruce*, V C, in *P Albert* v *Strange*, 2 De G & Sm 696.

and he can no longer insist that the whole world may not share them with him.

Where, however, the exhibition of the work to the public is for a particular purpose only, and that is notorious, a court of equity may restrain any act being an abuse of that exhibition; but this it seems upon the ground only of breach of an implied contract between the public and the exhibitor, for instance, where a picture has been publicly exhibited, but in places only where local regulations forbad copying, a court of equity will restrain copying. (a)

It cannot be objected to the owner of such a work, claiming therein copyright-before-publication, that the work has been published unless the very thing itself has been given to the world, e. g. the publication of an engraving of a picture is no publication of the painting, the publication of an abridgement is no publication of the original work, a publication of a plaster bust is no publication of a statue.

4. The reported cases bearing directly upon the subject of copyright-before-publication are by no means numerous, and it may be observed that in most of them fraud or breach of contract was an element; but it is obvious that a violation of the right may take place without either of those ingredients. The earliest case of such an infringement appears to be *Webb* v. *Rose*, (b) which was decided in the year 1732. Sir *Joseph Jekyll*, M.R., there granted an injunction against a conveyancer's clerk when he threatened to publish as legal precedents his master's conveyancing drafts, not having obtained

4 Early decisions on the right.

(a) *Turner* v *Robinson*, 10 Ir. Ch R. 121, 510
(b) Cited 4 Burr. 2330, 2 Bro. P. C. octavo ed. 1338. The Reports 'Cases temp. Talbot' seem to have been the piracy

the draftman's permission for such a proceeding. *Forrester* v. *Waller* (a) is another and somewhat similar case which occurred in the year 1741; an injunction then issued against printing, without his consent, the plaintiff's notes of cases; the notes, it is clear, had been obtained in a surreptitious manner. Again, in the year 1754, a clerk of Sir John Strange, while in that gentleman's employ, clandestinely made an abridgement of his master's unpublished MS. cases relating to evidence; Lord *Hardwicke*, C. did not hesitate to restrain the clerk, (b) from publishing them. *Macklin* v. *Richardson*, (c) decided in the year 1770 by Lords Commissioners *Smythe* and *Bathurst*, is another instance of an injunction against the unauthorised printing and publication of a private work. The subject of the copyright there claimed was Macklin's celebrated farce called ' Love à la Mode.' A peculiar feature in the case was the fact that the play had been publicly acted, and by the plaintiff's permission; the defendants employed one Gurney, a short-hand writer: he took down the words from the mouths of the players, the defendant corrected the short-hand notes by aid of his own memory, published the first act in a number of a magazine, and threatened to publish the second act in the next number. Of course there was a printed or written copy of the play; it was, however, only lent by the author to the prompter during and for the purpose of each performance. The Court restrained the threatened publication, and negatived a plea that the representation on the stage of the

(a) Cited 4 Burr 2330 , 2 Bro. P C octavo ed 1338.

(b) Dr Paley left certain manuscripts to be given only to his parishioners for their use A book-seller having obtained possession of them was restrained from publishing Cited by Sir S Romilly, 2 V & B 23

(c) Ambl 694

farce was such a publication of it by its author (a) as to estop him from complaining of another kind of dealing therewith, viz. the printing and selling, and so publishing the work. Lord Commissioner *Smythe* said : ' It has been argued to be a publication by being acted, and therefore the printing is no injury to the plaintiff; but that is a mistake, for besides the advantage from the performance, the author has another means of profit, from the printing and publishing, and there is as much reason that he should be protected in that right as any other author.' In like manner the performance at the English Opera of O'Keefe's comedy of the 'Young Quaker,' for the benefit of Maria Kelly, in the year 1820, was restrained by Lord *Eldon*, C. The plaintiffs were the proprietors of the Haymarket Theatre, then the assignees of the copyright in the manuscript. (b)

5. Modern decisions on copyright-before-publication have scarcely been called for. *P. Albert* v. *Strange* (c) is almost the only modern case on the subject; but in that the whole learning bearing upon this right was most fully brought forward, and one ground of the decision there was 'that any publication which communicates knowledge of a private work is an infringement of the owner's right of property therein, if the publication be against the consent, or without the authority of that owner;' the other ground of decision did not touch copyright, it was breach of trust.

The facts of *P. Albert* v. *Strange*, so far as it seems material here to narrate them, were these: Her Majesty

5 Modern decisions on the right.

(a) See *post.*

(b) *Morris* v *Kelly*, 1 Jac & W. 481 It is not quite clear that the manuscript of the ' Young Quaker' had not then been published.

Lord *Eldon's* allusion to *Power* v. *Walker* rather points to a previous publication

(c) 2 De Gex & Smale 652, 1 M. & Gor. 25.

and her Royal Consort had, solely for their own amusement, made certain etchings, and from these they had
struck off a few lithograph impressions for their own
use, but not for the purpose of publication; other impressions they had ordered to be struck off, and some of
these latter had been surreptitiously retained by one of
the pressmen employed in the operation, and from him,
through the instrumentality of a Mr. Judge, they had
passed into the possession of one Strange, a London
publisher; he (Strange) declared his intention of publicly exhibiting the impressions so improperly obtained,
and also of selling to the public a descriptive catalogue
of the lithographs. A bill was thereupon filed in the
Court of Chancery against him by the Prince; it prayed
delivery up to the plaintiff of the impressions surreptitiously taken, an injunction against any exhibition, engraving, copying, publication, or disposition of the same,
and any sale, or publication, of the catalogue, also delivery up to the Prince of all copies of the catalogue
then in the defendant's possession. On an ex parte
motion (supported, of course, by affidavit), and upon an
undertaking by the plaintiff and his solicitor severally
to abide by such order respecting damages as the
Court might thereafter make, an interim injunction was
granted by Sir *J. L. K. Bruce*, V.C. against the defendant
Strange, in the terms of the plaintiff's prayer. The injunction was subsequently extended to Mr. Judge, on
proof of his complicity in the matter. After putting in
his answer, Strange moved to dissolve the injunction, so
far only, however, as it restrained the publication of the
descriptive catalogue; his counsel contended in substance
that their client's act could not be put higher than a
breach of manners, and that it did not amount to an

offence against law; the Vice-Chancellor, however, thought otherwise. He considered that the act of the defendant Strange was not only a breach of manners, but an unlawful interference with another man's civil property, and that the means of composing and forming the catalogue had been obtained unduly, i.e. without the consent of the plaintiff, and without any right—moral, equitable, or legal. He accordingly refused the motion. On appeal, his judgment was affirmed by Lord *Cottenham*, C. that learned judge also coming to the conclusion, that the act of the defendant Strange was an interference with the Prince's property; he, however, observed that the case did not depend solely upon property, because, according to the evidence before him, the possession of the defendant Strange must have originated in a breach of trust. At the hearing of the cause, the defendant Strange consented to a perpetual injunction; the defendan Judge, who had been clearly privy to the surreptitious taking, resisted it, but in vain; his case the Vice-Chancellor characterised as one of entire and undissembled dishonesty. (*a*)

(*a*) By the decree it was declared that the plaintiff was entitled to have delivered to him the impressions (by the answer of Judge admitted to be in his possession) of such of the several etchings in the pleadings mentioned as in the catalogue and in the pleadings were stated to have been etched by the plaintiff, that is to say (they were described by reference to the numbers in the catalogue), and it was ordered that Judge should, within four days after the service of the decree, deliver up the impressions above specified on oath, and leave them with the Clerk of Records and Writs at the Record Office And it was ordered that the defendant Strange should, within four days after service of the decree, deliver to the Clerk of Records and Writs, at the said office, the twenty-three copies of the catalogue—being the same as were mentioned in the decree in the other suit of even date. And the decree contained similar directions as to six copies of the catalogue, admitted by Judge to be in his possession. And the Clerk of Records and Writs was ordered to

All to whom the doctrine of copyright-before-publication is interesting and new, and they may be many, should peruse and re-peruse in extenso, both in the regular reports and in the 'Jurist,' the case last cited. The vulgar intrusion of Strange and his co-defendant on the royal privacy awakened much public sympathy at that time for Her Majesty and the plaintiff, and elicited a clear judicial exposition of the principles of law upon which this copyright is based; but, in the legal world at least, those principles had long been well understood, the nature of the right of an author in his unpublished works had long been known to be analogous to the rights of ownership in other personal property.

The following extract from the judgment of the Vice-Chancellor proves clearly the pith of his decision in *P. Albert* v. *Strange*, and states his view of the law as to the origin, nature, and extent of the right then under consideration: 'Upon the principle, therefore, of protecting property it is that the Common Law, in cases not aided nor prejudiced by statute, shelters the privacy and seclusion of thoughts and sentiments committed to writing, and desired by the author to remain not gene-

destroy these copies of the catalogue, giving notice to the solicitors of the several parties of the time and place at which he intended to do so. And it was ordered that the defendants, their servants, &c., should be restrained from making, or permitting to be made, any engraving or copy of such etchings, or any of them, and from publishing the same, and from parting with or disposing of them, or any of them, except in obedience to the decree, and from selling, or in any manner publishing, the catalogue, or any work being or purporting to be, a catalogue of the etchings made by the plaintiff. And the plaintiff, waiving any costs against Strange, it was ordered that Judge should pay the plaintiff's costs to the 22nd of May, 1849 (when Judge obtained an order to defend in formâ pauperis) Liberty to apply was reserved.

rally known. This has been in effect often judicially declared, nor by any judge more distinctly than by Lord *Eldon*, upon several occasions. In particular, in Mr. Southey's case, (*a*) he said : " It is to prevent the use of that which is the exclusive property of another, that an injunction is granted; " and again, " I have examined the cases that I have been able to meet with containing precedents for injunctions of this nature, and I find that they all proceed upon the ground of a title to the property in the plaintiff." Such then being, as I believe, the nature and foundation of the Common Law as to manuscripts, independently of parliamentary additions and subtractions, its operation cannot of necessity be confined to literary subjects. That would be to limit the rule by its example. Wherever the produce of labour is liable to invasion in an analogous manner, there must, I suppose, be a title to analogous protection or redress. To consider, then, the case of mechanical works, or works of art executed by a man for his private amusement or private use, whatever protection these, or some of these may have by Act of Parliament, they are not, I apprehend, deserted by the Common Law. The principles and rules which it applies to literary compositions in manuscript must, I conceive, be to a considerable extent, at least, applicable to these also. Mr. Justice *Yates*, in *Millar* v. *Taylor*, said that an author's case was exactly similar to that of an inventor of a new mechanical machine; that both original inventions stood upon the same footing in point of property, whether the case were mechanical or literary, whether an epic poem or an orrery; that the

(*a*) *Southey* v *Sherwood*, 2   of *Queensberry* v *Shebbeare*, 2
Merv. 435, *post*, p. 19, and *Duke*   Eden, 329, *post*, p 15

immorality of pirating another man's invention was as
great as that of purloining his ideas.   Property in
mechanical works or works of art executed by a man
for his own amusement, instruction, or use, is allowed
to subsist certainly, and may before publication by
him be invaded, not merely by copying, but by
description or by catalogue, as it appears to me.   A
catalogue of such works may in itself be valuable.
It may also as effectually show the bent and turn of
the mind, the feelings and taste of the artist, especially
if not professional, as a list of his papers.   The port-
folios or the studio may declare as much as the writing-
table.   A man may employ himself in private in a
manner very harmless, but which, disclosed to society,
may destroy the comfort of his life, or even his success
in it.   Everyone, however, has a right, I apprehend, to
say that the produce of his private labours is not more
liable to publication without his consent, because the
publication must be creditable or advantageous to him,
than it would be in opposite circumstances.   Addressing the attention specifically to the particular instance
before the Court, we cannot but see that the etchings
executed by the plaintiff and his consort for their private
use, the produce of their labour, and belonging to
themselves, they were entitled to retain in a state of
privacy, to withhold from publication.   That right I
think it equally clear was not lost by the limited communications which they appear to have made, (a) nor
confined to prohibiting the taking of impressions without or beyond their consent from the plates, their

(a) Some copies had been given to a few private friends by Her
Majesty and the Prince.

undoubted property. It extended also, I conceive, to the prevention of persons unduly obtaining a knowledge of the subjects of the plates, from publishing (at least, by printing or writing), though not by copy or resemblance, a description of them, whether more or less limited or summary, whether in the form of a catalogue or otherwise. But I am satisfied, I repeat, that the means of composing and forming the catalogue in question must, upon the materials now before the Court, be taken to have been obtained unduly, that is, without the consent of the plaintiff, without that of his consort, and without any right, moral, equitable, or legal. Can I then deny it to be an interference with another's property? I think not. The defendant appears to me to have been seeking to make use for his own purposes of what does not belong to him. That the object of printing and publishing the catalogue was money, was gain, no man, of course, can doubt; and that it would be very saleable: that, were copies of it to be multiplied, edition after edition would find ready purchasers, (with or without the superfluous bait of the copied autograph,) is highly probable, for reasons sufficiently obvious. I do not say on account of the gentle address or graceful indirectness of the compliments, or the service to history of the memoirs, (those are merely the garnish,) but on account of the solid and substantial part of the publication, the simple catalogue. What, however, can be the defendant's right, or that of any person, but the owners of the plates, to this benefit? It is for them to use or bestow, or withhold, nor can a stranger be allowed to say that they do not want it: they alone are entitled to decide whether, and when, and how, and for whose advantage their property shall be made use of. I think, therefore, not only that the defendant here is unlawfully invading the plaintiff's right, but also, that the invasion is of such a kind, and affects such property, as to entitle the plaintiff to the preventive remedy of an injunction.' (a)

Prince Albert v. *Strange* may be termed the leading case on copyright before publication; but it may be well also to refer to another curious case in Ireland, which occurred in the year 1860. (b) A valuable picture, 'the Death of the Poet Chatterton,' painted by Wallis, had, after public exhibition at the Royal Academy, and elsewhere, been on view for the sole purpose of obtaining subscribers to an engraving of it. A person aware of the qualified purpose of the view, visited the place, minutely studied the picture, and afterwards, at his own house and from his own recollection, arranged figures and furniture, &c., so as exactly to represent the pictured scene in all its details. The ideas so stolen and embodied he then stereoscopically photographed. The Court of Appeal in Chancery scrupled not to restrain a publication of the photographs: one of the learned judges pertinently remarked 'that no court of justice could admit that an act, illegal in itself, could be justified by a novel and circuitous mode of effecting it.' The above-cited decision passed previously to the Act 25 & 26 Vict. c. 68, and when there was no statutory copyright in pictures.

(a) See 2 De G. & Sm 695. In *Millar* v *Taylor*, 4 Burr 2360, *Yates*, J. had long ago said 'If a stranger had taken his manuscript from him (an author), or had surreptitiously obtained a copy of his work, and printed it before him, he might then complain of injustice' See also *Mayall* v *Higby*, 1 H & C 148, but that was not a question of piracy of copyright, but of wrongful user of a published photograph borrowed for another purpose

(b) *Turner* v *Robinson*, 10 Ir Ch. R 510, but see 25 & 26 Vict. c 68.

It was evidently based on fraud, brought home to the defendant, but as copyright was discussed therein, this brief allusion to it may possibly be excused.

6. Copyright before publication, being an incident to personal property, is assignable; it may also doubtless be the subject of a bequest.

6 Transfer of the right.

On the death of the person to whom it belongs it devolves on his legal personal representative. (*a*)

After the death of an author, there is some ground for an argument that his executors may consent to the publication of his writing, though he himself never intended them to be published; (*b*) at all events, unless he has clearly prohibited the publication, they may publish, and their publication will be protected from piracy.

A transfer of the right will not be presumed, unless the intention of transfer is clearly manifested. That intention will not be inferred from a bare permission to take a copy of the subject, especially if the right be of great pecuniary value. A decision of Lord Keeper *Henley*, in a case of the *Duke of Queensberry* v. *Shebbeare*, (*c*) in the year 1758, seems to support this statement. There it appeared that Henry Earl of Clarendon, the son of the Chancellor, was, at his death, possessed of an original MS. of his father's History of the Reign of Charles II. In his lifetime he had given permission to Mr. Gwynne to take a copy of the MS., which Mr. Gwynne accordingly did. Mr. Gwynne's son and administrator, afterwards representing that he had a right to print and publish the copy, sold it to

(*a*) See *Thompson* v *Stanhope*, Ambl. 737, *Burnett* v *Chetwood*, 2 Meriv 444, n n , Dr Paley's case, cited 2 Swanst. 419.

(*b*) *Dodsley* v *M'Farquhar*, Mor. Dict of Decis 19, 20, app., part 1, p 1

(*c*) 2 Eden 329.

Dr. Shebbeare. The doctor attempted to print and publish, but was restrained by the Court of Chancery, at the suit of the Duke, as the legal personal representative of the author and of his son Henry. This injunction was afterwards continued to the hearing, the Lord Keeper saying 'that it was not to be presumed that Lord Clarendon, when he gave a copy of his work to Mr. Gwynne, intended that he should have the profit of multiplying it in print —that Mr. Gwynne might make every use of it but that.' This copy led to a great deal of litigation, for Dr. Shebbeare afterwards recovered, before Lord *Mansfield*, a considerable sum against the son and representative of Mr. Gwynne, for having held out to him that he could print and publish it.

One who agrees to write and supply another with a MS., in such a form as to enable the latter to publish it as his own composition, has no just cause of complaint in a Court of Equity if the latter mutilates the MS. This was decided in *Cox* v. *Cox*. (a) In the same case, Sir *W. P. Wood* intimated his opinion to be that in the absence of a contract for a qualified copyright, the purchaser of an unpublished MS. might mutilate and then publish it: the point did not, however, arise in that case.

7. Disposition in bankruptcy of the right.

7. The position of an unpublished MS., or other unpublished work, in reference to the creditors of its bankrupt author, has not yet been the subject of a reported legal decision, though it was just touched upon in *Millar* v. *Taylor*. *Willes*, J. there remarked: 'This is not the case of an unpublished MS., taken in execution by creditors, or claimed by assignees under a commission against a bankrupt author. When a ques-

(a) 11 Hare, 118

tion of that suit arises, the Court will consider what is right.'

In Mr. Turner's 'Treatise on Copyright,' it is stated that the right before publication adheres to the person of the author, and so escapes the claim of bankruptcy, whatever may become of the materials in which the right inheres. Mr. Bell, the Scotch commentator, also lays it down, that the property of unpublished compositions is not within the reach of creditors. (a)

Inasmuch, however, as such a copyright may frequently be converted by its owner into money, and so is in the nature of commercial property, there is some ground for contending that the right is within the reach of an English execution, or bankruptcy, whether the debtor be the author, or only the assign of the unpublished production. The prior intention of the debtor as to the disposition of his property can scarcely override the benefit of his creditors, and although the publication may be painful to him, or even prejudicial to his professional reputation, it is pretty clear that no court of law or equity in England will regard such injury per se as a ground of interference. (b) As to any prejudicial effects of such publication, they seem to be only an unfortunate consequence of the debtor's pecuniary embarrassments; if the work be unfinished and the publication be prejudicial only on that account, creditors would scarcely refuse to enter into some arrangement for its completion prior to publication; possibly, too, the author might prevent the use of his name as the parent of the work.

In a suit of *Atcherley* v. *Vernon*, concerning the will

(a) 1 Bell's Com p. 68   2 V and B 28, and Lord *Eldon*,
(b) See Sir *T. Plumer*, M R , in   C, in 2 Swanst 413, 426

of Mr. Vernon, the author of 'Vernon's Reports, it seems that this question of publication was, indeed, once discussed at the bar, but the Court passed no decision on it. The case is reported by Mr. Leech in his 'Modern Reports.' (a) It there appears to have been insisted, by Mr. Atcherley's counsel, that the manuscript reports found in the London house of Mr. Vernon, belonged to his heir-at-law, as guardian of the reputation of his ancestor. It was said that, if the tomb or monument of an ancestor be defaced or destroyed, an action lies for the heir-at-law; and that, by parity of reason, as those manuscripts were intended by the testator as a monument to transmit his learning and reputation to posterity, the law would intrust the heir with the care of them, that they should be printed in such a manner as would be most for the honour of Mr. Vernon's memory; that the printing or not printing these papers might as much affect the reputation of Mr. Vernon as any monument or tomb, that possibly they were not fit to be printed; that possibly they were never intended to be printed; that they were not in the nature of the thing fructuary, and did not, therefore, fall within a clause which gave the residue of the personal estate to trustees. The counsel argued: 'Suppose a man of learning should have the misfortune to die in debt: can the creditors come into this court and pray a discovery of all his papers, that they may be printed for the payment of his debts? And if creditors cannot do this, a fortiori not the trustees in the present case. If a minister of State should die, he may have a great number of papers that may be very curious, may print and sell well; yet, surely, these will not be considered as personal estate and go to the executor. As, therefore, papers found in

(a) 10 Mod 518

a man's study, not being in their nature fructuary, are not considered as personal estate, and, in case of no will, would not have gone to the administrators of Mr. Vernon, so they did not pass under that clause where the residue of his personal estate is given to the trustees.' The Court, however, determined nothing in *Atcherley* v. *Vernon* as to the position of the manuscript reports in reference to publication. All parties consented to have them printed, under the direction of the Court, without making any profit of them.

8. It is clear that an abandonment of copyright before publication must be unequivocal; the mere gift of copies of the work to a few friends is not considered as an abandonment of the right. (*a*)

8 Abandonment of the right

A question may hereafter recur, whether circumstances do not justify the conclusion that the original right has been abandoned, and so lost. Should such a question be again raised, it may be useful to refer to *Southey* v. *Sherwood*. The material circumstances of that suit were these:—In 1794, the poet Southey wrote his poem 'Wat Tyler,' and, by a friend, sent it up to London to Ridgway, the then well-known bookseller and publisher, for his consideration as to printing and publishing. Southey, himself, shortly afterwards followed the work to London, and conferred with Ridgway and one Symonds, as to printing and publishing it, but he soon returned to the country; Ridgway and Symonds were, or seemed to be, at first inclined to publish. The poet living away from town, and being much occupied by various literary works, omitted to ask for the return of his manuscripts. In 1817, the successors in business of

(*a*) See *P Albert* v. *Strange*, 2 De G and Sm 686, and see 4 Burr 2330

Symonds (then deceased) began to publish the poem, without the sanction or authority of Southey, and, thereupon, that gentleman commenced proceedings in the Court of Chancery against them. Upon a motion in that suit for an injunction to restrain the publication, Sir Samuel Romilly and Mr. Montague, being counsel for the defendants, insisted that the poem, by reason of its libellous tendency, was of such a nature, that there could be no copyright therein. They did not (according to the case as it is reported) object to the abandonment of the right, if any. The plaintiff's counsel contended that their client was entitled to the interposition of the Court, on account of the injury to his reputation, by the publication of a work, the sentiments of which he then disavowed and sought to discountenance. The Lord Chancellor (*Eldon*), at the conclusion of the argument, after alluding to the character of the poem, said: 'If the work be such a one as it has been described to be, it is extraordinary that with the change alleged to have taken place in Mr. Southey's opinions, there should be nothing stated to account for its having been left by him in Mr. Ridgway's hands to the present time, but " that Mr. Southey forgot it." It is impossible that Mr. Southey could have forgotten it. There must have been some other reason. If a man leaves a book of this description in the hands of a publisher without assigning any satisfactory reason for doing so, and has not enquired about it during twenty-three years, he surely can have no right to complain of its being published at the end of that period.' On the next day, Lord *Eldon* having meanwhile looked into all the affidavits, and having read the poem itself, stated that by reason of the character of the work, and its doubtful claim to be considered property, the original intention to publish, the subsequent abandonment of that intention, and the length of time during which the plaintiff had suffered the work to remain out of his possession without enquiry, he (Lord *Eldon*) could not grant the injunction until Mr. Southey should have established his right to the property by an action. (*a*) Many circumstances evidently combined to induce the denial of relief in the case just mentioned.

9. No one can have copyright-before-publication in a criminal work (i. e. a work calculated by publication to do injury to society, and to offend against the law).

Upon a motion for an injunction to restrain the publication of a literary work, Lord *Eldon*, C., said: 'If upon inspection the work appears innocent, I will act upon that submission; (*b*) if criminal, I will not act at all, and, if doubtful, I will send the question to law.' (*c*)

In *Southey* v. *Sherwood*, (*d*) in the year 1822, he adhered to that doctrine. The libellous tendency of 'Wat Tyler' appears to have been at least one of the reasons why he then refused to grant the injunction until Mr. Southey should have established his right of property in the poem by an action.

A dictum of Lord Chief Justice *Eyre* is also often quoted and properly so, to show that, in his opinion, the criminality of a work deprived it of the character of property. A Dr. Priestley had brought an action against a hundred for damages sustained by him in a riot at Birmingham, and claimed compensation for (among other

(*a*) See now 25 & 26 Vict c 42   (*c*) *Walcot* v *Walker*, 7 Ves 2
(*b*) A submission in the defen-   (*d*) 2 Merv 438, 439
dant's answer.

property alleged to have been destroyed) certain unpublished manuscripts; on behalf of the hundred, it was
alleged in reply, that the plaintiff was in the habit of
publishing works injurious to the government of the state,
but no evidence was produced to that effect; the Lord
Chief Justice thereupon observed : ' If any such evidence
had been produced, I should have held it was fit to be
received as against the claim made by the plaintiff.' (a)

In *Southey* v. *Sherwood* the criminality of the work
was only considered in its bearing on the question of
civil interest in Mr. Southey, but a decision more
curious than sound is mentioned in a note appended to
that case by Mr. Merivale. The decision is attributed
to Lord Chancellor *Macclesfield.* According to that
note, a bill was brought, in the year 1720, by a plaintiff,
as executor of Dr. Burnett, the author of two books, one
published in 1692, the other unpublished, to stay the
publication of an English translation of both books;
the defendant insisted that a translation was no violation of copyright, within the intent of the Act 8 Ann, c.
19; the Chancellor, however, granted the injunction,
and (if credit be given to the reporters for accuracy)
he said : ' Though a translation might not be the same
with the reprinting the original, on account that the
translator has bestowed his care and pains upon it, and
so, as a translation, the book might not be within the
prohibition of the Act ; yet, inasmuch as the book contained to his (the Chancellor's) knowledge (he having
read it in his study), strange notions, intended by the
author to be concealed from the vulgar in the Latin
language, in which language it could not do much hurt,
the learned being better able to judge of it, it was

(a) Priestley's case cited 2 Meriv 437

proper to grant an injunction to the printing and publishing it in English.' He then added, 'that the Court of Chancery had a superintendency over all books, and might, in a summary way, restrain the printing or publishing any that contained reflections on religion or morality. (*a*)

The law laid down by Lord *Eldon*, in *Walcot* v. *Walker*, as to granting or withholding an injunction, upon the application of the author of a work, mischievous in regard to the public, was again discussed in *Lawrence* v. *Smith*, (*b*) in the year 1822. The plaintiff had delivered at the College of Surgeons, and had afterwards published, a work under the title of 'Lectures on Physiology, Zoology, and the Natural History of Man.' The bill was filed to restrain the defendant from selling a pirated edition, and an ex parte injunction was obtained. The defendant then moved to dissolve the injunction, on the ground that the lectures were so hostile to natural and revealed religion, that they ought to have no protection. The character of the work, in its view of the Scriptures, was much disputed at the bar. Lord *Eldon* dissolved the injunction, and because he doubted whether the lectures did not contradict the Scriptures. His language was: 'The defendant comes into Court under singular circumstances. He says, that the work which he, as well as the plaintiff, has published, is so wrong, so immoral in its nature, that it ought to have no protection. As this Court has no jurisdiction in matters of crime, it has been said,

(*a*) 2 Meriv. 440, note *a* The facts alleged in the report of the case and in the report of the decree, differ from each other somewhat.

As the decree is set forth verbatim, preference has been above given to the facts alleged in the decree.

(*b*) 1 Jac. 471.

that if the injunction be refused, it has the effect of
increasing the number of copies. (*a*) The answer to that
is, that I have nothing to do with it as a crime.   The
question relates only to a civil right of property.   If the
one party has that right, the other must not invade it;
if he has not that right, the Court cannot give him the
consequences that belong to it.   Whether, if such a
defence were made upon a trial at law, there might or
might not be proceedings of a different nature against
both parties, that is a question that I have nothing to
do with; but the question is, whether it is so clear that
the plaintiff has this civil right, that on that ground he
is to have relief?   If, on reading the plaintiff's work I
thought it clear that he had that right, I should feel it
necessary to state the grounds of my opinion; for after
the argument at the bar, I should be unwilling to part
with the subject without telling you the view I take of
it.   But if I feel a rational-doubt whether an action
would lie, it will not be necessary to go into the grounds
of that doctrine; it might, perhaps, prejudice the trial if
I did.   Looking at the general tenor of the work, and
at many particular parts of it; recollecting that the
immortality of the soul is one of the doctrines of the
Scriptures; considering that the law does not give protection to those who contradict the Scriptures; and
entertaining a doubt, I think a rational doubt, whether
this book does not violate that law, I cannot continue the
injunction.   The plaintiff may bring an action, and
when that is decided, he may apply again.' (*b*)

From a note by Mr. Jacob in his report (*c*) of
Lawrence v. *Smith*, it appears that in *Murray* v.

(*a*) And see Lord *Eldon* in 2   (*b*) See 25 & 26 Vict. c. 42
Mern. 138   (*c*) 1 Jac 474, note

Benbow, February 1822, Mr. Shadwell, on the part of the plaintiff, moved for an injunction to restrain the defendant from publishing a pirated edition of Lord Byron's ' Cain,' and that Lord *Eldon*, after reading the poem, refused the motion on grounds similar to those stated in the above judgment. In the same book of reports, and in the same page, it is stated that Sir *John Leach*, V.C.E. dissolved in 1823, on similar principles, an injunction which had been obtained against the publication of a pirated edition of a portion of the poem of ' Don Juan,' ordering the defendant, however, to keep an account. (*a*)

It may well be doubted whether the above decisions would be considered guides in the present day; the existence of copyright can, however, be safely denied in works the publication of which would offend the law of the land.

Further, it has been held that no copyright can subsist in a book which seeks to obtain a sale by serious deception of the public in respect to authorship. If the misrepresentation be innocent, it is of course immaterial; but when its intent is serious and with a view to profit, the transaction ranges itself under the head of crimen falsi. (*b*)

10. Whether the author of an unpublished innocent work does or does not intend to seek profit by future publication, he is entitled to restrain an infringement of his copyright; because, according to *Prince Albert* v.

10 Protection of the right in equity and at law.

(*a*) The Acts against blasphemous and seditious libels are 9 & 10 Will 3, c 32, 53 Geo 3, c 160, 60 Geo 3 & 1 Geo 4, c 8, 9, 11 Geo 4 & 1 Will 4, c 73, 6 & 7 Will 4, c 76 The Act against publication of indecent books is 20 & 21 Vict c 83

(*b*) *Wright* v *Tallis*, 1 M Gr. & Sc. 893

Strange, any interference with his property is an unlawful act. (*a*)

As an American judge (*b*) has aptly remarked, ' A defendant is not to be enjoined from doing an act on account of the benefit which he expects to derive therefrom, but on account of the injury which it may occasion to the plaintiff. Here the plaintiff complains that his property is violated. Can the defendant resist the claim of the plaintiff by saying, " True it is I am about violating your property, but I seek not thereby any pecuniary benefit nor any advantage, but the gratuitous pleasure of working an injury." In foro legis the measure of relief or damage must be the same, whether any advantage be contemplated by the wrongdoer or not; while in foro conscientiæ his turpitude is surely the greater if none be expected. If a man is to be enjoined to print my letters, when he expects thereby to support his family, à fortiori when his only view is to do me harm.'

An action at law for damages lies after any infringement.

Where infringement was threatened and the plaintiff's legal title was clear, the Court of Chancery always gave relief. Where for any reason, prior to Rolt's Act, (*c*) the plaintiff's legal title was doubtful, a court of equity declined to restrain until that title had been established, (*d*) because the relief in equity was only ancillary to the right at law. (*e*)

(*a*) See also Lord *Eldon*, C , in 2 Meriv 437

(*b*) See *Denis* v *Leclerq*, 1 Martin, 305.

(*c*) 25 & 26 Vict. c 42

(*d*) It seems that Rolt's Act now compels the Ct of Chancery to determine for itself all questions of law and fact. (See *Re Hooper*, 11 W. R 797)

(*e*) *Lawrence* v *Smith*, 1 Jac 471 *Southey* v. *Sherwood*, 2 Meriv. 435.

11. The application of this copyright to private letters was first judicially considered in England in *Pope* v. *Curl,* (a) about the year 1741. Lord *Hardwicke,* C., in that case granted an injunction against a republication of the poet's private letters to Dean Swift. The letters had been, in fact, already published, not in England, but in Ireland; therefore the sole question for decision in the suit was copyright after publication, and that, under the statute 8 Anne, c. 19 (to which Act reference will hereafter be made). However, in the course of his judgment, the Chancellor apparently went out of his way to state what he considered to be the doctrine on the subject of copyright in private letters. (b) He observed: 'Another objection has been made by the defendant's counsel, that where a man writes a letter it is in the nature of a gift to the receiver; but I am of opinion that it is only a special property in the receiver: possibly the paper may belong to him, but this does not give a license to any person whatsoever to publish them to the world, for at most the receiver has only a joint property with the writer.' (c)

In the year 1774 occurred the first case which directly raised the question of Copyright in unpublished letters. It is *Thompson* v. *Stanhope,* (d) and it came before Lord Chancellor *Apsley.* He is there reported to have restrained on the application of Lord Chesterfield's executors, but until the hearing of the suit only, the publication of letters written and sent by that nobleman to his natural son. These letters the Earl had told one of the defendants (his son's widow) 'to keep,'

(a) 4 Burr 2330, 2 Atk 342 According to Dr Johnson, Curl was the victim of Pope in this publication See Johnson's 'Life of Pope.'

(b) See Lord *Eldon,* C, in 2 Swanst 425

(c) 2 Atk 342.

(d) Ambl 737.

when she at his desire gave up to him other letters also written and sent by him to his son. Lord Chesterfield had never approved of the publication, on the contrary, in reply to an observation by the widow to the effect 'that they (the letters) would form a fine system of education if published,' his Lordship had said, 'Why, that is true; but there is too much Latin in them.' This case has been often cited at the bar; but when closely examined does not prove much. It ended in a compromise at the recommendation indeed of Lord *Apsley*. (*a*) His observation at the hearing, 'that it was within the reason of several cases where injunctions had been granted, e. g. the case of Mr. Forrester, of Mr. Webb, of Mr. Pope's letters printed by Curl, and Lord Clarendon's Life (*b*) advertised to be published by Dr. Shebbeare,'(*c*) has not that weight which his words generally carry. Those cases have been already cited, and certainly do not involve any question as to the peculiar rights existing in private communications by letter. (*d*)

Again, and at a day much nearer to our own times, a dispute touching the right to publish confidential correspondence came before Sir *Thomas Plumer*, M R. Lord and Lady Percival had filed a bill in the Court of

(*a*) See Lord *Eldon*, C, in 2 Swanst 126

(*b*) It was Lord Clarendon's History of the reign of Charles II., from the Restoration to the year 1667—and not Lord Clarendon's Life, see 2 Eden, 329

(*c*) Ambl 740

(*d*) The letters in *Thompson* v *Stanhope* had been sold by the widow to Dodsley, the London bookseller, for 1,575*l* He afterwards published them in England, with the consent of the Earl's executors They appeared once more in litigation, and on that occasion became the subject of an interdict against certain Edinburgh printers (*Dodsley* v *M'Farquhar* Mor Dict of Dec 19, 20, app. part 1, p 1)

Chancery, praying an injunction against Mr. Phipps, to restrain him from printing or publishing certain letters written and sent by Lady Percival to Mr. Mitford, and from parting with them, or any copies of them, otherwise than to the plaintiffs; these letters the bill alleged to be of a private nature, and confidential between Lady Percival and Mitford. Lord *Eldon*, C., upon an ex parte motion had granted the injunction until answer; the defendant Phipps had then put in his answer, and thereby insisted that the letters had reference to articles which Lady Percival had sent through Mitford to Phipps for publication in his newspaper, and that the publication sought to be restrained was necessary to the public vindication of the defendant's character as the owner of that newspaper, publicly discredited by the plaintiffs. Upon an application to Sir *Thomas Plumer*, V.C., to dissolve the injunction, and at the close of counsel's argument, he stated his impression to be, 'That letters had the character of literary composition stamped upon them, so that they were within the spirit of the Act of Parliament protecting literary property: that a violation of the right in letters was attended with the same consequences as a violation of the right in an unpublished MS. of an original composition of any other description; that an injunction restraining the publication of private letters must stand upon the foundation of literary property, not of breach of confidence, not of wounded feelings; and that whatever degree of confidence, of reservation of property, might be implied from the transmission of a private letter, it would be too much to hold that the individual who receives it can in no case use it for the purpose of protecting himself from an unfounded imputation.'

Subsequently, and after a perusal of the bill and answer, the Vice-Chancellor dissolved the injunction, 'because upon the answer the plaintiffs had failed to establish either ground for the interference of a court of equity, copyright, or confidence.' (a)

It may not be amiss to remark that although the circumstances of *Percival* v. *Phipps* may have justified the decision made therein, there lurks in the language of the Vice-Chancellor, in reference to the Act of Parliament, that confusion between copyright-before-publication and copyright-after-publication, which has been deprecated at the commencement of this work. The decision was in the opinion of Lord *Eldon* simply this. 'Let it be ever so clear that the plaintiffs have either a sole or a joint property in the letters, the Court will not interfere between parties whose acts have supplied reasons for not interfering.' (b)

Once more the question of copyright in letters came before the Court of Chancery; it is reported and was raised in the year 1818. In that case (*Gee* v. *Pritchard*), on the authority of *Thompson* v. *Stanhope*, Lord *Eldon*, C. (c) restrained the publication of private letters written and sent by a lady to her husband's adopted son; a motion to dissolve the injunction which had been obtained on an ex parte application proved unsuccessful, and the Chancellor continued the relief; he believed that he was bound so to do by the law (although he doubted its soundness) laid down in similar cases in the Court of Chancery, 'that the receiver of a letter had only a joint property with the writer;' and he was also of

(a) *Percival* v. *Phipps*, 2 V & B 19.

(b) 2 Swanst 423, 427

(c) *Gee* v. *Pritchard*, 2 Swanst. 402.

opinion that, even if the defendant had originally had a right of publication in the letters, he had renounced that right.

In this last case, be it noted, the defendant had thought proper to return the original letters to the lady, but to keep copies of them without apprising her, while he assigned as a reason for the return, 'that he was unworthy of the sentiments and expressions of kindness contained in the letters.' So that undoubtedly breach of faith was an element in the case.

The latest case, (not yet reported,) on the subject of letters is the *Bishop of Exeter* v. *Shutte*. The defendant proposed to publish in a biography of the Bishop private letters written by that dignitary; at the suit of the Bishop he was restrained from so doing.

Of *Gee* v. *Pritchard*, the case above referred to, it has been said by an American Chancellor, that it may, perhaps, be doubted whether Lord *Eldon* in that case did not to some extent endanger the freedom of the press by assuming jurisdiction of the case as a matter of property merely, when, in fact, the object of the complainant's bill was not to prevent the publication of her letters on account of any supposed interest she had in them as literary property, but to restrain the publication of a private correspondence as a matter of feeling only. Lord *Eldon's* decision in that case has, however, received the unqualified approbation of the learned American commentator on equity jurisprudence, (Mr. Justice *Story*,) as the Chancellor himself could not but admit. (a)

A Scotch decision has also extended relief by interdict to assignees of copyright in private letters

(a) See *Brandreth* v *Lance*, 8 Paige, 2, 8

against a person who proposed, without authority from the writer, to publish them. The letters had been addressed and sent by the writer to a lady. The author was Robert Burns, the Ayrshire poet; the letters were confidential, and written by him to his 'Clarinda;' she, it may be observed, consented to their publication.

It is distinctly stated in 'Morison's Dictionary of Decisions' that in the case last cited there was little difference of opinion upon the Bench, and that the ground upon which the Court seemed to pronounce its decision was ' that the communication in letters is always made under the implied confidence that they shall not be published without the consent of the writer, and that the representatives of Burns had a sufficient interest for the vindication of his literary reputation to restrain the proposed publication.' (*a*)

Notwithstanding the above dicta of Lord *Hardwicke* in *Pope* v. *Curl*, and the decision in *Thompson* v. *Stanhope* (which last manifestly proceeded upon an imperfect recollection of the prior decisions upon private letters) (*b*) it may, perhaps, be fairly questioned, even now, whether a court of equity in England would not view the publication of a private letter by its lawful receiver rather as a breach of contract or trust on his part, than as a violation of copyright, or an invasion of property. (*c*) Lord *Eldon*, it is clear, entertained very grave doubts of the law enunciated somewhat unneces-

(*a*) *Cadell* v *Stewart*, Mor Dict of Dec app part 1, p 16

(*b*) See also Sir *J Romilly*, M R , in *Howard* v *Gunn*, 2 New Rep 256 , and as to the property in letters sent for insertion in a newspaper, see *Davies* v ' *Witness* '

newspaper 1 Jur N S pt 2, p 523

(*c*) See, however, Bell's Principles of Law of Scotland, p 518 He says that the law of England denies the right to publish letters on the ground of property alone

sarily in *Pope* v. *Curl* by Lord *Hardwicke*, and to
others it has seemed rather inexplicable that a joint
property in a letter should exist in its writer and
receiver, for the paper is but a chattel, and the property
therein must, it seems, pass on delivery; (*a*) the nature
of a private letter may, indeed, explain its transfer,
and so in equity control the use of the chattel by its
receiver, but it can hardly operate in contradiction of
the legal consequences of the act of transfer, so as to
divide the property in the letter between the possessor
and his correspondent, or even to constitute the
receiver simply a depositary in trust. Lord *Eldon*
himself said in *Gee* v. *Pritchard*, that the receiver of
a letter might destroy it; (*b*) this militates with the
notion of the joint property of the sender and receiver,
and is also opposed to any idea of fiduciary ownership in the latter, though the Chancellor there repudiated the idea of giving relief on the ground of breach
of trust, and carefully guarded himself against any
imputation of interference, because the letters were
written in confidence: his judgment seems solely
directed to the circumstances of that case 'wherein
the purpose of public justice publicly administered,
according to the established institutions of this country,
required the production of letters at the cost of wound-
ing the feelings of individuals.' (*c*) The language of

(*a*) *Oliver* v. *Oliver*, 10 W R
18 During the transit of a letter
by post, the property is in the
Postmaster-General.

(*b*) Lord *Mansfield* also, in
Millar v *Taylor*, alluding to the
transcript of Lord Clarendon's
History, in *D of Queensberry* v.

Shebbeare, said 'Mr Gwynne
might have thrown it into the fire
if he pleased.' 4 Burr 2397

(*c*) An injunction was, it seems,
afterwards granted in Ireland, and
also by Lord *Eldon* himself in
this country, restraining the publication of private letters from an

Sir *T. Plumer*, in *Percival* v. *Phipps*, appears to be capable of the same explanation, and the decision in *Prince Albert* v. *Strange*, already referred to, also tends to show that against the unauthorised publication of private letters by their possessor a court of equity may and will interfere upon the ground of breach of contract or trust, so that the writer of a private letter is not by any means remediless against its unauthorised publication.

To sum up, the conclusion seems to be this: if the property in the paper, the substantial element of a letter, pass by transmission or delivery, the right of publishing the ideas expressed upon that paper must pass with the property in the paper itself, however liable that right may be to restriction in its exercise by a court of equity, where publication would involve a breach of contract or confidence. (*a*)

old lady under the influence of a weak attachment to a young man who had contracted, for money paid him, not to publish, but to deliver up the letters to the lady 2 V. & B. 23, 27 This decision was clearly founded on contract

(*a*) The communication in private letters is, of course, always made under the implied confidence that they shall not be published without the consent of the writer (Mor Dict of Dec 19, 20, app pt 1 p 16) As to the old Roman right of property in letters, &c, the Civil Law says, Digest lib xli titl 1 §9 'Quâ ratione autem plantæ, quæ terra coalescunt, solo cedunt, eadem ratione frumenta quoque, quæ sata sunt, solo cedere intelliguntur Cæterum sicut is qui in alieno solo ædificavit, si ab eo dominus soli petit ædificium, defendi potest per exceptionem doli mali, ita ejusdem exceptionis auxilio tutus esse poterit qui (in) alienum fundum sua impensa consevit Literæ quoque, licet aureæ sint, perinde chartis membranisque cedunt, ac solo cedere solent ea, quæ ædificantur aut seruntur Ideoque si in chartis membranisve tuis carmen vel historiam vel orationem scripsero, hujus corporis non ego, sed tu dominus intelligeris Sed si a me petas tuos libros, tuasve membranas, nec impensas scripturæ solvere velis, potero me defendere per exceptionem doli mali utique si bonâ fide eorum possessionem nanctus sum' Cicero, in his second Philippic on M Antonium, writes 'At etiam litteras quas me sibi

12. In closing this chapter, it may be laid down as a rule, open to no exception, that possible injury to the feelings of others, from an exercise of this copyright, is not per se regarded in an English court of equity: the possible effect on reputation, unless connected with property, is not a ground of relief there, though it may be an ingredient for that court to consider when the question of a right of property is raised. (*a*)   Adverting to letters between friends or relations upon their private concerns, Sir *T. Plumer*, M.R. once remarked: 'It is not necessary here to determine how far such letters falling into the hands of executors, assignees of bankrupts, &c. could be made public in a way that must frequently be injurious to the feelings of individuals;' but he followed up this language by observing, 'I do not mean to say that would afford a ground for a court of equity to interpose to prevent a breach of that sort of confidence, independent of contract and property.' (*b*)

Lord *Eldon*, in *Gee* v. *Pritchard*, (*c*) repudiated, and that most distinctly, any notion of interference by the Court of Chancery with a publication, simply because it might wound feelings, and it seems abundantly clear from

misisse diceret recitavit, homo et humanitatis expers et vitæ communis ignarus Quis enim unquam qui paullum modo bonorum consuetudinem nosset, litteris ad se ab amico missas, offensione aliqua interposita, in medium protulit palamque recitavit? quid est aliud tollere e vitâ vitæ societatem, quam tollere amicorum colloquia absentium? quam multa joca solent esse in epistolis, quæ pro-

lata si sint ineptæ esse videantur? quam multa seria, neque tamen ullo modo divulganda?   Quod scribam tanquam ad civem, tanquam ad bonum virum, non tanquam ad sceleratum et latronem'

(*a*) See *Clarke* v *Freeman*, 11 Beav 112

(*b*) 2 V & B 28

(*c*) 2 Swans 113, 426

all the reported decisions that, except upon the ground of property, or of breach of contract or trust, no English court of law or equity will give relief in the case of an unauthorised publication.

In a Scotch text book of great authority ('Bell's Principles'), it is, however, stated that the Court of Session has always held itself competent to protect epistolary correspondence, not on the ground of copyright, but of right on the part of the writer to protect his reputation and his privacy, and that a like power has been exercised by the Court of Justiciary. (a)

The Act 3 & 4 Will. 4, c. 15 enacted that from and after the passing of that Act (June 10, 1833) the author of any tragedy, comedy, play, opera, farce, or any other dramatic piece or entertainment, composed and not printed and published by the author thereof or his assignee, or which thereafter should be composed and not printed or published by the author thereof or his assignee, or the assignee of such author, should have as his own property the sole liberty of representing or causing to be represented such production at any place or places of dramatic entertainment whatsoever in any part of the British dominions.

This enactment seems to be simply declaratory of the common law.

(a) An agent who has written and sent a letter expressly on behalf of his principal, and relating solely to that principal's affairs, cannot, of course, afterwards obtain relief from a court of equity, upon the ground that in fact the letter was his own private letter. *Howard* v *Gunn*, 2 New Rep 256 It is equally clear that no person has a right to open private letters not addressed to him, and that the Court of Chancery will grant an injunction against such a proceeding. *Scheile* v *Brackell*, 11 W R 797

CHAPTER II.

COPYRIGHT-AFTER-PUBLICATION.

*1 Origin and Present Foundation of the Right — 2 Extent and
Operation of the Right.*

1. THE Act 8 Anne, c 19, was the first statutory
dealing here with Copyright-after-publication. As its
name implies, the right commences from the moment
the eye of the public is allowed to rest upon any subject.
The Act of Anne only dealt with literary works. It was
by Lord *Hardwicke*, C. styled 'An universal patent for
authors.' But there is the authority of Lord *St. Leonards*
for saying that this patent was not scientifically framed,
and its ambiguous language certainly did not tend to allay
the great conflict of opinion which prevailed in the last
century, and even now may be said to exist, as to the
origin of the right. 'Perhaps,' said an American judge
(*M'Lean*), in allusion to that conflict, 'no topic in England has created more discussion among literary and
talented men than that of the literary property of authors.
So engrossing was the subject for a long time as to leave
few neutrals among those who were distinguished for
their learning and ability.' (*a*) In the time of Lord
Mansfield, C.J. the weight of authority was apparently
in favour of the foundation of the right in common law,

1. Origin of
the right.

(*a*) In *Wheaton* v *Donaldson*, 8 Pet 655

modern judicial opinions lean, however, to its statutory creation.

A glance at the cases wherein the arguments on both sides of the question have been raised and are now recorded may be useful, but their general tenor can thus be stated. The advocates of the common law origin have based their conclusions on the broad principles of right and wrong, which, rooted in natural equity, must, they say, govern civilised society. According to their view, 'the author of incorporeal ideas cannot claim the exclusive possession of those ideas after an authorised publication; but as a fair pecuniary return for his industry, he is exclusively and perpetually entitled to multiply copies of that which embodies his ideas, be it a book or any work of art; and the publication and sale by him of a single copy does not prejudice that right, because his intention and an equitable view of the transaction forbid such a construction. The answer generally given to this reasoning has been 'the interests of society over-ride the abstract rights of individuals; a perpetual copyright would be harmful to society; moreover, the absolute transfer of a chattel invariably passes at common law the entire property therein; in the absence of any restriction arising from express contract, or necessary implication, every use also of the chattel. There is no express contract between the author and purchaser of an ordinary publication that the latter shall not multiply it if he pleases, and the common law, in its hatred of a perpetual monopoly, will not imply such a contract.'

Perhaps the earliest reported dicta which touch the question are in *Midwinter* v. *Hamilton*. About the year 1746, Daniel Midwinter, Andrew Millar, and other

London booksellers, libelling upon the Act 8 Anne, c. 19, raised an action (*a*) in the Court of Session in Scotland against Hamilton and Balfour (Edinburgh booksellers), and Andrew Stalker (a Glasgow bookseller), by reason of their having printed, or having brought from England and published in Scotland, certain books the copyright property of the pursuers. The claim in the action was, that the defenders ought to pay the statutory penalties or damages for every surreptitious copy sold by them, and forfeit the remaining copies to be destroyed. In their process, however, the pursuers restricted their claim to the damages, and offered to prove the number of copies sold. They put the claim upon this footing: that by the Act of Anne a property was given to authors in the books published by them, which property of itself was sufficient to found a claim for damages, because every proprietor was entitled to damages at common law against those who encroached upon his property. The Court of Session ultimately decided that the action did not lie for damages. (*b*) The Court, in pronouncing its judgment, expressed an opinion that antecedent to the Act 8 Anne, c. 19, an author had no such property in a book composed and published by him, because 'the thought of an author's mind did not admit the notion of property, more than the invention of any machine or of gunpowder.' This judgment was appealed to the House of Lords; their decision clearly did not proceed upon the origin of

(*a*) *Midwinter* v *Hamilton*, Mor Dict of Dec 19–20, p 8295 It was alleged, but not sufficiently proved in this case, that Mr John Gray's executors had previously obtained damages in an action in England against James Watson for printing and publishing the opera of 'Polly,' or the second part of the 'Beggar's Opera,' in violation of the Act of Anne.

(*b*) See, however, *Cadell* v *Robertson*, 5 Paton, 493

copyright. The Lords do not appear to have even adverted to it. (a)

The question of property at common law in a literary work was afterwards discussed in the year 1761, in *Tonson* v. *Collins*, (b) upon the copyright of the 'Spectator,' and in the Court of King's Bench. That was, however, a collusive action. Lord *Mansfield*, C.J. suspected the collusion, and dealt with the litigation on that footing only.

The question was too important long to remain in the background, and it was again brought forward in *Millar* v. *Taylor*. (c) That was an action directed by the Court of Chancery, (d) and brought in the King's Bench, for the violation of a copyright which had survived the statutory period of protection then afforded to published literary works. The question was there ably argued, twice in the court of law, by very eminent counsel for the plaintiff and for the defendant. Upon the trial the jury found by a special verdict these facts, viz.: that the work alleged to have been pirated (Thomson's 'Seasons') was an original composition by a natural-born subject resident in England; that it was first published in London, and by the author, that Millar had, in the year 1729, purchased the work for valuable consideration from the author, and had ever since sold it as his own property, and exposed for sale a sufficient number of copies of the work at a reasonable price; that before the reign of Queen Anne (i.e. before any Act of Parliament had dealt with the subject) it was usual to purchase from authors the perpetual copyright of their books, and to assign the same from

(a) Mor Dict 19, 20, 8315
(b) 1 W Bl 301, 321, 315
(c) 4 Burr 2303

(d) *Osborne* v. *Donaldson*, 2 Eden, S C 2 Bro P. C. 129, Toml td

hand to hand for valuable consideration; and to make the same the subject of family settlements; that the Stationers' Company, in order to secure the assignment of copyright so far as in them lay, had passed bye-laws (set forth in the verdict) for a registry of books: that the work in question was upon purchase, and before publication or sale by the defendant Taylor duly entered in the register of the Stationers' Company as the sole property of the plaintiff Millar; and that Taylor had, in the year 1763, without the license or consent of Millar, published, exposed to sale, and sold in England, several copies printed without his license or consent, whereby he (Millar) had been and was damnified. As to the legal liability of Taylor upon these facts, the jury prayed the advice of the Court. The four judges of the Court of Queen's Bench were divided in opinion: Lord *Mansfield*, C. J. and *Willes* and *Aston*, JJ. ruled in favour of the right at common law, and therefore for the plaintiff. *Yates*, J. differed from his learned brethren. A writ of error was afterwards brought, but the plaintiff in error, after assigning errors, suffered himself to be non-prossed, and the Lords Commissioners then granted an injunction in support of Millar's right thus adjudged at law.

The decision in *Millar* v. *Taylor* was followed, as of course, by the Court of Chancery in *Donaldson* v. *Beckett*. (*a*)

About this period (that is to say in the year 1773) passed a contrary Scotch decision in an action of *Hinton* v. *Donaldson*. That action was brought in the Court of Session (*b*) in virtue of the pursuer's supposed common law copyright in an edition of Stackhouse's ' History of the Bible.' The Court, after a full discussion of the

(*a*) 1 Burr 2408   (*b*) Mor Dict of Dec 19–20, p 8307 question of copyright at law, came to the conclusion that no such right existed in authors or publishers, and assoilzied from the action.

An appeal was taken from the decree in *Donaldson v. Beckett* (in the year 1774) to the House of Lords: all the judges were then directed by the House to deliver their opinions upon five questions, viz.: (a)—1. Whether at common law an author of any book or literary composition had the sole right of first printing and publishing the same for sale, and might bring an action against any person who printed, published, and sold the same without his consent? 2 If the author had such right originally, did the law take it away upon his printing and publishing such book or literary composition, and might any person reprint, and sell for his own benefit, such book or literary composition against the will of the author? 3. If such action would have lain at common law, is it taken away by the statute 8 Anne; and is an author by the said statute precluded from every remedy except on the foundation of the statute, and on the terms and conditions prescribed thereby? 4. Whether the author of any literary composition and his assigns had the sole right of printing and publishing the same in perpetuity by the common law? 5. Whether this right is in any way impeached, restrained, or taken away by the statute 8 Anne? Upon these questions Lord Mansfield did not deliver an opinion to the House because he was himself a peer; but it is stated in Burrows' report of the case that the Chief Justice did not swerve from the opinion which he had given in the Court of Queen's Bench; the other eleven judges delivered their opinions seriatim. On question 1, ten judges against one

affirmed the copyright at common law there referred to,
i. e. copyright-before-publication; eight affirmed, one
denied that an action did lie for an invasion of the
right; two affirmed that it did lie only when the invasion was coupled with fraud or violence. On question 2,
seven judges against four replied in the negative. On
question 3, six against five judges were of opinion that
the act of Anne abolished the common law copyright-
after-publication; six against four were of opinion that
there was no remedy for an invasion of the right except
upon the act of Anne, and on the terms and conditions
prescribed thereby; one thought that there might be a
remedy in equity upon the Act, independent of the
statutory terms and conditions. On question 4, seven
judges against four replied in the affirmative. On
question 5, six judges against five replied affirmatively.
The House then, on the motion of Lord *Camden*, se-
conded by Lord *Apsley*, C. reversed the decree below,
and decided that whether copyright after publication in
literary works did or did not previously exist at common
law, the Act of Anne then in force had abolished the
common law right. This decision of the House of Lords
has never been reversed, and it is still law.

The question of property at common law in copyright-after-publication was, moreover, touched upon in
Scotland in the year 1787, in *Cadell* v. *Anderson* (a)
upon an alleged violation of the copyright in Blackstone's published 'Commentaries,' also in *Payne* v.
Anderson. (b) In the latter case the Court of Session
expressed its opinion that at all events literary property
was not then protected by the common law. In the

(a) Mor. Dict. of Dec 19-20, p   (b) *Ibid* p. 8316
8311

year 1811, in *Cadell* v. *Robertson,* (a) the House of Lords decided that an action did lie for damages, although the book was not entered pursuant to the Act of Anne. Lastly, the origin of the right was incidentally discussed in *Jeffreys* v. *Boosey.* (b)   The Act of Anne has since

(a) Piracy of Burns' works, Mor. Dict. of Dec. app part I. p. 18, S. C 5 Pat. 493

(b) 4 H. L Ca   The arguments for and against the common law origin in *Millar* v. *Taylor* and *Jeffreys* v. *Boosey* were as follow —

FOR.	AGAINST.
1 Long user of the right prior to the Act of Queen Anne.	1 No user by individuals is evidence of a general right, and no user of a right affecting an art (printing) not immemorial in this country is evidence of a legal customary right.
2 Recognition of the right in ordinances of the Stationers' Company.	2 Those ordinances were bye-laws of a corporation, only addressed to, and affecting its members, their enactment rather implied that such a right was not recognised at law, a corporation cannot create a new kind of legal property
3 A recognition of the right in a royal proclamation of September 25, 1623	3. That proclamation only enforced a Star Chamber decree in support of the privileges of the Stationers' Company, who were but literary constables for the suppression of seditious or improper books
4 Recognition of the right in ordinances of Parliament during the usurpation	4 Those ordinances were directed to political objects, and did not in fact recognise the existence of such a right
5. Recognition of the right in decrees of the Star Chamber.	5 These decrees emanated from an illegal and arbitrary court in its exercise of a political and criminal jurisdiction, and did not touch any civil rights of subjects inter se, or recognise this right
6 Milton's speech in 1644,	6 A somewhat vague dictum by

been to a certain extent repealed, and other statutes giving further protection to published works of literature

upon an ordinance of Parliament against unlicensed printing, wherein he spoke of 'the just retaining of each man his several copy, which God forbid should be gainsaid'

7 The recognition of the right in the Licensing Act 13 & 14 Car. 2.

8. *Atkinson* v *Stationers' Company*, Carter, 89

9. *Roper v. Streater*, Skinner, 234

10 Dicta of the Court in the *Stationers' Company* v. *Seymour*, 1 Mod 256

11 The language of one of the cases given to certain members of Parliament in support of a bill introduced in 1709, for securing the property of copies of books to the rightful owners

12 The jurisdiction exercised by Chancery against the violation of the right, since the Act of Queen Anne, and without regard to the statutory terms and conditions (see *Eyre* v *Walker*, *Motte* v *Faulkner*, *Walthoe* v *Walker*, *Tonson* v *Walker*, *Tonson and another* v *Walker*), which jurisdiction could stand on no other footing than the original common law right, or the statutory confirmation for a term of that right

13 The *Stationers' Company* v *Parker*, Skin 233

a great author, whose opinion on a point of law, even if more clearly proved, could not per se carry much weight

7 That act only supported the privileges of the Stationers' Company, and did not recognise the right

8 That was a case of Crown right, based on prerogative, and did not decide general right

9 That was a case on the law patent, and not on the common law right of a subject

10 Those dicta had reference to the law patent, not to the common law.

11 The language of persons anxious to get the statutory security of a penalty

12 The Court of Chancery could and did give relief only upon the right created by the Act of Queen Anne, the terms and conditions of that Act merely applied to statutory actions for penalties *Motte* v *Faulkner*, *Eyre* v *Walker*, *Tonson* v *Walker*, and *Tonson and another* v *Walker*, were injunctions on the statutory right *Walthoe* v *Walker*, and *Eyre* v *Walker*, were moreover only interim injunctions, and therefore did not decide or profess to decide the legal right.

13 That was a case of Crown right and of patent law, not of general common law right

and art have been successively passed; but that no common law right results after the expiry of the pre-

14 A judicial dictum in *Manley* v. *Owen*, cited 4 Burr 2329, 2404.

14. The dictum had reference to a customary and exclusive right in the Lord Mayor of London

15. *Webb* v. *Rose, Pope* v. *Curl, Queensberry* v *Shebbeare*, and *Forrester* v. *Waller*.

15 *Webb* v *Rose, Queensberry* v. *Shebbeare*, and *Forrester* v *Waller* were all cases of copyright before publication.

16 The existence of copyright-before-publication.

16 That right is very distinct from copyright-after-publication, and stands on principles wholly different

17 The existence of Crown copyright-after-publication.

17 That is a prerogative right

18. The preamble of the Act of Queen Anne, 8, c 19, declaratory of a general common law right

18 The preamble was the reverse of such a declaration

19 The original title in committee of the Act of Queen Anne as a bill to secure the undoubted property of copies for ever, and the change of that title in Parliament

19 The ultimate change of the title was evidence of the denial by Parliament of the existence of such a property at law.

20 The technical recognition of the copyright at law by the enacting words of the Act 8 Anne, c 19

20 From the title to the end that Act was a plain declaration that the right did not exist at common law

21 Principles of natural justice and public policy, which principles gave to an author a property in the fruit of his mental labour, although such fruit might not have all the characteristics which were attributed to property long established by legal precedent

21. Incorporeal ideas could not in their nature be the subject of property; therefore an author could not suffer legal injury in his property by an invasion of his ideas, further, to give a property in all ideas, however mean, would lead to absurdity

22. The recognition by the common law of all principles of natural justice.

22 The common law did not claim so wide a field.

23. The plain, though tacit intent of an author in publication of his work, and the absence of any express renunciation by him

23 Publication of a work embodying ideas ipso facto makes them common stock, and irrevocably lays them open to the world.

sent statutory right, and that no such common law right co-exists with the statutory seems now to be indisputable. (a)

2. Admitting copyright-after-publication at the present day to be simply a creature of statute law, its nature, extent, and operation must of course be examined by reference to that law. By several Acts of Parliament this exclusive privilege has been conceded to workmen in many different fields of mental labour; to various artists as well as to the composers of literary and musical works; but, unfortunately, though the several Acts have a certain degree of family likeness to each other, then features are so far dissimilar, that the law regulating copyright in the various offspring of the busy brain must be looked for in many scattered pages of the Statute Book. The only safe path in the further consideration of copyright law now seems to be to adhere to the course taken by the Legislature, and so separately to treat of the privilege as it exists in the several subjects to which it now extends.

2 Nature, extent, and operation of the right.

in the act of publication of a just control over his property.

No tacit reservation by the publisher can control the necessary consequences of his act A man cannot retain what he parts with

24 Patent right.

24. Patent right and copyright stand on different foundations, and arguments taken from the former cannot be applied to the latter

See also *Cadill* v *Robertson*, 5 Pat. 504, n.

(a) See judgment in *Reade* v *Conquest*, 9 C B. n s 755, Right Honourable *T B E. Smith*, M R, 10 Ir Ch R 121 (See, however, *Boosey* v *Tolkien*, 5 C. B 476)

CHAPTER III.

COPYRIGHT-AFTER-PUBLICATION IN LITERARY AND MUSICAL WORKS.

1 Present regulation of the right

1. COPYRIGHT-after-publication in literary works is now regulated by an Act 5 & 6 Vict. c. 45 (commonly called Talfourd's Act), which, beginning with a recital 'that it is expedient to amend the law relating to copyright, and to afford greater encouragement to the production of literary works of lasting benefit to the world,'

repeals the former legislation on the subject, except so far as the continuance of either of the previous Acts (*a*) might be necessary for carrying on, or giving effect to, any proceedings at law or in equity pending on July 1, 1842 for enforcing any cause of action or suit, or any right or contract then subsisting.

It was proposed to include engravings in this Act; they were, however, omitted by the advice, it is said, of the late Sir Robert Peel, who then contemplated further legislation as to copyright in works of the fine arts.

2. The definition of this right is given by the Act 5 & 6 Vict. c. 45. It is the sole and exclusive liberty of printing, or otherwise multiplying copies of any subject to which the word copyright is in that Act applied. The word is there applied to a book only, viz. every book published prior to July 1, 1842, and then entitled to copyright, and every book thereafter published. By every book (*b*) is meant and included every volume, part or division of a volume, pamphlet, sheet of letter-press, (*c*) sheet of music, (*d*) map, plan, or chart, separately published. No other work, therefore, than such a book can be the subject of this copyright.

This definition does not extend to prints or designs separately published, but where designs form part of a book, in the text of which a person has copyright under the Act of Victoria, that copyright extends to any illustrations in the book as well as to the letter-press. This, at least, was the opinion expressed by

2 Definition of the right

(*a*) The previous Acts are in the appendix, and are 8 Anne, c 19, 41 Geo 3, c 107, 54 Geo 3, 156

(*b*) See 54 Geo 3, c 156, and *White* v *Geroch*, 2 B & Ald. 300

(*c*) See *Hine* v *Dale*, 2 Campb 27, n , *Clementi* v *Goulding*, 2 Campb 25 , 11 East, 244

(*d*) Written music was held to be within the Act of Anne (*Bach* v *Longman*, Cowp 623).

Sir *J. L. K. Bruce*, V.C. upon a motion to restrain the piratical publication of an original work embracing letter-press and illustrations. The original work referred to ('The Comical Creatures from Wurtemberg') contained twenty illustrations (drawn from the stuffed animals contributed by Herman Plocquet to the Exhibition of 1851), and a story of ' Reynard the Fox.' The alleged piracy was a number of a serial work entitled 'The Story Book for Young People, by Aunt Mary.' In the original work the illustrations were actually printed on the same paper as the letter-press itself, but that fact does not seem necessary to bring the picture-part of a story-book within the Act. (*a*)

A book to be within copyright legislation need not consist of original or speculative matter; (*b*) mere compilation and arrangement, (*c*) as in a Court Calendar or Almanack; the mere results of enquiry, as in a Road Book or Guide Book, and so on, may be the subjects of copyright. (*d*) The Reports show that a spelling book, (*e*) a book of elementary lessons in arithmetic, (*f*) a map, (*g*) an annotated catalogue, (*h*) a book of chronology, (*i*) have each of them been held to be within the enactments of the Legislature upon literary property; a mere collec-

Rogue v *Houlston*, 5 De G 275

(*b*) Lord *McKenzie*, 20 Dec of Court of Sess 2d series, p 1161, note

(*c*) Sir *John Leach*, in *Burfield* v. *Nicholson*, 2 S & S 7

(*d*) Dec of Sess 2d series, p 1161, note, Lord Deas, *ibid* p 1160, and see *Taylor* v *Bayne*, Mor Dict. of Dec 19-20, app pt I p 7, and *Carnan* v *Bowles*, 2 Bro C C 80 and Story, 3, *Gray*

v *Russell*, 1 Story, 11, and *Emerson* v *Davies*, 3 Story, 781

(*e*) *Lennie* v *Pillans*, S & D 416, *Constable* v ——, 3 S 216

(*f*) *Emerson* v *Davies*, 3 Story, 763, and see *Baily* v *Taylor*, 1 Tamlyn, 305

(*g*) See Lord *Eldon*, in *Wilkins* v *Aiken*, 17 Ves 425

(*h*) *Hotten* v *Arthur*, 11 W R 934

(*i*) *Trusler* v *Murray*, 1 East, 363 n

tion of receipts for cookery, a task requiring no mental labour, cannot, it has been said, claim copyright. (a)

'In truth,' writes *Story*, J. (b) 'in literature, in science, and in art, there are and can be few if any things which, in an abstract sense, are strictly new and original throughout. Every book in literature, science, and art borrows, and must necessarily borrow and use much which was well known and used before. No man creates a new language for himself, at least if he be a wise man, in writing a book. He contents himself with the use of language already known, and used, and understood by others. No man writes exclusively from his own thoughts, unaided and uninstructed by the thoughts of others. The thoughts of every man are more or less a combination of what other men have thought and expressed, although they may be modified, exalted, or improved by his own genius or reflection. If no book could be the subject of copyright which was not new and original in the element of which it is composed, there could be no ground for any copyright in modern times; and we should be obliged to ascend very high even in antiquity to find a work entitled to such eminence.'

Another learned writer (Burton) has still more broadly laid it down 'that books are like medicine, which the apothecary composes by pouring from one phial into another.' This dictum, however, should perhaps be restricted to books in the nature of compilations.

A work already given to the world cannot, of course, be again published; the previous publication abroad of a book disqualifies it for copyright under the Act of

(a) See Lord *Eldon*, C., in *Rundell* v *Murray*, Jac 314

(b) In *Emerson* v *Davis*, 3

Story, 779, and see same *Judge* in *Gray* v *Russell*, 1 Story, 16

Victoria: this is no new doctrine. Long prior to the operation of that Act it had been held that a foreign publication vitiated a claim to copyright here. (a)

If, however, the publication here and abroad be simultaneous, the publication abroad will not stand in the way of copyright in this country. (b)

3 Non-existence of the right in criminal publications

3. The right does not subsist in any book of which the publication is itself an offence against the law. This was the decision of the Court of King's Bench in *Stockdale* v. *Onwhyn*. (c) An action had there been brought for the purpose of recovering compensation in damages for piracy of a publication entitled 'The Memoirs of Harriette Wilson.' The work was libellous and licentious. *Abbot*, C.J. said 'it would be a disgrace to the common law could a doubt be entertained upon the subject.' The printer of the book above referred to bringing an action for his bill against the publisher was also non-suited by *Best*, C.J (d) who said that it would be strange if a man could be fined and imprisoned for doing that for which he could maintain an action at law. The printer and publisher were of course participes criminis, but the Chief Justice, quoting Lord *Kenyon*, met that objection by saying, 'I will not sit here to take an account between two robbers on Hounslow Heath.'

4 Duration of the right

4. The statutory period of duration of this copyright in a book published since July 1, 1842, or published thereafter in the lifetime of its author, is the life of such author and the further term of seven years commencing

(a) See *Clementi* v *Walker*, 2 B & Cr. 861, *Guichard* v *Mori*, 9 Law, J ch 227, and *Hedderwick* v *Griffin*, S & D. 383

(b) *Erle*, J at Nisi Prius, in *Cocks* v *Purday*, 2 C & K 269

(c) 5 B & Cr

(d) *Popleton* v *Stockdale*, R & M 337

at his death; if, however, the term of seven years expires within forty-two years from the first publication (*a*) of the book, the right endures for such forty-two years.

The period of duration of the right in every book published since July 1, 1842, or published thereafter, but after the death of its author, is forty-two years from the first publication of the book.

The period of duration of the right in every book published prior to July 1, 1842, and in which copyright then subsisted, is the same as that of a book published after July 1, 1842, where the old copyright belonged on that day in whole or in part to a publisher or a person who had acquired it for other consideration than that of natural love and affection. The author of the book, or, if he on July 1, 1842, was dead, his executor, administrator, or next of kin entitled to administration, and the proprietor of the old right, must, before the expiration of such right, consent to accept the benefits of the Act of Victoria in respect of such book, and cause a minute of such consent to be entered in a certain form in the book of Registry at Stationers' Hall; failing so to do, the property in such book under the Act only lasts during the term of the ancient right therein.

The right so limited in duration ought, perhaps, to satisfy the fair claim which every busy brain has to the fruit of its own toil. This it must, however, be admitted is not the unanimous verdict (*b*) of the legal or literary world; but the limit which would satisfy every mind it would be difficult to fix.

(*a*) A sale of copies of a MS is a publication of the MS. See *Abbot*, C. J. in *White* v *Geroch*, 2 B & Ald 298.

(*b*) See *Williams* on Personal Property, p 202.

The late Mr. Bell, in the last edition (*a*) of his 'Principles of the Law of Scotland,' writes: 'Although the foundation on which a right of exclusive privilege may be argued at common law is the same in the case of a mechanical invention and of a literary composition, there is a remarkable difference in the consideration on which the limited monopoly of each ought to stand.   In the arts the public is concerned in the invention being opened to them at no very distant period, for no use being derivable from the invention without the absolute possession of the individual machine or manufacture, the public is entirely in the power of the monopolist, and yet the invention would probably have been made by others if not restrained.   But in the case of a book, not only is it impossible that any other person could have composed the same book, but it is a kind of production of which the public has the benefit by the knowledge diffused; and the value of which, and consequently the power of keeping up extravagant prices, is restrained by the interest of the author himself. There are not, therefore, the same reasons for limiting the monopoly of an author as there are in setting bounds to that of the inventor.'

The difference pointed out by the learned writer no doubt exists to a certain extent, and cannot be wholly disregarded

It was argued at the bar of the Court of Session, in *M'Lean* v *Moody*, (*b*) in the year 1858, that the object of the statute of Victoria was to encourage literary merit, that intellectual labour constituting authorship was alone thereby protected, that there could be no authorship without an author, and that the life of the author afforded the only criterion which the statute gave for measuring the endurance of the privilege, and that without the statutory means of measuring the privilege the privilege itself could not exist. This argument Lord *Deas* pronounced unsound; he declared it to be his opinion that the Act did not confine the privilege to cases in which there was a known author, whose life should afford a measure for the endurance of the privilege; that the work might be the joint production of two or more authors, whose contributions to it were undistinguishable, so that the life of one of them could not be the criterion for measuring the privilege; that a person might find a MS. in his ancestor's repositories, or get a gift of it, and publish it, and he might be entitled to copyright, although he could not tell who was the author, nor whether the author was living or dead; that the Crown might get up a publication, and be entitled to publication, and yet the Crown never died: that it was assumed in section 16 of the Act that there might be cases in which the first publisher might be entitled to copyright although no author had been or could be named; that the endurance of the privilege in such cases must be for forty-two years after the first publication.

5 The nature of this right is that of personal property It is transmissible by bequest, and, in case of intestacy, it is subject to the same law of distribution as other personal property; it is a local right only. embracing Great Britain and Ireland, the islands of Jersey and Guernsey, the British dominions in the East and West Indies, and the colonies, settlements, and possessions of

5. Nature of the right.

the British Crown, acquired on, or since, the first day of July 1842, or which hereafter may be acquired. (a)

The absence of any intention on the part of an author to publish his literary production will not, it seems, prevent his executors from consenting to and authorising the publication; and this copyright may be acquired in a work so submitted to the world. This conclusion may be gathered from the report of the Scotch case of *Dodsley* v. *M'Farquhar*. (b) It there appears that the work now known under the title of 'Lord Chesterfield's Letters to his Son' was published by the assignee of the son's executrix, with the consent of the Earl's executors. Neither the Earl nor his son had given any assent whatever to that proceeding. Dodsley, the London bookseller, was the assignee, and he obtained an interdict against M'Farquhar and others who had in Edinburgh pirated the work.

6 Registry of every subject of the right.

6. One of the provisions of the Act 5 & 6 Vict. c. 45, is for registry; the object of such registry is clearly to prevent, as far as possible, any offences against the Act through ignorance. (c) The enactment (d) declares, that a book of registry, wherein may be registered the proprietorship in the copyright of books and assignments thereof, and in dramatic and musical pieces, whether in manuscript or otherwise, and licences affecting such

(a) 5 & 6 Vict c 45, s 3
(b) Mor Dict. of Dec 19-20, p 8308.
(c) See also 8 Anno, c 19, s. 2 To provide the means of discovering the authors of every publication, in order that they might be made answerable for its contents, the Act 39 Geo 3, c 79, has also directed that all parties concerned in bringing a publication into the world, whether printers or publishers, shall be made known Therefore a printer, who sends out his work without his name, can never recover for his labour or materials used in printing. *Beasley* v *Bignold*, 5 B. Ald 335.
(d) 5 & 6 Vic c 45, s 11

copyright shall be kept at the Hall of the Stationers' Company, by an officer appointed by the company, for the purposes of that Act; that the book shall at all times be open to the inspection of any person, on payment of one shilling for every entry which shall be searched for, or inspected, in the book; and that such officer shall give a copy of any entry in such book (certified under his hand, and impressed with a stamp of the company), to any applicant, on payment of five shillings.

The Act further provides that such copies, so certified and impressed, shall be received in evidence in all courts and in all summary proceedings, and shall be primâ facie proof (a) of the proprietorship or assignment of copyright, or licence, as therein expressed, but subject to be rebutted by other evidence, and in the case of dramatic or musical pieces, shall be primâ facie proof of the right of representation or performance, subject to be rebutted as aforesaid.

The Act makes (b) a false entry in the book of registry a misdemeanour, and permits (c) the proprietor of copyright in any book to enter therein the title of his book, the time of its first publication, the name and place of abode of its publisher, and, lastly, the name and place of abode of the proprietor of the copyright, or of any portion of the copyright; this upon payment of five shillings to the officer of the Stationers' Company. The Act also permits such registered proprietor to make entry of any assignment of his interest, or any portion of his interest, in the copyright; this entry also on

(a) M'Lean v Moody, Dec in Ct of Sess vol xx 2d series

(b) 5 & 6 Vict c 45, s 12
(c) Ibid s 13

payment of five shillings. The Act gives, in a schedule thereto, the forms of such entries.

Previously to the Act 5 & 6 Vict. c. 45, although there was no entry of a work at Stationers' Hall, a person entitled to the copyright therein might protect his right by action or suit; but, prior to registration, he could not recover the statutory penalty for violation of his right. The Act of her present Majesty has, according to its construction by Vice-Chancellor *Kindersley*, made an alteration in the law in this respect. (a) the 24th section of the Act declares that no proprietor of copyright in any book, published since July 1, 1842, can maintain any action or suit, or any summary proceedings, in respect of any infringement of such copyright, unless he shall, before commencing such action, suit, or proceeding, have caused an entry to be made in the book of registry of the Stationers' Company of such book, pursuant to the Act.

A separate article for a periodical publication is not a book to be registered under this section. (b)

To whatever extent a second edition published after the passing of the Act 5 & 6 Vict. c. 45, of a copyright work published before the Act, is substantially a new work, to that extent it cannot be protected until registration. This was decided by Sir *R. Kindersley*, V.C., upon a bill filed (by John Murray, of guide book celebrity, against Mr. Bogue, the publisher) to restrain the piracy of the plaintiff's 'Handbook for Travellers in Switzerland.' (c)

(a) Sir *R. Kindersley*, V C in *Murray* v *Bogue*, 1 Drew, 364

(b) *Murray* v *Maxwell*, 3 L. T n s. 466 Ch

(c) *Murray* v. *Bogue*, 1 Drew, 364, but see *Beckford* v. *Hood*, 7 T R 628, *Novello* v. *Sudlow*, 16 Jur 689.

Any person associated by the proprietor of a copyright with himself in an entry in the Book of Registry has a primâ facie right to sue jointly with him in respect of a violation of the right. (a)

By the Act of Victoria, it is further enacted (s. 14) that if any person shall deem himself aggrieved by any entry made under colour of that Act in the Book of Registry, he may apply by motion to the Court of Queen's Bench, Common Bench, or Exchequer, in term, or by summons to any Judge of such Court in vacation, for an order that such entry may be expunged or varied; and upon any such application, such Court or Judge shall make such order for expunging, varying, or confirming such entry, either with or without costs, as to it or him shall seem just. And the officer appointed by the Stationers' Company for the purposes of that Act shall, on the production to him of any such order for expunging or varying any such entry, expunge or vary the same according to the requisitions of such order

The evidence adduced in support of such application should be as direct and clear as possible.

A rule nisi (b) was obtained in the Queen's Bench, under section 14, by one Davidson, calling on Robert Cocks to show cause why certain entries in the Book of Registry should not be varied or expunged. The rule was obtained upon a simple affidavit of belief by Davidson that the persons named in the entries were not the authors. Cocks, by his counsel, refused to give any undertaking not to use the entries as evidence on the

(a) *Stevens* v *Wildy*, 19 L J   (b) 2 Ell & Bl 577
Ch. n s. 190

trial of an action brought by Cocks against Davidson, for violation of the copyright to which the entries referred. Lord *Campbell*, C.J., in giving judgment said 'We are not prepared to expunge these entries, but we think that there is enough to justify us in ordering "proprio vigore," and without consent, that the rule be enlarged until the trial of an issue in which Cocks shall be plaintiff, and on the trial of which he shall not use these entries as evidence.' (a)

This course the Court of Common Bench declined to follow in a subsequent case (b) as being beyond their power, and refused to expunge an entry because its falsity was not clearly proved.

In the last case, it was also mooted whether the party showing cause was a party aggrieved within the meaning of the Act 5 & 6 Vict. c. 45, s. 14, the fact being that at the date of the piracy, the name of another person, his agent, was, by mistake, entered in the Book of Registry as proprietor, though the error had since been rectified.

In ex parte Baston (c), upon the application of A., the sole registered proprietor of a copyright, which application A. supported by an affidavit of his pro-

---

(a) The following order is reported to have been made —'The rule shall be enlarged until the trial of an issue in which Cocks shall be plaintiff and Davidson shall be defendant, and the question to be tried shall be, "whether there was any copyright in all or any, and which of the pieces of music in question, and whether Cocks was proprietor of the copyright in all or any, and which of the pieces" The entries made at Stationers' Hall shall not be set up at the trial of the issue, and the proceedings in the action between the above-mentioned parties shall be stayed, unless Cocks elects, within a week, not to use the entries, or any of them, at the trial.'

(b) *Ex parte Davidson*, 18 C B 310.

(c) 14 C B 631

prietorship and belief, 'that B., under colour of an agreement with him for publication, had caused an entry to be made in the Book of Registry,' a rule absolute to expunge the entry was granted by the Court of Common Bench.

It seems that neglect in registry on the part of the officials at Stationers' Hall may deprive an author of the benefit of the Act as against the public. (a)

If the defendants in an action for piracy object the non-registration of the original work at Stationers' Hall pursuant to the Act, they should, it seems, distinctly plead such non-registration. (b)

7. A very few words may suffice upon the parliamentary provisions for the deposit and delivery in certain quarters of copies of every subject of literary copyright.

In return for the statutory protection, and to secure a deposit accessible to literary persons for books which may be of such considerable price as not to be easily attainable by scholars of ordinary means, (c) the Legislature requires the publisher of every literary work to deliver a copy of the work at the British Museum, and a fixed number of copies after demand at Stationers' Hall; it also declares the mode of delivery, and enforces that delivery by penalty; the requisitions are contained in ss. 6, 7, 8, 9, and 10 of the Act 5 & 6 Vict. c. 45. (d)

7 The necessary deposit and delivery of copies of every literary publication

(a) *Cassell* v *Stiff*, 2 Kn & Jo 79

(b) *Chappell* v *Davidson*, 18 C B 194

(c) See 8 Anne, c 19, s 5, and Lord *Ellenborough*, C J, in *Cambridge University* v *Bryer*, 16 East, 321, and *Le Blanc*, J *ibid* 328

(d) See appendix See also, 54 Geo 3, c 156, s 2, and *British Museum* v *Payne*, 4 Bingh 540, as to delivery of part of a work, and 5 & 6 Vic c 45, s 2, 'book'

8. The next point perhaps for consideration is the assignment of literary copyright.

Every registered proprietor may assign his legal interest, or any portion of his interest in the copyright by any writing in pais, (a) or by an entry in the Book of Registry; the particulars of entry are the date of the entry, the title of the subject, and the names and places of abode of the assignor and assignee; the form of the entry is given in the schedule to the Act 5 & 6 Vict c. 45. An assignment so entered is effectual in law to all intents and purposes whatsoever, without being subject to any stamp or duty. It is expressly declared by the Act that an assignment by deed would not be more effectual by way of estoppel. (b) Want of express consideration cannot, therefore, be objected to such an assignment

In Viner's 'Abridgement,' it appears that a bill was filed that the plaintiff might be quieted in the enjoyment of the right of sole printing Dr. Prideaux's 'Directions to Churchwardens,' and for a perpetual injunction against the defendant to prevent his printing and publishing the same An objection by the defendant that he had title by plaintiff's delivery of a copy to the original printer was over-ruled by Lord *Macclesfield*, C such qualified delivery of a copy not being in the nature of an assignment of the right.

A simple assignment of the copyright in any book

(a) See 8 Anne, c 19, *Davidson v Bohn*, 6 C B 456, *Cumberland v Copeland*, 7 H & N 118, and *Parke*, B in *Jeffreys v Boosey*, 4 H L C 931 But see also Lord *Ivory* in *Jeffreys v Kyle* 18 Dec of Ct of Sess 2d series, p 911 See also 8 Jur n s pt ii p 148 A writing attested by two witnesses was formerly necessary

(b) 5 & 6 Vict c 45, s 13

consisting of a dramatic piece or musical composition does not convey to the assignee the right of representing or performing such piece or composition, unless entry of that intention is made in the Book of Registry. (a) The decision in *Cumberland* v. *Planché* (b) appears to have led to the enactment of this law.

The House of Lords held in the year 1859, upon a bill of exceptions that a pursuer in the Court of Session claiming as the assignee of a copyright might, the primâ facie evidence of his proprietorship having been rebutted, support his title without production of a formal deed of assignment attested by two witnesses. (c)

A legal assignment must it seems be in writing; this was the opinion of the Court of King's Bench in an action on the case (d) brought in the year 1814, when the Act 8 Anne, c. 19, was in full operation; the reasons given by Lord *Ellenborough*, C.J. and *Dampier*, J. for the decision, were 'that the Act 8 Anne, c. 19, having required that the consent of the proprietor, in order to authorise the printing or reprinting of any book by any other person should be in writing, the con-

(a) *Ibid* s 22, and see Lord *Eldon*, C Jac 315, *Morris* v *Kelly*, J & W 481, *Moore* v. *Walker*, 1 Camp 9

(b) I. A & E 580 The Ct of K B there decided that the assignee of the copyright in a play printed and published within ten years before 3 & 4 Will 4, c 15, was an assignee of the right of representation

(c) *Kyle* v *Jeffrys*, 21 Dec of Ct of Sess, 2d series, p 18

(d) *Power* v *Walker* 4 Camp 8

& s c , 3 M & S 7, *Clementi* v *Walker*, 2 B & Cr 861 Lord *Eldon* refused an injunction to an assignee of copyright when the bill did not state an assignment in writing He afterwards assumed the assignment upon an affidavit that the plaintiff could not say whether there ever had been any written assignment by the author to this deponent's vendor, but that his vendor had assigned to him by deed *Morris* v *Kelly*, 1 J & W 481

clusion from it seemed almost irresistible that the assignment must also be in writing, for if the license, which is the lesser thing, must be in writing, à fortiori the assignment, which is the greater thing, must be.'

The provisions in the Acts 8 Anne, c. 19, and 5 & 6 Vict. c. 45, on this subject, as to the necessity of writing, are similar. (a)   Lord *Eldon* (b) thought it would be difficult to maintain that there must be an assignment in writing between a bankrupt and his assignees. Clearly it is not necessary in that case.

The absence of an assignment in writing must be specially pleaded at law, (c) unless, of course, admitted by the other party. (d)

As to the extent of an assignment in general terms it appears that an author was not presumed to have assigned his contingent right in case of his surviving the first statutory term of copyright given by the Act 8 Anne, c. 19, unless the assignment was so specially expressed. (e)

It has never, however, been decided at law or in equity that an assignment of the copyright must be by deed, and a deed seems unnecessary, (f) though a contrary opinion is attributed to *Tindal,* C J in *De Pinna* v. *Polhill.* (g)   In reference to an assignment of the right, a deed is referred to in the thirteenth section of

(a) See Sir *W P Wood,* V C in *Cassell* v *Stiff,* 2 Ka & Ju 279 , *Lover* v *Davidson,* 1 C B N S. 182

(b) In *Newman* v *Tegg* 2 Rup

(c) *Barnett* v *Glossop,* 1 Bingh N C 633 , *Latour* v *Bland,* 2 Stark, 382 , *De Pinna* v *Polhill,* 8 C & P 78 , *Cocks* v *Purday,* 5 C B 860

(d) *Moore* v *Walker,* 4 Campb 9 n

(e) *Rundell* v *Murray,* Jac 315   See also *Carnan* v *Bowles,* 2 Bro C C 80

(f) *Wightman,* J in *Jeffreys* v *Boosey,* 4 H L Ca 891 , *Stevens* v *Benning,* 1 K & Jo 168 S C 6 De G M & G 223

(g) 8 C and P 78

the Act of Victoria, that seems to have reference only to the doctrine of estoppel.

Since the repeal of the Act of Anne, an assignment in writing need not, it seems, be attested; (a) this proposition has been disputed in a legal journal. (b)

In *Jeffreys* v. *Boosey*, (c) Lord *St. Leonards*, Sir *F. Pollock*, L.C.B. and *Parke*, B. expressed decided opinions against the validity of an assignment limiting the enjoyment of a copyright as to locality; but under the Act 5 & 6 Vict. c. 45, s. 13, it is clear that an assignment may be valid limiting the enjoyment in point of time. (d)

In *Howitt* v. *Hall*, (f) there was a sale for four years of an English literary copyright, and a question arose, 'whether by the terms of the agreement between the author and his assignee, the latter could, after the four years, sell copies of an edition printed and published by him within that period. The only evidence in writing of the agreement was the following memorandum signed by the author and addressed to the publishers: — 'Gentlemen, I confirm the agreement entered into with you by Mrs. Howitt, on March 14, 1854, for the publication of a " Boy's Adventures in Australia," being copyright of four years from that date;' there was also a receipt (g) for the money paid for the copyright and sole right of sale for four years. Sir

(a) *Crompton, Erle, Wightman,* JJ *Parke,* B *Jervis,* L C J 4 H L Cᵢ, 855, 881, 891, 931, 943

(b) See 8 Jur N S. pt 2, p. 148 And see *Power* v *Walker,* 3 M & S 8 , and *Bohn* v *Davidson,* 6 C B 458 Lord *Ivory,* in *Jeffreys* v *Kyle* (18 Dec of Ct of Sess 2d series p 911), and others have thought that *Power* v *Walker* is well as *Bohn*

v *Davidson* were wrongly decided, but see Lord *St Leonards,* 4 H L Cᵤ 995, and *Alderson,* B 4 H L Cᵤ 915

(c) 4 H L Cᵢ 933, 940, 993

(d) See *Maule,* J in *Davidson* v *Bohn,* 6 C B 456

(e) 10 W R 351

(f) See *Latour* v *Bland,* 2 St ukᵤ, 382

W. P. Wood, V.C. held that the purchase of the copyright carried with it the right of printing and publishing, and that the defendant was entitled to continue selling after the expiration of the four years' term the stock printed by him under his purchase. In answer to a suggestion that the effect of such a sale might be to destroy the copyright in the author altogether, as the publisher, who had purchased the copyright for a limited period only, might, during that period, print off copies enough to last for all time, the Vice Chancellor said: 'A nice question might, indeed, arise as to the number of copies of which an edition might consist, but a publisher was not likely to incur the useless expense of printing copies enough to exhaust the demand for all time, and have them lying upon his hands unprofitably. Besides this, even if the effect of a sale for four years might operate in this way to deprive the author of all copyright in his work, the answer was that he had not guarded himself against such a contingency.'

Where, in an action for piracy, it appeared that the work alleged to be pirated had been for several years sold by the defendant, with the acquiescence of the plaintiff, *Abbott*, J. thought it might be inferred that the defendant once had authority to sell, but that it was impossible thence to infer for what time that authority might have been given, and whether it subsisted at the time of the publication of which the plaintiff complained. (a)

An agreement in writing between an author and publisher, (b) 'that the latter should print, reprint, and

---

(a) *Latour* v *Bland*, 2 Stark 382, and see *Randell* v *Murray*, Jac 311

(b) As to account of profits between author and publisher, see a recent case, *Barry* v *Stevens*, 31 Beav

publish his book, and that he and they should equally share the net profits of the publication, and that he should write, and they should print and publish on the same terms any subsequent edition of the book which the public might require, and that if all the copies of any edition should not be sold within five years from publication, the publishers might sell the remaining copies in order to close the account,' is not a contract for an assignment of the copyright, but a mere personal contract not assignable by either party. (a)

A contract for the sale of copyright is enforceable in equity. (b)

In *Leader* v. *Purday*, (c) which was an action upon the case for an infringement of copyright, the defendant objected that the plaintiffs agreed to assign it to one of them : this objection was overruled; it was at law and when equitable pleas were unknown there.

In the Court of Chancery it has always been held sufficient if the plaintiff established an equitable title to the copyright violated. (d)

It was considered in *Cocks* v. *Purday*, (e) that a sale

258. Sir *J Romilly*, M R observed 'I am very far from saying that the author of a book may not come into a court of equity for an account, when such an account is refused' In that case he refused the relief prayed, because it amounted to a mere money demand, which could be dealt with at law, and a reference on the subject was then pending at law   The issue of an edition of a work as an edition by its author, when it is not so, may lead to an action for damages by him against the publisher (*Archbold* v *Sweet*, 5 C & P 219)

(a) *Stevens* v *Benning*, 1 Ku & Jo Affirmed on appeal, 6 De G. M & G 223   An action lies for damages against an author failing to supply a publisher with MS according to contract   (*Gale* v. *Leckie*, 2 Stark 107, but as to specific performance of such a contract, see *Clarke* v *Price*, 2 Wils. C C 157.)

(b) *Thombleson* v *Black*, 1 Jur. 128

(c) 7 C B 14

(d) *Sweet* v *Shaw*, 3 Jur 217, *Sweet* v *Maugham*, 4 Jur 156

(e) 5 C B 885

of the copyright in an unpublished musical work by the author (a foreigner), the sale being evidenced by writing and valid abroad, so vested the interest of the vendor in the purchaser afterwards publishing in England as to make the latter an assignee of the copyright within the meaning of section 3 of the Act 5 & 6 Vict. c 45; but, in *Jeffreys* v. *Boosey*, common law Judges were divided on this point, and Lord *St Leonards* held it to be perfectly clear, that no assignment of an English copyright could be held good in this country, unless it satisfied the requisition of the law of England in respect to an assignment of such copyright. Sir *J. Coleridge*, J. in the same case, was of opinion that the sale abroad gave an inchoate right to the purchaser. The decision, however, of the House of Lords in *Jeffreys* v. *Boosey* (*a*) overruled the actual decision in *Cocks* v. *Purday*.

For an instance of a limited assignment of copyright *Sweet* v. *Cater* may be looked at. (*b*)   That case proceeded upon a written agreement between Lord St. Leonards (then Sir E. Sugden) and Mr. Sweet (the law bookseller and publisher). The agreement ran as follows: —'The Right Honourable Sir Edward Sugden having prepared a new edition (the 10th) of the "Treatise of the Law of Vendors and Purchasers," and S. Sweet being desirous of purchasing the same, it is agreed that Messrs Hansard shall print 2,500 copies of the work in type and page corresponding with the 6th edition of the "Treatise of Powers," at the sole cost of S. Sweet, and S. Sweet shall pay to Sir E. Sugden for the said edition, the sum of   '. (the sum to be paid, and the

---

(*a*) 4 H L Ca 977   (*b*) 11 Sim 573

instalments by which it was to be paid, were then mentioned): the first instalment was to be paid in cash as soon as the edition was ready for publication, the second instalment by a bill payable four months after date, the last instalment by a bill payable eight months after date; both bills were to be dated at the time the edition was ready for publication; the work to be divided into three volumes, and to be sold to the public for 3l. in boards; but, should it exceed 111 sheets or 1,776 pages, a proportionate increase to be made in the charge to the public, and a proportionate addition to the consideration to be paid to Sir E. Sugden by S. Sweet; fifteen copies in boards to be delivered to Sir E. Sugden, free from all charge or expense.' The bill (to restrain the defendant from piracy of the treatise) was demurred to for want of equity, on the ground that the plaintiff had a mere license under the agreement to publish and sell 2,500 copies, not even an exclusive license for any definite time, and therefore no interst, legal or equitable, in the copyright. Sir *L. Shadwell*, V.C.E (without hearing the plaintiff) overruled the demurrer, because he considered that under the agreement Sweet was an assign of the copyright in the limited sense of having the exclusive right to publish and sell the whole edition of 2,500 copies.

9. It seems that there are no reported judgments on the extent to which the law implies a warranty upon the sale of a copyright, therefore the point must be decided by analogy to the sales of other personal property. *Sims* v. *Marryat* (a) is, however, a case where an express warranty was collected from the language

9 Warranty on sale of the right

(a) 17 Q B 281.

of a letter and receipt which passed between the vendor and purchaser of a copyright.

10. Attention may here, perhaps, be properly called to *Reade* v. *Bentley*. (*a*)   There were two agreements in that case, exactly similar, between the plaintiff and defendant, relating to two different works.   The agreements were couched in the following language :—' It is agreed that Rd. Bentley shall publish, (*b*) at his own expense and risk, a work at present entitled, &c.; and after deducting from the produce of the sale thereof the charges for printing, paper, advertisements, embellishments (if any), and other incidental expenses, including the allowance of ten per cent. on the gross amount of the sale for commission and risk of bad debts, the profits remaining of every edition that shall be printed of the work are to be divided into two equal parts, one moiety to be paid to C. Reade, and the other moiety to belong to Rd. Bentley, the books sold to be accounted for at the trade sale price, reckoning 25 copies at 24, unless it be thought advisable to dispose of any copies or of the remainder at a lower price, which is left to the judgment and discretion of Rd. Bentley.'   The defendant had stereotyped the works, had published a first edition of the earlier work at a price fixed by himself and the plaintiff, a second edition of that work at a lower price fixed by himself alone, three editions of the later work at a price fixed by himself and the plaintiff, and a fourth edition at a lower price fixed by himself alone.   On the defendant's communicating to the plaintiff his intention of publishing another edition of both works at a still

(*a*) 4 K & Jo 656
(*b*) Publication of a book by its author or his assignee, in breach of his agreement with another person, may be restrained *Brook* v *Wentworth*, 3 Austr 881

lower price, the plaintiff gave to the defendant notice of
his objection to such a publication ; the defendant per-
sisted in his intention, and thereupon the plaintiff filed
a bill against him, and thereby prayed that the joint
adventure, or partnership, between himself and defendant might be dissolved; that accounts might be taken,
and that it might be declared that he (the plaintiff) was
absolute owner and proprietor of the copyright; that the
agreements might be delivered up to be cancelled, and
that the defendant might be restrained from publishing,
&c. any new editions of the works without the plaintiff's
written sanction or consent. Sir *W. P. Wood*, V.C. made
the declaration prayed, and decreed the consequent accounts, but gave no costs, the whole litigation having
arisen, in his opinion, from the defective form of the
agreement, for which both plaintiff and defendant were
to blame.   In the course of his judgment, the learned
Vice-Chancellor observed: 'The question then was as
to what is the exact character of the contract.   It had
been said that it was a simple agency, but clearly it was
something more than that, the publisher taking upon
himself the whole risk of bringing out the work, while
a mere agent never embarked in the risk of the undertaking, then it had been regarded partly as a joint
adventure, and partly as a license to publish, which,
according to the defendant's contest, was irrevocable ...
The plaintiff contended that the defendant's duty had
been fulfilled when any one edition had been published,
but that, as to the particular edition, he could not interfere with that edition after expense had been incurred
upon it.   If, however, the plaintiff were not entitled to
exercise a control and determine the arrangement as to
any subsequent edition, he would be in this position,

that he would not be able to assert any right of publishing his works himself, and would in effect have parted
with the copyright for the life of the defendant. At all
events, the contract would be personal and would not
extend to the defendant's representatives; but during
the defendant's own life, the plaintiff's interest would
have become divested, and all right of interference gone
so long as the defendant was ready and willing to publish continued editions. At the same time, the author
would not be able to compel the publisher to publish
any second edition, which would be leaving the author
in a position of great hardship. The publisher was the
proper person to fix the price, as he had been at the
expense of advertisements, agency, printing, and paper;
then, as to the time of bringing out a fresh edition, the
publisher might not refuse definitely so to do, but might
think that the proper period had not yet arrived. If
the proper person to fix the price, it must be held by a
parity of reasoning that the publisher was the proper
person to fix the time, though this result would be one
of considerable hardship and difficulty upon the author,
if he had no power of determining the arrangement.
On the other hand, when was the author's right of
determining the arrangement to commence? The
publisher had expended his capital and given the benefit
of his talents and position, considerations by no means
to be overlooked, with the expectation that the work
would run to several editions. The defendant also
relied upon the circumstance that he had stereotyped
the work, a process in itself involving considerable
expense. The Court did not concur in the plaintiff's
view that there had been any fraud in stereotyping the
work; it would not be influenced by the accident of its

being in stereotype rather than moveable type, and was equally powerful to restrain any unfair use of the one or the other. The period fixed by the word edition seemed to refer to the time for having a periodical statement of accounts and profits. It was said that when the work was stereotyped, the edition, in the technical sense, was at an end; a question of right like this was not, however, to be governed by the pedantry of etymology, but by the facts of the case. He (the Vice-Chancellor) apprehended that, if a publisher chose to print 20,000 copies, keeping in his storehouse a large quantity, and periodically issuing them to the world, by thousands, for instance, every such issue would be an edition. There would be no substantial difference between this course and printing a new set of 1,000 for an issue. The profits of every edition meant that the time at which each edition was issued was the period for taking and terminating the accounts. No new expense had been incurred in printing or embellishment since the second edition of the earlier work and the fourth of the latter work. On a balance of the difficulties, it appeared that the onus was thrown upon those who contended that the necessary construction of this agreement, which on the face of it contained no such stipulation, was a parting by the author with all control as to all publication and all right to determine the arrangement, a conclusion to which the Court could not come.'

Whether a purchaser of a foreign work can here insist on copyright therein, when an unauthorised publication of the work in this country has preceded a written assignment of the right to himself, was a question which, in *Chappel* v. *Purday*,(a) Lord *Abinger*, L.C.B. thought too important and too doubtful to be decided on a motion for an injunction.

11. There is no statutory enactment as to the form of licenses affecting this copyright; but, as already stated, they should be registered at Stationers' Hall. (b)

A license to print a book ordinarily conveys by the trade custom the privilege of printing a certain number of copies, called an edition.

12. The only persons who can lay claim to this copyright are, in the case of a book published before July 1, 1842, the proprietor on that day of the copyright therein or his assigns; and in the case of a book since published, the author or his assigns. No other person can claim this right.

The only qualification of the word 'author' in the Act 5 & 6 Vict. c. 45, seems to be the decision of the House of Lords in *Jeffreys* v. *Boosey*. (c) It was there ruled that a foreigner, although he be the author of a book first published here, is not, if absent from this country at the date of publication, an author within the protection of our copyright law.

That case was determined upon the Acts 8 Anne, c. 19, & 54 Geo. 3, c. 156; but the Act 5 & 6 Vict. c. 45 is open to the same construction (as to the claim of a foreigner to copyright here) as that put upon the earlier Acts.

(a) 4 Y & C 485, but see now *Jeffreys* v *Boosey*, 4 H L Ca

(b) 5 & 6 Vict c 45, s 11 For an instance of an agreement to sell a certain number of copies of a work, see *Benning* v *Dove*, 5 C & P 427 A reprint of a portion of a work, to replace copies destroyed by fire when in the publisher's hands, is not an edition entitling the editor to insist on superintending its issue, and receiving remuneration (*Blackwood*, 1860,p.142) As to an implied license prior to the Act of Victoria, see *Sweet* v *Archbold*, 10 Bingh 133

(c) 4 H L Ca. 977

Contrary doctrine had been previously held by the Court of Common Bench in *Cocks* v. *Purday*, (*a*) in that case the decision was given upon the authority of *D'Almaine* v. *Boosey*, (*b*) *Bentley* v. *Foster*, (*c*) the expression of judicial opinion in *Clementi* v. *Walker*, (*d*) and upon the principle of our law, that an alien may in this country acquire personal rights, and may in this country maintain personal actions in respect of injury to such rights.

Prior to the decision in *Cocks* v. *Purday*, Sir *L. Shadwell* had, however, observed in *Delondre* v. *Shaw* (*e*) (not a copyright case be it remarked, but a motion to restrain the imitation of trade marks): 'The circumstance that he was the inventor of the seals will not justify the Court in interposing in his behalf, for he

(*a*) 5 C B 860

(*b*) 1 Y & C 288 *D'Almaine v. Boosey* was only a decision by the Court of Exchequer that an English assign and first publisher in England of the musical composition of an alien amy might bring an action on the case against any one pirating the composition in this country Lord *Abinger*, L C B, had, however, observed in his judgment therein 'The point whether the copyright of a foreigner is protected at all in this country does not arise in the present case, because the plaintiff D'Almaine is not a foreigner'

(*c*) 10 Sim 329 *Bentley* v *Foster* was a motion to dissolve an injunction restraining the defendant from pirating a work, the copyright of which the plaintiff, an English-man, had purchased of a citizen of the United States of America resident there Sir *L Shadwell*, V C E, observed in that case, that protection was given by the law of copyright to a work first published in this country, whether written abroad by a foreigner or not, but as the question was legal, he directed the plaintiff to try it at law, and meanwhile he continued the injunction; the plaintiff brought the action, and the defendent consented to a verdict against himself

(*d*) 2 B & Cr 861, by *Bayley*, J 'that after publication abroad, copyright was acquired by first publication in England, if the publication here followed promptly the foreign publication

(*e*) 2 Sim 240

was a foreigner, and the Court does not protect the copyright of a foreigner.'

After the decision in *Cocks* v. *Purday*, in the Court of Common Bench, a motion was heard in a case of *Chappel* v. *Purday* by the Court of Exchequer; (a) the motion was to dissolve an injunction obtained ex parte by a plaintiff to restrain a defendant from publishing and selling the overture and airs of an opera composed abroad by a foreigner there resident, the plaintiff, though the purchaser and first publisher in England of the overture and airs, had omitted to get a conveyance to himself of the copyright therein until after their publication in England by another; the only point decided in that case was apparently this: 'that the question involved in the application was too important and too doubtful for an interlocutory order.' In delivering judgment, however, Lord *Abinger*, L.C.B. expressed his own individual opinion that a foreigner, author of a work unpublished abroad, might communicate such right as he had therein abroad to any British subject, at least, for the period prescribed by the statute of Anne.

In *Boosey* v. *Davidson* (b) the Court of Queen's Bench had given judgment expressly in accordance with the decision in *Cocks* v. *Purday*, but did not more particularly state the grounds of its judgment. In the subsequent case of *Boosey* v. *Purday*, (c) the plaintiff as assign and first publisher in England of an opera composed abroad by a foreigner, had brought an action on the case for infringement of his copyright therein in this country; the judgment was delivered by Sir *F.*

(a) 1 Y & C 485

(b) 13 Q B 257

(c) 4 Exch 145

Pollock, L.C.B. The Court of Exchequer had there held that the Copyright Acts give no property in England to a foreigner composing a work abroad; that a foreigner, therefore, could transfer no such right to the plaintiff.

Boosey v. *Jeffreys* followed this last decision: it was an action on the case brought in the Court of Exchequer in order that the matter might be taken by way of appeal to the House of Lords; it was tried by *Rolfe*, B., (now Lord *Cranworth*). The following facts then came out : an opera had been composed at Milan, by an alien ; the composition gave to its author a copyright at Milan, assignable by him; he had at Milan, and according to Milanese law, assigned his right in part of the opera to another alien there, who had afterwards in London, and by deed, assigned his interest to the plaintiff, but for publication in the United Kingdom only. The plaintiff had been born in England and was resident here; he had been the first publisher in England of the work of which he had duly registered himself assignee. The defendant had also published and sold here copies of the opera. *Rolfe*, B. in conformity with the decision in *Boosey* v. *Purday*, directed the jury to find for the defendant · a bill of exceptions to that direction was tendered, and the Court of Exchequer Chamber declared the direction to be wrong : (*a*) the grounds given for the reversal were that the British Parliament could legislate within British territory for aliens, and if it used general words, which would cover aliens as well as natural-born subjects, it must be presumed to be legislating for aliens ; that the words of the Copyright Act were general ; that

(*a*) *Boosey* v *Jeffreys* 6 Exch 593

the Act 8 Anne, c 19, was for the encouragement of learning (see title of the Act 8 Anne, c. 19), and that it was consistent with the uniform policy of Parliament to promote the importation of foreign literature.

The cases of *Cocks* v *Purday* and *Boosey* v. *Purday* had been brought to the notice of Sir *J. L. K. Bruce*, V.C. in *Ollendorff* v. *Black*, (*a*) upon a motion by the plaintiffs to restrain the defendant from selling an edition of a work written by one of the plaintiffs, a German, and first published in London while the author was temporarily resident there; that learned Judge granted the motion, expressing on the occasion his preference for the decision in *Cocks* v. *Purday*, and founding thereon, to some extent, his judgment, but distinguishing the case then before him from *Boosey* v. *Purday* by this point of difference, viz. that in *Ollendorff* v. *Black*, the first publication in England took place when the author, though domiciled abroad, was in England.

From the judgment of the Court of Exchequer Chamber in *Boosey* v. *Jeffreys* a writ of error was brought in the House of Lords, (*b*) and after taking the opinion of the Judges, (*c*) the House, in *Jeffreys* v.

(*a*) 4 De G & Sm 209

(*b*) Pending the appeal from the judgment of the Court of Exchequer Chamber, a somewhat similar case, *Buxton* v *James*, 5 De G & Sm. 80, was decided by Sir *J Parker*, V C, upon the authority of that judgment The Vice-Chancellor on that occasion observed that he had himself never doubted the law as laid down by the Exchequer Chamber in *Boosey* v *Jeffreys*

(*c*) The following statement and questions were submitted to the judges for their opinions —

STATEMENT

Vincenzio Bellini being an alien friend, while living at Milan composed a literary work, in which, by the laws there in force, he had a certain copyright He there, on the 19th February 1831, by an instrument in writing, bearing date on that date, not executed in the

COPYRIGHT-AFTER-PUBLICATION IN BOOKS.

Boosey, reversed the judgment of that Court, and affirmed the ruling of the Court of Exchequer. The Law Lords who spoke were Lord *Cranworth,* C.,

presence of or attested by two witnesses, made an assignment of that copyright to Giovanni Ricordi, which assignment was valid by the laws there in force. Ricordi afterwards came to this country, and on January 9, 1831, by a deed under his hand and seal, bearing date on that day, executed by him in the presence of and attested by two witnesses, for a valuable consideration, assigned the copyright in the said work to the defendant in error, his executors, administrators, and assigns, but for publication in the United Kingdom only, the said defendant then printed and published the work in this country before any publication abroad, the plaintiff in error, without any license from the defendant in error, then printed and published the same work in this country.

QUESTIONS

1. Did this publication by the plaintiff give to the defendant any right of action against him?

2. If the assignment to Ricordi had been made by deed under the hand and seal of Bellini, attested by two witnesses, would that have made any and what difference?

3. If Bellini, instead of assigning to Ricordi, had, while living at Milan, assigned to the defendant in error all his copyright by deed, similar in all respects to that executed by Ricordi, would that have made any and what difference?

4. If the work had been printed and published at Milan before the assignment to the defendant, would that have made any and what difference?

5. If the work had been printed and published at Milan after the assignment to the defendant, but before any publication in this country, would that have made any and what difference?

6. If the assignment to the defendant had not contained the limitation as to publication in this country, would that have made any and what difference?

7. Looking to the record as set out in the bill of exceptions, was the learned judge who tried the cause right in directing the jury to find a verdict for the defendant?

The substance of the several answers of the judges was as follows —
Crompton, J. He thought it unnecessary to consider either the possible effect of the decision in *Jeffreys* v *Boosey* upon our literary relations with other countries, or the existence of a common law copyright anterior to the Act 8 Anne, c 19, or the rights of an author against parties having illegally or surreptitiously taken or used his manuscripts or copies copyright was a territorial monopoly, bounded and regulated by the Copyright Acts, and not a property derived from or carved out of a general right of property or foreign copyright, publication was

Lord *Brougham*, and Lord *St. Leonards*: they were unanimous as to the reversal.

the commencement and foundation of English copyright (*Beckford* v. *Hood*, 7. T. R 620), by publication was meant a bonâ fide publication in this kingdom, the right might be acquired by a foreign author, although he resided abroad, and did not personally come to England to publish *Clement* v *Walker* had tacitly recognised this last conclusion to be law, if such was not law   A foreigner residing at Calais, and composing a work there upon an English subject and for the English reading market, could not write to his agent in London to publish it, and so acquire copyright, but might acquire it by crossing to Dover and sending his publication thence to be published in London during his stay here   There was nothing in the Act 8 Anne, c 19, to exclude friendly foreigners, if the Act was to be read, inserting 'British' before 'author,' it would also seem necessary to insert 'British' before 'assigns,' otherwise a British author could not assign the right to a foreigner, such foreigner could not assign it to a British subject, and there would be created by the Act, contrary to the general rule of law, a species of personal property which an alien friend would be incapacitated from taking, it was improper to introduce into an Act words, when the intention of Parliament was not more clearly expressed than in the Act 8 Anne, c 19 The answer to the query,

'Why is the publication to be construed British, and the author not to be construed British?' was this 'the publication being made the commencement of the period of the monopoly, and that publication giving rights confined to Britain, and the enactments as to the entries at Stationers' Hall, and the obligation imposed of delivering copies to British institutions, together with the authority of *Clements* v. *Walker*, satisfactorily show that the publication must be intended to be in England, whilst there seems nothing in the Act to show that the Legislature, in using the words "author" and "assigns," had any intention of restricting the place of composition or the personal capacity of the author or assigns' it was not clear if a composition like that in *Boosey* v *Jeffreys* had occurred to the Legislature, it would have excluded it, *Bentley* v *Northouse*, Moo & Mal. 66, *Milne* v Graham, 1 B & Cr 192, *De la Chaumette* v. *Bank of England*, 2 B & Ald. 385 (cases which established the application of the general words in the Act 3 & 4 Anne, c 9, to notes and endorsements abroad), opposed a limited construction of similar words in the Act 8 Anne, c 19 there was no absurdity in giving copyright to a foreigner having his work first bonâ fide published here the alleged presumption in favour of legislation by Parliament for British subjects only, and the

Lord *Cranworth*, C. in moving the reversal, said, in effect, that the Act 8 Anne, c. 19, must be construed

unlikelihood of an enactment in the reign of Queen Anne to protect foreign productions, were insufficient reasons for restricting the general words, for the Act 8 Anne, c 19, protected foreign productions only as English publications That an assignee might acquire copyright by first publication was clear from the words of the Act 8 Anne, c 19 · the author or his assignee shall have the sole liberty, &c from the day of the first publication ' The assignment of English copyright must be such as our law required, because the right was local, and created or regulated by statute law, but the attestation of two witnesses to such assignment was unnecessary since the Act 51 Geo 3, c. 156, the decision to the contrary in *Davidson* v *Bohn* was wrong With these observations, *Crompton*, J. coupled these categorical answers to the questions 1 Although on the state of facts assumed, Bellini appeared to him an author who might have sent his work over here for first publication, yet that it did not sufficiently appear that there was any sufficient assignment of his right to publish, so as to obtain English copyright. It was stated with reference to the first question, that Bellini had, by the law of Milan, a right to a certain copyright, by which he (*Crompton*, J) understood some copyright in a foreign country, to be enjoyed there according to the

law of the country; but to what extent or for what time, did not appear, and it was stated that the assignment was of that copyright; Bellini's right to clothe himself with the English monopoly arose from his authorship, and not at all as being parcel of or carved out of any foreign copyright. Could an assignment, stated to be of foreign copyright, pass a right under the English statutes ? On the supposition, then, that the assignment mentioned in the first question was intended to apply to the foreign copyright solely, he (*Crompton*, J) answered the first question in the negative, on the ground that the assignment referred to in that question did not appear to be an assignment of any English right 2 If the assignment by Bellini had been by deed attested by two witnesses, the defect in the title would not be cured, as the assignment was stated to have been of the foreign copyright, and did not appear to have included any other right 3 If Bellini had assigned either to Ricordi or immediately to the defendant in error by deed, similar in all respects to that executed by Ricordi, and therefore comprising and assigning the right as to this country, the defendant in error would have had a good title to the copyright. 4 If the work had been printed and published at Milan before the assignment, the right to publish in England so as to acquire the English copyright

G

as referring to the authors being British subjects, i. c. at least within the Queen's dominions, and so owing to

would have been lost.   5. The same consequence would have ensued, if the publication at Milan had been made after the assignment, but before the publication in England.   There would have been nothing in the assignment of the English copyright to prevent the publication at Milan, and that publication not giving the monopoly in England, would make it lawful to publish the foreign work in England, and if once lawful for any one to publish, the right of acquiring the English copyright in the work was gone   6 The limitation of the exercise of the right to this country did not seem material   If the right was an entire right it could not be divided, so, for instance, as to make an assignment of English copyright to one person in Yorkshire, and to another for Middlesex, and in such case there would be great difficulty   In the present case, the right of the author to the English copyright was an entire thing under our municipal statutes, and was not parcel of or derived out of anything else, the author in this case had the right here as author, and not by the law of Milan, and if, having that entire thing under our law, he, by assignment, passed that right as to this country, there was no subdivision of the copyright, unless, indeed, the Act 54 Geo 3, extending the privilege to all the British dominions, might make a difference in

that respect.   *Lastly*, The question upon this record arose upon a bill of exceptions to the ruling of the learned judge directing a verdict for the defendant below   The Act 5 & 6 Vict. c. 45, s. 11, made the copy of the entry primâ facie evidence of the title of the plaintiff, who was, therefore, entitled to the verdict unless his title was destroyed by the defendant's evidence. If the supposed defect in the plaintiff's title depended only upon the form or nature of the assignment, his primâ facie title might not be so entirely destroyed as to warrant the direction that the finding must be for the defendant, as though the proof of such defective assignment might be strong and cogent proof that there was no other, yet, as it was not found that there was no other, there would be evidence both ways, and the direction could only be supported if there was no evidence for the consideration of the jury As to the supposed defect on the ground of the author being an alien, and not having been in this country, as that fact was directly negatived, the defect, if available, would directly negative the title of the plaintiff, and the direction to find for the defendant would be right.   As, under the circumstances stated in the record, the title might be gained by the foreign author or his assignee, and an assignment in writing, though without witnesses, would be suffi-

her temporary allegiance; because primâ facie the Legislature of this country must be taken to make laws

cient, and as the assignment in question, though ambiguously stated in the bill of exceptions, might have been sufficiently general to pass to the assignee the right of clothing himself with the English copyright (as from the recital of it in the deed to the plaintiff it seemed really to have been), and as there was nothing to negative the primâ facie title of the plaintiff under the entry in this respect, by showing that there had not been a sufficient assignment by this or some other instrument, the statement upon the record not being inconsistent with the existence of a good assignment, the learned judge was not right in directing the jury to find a verdict for the defendant —— *Williams*, J. 1 The publication by the plaintiff in error gave to the defendant in error a right of action against him The authorities in favour of the proposition ' that a foreign author might gain an English copyright by publishing in England before any publication abroad, though he might be resident abroad at the time,' were not mean Neither to the counsel nor to the judges in *Clementi* v *Walker* did the doctrine occur that ' copyright could not be gained by a foreigner who was resident abroad at the time of the publication,' though this doctrine would have disposed of one point at least in that case In *D'Almaine* v. *Boosey*, Lord *Abinger*, L.C.B, granted an injunction to protect

the copyright of a foreigner who had first published in England. In *Chappel* v *Purday*, Lord *Abinger*, LCB adhered to his decision in *D'Almaine* v. *Boosey*. In *Bentley* v *Foster* the precise point arose, and Sir *L Shadwell*, VCE, there said that, in his opinion, protection was given by the Law of Copyright to a work first published in this country, whether it was written abroad by a foreigner or not. In *Chappel* v. *Purday*, Sir *F Pollock*, L.C.B. stated the result of the decisions to be, that if a foreign author, not having published abroad first, published in England, he might have the benefit of the Copyright Acts The decision in *Cocks* v *Purday* was, that an alien amy, resident abroad, being the author and first publisher in England of a work not previously published abroad, had a copyright therein, whether composed here or abroad , and that decision was followed in *Boosey* v. *Davidson* The only authority conflicting with these cases was an intimation by the Court, in *Chappel* v *Purday*, that, on a proper construction of the Copyright Acts, a foreign author, or the assignee of a foreign author, could not gain English copyright , and a decision to that effect in *Boosey* v *Purday* There were no words in the Act 8 Anne, c 19, which confined its benefits to British subjects by birth or residence ; though the context, and other provisions of the Act, showed

for its own subjects exclusively, and where, as in the Act 8 Anne, c. 19, an exclusive privilege was given to a

that the publication must be British. The title of that Act did not require such a construction of its provisions; and Parliament might legislate for foreigners in respect of the legal consequences in Great Britain of an act done in Great Britain. The Legislature could scarcely mean that a foreign author should have no copyright if he remained at Calais, but should gain it if he crossed to Dover, and there gave directions for, and awaited the publication of, his work; or that a foreign author, who, during a residence in England, had composed a work which was afterwards first published in England by his order and at his expense, should have no capacity to acquire a copyright therein, if the exigencies of his affairs constrained him to quit England just before the work was published; but that a foreign author, who, during his residence abroad, had composed a work which was afterwards first published in this country, should have the copyright if he happened to come to England just before the publication, and abided here till it was complete. Harsh consequences would also result from such construction to the trade of booksellers (for whose protection, as well as for authors', the Act purported to be passed), for if a bookseller should purchase a literary work in manuscript from a foreign author resident here in England, the copyright would be lost to the bookseller if the author should choose to leave this country, and be absent from it even without the knowledge of the bookseller at the time of publication; and if the bookseller should think it best to publish the work in several volumes, at several times (as it had happened in many well known instances), he might have copyright in some of the volumes, and not in others—because the existence or non-existence of the right would vary with the accident of the author's being, or not being, in this country at the dates of the respective publications of the volumes. Further, no little difficulty would arise in deciding on the rights of the bookseller, supposing the author were to die between the time of selling his work to the bookseller and the time of the publication of the work in England. The defendant in error was the assignee of the author, because the law of Milan recognised in Bellini an assignable right of property in an unpublished work, which right Bellini, in conformity with that law, assigned at Milan to Ricordi, by whom the monopoly only in England was duly assigned to the defendant. The assignment to the defendant was not void, because limited to the English copyright. An English author might limit the right of his assignee to publication in Great Britain,

particular class at the expense of the rest of Her Majesty's subjects, the object of giving that privilege must be taken

and there was no distinction on this point between an English and a foreign author 2, 3 If the assignment to Ricordi had been made by deed, under the hand and seal of Bellini, attested by two witnesses, or if Bellini, instead of assigning to Ricordi, had, while living in Milan, assigned to the defendant his copyright by deed similar in all respects to that executed by Ricordi, that would have made no difference, provided the supposed assignments had been operative according to the laws of Milan 4, 5 If the work had been printed and published at Milan before the assignment to the defendant, or after the assignment to the defendant, but before publication in this country, the defendant by his subsequent publication in England would have gained no copyright The reasons for this opinion may be found fully and clearly stated in the judgment of the Court of Exchequer, delivered by Chief Baron *Pollock*, in *Chappel* v *Purday* 6 If the assignment to the defendant had not contained any limitation as to publication in this country, that would have made no difference *Lastly*, Looking at the record as set out in the bill of exceptions, the learned judge who tried the cause was wrong in directing the jury to find a verdict for the defendant —— *Erle*, J. 1 The publication by the plaintiff gave to the defendant a right of action against him (1) All authors

had by common law copyright and all other rights of property in their written works (2) The statute of Anne embraced alien authors and their assigns first publishing in England In support of proposition (1) the origin of an author's property in his work was in production, the subject of the property was the order of words in the composition, not the words, nor the ideas expressed by the words. The nature of the property was analogous to property in other personalty, and extended beyond the right to control copies after publication of the work in print, to which right only the Act 8 Anne, c. 19, related· thus an author had for wrongful abstraction of copies of his unpublished works, remedies analogous to those of an owner of other personalty in like case, he might prevent publication, claim copies wrongfully made, sue for damages, and stop the sale of copies wrongfully made and published abroad and innocently imported. The right of an alien or native author in respect of publication here of his private work wrongfully copied abroad would be equally protected, because it was a personal right, based on principles common to all nations who read, and analogous to the right of an alien while residing abroad to prohibit the publication here of words defamatory of his character (see *Pisani* v *Lawson*, 6 Bingh N C. 90) The right of disposition of an

to have been a national object, and the privileged class must be confined to a portion of that community for

unpublished work was similar to the right of disposition of other personalty, the disposition might be absolute or qualified in any degree. Publication did not affect the author's common law right, because the printing, i.e. copying, had no legal effect upon the previous right to control copying, and because a contrary doctrine would make the labours of an author profitless in a pecuniary point of view, and would, to that extent, discourage productions useful to the community. Objectors to the common law right of an author after publication relied mainly on three grounds. *first*, that copyright after publication could not be the subject of property, *second*, that copyrigh' was a privilege of prohibiting others from the exercise of the right of printing, and a monopoly lawful by statute, *third*, that by publication the property of the author was given to the public. Now, as to the *first* objection, copyright could be the subject of property, it was a claim to the order of words, which order had a marked identity and a permanent endurance. It was also indeed a neutral abstraction, but that might be property, e.g. a right to a flow of water. It might be that in an early stage of society nothing was property which could not be earmarked and recovered in detenue or trover, but this was not true in a more civilised state of society. As property must precede the violation of it, so the rights of property

must precede the remedies for violation of such rights. To seek, therefore, the law of the rights of property in the law of procedure for the remedies for their violation was the same mistake as to suppose an ear mark is a cause not a consequence of property in the ear. The difference in the judgments of *Yates*, J. and Lord *Mansfield* on this point was the difference between following precedent in its unimportant forms and in essential principles. if precedent in its unimportant forms was to be followed, there was no precedent, of course, relating to printing before printing was known; printing, however, was but a mode of production. if the growth of law could be traced in words actionable or indictable, there should be similar growth of law in respect of the interest connected with the investment of capital in words. In other matters the law had been adapted to the progress of society, according to justice and convenience, and by analogy it should be for literary works, then they would become property with all its incidents, on the most elementary principles of securing to industry its fruit and to capital its profits. As to the *second* objection, copyright was property, not a personal privilege in the nature of a monopoly, a printer might not print everything published; the supposition of the objector was that there was a demand for books, that the supply was produced by labour,

the general advantage of which the enactment was made; publication of a work was the overt act, esta-

skill, and capital for the sake of profit, that the profit began to arise upon the sale of the production, and that, as soon as the sale had commenced, the law gave to the printer an equal right to the profits with the producer, i e. the law gave up the most important production of industry to spoliation a printer might not print anything already in print, he might (see Stationers' case, 1 Mod 256) print all that had been made common, but not that which had remained enclosed, he clearly might not print words of blasphemy, sedition, or defamation, and he might not infringe the Queen's copyright, his liberty of printing was so far restrained, the principle of liberty in printing would not be more invaded if restricted also as to the property of an author As to the *third* objection to say that by publication an author intended a gift to the public was contrary to fact, and to say that publication operated in law as such gift was begging the question In the argument of Wedderburn in *Tonson* v *Collins*, in the judgments of Lord *Mansfield* and of *Aston* and *Willes* JJ, in *Millar* v. *Taylor*, and in the summing up of the argument on this point in *Donaldson* v. *Beckett*, 2 Bro. P C, 129, the governing question was whether authors had a perpetuity of copyright since 8 Anne *Donaldson* v *Beckett* decided that the Act 8 Anne, c 19, had restricted the right to the period therein mentioned, but left the question of copyright at common law undecided, authorities preponderated in favour of copyright at common law The cases prior to Charles II, cited in *Millar* v *Taylor* and *Donaldson* v. *Beckett*, though not decisions upon the right, were good evidence that the right was from the beginning of printing known and supported the Act 13 & 14 Car 2, c. 33, s. 6, also recognised the right, and in 16 Car. 2, *Roper* v. *Streater* (Skinn 234), decided that the assignee of the executor of an author had copyright in his law reports against the law patentee—a decision indeed reversed, but only on the ground of the character of the reports The Act 8 Anne, c 19, was decisive that copyright existed previously thereto, it spoke of it as having been he subject of sale and purchase, therefore as property, and of the then usual manner of ascertaining title to it. Each of the Acts 13 & 14 Car. 2, c 33, and 8 Anne, c 19, secured it against piracy, and referred to registration as a mode of proving the right. The Act 8 Anne, c 19, was for the encouragement of both readers and authors, and arose from their conflicts, for the clause therein which appeared to promote the interest of authors by vesting their property in them for a term, and giving them stringent remedies for its protection, contained the expression which in *Donaldson* v *Beckett* was held to have destroyed the perpetuity of

blishing authorship; then copyright arose; if a foreign author was not then in this country he was not a

their property—a result so inconvenient that the Legislature had since twice interposed to extend the term All the actions on the case, and all the injunctions for infringement of copyright during the first fourteen years after publication, were authorities that the right had continued at common law since the Act 8 Anne, c 19, no otherwise affected thereby than limited in duration, for if the Act created a new right for 14 years, it created also a new remedy, which would be the only remedy, and the point on which the plaintiff succeeded in *Beckford* v *Hood*, viz that the new remedy did not extend beyond 14 years (but see *Beckford* v *Hood*, 7 T. R 620, the plaintiff had copyright for 28 years, the piracy was not within 14 years of the first edition), would have been of no avail in reasoning for the 14 years In the conflict ending with *Donaldson* v *Beckett*, the great majority of the judges were for copyright at common law—3 to 1 in *Miller* v *Taylor*, 10 to 1 in *Donaldson* v *Beckett* The judgment of *Yates*, J, in *Miller* v. *Taylor*, was the sole judgment against such copyright Lord *Kenyon* extra-judicially expressed his concurrence in the opinion of *Yates*, J, but his judgment in *Beckford* v *Hood* was inconsistent, admitting the common law remedy, he derived the right from the Act 8 Anne, c 19 Lord *Ellenborough's* opinion, incidentally expressed in

Cambridge University v. *Bryer*, 16 East. 317, also seemed against such copyright; but the opinions of Lords *Kenyon* and *Ellenborough*, so extra-judicially expressed, are outweighed by Lord *Mansfield's* judgment in *Millar* v *Taylor* those successors of Lord Mansfield had turned away from that source of the law to which he habitually resorted with endless benefit to his country.   The absence of any record of an action on the case for infringement of copyright prior to the Act 8 Anne, c 19, was no presumption against the right, if piracy was then rare, or if a more ready remedy then existed now printing was here originally controlled by the tyrannical Star Chamber, the High Commission Court, &c, and even in the reign of Charles II. the number of printers was limited by an Act to 20, further, it was noticed by *Willes*, J in *Millar* v *Taylor*, that in Queen Anne's reign the poverty of the pirates was such as to make an action for damages against them futile, and that therefore the booksellers petitioned for the Act 8 Anne, c 19. Even if copyright after publication was derived only from the Act 8 Anne, c 19, the plaintiff below had a cause of action, for that Act did not express an intention to destroy the property which an author clearly had before publication (*P Albert* v. *Strange*, 1 M & G 25) effect could be given to all the provisions

British subject, and therefore not a person within the protection of the Act: from this view the apparent

of the Act, without coming to that conclusion. The right to prohibit piracy was incidental to the ownership of the property in the work pirated ownership prohibited user of property against the owners' will, even if the Act annulled the property after publication, it left the property before publication as it was. it touched not the plaintiff, an assignee before publication The Act was intended to encourage learning, and to induce learned men to write useful books now learning was encouraged by supplying the best information at the cheapest rate, therefore the learner should have free access to the advances in literature and science to be found in the useful books of learned men of foreign nations This was the scope of the Act it was not to be supposed that the Legislature regarded all foreign literature as bad, and all British productions as good, or that it planned the release of British authors from competition with foreigners, or the restriction of readers to British productions inferior to foreign and dearer, or a small premium to British authors of mediocrity at the cost of depriving British printers and booksellers of the profit from printing and selling excellent works by foreigners If such was its plan, the Act did not execute it It provided for 'authors,' a word which had relation to works exclusive of country The construc-

tion 'British authors' emanated from the Court in *Chappel* v *Purday*, but though years had since elapsed, no one could, with practical precision, express in what sense the authors must be British Perhaps Irish authors were not excluded, but how were they included in British authors? Perhaps alien authors in British allegiance by residence in Britain, were included, but if so, what residence would qualify? Must it be during education, so that the mind should be British, or during composition, so that the work should be British? No, that construction was too vague to be practical If an alien author within our frontier at the publication or assignment of his work was British within the Act, this inconsi tency resulted, that the Legislature planned a British monopoly, and made it defeasible by any alien who would go through a senseless formality, further, such construction would be too vague for practice, as to the subject of copyright, for ancient MSS by foreign authors, if now transcribed and published in England, would be thereby excluded from copyright, unless the transcriber of a difficult MS being equal in merit with an author should be considered as an author; but to what practical uncertainty would this lead? If a collection of letters, &c 'of a distinguished foreigner might be published with notes and narrative, and so be

absurdity resulted, that a foreigner having composed a work at Calais gained a British copyright if he crossed

protected, was not the protection illusory, if the letters might be transcribed and published with other notes and narrative? In short, the construction of the plaintiff in error was wrong, because it was contrary to the general rule requiring effect to be given to words according to their ordinary acceptation ; because it was contrary to justice and expediency, in depriving learners of information, and booksellers of profit ; and because it gave to British authors a protection from competition which was more degrading than gainful to them   The opposite construction gave no extra-territorial effect to the Act. The copyright at Milan of the alien author in his MS which was assumed in the question was recognised in England on the authorities collected in *Cocks v Purday* (5 C B 860), the MS was by him assigned at Milan, brought to England by the assignee before publication abroad, and then by him assigned to the plaintiff before publication, i e before the statutory term of copyright began ; the plaintiff published here, and after such publication claimed the operation of the Act in England to protect his right here, in so doing, he only claimed an intra-territorial effect from the Act   If the Act made void the assignment in Milan, it would have an extra-territorial effect, by depriving an alien abroad of a personal right in England, which, but for the Act,

the common law would have given him here   2. If the assignment from Bellini had been by deed under the hand and seal of Bellini, attested by two witnesses that would not have made any difference.   The assignment by Bellini was valid by the law of Milan, therefore valid in England even if the law of England operated in respect of the assignment it was valid, for since the Act 54 Geo 3, c. 156, s 4, no attestation was necessary   That Act was not on this point adverted to in *Davidson v Bohn* 6. C B 456   3 If Bellini, instead of assigning to Ricordi, had, while living at Milan, assigned to the defendant in error all his copyright by deed, similar in all respects to that executed by Ricordi, that would not have made any difference   the assignment in the form valid at Milan would be valid in England, so would an assignment in the form valid in England, if made to an Englishman, to be used in England   4 If the work had been printed and published at Milan before the assignment to the defendant, that would have made a difference   it would have defeated the right of the plaintiff below   There was no copyright in England for a work already published abroad   this proposition of law was recognised by the Act 8 Anne, c 19, s 7, and by the statutes on international copyright   5 The same answer as to 4 the lawful publication abroad would

to Dover and there first published his work, whereas he would have no copyright, if he should send it to an agent

defeat any claim to copyright in England. 6 If the assignment to the defendant had not contained the limitation as to publication in this country, that would not have made any difference, the owner of copyright might dispose of the whole or any part of his interest as he might choose. *Lastly*, Looking to the record as set out in the bill of exceptions, the learned Judge who tried the cause was not right in directing the jury to find a verdict for the defendant —— *Wightman*, J 1 The plaintiff had right of action against the defendant. Ten if not eleven judges against one judge in *Donaldson v Beckett* were of opinion that by the common law the author of a literary composition was entitled, from composition, at least, till publication, to the incorporeal right, to the sole printing and publishing such composition, and by the Act 8 Anne, c 19, from first publication for and during the term specified in that Act and the Act 54 Geo 3, c 156 an alien might in England hold and defend all other personal property, therefore he might hold and defend this incorporeal right, for it was merely personal property (*Tuerloote v Morrison*, 1 Bulstr 134, *Pisani v Lawson*, 8 Scott, 182, Anon. Dyer, 2 b.) The Act 8 Anne, c 19, recognised proprietors at common law of literary property, and contained no language indicative of exclusive benefit to authors being British sub-

jects · it also professed to be an Act to encourage literature and learned writers, and referred not to country or persons. To limit the Act to native authors would be to lessen its beneficial operation, first publication in England of a work by a foreign author was not a matter 'extra fines,' therefore the municipal law might deal with it. Bellini, i s an author, had in his work an incorporeal right, recognised by the law of England; he assigned that right to Ricordi. Upon modern authority (*Chappel v Purday*, *D'Almaine v Boosey*, *Cooks v Purday*, *Boosey v. Davidson*, *Boosey v Purday*) there was a preponderance in favour of the proposition that a foreign author resident abroad could by first publication in England acquire a copyright here, the assignment by Ricordi was valid by the law of Milan, and in England attestation was unnecessary since the Act 54 Geo 3, c 156 2 3 It would not have made any substantial difference in the case if the assignment to Ricordi had been by deed attested, or if the assignment had been direct at Milan from Bellini to Boosey, by deed attested. 4, 5 If the work had been printed and published at Milan before the assignment to Boosey, or after the assignment to him, but before publication here, neither the author nor his assignee would have been entitled to copyright in England first publication

to publish for him; but this was not really absurd, for whenever it was necessary to draw a line, cases border-

in England was essential to statutory protection of copyright *Chappel* v. *Purday* decided that First publication at Milan by the author after assignment would not have wronged Boosey, as the assignment to him was limited to publication in England 6. The limitation in the assignment made no difference under the circumstances of the case A first publication in England under such an assignment would entitle the assignee to the benefit of the statute No terms, however general, could restrain a publication abroad where the English law had no operation, and there was no rule of law which would make such a restricted assignment invalid, though it might be that, as far as copyright in the British dominions was concerned, a restricted assignment would exhaust the whole power of the assignor, and that he could not make another assignment to take effect in another place *Lastly*, Looking to the record as set out, the learned Judge who tried the cause was wrong in directing the jury to find a verdict for the defendant —— *Maule*, J 1 The publication by the plaintiff in error gave the defendant in error a right of action against the plaintiff 2 It would have made no difference, supposing the other circumstances in the first question to be the same 3 It would have made no difference Question 2 did not state that such a deed would have been operative

by the law of Milan, but as the subject of it was expressed to be and actually was the right of publishing, or that of acquiring of such right by proper means in the United Kingdom only, and as the deed was in a form which, by the law in this country, was proper to operate on such a subject, and was executed by an author on whom the Acts conferred the British right and the power of transferring it, such deed was effectual for the purpose of constituting an assignee within the Acts. 4, 5. In the cases supposed in these two questions, the defendant in error would have had no right of action against the plaintiff in error. 6 Whether the words limiting the right to the United Kingdom were or were not contained in the assignment, the defendant in the case supposed in the first question would have had a right of action against the plaintiff *Lastly*, The learned Judge was not right in directing a verdict for the defendant. Copyright, in common acceptation, comprehended (1) the right belonging to an author *before* publication, i e the right to publish or not, as he thought fit, and to restrain others from publishing, (2) the right belonging to an author *after* publication, i e the right to re-publish and to restrain others from re-publishing The right *before* publication arose out of the nature of the thing, as the right of exclusive use of personal chattels arose out of

ing it on either side were so near to each other, that it was difficult to imagine them as belonging to separate

their nature in respect of their mode of acquisition and capacity of exclusive use. This part of copyright not only existed at common law, but it must be presumed to exist in Milan, and in every country where it was not shown to be restricted. The right *after* publication had not the same origin. it rather derogated from the natural right of the owner of a copy of a published book to make what use he would of his own property. It was unnecessary to decide whether this right existed at common law, but it was very clear that no such right existed there in respect of the first publication in England of a book which had been *previously* published in a foreign country. To admit such a right would imply that the law gave without any distinction to a re-publisher of a book, which anyone might and could re-publish, the same monopoly as to an author of an unpublished work. Whatever might be the common law, a right *after* a first publication was given by the Acts 8 Anne, c 19, and 54 Geo 3, c 156, and to aliens as well as natives, for the right was a personal right, and an alien might exercise any such right; further, the Acts did not expressly exclude aliens. Assuming that the intent of the Acts was restricted to the encouragement of British industry and talent (which was contrary to his, J Meade's, belief), the general words of the Legislature could not

be construed so narrowly. The gift by Parliament of copyright to a foreign author publishing in this country was within the province of Parliament. it was a dealing with British interests, and a legislation for British persons. The general words in the Act with respect to the extent of the sole liberty of printing were necessarily confined to the local jurisdiction of the Legislature; further, they were explained by the words prohibiting importation; but the words 'author,' 'assignee,' and 'assigns' naturally comprehended aliens. *Lastly*, To deny copyright to an alien would be an inconvenient exception to the rule which, in personal matters, placed an alien in the same situation as a natural-born subject. Bellini was, therefore, within the Acts of Anne and George 3; his copyright included the right *before* publication; Bellini duly assigned it to Ricordi; he acquired by the assignment the right of obtaining to himself, or his assignees, by a first publication, the sole liberty of printing here, and he duly assigned it to the defendant; the words of limitation did not prejudice the assignment to the defendant, because, if omitted, the assignment would have passed no greater British right. ——*Coleridge*, J 1. The defendant had a right of action against the defendant in error 2, 3 No 4 If the work had been printed and published at Milan before the

classes, however distinguishable they might be.   If the object of the Act 8 Anne, c. 19, was to give at the

assignment to the defendant it would have made a difference, for that publication would have made it lawful for anyone to publish in England   Bellini or his assignee in Milan had not directly copyright in England.   If either of them brought an unpublished manuscript to England, then the English copyright arose, but if the manuscript had been published before, and so put within the power and the right of all other persons as to copyright out of the Milanese territory, Bellini or his assignee would have been on the same footing as any one of the public, an Englishman would have had the same right to publish Bellini's work as he would to publish Dante's, and that state of things was inconsistent with any exclusive right in Bellini or his assignee   5 Same answer as to question 4   6. The limitation as to publication in this country made no difference   *Lastly*, The learned Judge was wrong in directing the jury to find a verdict for the defendant.   Assuming that 'a certain copyright' in the statement made a copyright without any limitations in the contract material to be stated, that 'copyright' was used in the sense in which an English judge would define it according to English law to an English jury, and that Ricordi was an alien friend   Ricordi when he came to England was the owner of two distinct properties, a manuscript (i o a personal chattel), and a copyright (i e an incorporeal right to sole printing and publishing), as an alien, he could by the law of England hold and defend such properties ; he was, therefore, in respect of them, in the same position as a natural-born subject   It was objected that from its nature the property in a Milan copyright was confined to Milan, further, that a prior publication abroad prevented an alien amy from having a copyright in England, whereas it had not that effect in regard to a natural-born subject   Now, to rob the alien in England of the MS was indictable ; he might also sue for it here in detenue or trover   It was also admitted that he might prevent anyone from seeing, reading, or multiplying copies of it; yet if this last should be done unlawfully, because he had no right to multiply copies exclusively, it was a 'damnum sine injuriâ,' yet an alien amy correspondent abroad of an Englishman might, being in England, restrain by injunction a publication here by the Englishman of the correspondence, and get an account of the profits of such publication, and on the ground of his (the alien's) property therein. The argument on the intra-territorial operation of municipal laws was beside the case. Ricordi's rights in England were not founded on Milan law   he was by the Milanese assignment the lawful owner as against Bellini, and

expense of British subjects a premium to those who laboured, no matter where, in the cause of literature,

through him against all the world of the MS., with all the rights incident to such ownership by English law. As such owner, he therefore acquired (setting aside his foreign origin) the exclusive right of multiplying copies of the MS., with the necessary remedies for the vindication of that right in our courts of law. That copyright for the author of a literary or musical composition existed by the common law, unless taken away by the Act 8 Anne, c 19, or some succeeding Act, was settled by *Millar* v *Taylor*, and the opinions of the majority of the judges in *Donaldson* v *Beckett*. Next, the foreign origin of Ricordi was immaterial at common law, because in regard to such property he was by that law in the same situation as a natural-born subject. Then how was the case affected by statute law? That law applied, or it did not. If it applied, the case was within the new statutory right, if it did not apply, the right at common law remained. It would be simply unreasonable and unjust to say, 'you are not within our contemplation for the purpose of protecting the new right, but you are for that of extinguishing the old.' If the right of an alien in England existed at common law, the construction of the statute was immaterial, if the right did not exist at common law, why was Ricordi, being in England, excluded when it was admitted that if Bellini had

been here he might, within the Acts of Anne and George, have assigned to Ricordi? The Act of Anne spoke of books already printed, and of books not printed and published. In both cases it was silent as to any special form of assignment, and used words which embraced assignees in law and by devolution, because in the penal clause an exception was made in favour of those who were licensed by a consent in writing, attested by two witnesses. It was held in *Power* v *Walker* and *Davidson* v. *Bohn*, that an assignment must be so attested, the reason of those decisions was anything but satisfactory. The judgments in *Millar* v *Taylor* and *Donaldson* v *Beckett* left many supposable cases undecided. Suppose the case of a purchaser, prior to the Act 8 Anne, c. 19, from a legatee, or executor, or administrator after it passed, surely the Act did not affect their title because derived from an instrument unattested by two witnesses. The language of those judgments showed that the judges had in contemplation only the precise cases before them, those judgments, therefore, did not govern the present case. The principle of those judgments was this 'where the assignee and the licensee both claim under instruments executed in England, let the requirements of the statute as to one govern in regard to the other,' but where one purchased or acquired, or became

there was no adequate reason for the exception which it was admitted on all hands must be introduced against

assignee of the author's right in a country in which the statute had no operation, the ground of the reasoning failed. Suppose an English owner of English copyright licensed, at Milan, by an unattested document valid there, another person to print and sell in England —could it be maintained that the printing and selling would be piratical, and within the penalty clauses of the Acts of Anne and George? Ricordi was, by a document valid at Milan, substituted for the author. He claimed to have been clothed by that document with the author's rights, so that when he (Ricordi) came to England, he was, by the joint operation of it and the English law, entitled to the statutory rights. He was clearly within the enabling words of the statute: he was the 'assignee of an author,' and it had not been decided that 'assignee' must in all cases mean, 'assignee under an instrument in writing attested by two witnesses.' larger words and less restrained the Legislature could scarcely have used. On what sound principle was restraint by implication to be imported? *Chappel* v *Purday* differed from the present case, inasmuch as there the composition at the date of its assignment had been published in Paris, and so made common in England, and was therefore not a subject of copyright. There was a remarkable and not immaterial inaccu-

racy in the reported judgment in *Chappel* v *Purday*, 14 M & W 316. The question was stated to be, 'whether a foreigner, residing abroad and *composing* a work, had a copyright in England?' And that was answered by saying, 'that a foreign author residing abroad, and there *publishing* a work, had not any copyright here,' as if composing and publishing were the same thing. Dicta in that judgment as to the intent of the British Legislature in the Acts of Anne and George were not law. It would be more true to say that the statutes were intended to extend to all persons who could bring themselves within their requirements. Many of those might be inapplicable to a foreign author resident abroad. Thence it was logical to infer that the statutes were not made for *him*, but it was illogical to infer that the *assignee*, whether British subject or not, of a foreign author might not come within their protection. The supposition was not absurd that the author could possess a subject-matter which, from his personal incapacity to comply with the English municipal law, might be no property in him here, yet which he might pass to another in whom it might be property. There was no legal or philosophical ground for narrowing the construction of large statutory words capable of a liberal construction, and the political or economical ground, 'that the more

those who not only composed but published abroad.
If ' author ' in the Act 8 Anne, c. 19, included ' foreign

tightly we drew the limits round the law of copyright, the more likely we were to induce foreign governments to enter into treaties for international copyright,' could not influence a court of law in determining the common law or the construction of an Act   *Cocks* v *Purday* went beyond what was necessary for the present case The grounds of that decision were that an alien amy, the author of a work unpublished elsewhere, and first published by him in England, had copyright in it by our law, and that any claiming under him, by an instrument valid for the purpose, where made before publication, and first publication here, was an assignee within the Act 5 & 6 Vict c 45, s. 3. The language of that Act was not more favourable than the Acts of Anne and George to foreign authors, but the language of the Acts of George and Victoria as to licenses was less restricted than that of the earlier Act, inasmuch as they did not require the attestation of witnesses ——*Alderson*, B 1 No. 2 If the assignment to Ricordi had been made as suggested, it would have removed one difficulty in the case, but the result would have been the same—the plaintiff could not have recovered   3. No 4 It seems admitted by the Court below that, according to the previous cases, a previous publication abroad would have put an end to the plaintiff's right   But why should

it do so if a foreigner and a British subject are in pari casu, as the Court below seemed to say they were? A publication by an English author abroad did not prevent his acquiring a copyright in England. It might possibly affect its duration, for the statute of Anne did not date the commencement of the term given from the first publication in England, but from the first publication   The clauses as to entry in Stationers' Hall, which no doubt pointed to a publication in England, were added to give a new and further remedy against those who infringed the right, and this remedy could not be had till that was done The fact that a previous publication abroad took away the right of a foreigner seemed to show that the law only applied to persons who, when they *first* published in England, had the right of then acquiring an English copyright This qualification was everywhere, at all times, and under all circumstances possessed by a British subject, but if it was not possessed by an alien amy till he came to England with an unpublished work, he could not, if he had before published it abroad, acquire by a publication here a copyright in England this was admitted to be so in fact, and this seemed to show that the English subject and the alien amy were not in pari casu till the latter came to this country 5 The same answer as to question 4.

II

authors living and composing abroad,' why should 'first published' be not equally extended? There was no

6 The suggested fact would make a difference, for then it would have been an assignment of the copyright, and not a mere license to publish, but, as in the second question, it only removed one out of several objections to the plaintiff's case Lastly, The direction of the Judge and the verdict were right. The question 'whether copyright, i e the sole right of multiplying copies of a published work, existed at common law, or was created by statute,' was beside the present case, it was strange to discuss the question in the case of a foreigner who, while abroad, was not subject to the common law, and it seemed settled that copyright was created or now depended on the Act of Anne An Act was territorial, and extended only to persons under legiance of this country, unless a contrary construction of the Act was shown to be necessary Such contrary construction of the Act 8 Anne, c. 19, cannot be shown to be necessary, therefore this copyright (which was a profitable monopoly) must be regulated by the Act 8 Anne, c 19 An alien amy might make himself capable of obtaining this right by coming to England and first publishing his work here, but until he did so he had not the right, ergo could not transmit it Copyright was different from the ownership of a MS, and from the power over its first publication The Act gave to the author and the assignee copy-

right, not in respect of his possession of the MS., but of his right to multiply copies of it if the author had not this right until he became a British subject (and he did not become such subject before he assigned), his assignment was inoperative· that was the case here Further, Bellini had copyright in Austria. this only he assigned to Ricordi, Ricordi affected to assign to Boosey a different right (no part of his Austrian copyright), i e a right of solely publishing in England even if Ricordi's assignment had been general, it was at most a local license to Boosey by the assignee of the copyright, together with a covenant that he (Boosey) should alone be allowed to publish the work here Now such a license could not, or in any event could not in his own name maintain this action Further, Ricordi was not Bellini's agent the assignment to Ricordi was also bad, because unattested, on this point Davidson v Bohn was decisive An alien amy might maintain an action here for injury to his personal property or to his person, but in that action the property of the alien was admitted, here it was not The dictum of Lord Thurlow when counsel in Tonson v Collins was no authority Bach v Longman proved only this, that in arguing that case, Baron Wood said nothing about a point which had no relation to the point there in question.

analogy between copyright and patent right, for the
Act 21 Jac. 1, c. 2, though it limited the exercise by

The dictum of Lord *Abinger*, in *D'Almaine* v. *Boosey*, was only to this effect, 'that a foreigner *residing here* and publishing might have a copyright.' *Clementi* v. *Walker* might be classed with those authorities; the cases in Simons might be set off against each other. In *Chappel* v *Purday* there was a distinct opinion on this subject, which was questioned in *Cocks* v *Purday*, but in neither of those cases was there a *decision* on it. *Boosey* v *Davidson* simply followed *Cocks* v *Purday* —— *Parke*, B. 1 The defendant in error had no right of action against the plaintiff in error. 2, 3 The attestation of the deed in each case would have made no difference. 4, 5. No. 6 If the assignment to the defendant in error had not contained the limitation as to the publication in this country, it would have made no difference in that respect, as the defendant had no copyright to assign, but if he had such a right, it was the statutory right, by 54 Geo 3, c 156, to the sole privilege of printing copies in the United Kingdom, or any part of the British dominions, that was an *indivisible* right, and the owner of it could not assign a part of the right, as to print in a particular county or place, or do anything less than assign the whole right given by English law. It was analogous to an exclusive right by patent, which could not be parcelled out, though licenses under it might. *Lastly*,

Looking at the Record as set out in the bill of exceptions, the learned Judge who tried the cause was perfectly right in directing the jury to find a verdict for the defendant; the only doubt arose from the form of the question lastly proposed. In the record a certified copy of the register book of the Company of Stationers was stated to have been produced, and that by the 5 & 6 Vict c 45, s. 11, was made primâ facie proof of the proprietorship therein expressed; thereon arose a question whether the other evidence produced by the plaintiff below did rebut it. The evidence of Bellini, a foreigner, did, however, rebut it, for a foreigner resident abroad could not have English copyright. The evidence set out on the bill of exceptions sufficiently rebutted the title of the plaintiff, because it appeared that he claimed under the said partial assignment. Copyright might be understood in two senses 1st, an author's common law right to his MS., and to the actual copies thereof made by himself; 2nd, the exclusive right of multiplying copies of a MS Copyright in the second sense was alone now for consideration. Its existence at common law was not the question in the present case, but the rational view of the subject. The weight of authority and the opinions of foreign judges administering English law were against its existence. The opinions of Lord *Kenyon* in

the Crown of its claim to grant to any person (native or foreigner) a monopoly, left the persons unto whom the

Beckford v *Hood*, of Lord *Ellenborough* in *Cambridge University* v. *Bryer*, and of the majority of the American judges in *Wharton* v *Peters*, 8 Peters, 591, were all against its existence; certainly it could not exist in favour of an alien, for the common law did not extend to aliens, further, an alien could not claim it on principles of natural law, or by the comity of nations the only question then was, 'could an alien claim it under the statute law, i e under the Acts 8 Anne, c 19, and 51 Geo 3, c 156?' There had been no decision on this question *Tonson* v *Collins* and *Bach* v *Longman* were no authorities on the point In *Tonson* v *Collins*, *counsel* remarked, that if authors resident in England composed a work, it mattered not as to the right to copyright whether they were natural-born subjects or not. In *Bach* v *Longman*, *counsel* did not object to the plaintiff's common law right, but it did not appear that Bach was an alien or non-resident in England at the date of the publication of his work, he was, indeed organist in the Chapel Royal, and probably resident here Further, the objection would not have been tenable, because the sole issue in that case was, 'whether a musical composition was a work within the Act 8 Anne, c 19' *D'Almaine* v *Boosey* was no authority it was decided hastily, and on a mistaken impression of *Bach* v *Longman* The dictum of

Sir L. *Shadwell*, V C E in *Delondre* v *Shaw* was no authority, and it was contradicted by his dictum and conduct in *Bentley* v *Foster* *Clementi* v *Walker* only decided that an assignment by an alien author of his copyright in England was ineffectual, if a prior publication abroad had occurred *Page* v. *Townsend* was no authority. it was decided upon the Acts for the protection of engravers. The Legislature had no power over persons beyond its jurisdiction, and must be presumed to legislate for the benefit of those only who owed obedience to our law, and therefore were entitled to protection under it. General words might have a limited construction 'person' in the Legacy Acts had been construed 'English domiciled subject' (*Thompson* v *Advocate-General*, 12 Cl & Fin 1, *Attorney-General* v *Forbes*, 2 Cl & Fin 48, Lord *Cottenham*, C. in *Arnold* v *Arnold*, 2 M & Cr 270) The construction which was in Queen Anne's reign put on the Act 8 Anne, c. 19, must be adhered to, the Parliament of Queen Anne could scarcely have meant to encourage foreign authors at the expense of the British public The clear intention and expressed object of that Act was the encouragement of British authors, not of book importers, in the category of British authors were included, not merely subjects of the Crown by

grant might extend untouched; further, it was no objection to a patent that the subject of it had been in

birth, but by domicile or residence, or even perhaps by personal presence at the time of first publication, for even those last owed temporary allegiance It might be easy for an alien to procure the title by journeying to England and remaining for a short time, and so to evade the intention of the Act, but in Queen Anne's reign that would have involved much cost and trouble, and some now that could only be an argument against construing the Act in favour of aliens coming here not to reside, but merely to publish The construction of the Patent Acts was inapplicable to the Copyright Acts there might be a patent of a manufacture new only within the realm (*Edgibury* v. *Stevens*, 2 Salk 447) The gift of a patent might also perhaps be to an alien resident abroad, and for this reason, viz. prior to 21 Jac 1, c 3, the Crown might by prerogative have given a monopoly to 'anyone who had brought a new invention and new trade within the kingdom' (Clothworkers of Ipswich case, Godb 252), and the grants excepted by that Act from abolition were not expressly restricted to subjects further, in author had a right, the gift of a patent was in the discretion of the Crown. If aliens living abroad could obtain copyright under the Acts of Anne and George by first publishing in England, they might, by a simultaneous publication abroad and in England,

put an end to the advantages which this country could offer to a foreign country (e g. to the States of America, which recognise no copyright but in their citizens) as an equivalent for a copyright in that country, however, that argument of political expediency must not affect a judicial construction of Acts of Parliament. Even if the above reasoning was incorrect, and Bellini had an English copyright, he, according to the statement introducing the 1st question, assigned his *Milanese* copyright *only* to Ricordi, if Bellini did in terms assign the English copyright, the assignment was not void, as not made in the presence of two witnesses the Act 54 Geo 3, c 156, by implication repealed the clause in the Act 8 Anne, c 19, which was the ground of the decision in *Power* v *Walker*, avoiding such an assignment, *Davidson* v *Bohn*, indeed, occurred after the Act 54 Geo 3, c 156, but that Act was not noticed in that case, probably because the *assignment* there was *before* the Act Although by international law, generally speaking, personal property passed by transfer conformable to the law of the domicile of the proprietor, yet, if the law of any country required a particular mode of transfer with respect to any property having a locality in it, that mode must be adopted (*Story's* 'Conflict of Laws,' ss 383, 398, Lord *Kenyon*, in *Hunter* v *Potts*,

pub he use abroad, but previous publication abroad con-
fessedly interfered with copyright in this country.

4 T R. 182, 192) This copyright
was of a local nature, and therefore
must be transferred in the English
way —Sir *Fred Pollock*, L C. B
1 Assuming the facts stated in
this question to be true, the publication by the plaintiff in error did
not give the defendant in error any
right of action against him 2, 3,
4, 5, 6 Assuming the facts to be
true which in questions 2, 3, 4, 5, 6,
respectively were supposed, they
would not have made any difference *Lastly*, Looking to the record,
the learned Judge who tried the
cause was right in directing the
jury to find a verdict for the defendant—now the plaintiff in error
The weight of authority was against
the existence of copyright at common law *Willes*, J was in error
when in *Taylor* v *Millar* he argued
that it should be held to exist at common law, because, on principles of
private justice, moral fitness, and
public existence, the right ought to
exist there, the common law could
not create new rights and limit and
define them.   This was not indeed
the argument for the defendant in
error his ground was that an author had the same property in his
composition, being his own creation
or work, as a man had in any physical object produced by his personal labour But if such a property existed at common law, it
must commence with the act of
composition be independent of
reduction into writing, and be
liable to be withheld from or

offered at an unreasonable price to
the public. It must exist in every
offspring of man's imagination,
however important or mean, e.g in
the discovery of the scientific man,
or in the grimace of the clown
Copyright did not exist at common
law   What was the true construction of the Copyright Acts? They
did not apply to a foreigner resident
abroad or his assigns (see the judgment in *Boosey* v. *Purday*) English statutes had no force beyond
the realm, not even to bind British
subjects, unless expressly mentioned, or necessarily implied. It
was therefore a rule in construing
statutes not to extend them beyond
the realm.   An alien resident here
was the Queen's subject, owing
obedience to the law, and therefore
entitled to the benefit of it, not so
an alien abroad   It was conceded
that if a foreign author first published his work abroad he could
not have copyright in England,
but why? if such author was
within the Act   The third section
of the Act (which section conferred
copyright) made no distinction in
words between a publication 'in
the lifetime of the author' in this
country and anywhere else again,
the sixth section, as to delivery
of copies to the British Museum,
seemed to confine the operation of
the Act to the British dominions
The tenor of all the Copyright Acts
showed that a foreign author resident abroad was not in the contemplation of the framers   If

There was nearly an equal array of authorities on the one side and on the other. His (the Chancellor's)

Bellini had any English copyright, it being 'personal property' by the Acts, his assignment, valid by the law of Milan, was sufficient It was doubtful whether copyright could be partially assigned, certainly here the proprietor of copyright could not assign it with reference to one county to one person, and with reference to another county to a different person, so as to give to each a right to maintain an action for infringing the copyright The Act 54 Geo 3, c. 156, in force at the time of this transfer, made copyright commensurate with the British dominions, so it was indivisible into parts according to local boundaries, the assignment to the defendant in error could therefore operate as a license only, which would not enable him to sue as proprietor. A publication at Milan, subsequent to the assignment, but before publication here, would have defeated it —Sir *John Jervis*, C J 1 No, because the question assumed that Bellini only assigned to Ricordi the copyright which Bellini had by the law of Milan, and further, because Bellini had under the circumstances stated no copyright in England, which he could assign 2 No, because, first, two witnesses would not be required to attest the assignment of an English copyright, if Bellini had such copyright to assign, secondly, because Bellini did not profess to assign the English copy-

right, if he had it, and thirdly, because he had no English copyright which he could assign 4, 5 No, because Bellini under the circumstances having no English copyright to assign, it was immaterial whether the work was published abroad or after the assignment, and before publication in this country In *Clementi* v. *Walker* it was decided that a prior publication abroad would prevent a foreign author resident in this country from having copyright here 6 No, under the particular circumstances of this case, because Bellini had no English copyright to assign *Lastly*, Yes, because technically the assignment to Ricordi passed only the Milanese copyright, and because substantially Bellini had no English copyright to assign , the certified copy of the register, by 5 & 6 Vict c 45, primâ facie evidence of proprietorship in copyright, was rebutted by other evidence upon the record .A slip in the bill of exceptions, however, decided the writ of error it was in the bill stated that Bellini assigned to Ricordi the 'said' copyright, which must be referred to the copyright previously alluded to, i e the Milanese copyright Passing over this slip, the assignment was not void because unattested, the necessity for attestation was abolished by the Act 51 Geo 3, c 156, which, in enacting that all booksellers and others who printed

opinion was founded on the general doctrine, that a British statute must primâ facie be understood to

and published *without* the consent in writing of the proprietor should be liable to an action, was inconsistent with the Act 8 Anne, c 19, and so by implication repealed it, and the reasoning in *Power* v. *Walker* and *Davidson* v *Bohn* on the Act 8 Anne, c 19, from a license to an assignment, was applicable to a case within the Act of George As to the main point, 'copyright' must here be considered only as the exclusive right to multiply copies of a manuscript, not as a right to the manuscript itself, or any copy or copies of it this right attached not to chattels, the exclusive privilege of making them was not an incident to the property in them, but sprung from the prerogative of the Crown. It was not necessary then to decide whether a British author had copyright at common law, but he (the Chief Justice) agreed with Lord *Kenyon* in *Beckford* v *Hood*, Lord *Ellenborough* in *Cambridge University* v *Bryer*, and the majority of the American judges in *Wheaton* v *Peters*, that no author had At all events, the common law was confined to British authors and authors resident in England, and within the protection of the law of this country Was the right conferred upon a foreigner resident abroad by statute law? No, the question turned on the construction of the Act 8 Anne, c 19 In expounding it, policy must be disregarded, the intention

of the framers must if possible, be arrived at Statutes in general applied only to those who owed obedience to the laws, and whose interests it was the duty of the Legislature to protect. With aliens resident abroad the Legislature had no concern. The Act of Anne did not show that it was intended to apply to all authors, foreign or British, wherever resident, the object of the Act was the advancement of learning, by rewarding authors, at the cost of the public In the case of British authors, the object of the Act might be worth the price paid by the public for it But Bellini had a Milan copyright, deemed at Milan a sufficient encouragement for the advancement of learning It might be that a simultaneous publication in every country in Europe would more richly reward an author But such a publication was not contemplated by Queen Anne's Parliament Having that Milan encouragement, why should Bellini be encouraged to publish here works (which might be imported) at the cost of the British public? It was asked, 'why, if a foreigner might acquire the right by coming to England, might he not have it while resident abroad?' The answer was, 'whilst he was out of the realm, he was not subject, nor entitled to, the benefit of the laws of this kingdom' It was urged 'that copyright was analogous to patent right, and that the same

legislate for British subjects only, and there were no special circumstances in the Act 8 Anne, c. 19, leading to the notion that a more extended range was meant to be given to its enactments.

Lord *Brougham* argued that copyright was the mere creature of legislative enactment, and had no existence at common law: that therefore it could not be that

construction should be put upon the several statutes applicable to each' No, it was held that the words in the Act 21 Jac. 1, c. 3, 'new' manufactures within the realm, meant manufactures known abroad, but 'new within the realm,' because the latter manufactures had been the subject of grants of monopolies at common law, and the words of the Act did not *expressly* exclude them, but there was no copyright at common law for foreign authors which could give a larger meaning to the natural import of the words of the Act 8 Anne, c 19 The assertion in *Tonson v Collins*, by counsel, that 'if an author, *resident in England*, composes a work, it is immaterial whether he is an alien or a British subject,' was not in point. *Bach v Longman* was also no authority It was not objected there, that the plaintiff was a foreigner, but the *only* point for determination was 'whether a *musical* book was within the statute' *D'Almaine v Boosey* was decided upon a misunderstanding of *Bach v. Longman*, and was therefore inconclusive Vice-Chancellor *Shadwell's* opinions in *Delondre v Shaw* and *Bentley v*

Foster contradicted each other Clementi v Walker, so far as it went, was an authority for the plaintiff in error. The point there decided was that a *prior publication in France* destroyed any copyright which a foreigner coming to this country *might have* here, but the Court intimated an opinion that the statute of Anne was passed for the advancement of *British* learning The question was first pointedly raised in *Chappel v Purday*, where the Court of Exchequer held, under circumstances like the present, that a foreigner resident abroad had *no* copyright, for that the Act 8 Anne, c 19, was confined to British authors. The Court of Common Pleas took a different view in *Cocks v Purday*, and that view was followed by the Court of Queen's Bench in *Boosey v Davidson*, in which last case *Cocks v Purday* was fully considered, as shown by the judgment of Lord *Campbell* In the latest case on the subject, *Boosey v Purday*, the Court of Exchequer adhered to their decision in *Chappel v Purday*. The learned Judge who tried this cause took the view of the Court of Exchequer.

the Legislature had it in contemplation to vest the right in any but its subjects and those claiming through them; the object of the Act 8 Anne, c. 19, was the encouragement of learning by encouraging learned men to write useful books—an encouragement given at the expense of British subjects, to whom the monopoly raised the price of books; it was also a legal presumption that a Legislature confined its enactments to its own subjects, over whom it had authority, and to whom it owed a duty in return for their obedience. When the Act 8 Anne, c. 19, was passed, the principles of Parliament were very crude and narrow, for that Act absurdly attempted to keep down the price of books; it was therefore difficult to attribute to the framers of the same Act such large and enlightened views as they must have had if it encouraged foreigners (the case of foreigners was not a casus omissus, see the Act 8 Anne, c. 19, s. 7) at the temporary and immediate cost, at all events, of British subjects, for the sake of multiplying generally the number of useful works, and so benefiting those subjects on the whole (but see 1 Rich. 3, c. 9). The objection 'that the consequence of confining the statute to one territory would be to make a foreign author come over to Dover, in order to have the exclusive privilege, for if he stopped at Calais he would not have it,' was more showy than solid; it was only one of the consequences of a law bounded in its operation by territory. *Cocks* v. *Purday* was apparently decided, not so much upon the consideration of the Copyright Acts, as upon the erroneous assumption that the Court of Exchequer had in *Chappel* v *Purday* questioned the personal right of an alien in England. The Milanese copyright had no existence beyond Milan, and though property by the Milanese law, it was not recognised as property here : the foreign right in a slave was an analogous right—it was not recognised as property here which the law would protect.

Lord *St. Leonards* expressed his agreement with the Lord Chancellor and Lord *Brougham*, and said that he had long since arrived at the conclusion that no common law right existed after publication of a literary work. He thought that the Patent Law was also in favour of that view, but whether that view was right or wrong, a common law right could never be held to extend to a foreigner abroad. The question then came upon the Copyright Acts. It was clear, as an abstract proposition, that an Act of Parliament of this country having within its view a municipal operation, having as in the case before the House territorial operation, and being therefore limited to this kingdom, could not be considered to provide for foreigners, except as both statute and common law provided for foreigners when they became resident here and owed a temporary allegiance to the Sovereign, and thereby acquired rights just as other persons did; not because they were foreigners, but because being here they were entitled (in so far as they did not break in upon certain rules) to the general benefit of the law for the protection of their property in the same way as if they were natural-born subjects. The Act 7 Anne, for generally encouraging the settlement here of foreign Protestants, showed that just before the Copyright Act 8 Anne, c. 19, Parliament, under the idea that population was wealth, wished to attract foreigners to this country, and further, in two different Acts of 8 Anne, whereby it was intended to provide expressly for foreigners, the words

'natives and foreigners' were inserted. The Act
8 Anne, c. 19, was by no means scientifically framed:
its heading was singular, the word 'copies' in the
heading was used to represent 'the exclusive right to
the copies;' the necessity of printing here, and of first
publication here, clearly appeared from the intent of
the Act, which was to benefit authors and not importers,
particularly from section 7, but only by implication;
and the Act 12 Geo. 2, c. 36, prohibiting generally the
importation of books reprinted abroad, which had been
first composed or written and published here, forced
this conclusion, 'that the Legislature then assumed
that the books within the protection of the Act 8 Anne,
c. 19, were books printed in this country.' If a book
composed abroad by a foreigner must be first published
here, it necessarily and naturally followed that the
foreigner should himself be here, to superintend that
publication. Unless that construction was put upon
the Act 8 Anne, c. 19, a foreigner might after that
Act have imported books printed abroad, and have
had copyright therein in evasion of that Act. The
case put, 'that a man might pass over from Calais
and obtain the copyright here, whereas by remaining at Calais he could not acquire it,' had no bearing
on the question before the House. The real distinction was between a foreigner in temporary allegiance
to this country, and claiming the right of a subject, and a foreigner owing no such allegiance, yet
claiming that right The question must be decided
without reference to the relation in which this country
stood to the United States, and without reference to
the law of any other country; but it might be re-

marked that the United States did not give copyright to a foreigner not resident in the States, so reciprocity did not call for a strained construction of the Act in their favour. *Page* v. *Townsend*, 5 Sim. 395, bore on the subject: it was there held that prints engraved and struck off abroad, but published here, were not protected from piracy under the Act; if books could be printed abroad, and could then, being imported, obtain copyright here, a right would subsist in books which did not subsist in prints and engravings. The foreign composer, in the case before the House, was not in this country when his work was published here; he therefore never had the copyright in England, so could not assign it to the plaintiff. A fatal objection to the plaintiff's case also arose from the language of the bill of exceptions assuming that the plaintiff's assignor had a general copyright in the British dominions; the assignment to the plaintiff was by the bill stated to be confined to the United Kingdom: it was consequently an assignment of part only of the copyright, but copyright was indivisible: the assignment was therefore void, the assignment was also void on the authority of *Davidson* v. *Bohn*, 6 C. B. 456, because it was not attested by two witnesses.

In an action relating to the assignment of a copyright, (*a*) Sir *John Jervis*, C.J incidentally remarked that the Court did not think it necessary on that occasion to express any opinion, ' whether under any circumstances the copyright in a literary work could become vested ab initio in an employer other than the composer.'

In a recent case, wherein it appeared that Mr.

_____

(*a*) *Shepherd* v *Conquest*, 17 C B 427

Charles Kean, the well-known actor and dramatist, had designed the adaptation of one of Shakespeare's plays to the stage with the aid of scenery, dresses, and music, and had paid a person to compose the music, the Court of Common Bench held that the music, being only accessory to the principal design, the copyright in the music did not belong to the paid composer. (*a*)

A person who composed words to a well-known air, and added a prelude and an accompaniment of his own, has also been held to have acquired a copyright in the combination. (*b*)

No private arrangement can interfere with the author's statutory right; (*c*) and, in view to that protection, it is not necessary that he should affix his name to the production of his pen. (*d*)

13 What amounts to an infringement of the right

13. Whilst all men are entitled to common sources of information, none are entitled to save themselves trouble and expense by availing themselves, for their own profit, of other men's works; when those are the subject of copyright, they are entitled to legal protection. (*e*) Said a Scotch judge 'A person might as well steal books, as appropriate their contents and transcribe them into his own publication.' (*f*)

It now, therefore, becomes necessary to consider what amounts to an infringement of the right by piracy of its subject. The case and dicta on this point seem to warrant the conclusion that any unauthorised use of a copy-

(*a*) *Hatton* v *Kean*, 8 W R 7

(*b*) *Lover* v *Davidson*, 1 C B. n s 182, and see *Leader* v *Purday*, 7 C B 4

(*c*) *Storace* v *Longman*, 2 Campb 27, n , but see also *Shepherd* v *Conquest*, 17 C B 427

(*d*) See *Beckford* v *Hood*, 7 T R 620

(*e*) See Lord *Langdale* in *Lewis* v *Fullarton*, 2 Beav 8

(*f*) Lord *M'Kenzie* in *Walford* v *Johnstone*, 20 Dec. in Court of Sess 2d series, 1161

right book in a later publication is an infringement of the earlier, unless that use involves a fair amount of thought and judgment.

In allusion to a literary copyright work (then before him), giving an account of natural curiosities and such articles, Lord *Eldon* said that it was equally competent to any other person to set about a similar work bonâ fide his own, but that it must be in substance a new and original work, and must be handed out to the world as such. (*a*)

The same learned Judge observed in a subsequent case, (*b*) 'all human events are equally open to all who wish to add to or improve the materials already collected by others, making an original work.'

Again, in *Longman* v. *Winchester*, (*c*) upon a similar application, Lord *Eldon* states the question before him to be, 'whether it is not perfectly clear that in a vast proportion of the work of these defendants no other labour has been applied than copying the plaintiff's work.' He added: 'from the identity of the inaccuracies, it is impossible to deny that the one was copied from the other verbatim and literatim. To the extent, therefore, in which the defendant's publication has been supplied from the other work, the injunction must go; but I have said nothing that has a tendency to prevent any person from giving to the public a work of this

(*a*) In *Hogg* v. *Kirby*, 8 Ves 222 This case was not decided on the ground of copyright, but of fraud, the Chancellor concluded that the defendant falsely represented to the public that his work was a continuation of the plaintiff's, and therefore restrained him See also *Webb* v *Powers*, 2 Woodb & Min 46

(*b*) *Matthewson* v *Stockdale*, 12 Ves 275, reported by Mr Vesey upon a motion to dissolve an injunction which stayed the publication of an Indian Directory The Lord Chancellor restrained the later work, because it was in his opinion a fac-simile copy of the original

(*c*) 16 Ves 272

kind, if it is the fair fruit of original labour; but if it is a mere copy of an original work, this Court will interpose against that invasion of copyright.' The motion was accordingly refused.

In a recent case, it was also clearly laid down by Sir *W. P. Wood*, V.C. that a man is fully at liberty to avail himself of matters patent to all the world, as a skeleton or starting-point, when he employed his own labour upon the subject-matter. (*a*)

Whenever infringement of copyright is the subject of complaint, Lord *Eldon* said the question is, ' whether it is a legitimate use by the defendant of the plaintiff's publication in the fair exercise of a mental operation deserving the character of an original work.' (*b*) This last dictum Lord *Cottenham* declared put the question upon a proper footing. (*c*)

' A copy is one thing,' remarked *Story*, J. in *Emerson* v. *Davies*, ' an imitation or resemblance another. There are many imitations of Homer in the Æneid, but no one would say that the one was a copy from the other. There may be a strong likeness without an identity; and, as was aptly said by the learned counsel for the plaintiff—

> Facies non omnibus una,
> Nec diversa tamen, qualem decet esse sororum.'

Upon piracy, and especially upon piracy of such books as are incapable of much originality in matter, the opinion of the talented Lord *Jeffreys* has fortunately been recorded on an application made to him in the Court of Session, in the year 1847, for an interdict against the

(*a*) *Cornish* v *Upton*, 4 Law T   422
n s 863   (*c*) In *Bramwell* v *Halcomb*, 3
(*b*) *Wilkins* v *Aikin*, 17 Ves   M & Cr 738

violation of copyright. In a collection of statutory precedents he appears to have thus expressed his views: (a) 'This is a case in which it is evident, from what has fallen, that there are involved principles of some delicacy. In a great number of preceding cases which have been tried, this sort of delicacy has arisen from the necessity of maintaining the policy of the Copyright Acts, and of affording the protection contemplated to parties who fall within the principle of those Acts on the one hand, and on the other, of avoiding the inexpediency of stretching that principle to cases where absolute originality cannot be pretended, and where the pretensions of the claimant of such copyright may tend to prevent all other parties from having recourse to the common and public materials from which his work has been taken or compiled. At the same time I must confess that I do not think any very clear general rules exist on this subject. . . . First, then, I hold clearly that, notwithstanding the difficulties I referred to as arising out of the policy of the Copyright Acts, we are bound to give the protection necessary to prevent literary men, the result of whose intellectual labour is embodied in certain useful works, from losing the fair reward of their industry by the misapplication of its products by others. This I hold to be clearly settled, that even though the materials from which such a work is taken be "in medio," as it is called, yet if those materials be arranged in a new form, the effect of that will be to afford the author the protection of copyright in that form. In all cases, in short (although the materials are expressly "in medio," and open to everybody), when a particular degree of judg-

(a) Alexander v M'Kenzie, Dec in Court of Session, vol ix, n s 748

I

ment in the selection of those materials has been used,
and when the subject "in medio," so open to the world
at large, has been to a certain extent snatched at and
appropriated, such selection is in itself recognised as a
certain degree of mental effort, which is entitled to the
benefit of copyright.   Again, while there is no doubt
that it would be dangerous to encroach on the liberty of
all who are disposed to make a selection from materials
' in medio," with a view similar to that of any person
who has previously made a selection from those materials, still the question comes to be " whether any second
party, making such selection, has gone into the matter
'in medio,' for himself, and has not merely followed in
his predecessor's traces?"   But while the second party
is not bound to shut his eyes to the advantages presented by the exertions of his predecessors, or of others
who have been labouring in the same field, the question
still comes to be, " Is there reasonable evidence that the
two works produced are identical, and that the last
author did not mount upon the back, and walk on the
crutches of his predecessor, but actually used his own
muscular exertions in traversing the field in which he
made his observations?   Did he, on the whole, do so
fairly and honestly for himself, although he may occasionally have followed in the vestigia left by his pre-
cursor?   Or is there evidence that the second writer's
not going over the ground for himself is not the very
cause why he arrived at almost identical conclusions with
his predecessor?"   I think that is the case here. but the
point is perhaps of such a kind that piracy is not to be
presumed from the mere coincidence in the substance of
the works.   It may often be a matter of great delicacy to
substantiate such a charge.   Perhaps, from the subject to

which both works relate being "in medio," the second party may be entitled to a favourable interpretation, and the mere fact of great similarity between the second and first work may not of itself warrant the inference that the second work is a mere copy. Thus piracy is not to be easily presumed from a similarity in matter in the case of spelling-books, or such elementary works; but if a second party issues a spelling-book which is nothing but a reprint of a spelling-book by another, with a new title page substituted for the old one, that is clearly piracy. If it is quite plain that the similarity of the substance of a second work and of a first is not a mere coincidence, which is the result of similar observation; but if the second work is substantially a transcript of the first, with merely colourable alterations, then there is an undoubted infringement of the copyright in the first work, and the alterations only make the case worse, as they indicate that the party has resorted to a device like that used in regard to stolen goods, of altering the marks on them to prevent identification.'

The really difficult question in cases where it must be admitted that the matter is not original is, said Sir W. P. Wood, V.C. in *Jarrold* v. *Houlston*, (a) 'how far the author of the work in question can be said to have made an unfair or undue use of previous works protected by copyright. As regards all common sources, he is entitled to make what use of them he pleases; but, as Lord *Langdale* said, in *Lewis* v. *Fullarton* (2 Beav. 6), he is not entitled to make any use of a work protected by copyright which is not what can be called a fair use.' The Vice-Chancellor then gave several instances of unfair or undue use, and the contrary, and remarked,

(a) 3 Kn & Jo 708

I 2

'that in writing for publication a work in the form of question and answer on a variety of scientific subjects, the author had a right to look to all those books which were unprotected by copyright, and to make such use of them as he thought fit, by turning them into questions and answers, he had also a right, if in reading a similar scientific work he observed that the writer had been led up to particular questions and answers by the perusal of some other work, to have recourse himself to that work; and so it would be a legitimate use of a scientific work if the author of a subsequent work, after getting his own work, with great pains and labour, into a shape approximating to what he considered a perfect shape, should look through the earlier work to see whether it contained any heads which he had forgotten.' And then the Vice-Chancellor added, 'now for trying that question (the question of fair use) several tests have been laid down; one, which was originally expressed, I think, by a common law judge, and was adopted by Lord *Langdale*, in *Lewis* v. *Fullarton*, is, whether you find, on the part of the defendant, an *animus furandi*, (*a*) an intention to take, for the purpose of saving himself labour. I take the illegitimate use as opposed to the legitimate use of another man's work on subject matters of this description to be this, that if knowing that a person, whose work is protected by copyright, has, with considerable labour, compiled from various sources a work in itself not original, but which he has digested and arranged, you being minded

(*a*) The *animus furandi* is only a proper test of piracy in cases where the materials are necessarily common to all mankind, and where the amount of independent labour bestowed by a man upon such materials to make them his own is in question (*Reade* v *Lacy*, 1 J & H 524)

to compile a work of a like description, instead of taking the pains of searching into all the common sources, and obtaining your subject matter from them, avail yourself of the labour of your predecessor, adopt his arrangements, (a) adopt, moreover, the very questions he has asked, or adopt them with but a slight degree of colourable variation, and thus save yourself pains and labour by availing yourself of the pains and labour which he has employed, that I take to be an illegitimate use.'

Perhaps, however, the best judicial answer given to the question, 'What is an infringement of copyright?' appears in the report of the judgment of Sir *W. P Wood*, V.C. in *Spiers* v. *Brown*.(b) That judgment is mainly directed to the somewhat peculiar case of a dictionary, but it has a bearing on the infringement of other literary works, and for that reason the judgment should be attentively read. In this little book the following extracts may be considered sufficient. He says. 'All cases of copyright were very simple when a work of an entirely original character was concerned, being a work of imagination or invention on the part of the author, or original in respect of its being a work treating of a subject common to mankind, such as history or other branches of knowledge, varying much in their mode of treatment, and in which the hand of the artist could readily be discerned. But the difficulty that arose in this class of cases was that they not only

(a) Where the scheme of two guide books was quite different, the plan of the latter being more limited than that of the earlier work, and the scheme of the routes therein set forth different, and the latter book mentioned some places on the routes, which places were not mentioned in the earlier book, Sir *R Kindersley*, V C very properly refused to restrain the publication of the latter (*Murray v Bogue*, 1 Drew, 353)

(b) 6 W R 352

related to a subject common to all mankind, but that
the mode of expression and language was necessarily so
common that two persons must to a very great extent
express themselves in identical terms, in conveying the
information or instruction to society which they were
anxious to communicate.   The most obvious case was
that of figures, such as the table of logarithms (the
case before Sir *John Leach*), where it would be impossible to deviate in the calculations or to vary the
order, and the result must be identical.   The same
might be said of directories, calendars, Court guides,
and works of that description.   Those were cases in
which the only mode of arriving at the amount of
labour bestowed was by the common test resorted to
of discovering the copy of errors and misprints, in-
dicating a servile copying. . . . As to dictionaries,
the matter stood in a somewhat different position. . . .
Of course there could be no copyright in much of the
information contained in the numerous dictionaries
published, each necessarily having a large number of
words identically similar.   In a large part of his work
Dr Spiers could have no copyright as to words and
expressions, though he might have it as to new words
introduced, or new acceptations, or as to the order and
arrangement by which he improved the particular work
he had in hand.   There were only one or two cases
which seemed to lay down the principles applicable to
this subject with sufficient clearness.   In the case of
Cary v. *Kearsley*, 4 Esp. 168, Lord *Ellenborough* laid
down the law in a manner which had not been questioned.   He said: " That part of the work of an author
found in another is not of itself piracy, or sufficient
to support an action, a man may fairly adopt part

of the work of another; he may also make use of another's labours for the promotion of science and the benefit of the public; but, having done so, the question will be, was the matter so taken used fairly with that view, and without what I may term the animus furandi?(a) Look through the book, and find any part that is a transcript of the other; if there is none such, if the subject of the book is that which is subject to every man's observation, such as the names of places and their distances from each other, the places being the same, the distances being the same; if they are correct, one book must be a transcript of the other; but when in the defendant's book there are additional observations, and in some parts of the book I find corrections of misprinting, while I shall think myself bound to secure every man in the enjoyment of his copyright, one must not put manacles on science." Then there was the case of *Longman* v. *Winchester*, 16 Ves. 269, in which Lord *Eldon* said: "Take the instance of a map describing a particular county, and a map of the same county afterwards published; if the description is accurate in both they must be pretty much the same · but it is clear that the latter publisher cannot on that account be justified in sparing himself the labour and expense of actual survey in copying the map previously published by another. So as to Paterson's 'Road Book:' it is certainly competent to any other man to publish a book of roads, and if the same skill, intelligence, and diligence are applied in the

(a) Animus furandi arises properly, in cases upon dictionaries, directories, and the like, where the materials are common, and the test is the amount of independent labour bestowed by a man upon such materials to make them his own (Sir *W. P. Wood*, V.C. in *Reade* v. *Lacy*, 9 W. R. 532.)

second instance, the public would receive nearly the same information from both works; but there is no doubt that this Court would interpose to prevent a mere re-publication of a work which the labour and skill of another person had supplied to the world. So in the instance mentioned by Sir *Samuel Romilly*, a work consisting of a selection from various authors, two men perhaps might make the same selection, but that must be by resorting to the original authors, not by taking advantage of the selection already made by another." Again, "The question before me is, whether it is not perfectly clear that in a vast proportion of the work of these defendants no other labour has been applied than copying the plaintiff's work. From the identity of the inaccuracies it is impossible to deny that the one was copied from the other verbatim et literatim. To the extent, therefore, in which the defendant's publication has been supplied from the other work the injunction must go, but I have said nothing that has a tendency to prevent any person from giving to the public a work of this kind if it is the fair fruit of original labour, the subject being open to all the world." Another case, which seemed to condense into one point the view taken by the Courts in cases where actual use is avowed (and the only question is, whether it is a fair use) is *Wilkins* v. *Aikin*, 17 Ves. 422, where Lord *Eldon* says this: " Upon inspection of the different works, I observe a considerable proportion taken from the plaintiff's that is acknowledged, but also much that is not; and in determining whether the former is within the doctrine upon this subject, the case must be considered as also presenting the latter circumstance " The question upon the whole is, " whether there is a legitimate use of the plaintiff's publication in the fair exercise of a mental operation deserving the character of an original work." Those were the words which had been relied on by Lord *Cottenham* in *Bramwell* v. *Halcomb*, 3 M. & Cr. 737; and it was with the view thus taken by those learned judges that I have gone through a very laborious investigation of the works now in question.'

'The true test of piracy or not,' said an American Court, (*a*) 'is to ascertain whether the defendant has in fact used the plan, arrangements, and illustrations of the plaintiff as the model of his own book, with colourable alterations and variations only to disguise the use thereof, or whether his book is the result of his own labour, skill, and use of common materials and common sources of knowledge open to all men, and the resemblances are either accidental or arising from the nature of the subject.'

In *Webb* v. *Powers* (*b*) (a suit to restrain the invasion of copyright in a floral dictionary) an American judge (*Woodbury*) observed . 'Again, there is much discrimination to be used in enquiries of this character between different kinds of books, some of which from their nature cannot be expected to be entirely new. Thus, dictionaries of all descriptions, when on like subjects, philological, lexicographical, professional, or scientific, must contain many descriptions and definitions almost identical, as must gazetteers, grammars, maps, arithmetics, almanacks, concordances, cyclopædias, itineraries, guide books, and similar publications. In these, if great errors have not previously existed or unusual ignorance to be corrected, no great novelty is practicable or useful unless

(*a*) *Emerson* v *Davies*, 3 Story, 768   (*b*) 2 Woodb & Min 512

it be to add new discoveries or inventions, new names,
or words, or decisions, so as to post up the subject to
more recent periods; or unless it be to abridge and
omit details, and condense a more voluminous work
into a smaller and cheaper form, so as to bring its
purchase within the reach of new and less wealthy
classes in society. Some similarities, and some use of
prior works, even to copying of small parts, are in such
cases tolerated, if the main design and execution are in
reality novel or improved, and not a mere cover for
important piracies from others. . . . While, on the one
hand, a prior compiler is not permitted to monopolise
what was not original in himself, and what must be
nearly identical in all such works on a like subject, yet
he who uses it subsequently to another must not employ
so much of the prior arrangement and materials as to
show that the last work is a substantial invasion on the
other, and is not characterised by enough new or improved to indicate new toil and talent, and new property
and rights, in the last compiler. That is the cardinal
distinction.'

The question of infringement of copyright is indeed
a question 'not so much of kind as of degree,' (a) and
doubtless it is difficult to draw the line where the
use that is made of a work is fair and reasonable, or is
substantially what is unlawful and forbidden, and only
colourable and evasively different from it. (b)

Sir *R. Kindersley*, V.C. has defined unfair use of an
original work to be the extraction of its vital part. (c)

(a) *Maule, J in Sweet v Benning*,
16 C B 185, and see Lord
Jeffreys in Alexander v M'Kenzie,
9 Dec of Court of Session, 751

(b) *Ibid*
(c) *Murray v Bogue*, 1 Drew,
369

It is clearly not necessary that a piracy should be so far a copy as to be a substitute for the original work. (a)

Where a work, entitled 'A Practical Treatise of the Law Relative to the Sale and Conveyance of Real Property, with an Appendix of Precedents, comprising Contracts, Conditions of Sale, Purchase, and Disentailing Deeds, &c.' contained extracts from an earlier standard work, which was entitled 'A Practical Treatise of the Law of Vendors and Purchasers of Estates,' Sir *L. Shadwell*, V.C.E. remarked: 'In cases of this nature, if the pirated matter is not considerable, that is, where passages which are neither numerous nor long have been taken from different parts of the original work, this Court will not interfere to restrain the publication of the work complained of, but will leave the plaintiff to seek his remedy at law. But in this case it is plain that the passages which have been pointed out have been taken from the plaintiff's book, and they are so considerable, both in number and length, as to make it right that this Court should interfere.' (b)

The dicta of the Vice-Chancellor, in the case last cited, must not, however, be relied on as an argument that piracy is to be judged solely by the quantity taken from the copyright work. Lord *Cottenham* has said, in reply to an argument of that description 'When it comes to a question of quantity it must be very vague, one writer may take all the vital part of another's book, though it might be a small proportion of the book in quantity: it is not only quantity but value that

(a) *Bohn* v *Bogue*, 10 Jur 420
(b) *Sweet* v *Cator*, 11 Sim 580, and see *King's Printer* v *Bell*, Morison, 8316, and *Murray* v *Farquhar*, Morison, 8309 both instances of too copious extracts

is always looked to. It is useless to refer to any particular case as to quantity.' (a)

Where the matter pirated formed an exceedingly small part of the plaintiff's work, but constituted the bulk of the defendant's work, Sir L Shadwell, V.C.E. granted an injunction, but ordered the plaintiff forthwith to bring such an action as he might be advised. (b)

Mr. Turner, in his valuable little treatise on 'Copyright in Design,' pertinently observes. 'As to the estimating the injury by quantity (as when in Roworth's case (c) the pages were counted), we may remember Lieber's observation, that the thief only takes the wheat, not the straw, which is the bulk of the crop.' (d) And said Story, J. in Gray v. Russell, (e) 'Extracts non numerantur sed ponderantur. The quintessence of a work may be piratically extracted so as to leave a mere caput mortuum, by a selection of all the important passages in a comparatively moderate space.'

11 As to piracy by quotation

11. Quotation for the purpose of reviewing is not to have the appellation of piracy affixed to it; but quotation may be carried to the extent of manifesting piratical intention. This dictum is ascribed to Lord Eldon in Mawman v. Tegg. (f) 'There is no doubt,'

(a) In *Bramwell v Halcomb*, 3 M & Cr 738, and see Sir W P Wood, V C in *Tinsley v Lacy*, 11 W R 877

(b) *Kelly v Hooper*, 1 Jur. 21

(c) *Roworth v Wilkes* was a case in which 75 pages of a treatise consisting of 118 pages were taken and inserted in a very voluminous work—the *Encyclopædia Londinensis*, and although the matter taken formed but a very small proportion of the work into

which it was introduced, the jury found for the plaintiff, who was the author of the treatise —1 Campb 94

(d) P 38

(e) 1 Story, R 11

(f) 2 Russ 393   See also Lord Eldon, C in *Wilkins v Aikin*, 17 Ves 424, *Bohn v Bogue*, 10 Jur 420, *Whittingham v Wooler*, 2 Swanst 428, *Bell v Whitehead*, 3 Jur 68

said Lord *Eldon* on another occasion, 'that a man cannot under the pretence of quotation publish either the whole or part of another's works, though he may use what it is in all cases very difficult to define, fair quotation.'

Admitted quotation may amount to piracy. This was ruled in *Bohn* v. *Bogue.* (a) The learned Judge there observed: 'Confession may at the time that it is made be so far a proof of honesty, but a confession from the very nature of it does not diminish the previous theft; if a theft has been committed, it may save trouble in conviction, but it neither excuses nor justifies.'

To hold that extracts from a work for the sole purpose of criticism are piratical would, it has been truly observed, fetter public discussion, and such discussion is in this country considered beneficial to the public; further, a common result of extracts by way of criticism is far from injurious to the author or proprietor of the work criticised: they frequently extend its sale.

In *Carey* v. *Kearsley* (b) a test of fair quotation is given. Lord *Erskine* there remarked: 'Suppose a man took "Paley's Philosophy" and copied a whole essay with observations and notes or additions at the end of it, would that be piracy? That would depend upon the fact whether the publication of that essay was to convey to the public the notes and observations fairly, or only to colour the publication of the original essay, and make that a pretext for pirating it; if the latter, it could not be sustained.'

'In short,' to borrow the language of J. *Story,* 'we must, in deciding questions of this sort, look to the

(a) 10 Jur 420   (b) 4 Esp. 168

nature and objects of the selections made, the quantity
and value of the material used, and the degree in
which the use may prejudice the sale, or diminish the
profits, or supersede the objects of the original work.
Many mixed ingredients enter into the discussion of
such questions. In some cases a considerable portion
of the materials of the original work may be fused, if
we may use such an expression, into another work so
as to be undistinguishable in the mass of the latter,
which has often professed and obvious objects, and cannot
fairly be treated as piracy, or they may be inserted
as a sort of distinct and mosaic work into the general
texture of the second work, and constitute the peculiar
excellence thereof, and it may be a clear piracy. If a
person should, under colour of publishing elegant extracts
of poetry, include all the best pieces at large of a
favourite poet, whose volume was secured by a copyright, it would be difficult to say why it was not an
invasion of that right, since it might constitute the
entire value of the volume.' (a)

The law laid down by Lord *Erskine* in *Carey* v.
Kearsley was followed in *Campbell* v. *Scott,* (b) where
the Vice-Chancellor of England granted an injunction
against the publication by the defendant of certain of
Campbell's poems, in a collection of poetry entitled
'The Book of Poets,' and 'The Modern Poets of the
Nineteenth Century.' He on that occasion observed
'Then, is the work complained of anything like an
abridgement of the plaintiff's work, or a critique upon
it? Some of the poems are given entire, and large
extracts are given from other poems, and I cannot

(a) *Story, J* in *Folsom v Marsh*   (b) 11 Sim 31
2 Story 116

think that it can be considered as a book of criticism when you observe the way in which it is composed. It contains 790 pages, thirty-four of which are taken up by a general disquisition upon the nature of the poetry of the nineteenth century; then, without any particular observation being appended to the particular poems and extracts from poems which follow, there are 758 pages of selections from the works of other authors; and therefore I cannot think that the work complained of can in any sense be said to be a book of criticism. If there were critical notes appended to each separate passage, or to several of the passages in succession, which might illustrate them, and show from whence Mr. Campbell had borrowed an idea, or what idea he had communicated to others, I could understand that to be a fair criticism. But there is first of all a general essay, then there follows a mass of pirated matter, which, in fact, constitutes the value of the volume.'

In *Whittingham* v. *Wooler* (a) the publication of extracts (occupying six or seven pages) from different parts of Poole's farce of 'Who's Who, or the Double Imposture' (occupying forty pages), in a critical work called 'The Stage,' was not considered piracy clear enough for the interference of a court of equity. (b)

15 The publication of an unauthorised but bonâ fide abridgement or digest of a published literary copyright work is, it seems, no piracy of the original.

15 Piracy by abridgement or digest

First, as to an abridgement; that conclusion was reached many years ago in *Newbery's* case, by Lord *Apsley*, C. and *Blackstone*. (c) Later, but as far back as the year 1740, a bill (a) was brought

(a) 2 Swanst 128.
(b) For a case of too copious extracts see *Murray* v *M'Far-*
quhar, Mor Dict of Dec 19, 20, p 8309
(c) Lloft. R 775

by Fletcher Gyles, a bookseller, for an injunction to stay the printing of a book entitled 'Modern Crown Law,' it being suggested by the bill to be colourable, and, in fact, borrowed verbatim from Sir Matthew Hale's 'Pleas of the Crown,' only some repealed statutes having been left out, and the Latin and French quotations translated into English. Upon the hearing, Lord *Hardwicke*, L.C. said: 'The question is whether this book of the new Crown law which the defendant has published is the same with Sir Matthew Hale's "Historia Placit Coronae," the copy of which is now the property of the plaintiff. (*b*) Where books are colourably shortened only, they are undoubtedly within the meaning of the Act of Parliament, and are a mere evasion of the statute, and cannot be called an abridgement. But this must not be carried so far as to restrain persons from making a real and fair abridgement, for abridgement may with great propriety be called a new book, because not only the paper and print, but the invention, learning, and judgment of the author is shown in them, and in many instances are extremely useful, though in some instances prejudicial, by mistaking and curtailing the sense of an author. If I should extend the rule so far as to restrain all abridgements, it would be of mischievous consequence, for the books of the learned " Les Journals des Savans," and several others that might be mentioned, would be brought within the meaning of this Act of Parliament. In the present

(*a*) *Gyles v Wilcox* 2 Atk 141
(*b*) The 'Pleas of the Crown' were left in manuscript by Sir Matthew Hale at his death. He died in 1676, and in 1680 the House of Commons desired his executors to print and publish the MS. Various accidents, however, prevented the publication till 1736 when the copyright was assigned to Gyles. See Mor Dict of Dec app pt 1 p 5

case it is merely colourable; some words out of the " Historia Placitorum Coronæ" are left out only, and translations given instead of the Latin and French quotations that are dispersed through Sir Matthew Hale's works.' (a)

Again, in 1753, Lord *Eldon* said in *Tonson* v. *Walker*: 'A fair abridgement would be entitled to protection, but this is a mere evasion.' (b)   *Tonson* v. *Walker* did not itself raise a question of piracy by simple abridgement. In that case the plaintiff's edition of ' Milton,' with Dr. Newton's 1,500 compiled notes, had been copied by the defendant's edition which merely added twenty-eight more notes.

The same doctrine was held by Sir *T. Sewell*, M.R. sitting for the Lord-Chancellor, about the year 1785, to hear a suit for piracy of the 'Memoirs of the Life of Mrs. Bellamy.' (c)

Dodsley v. *Kinnersley* has been sometimes quoted as an authority upon piracy by abridgement, but it was, as Sir *T. Plumer*, M.R. said in *Whittingham* v. *Wooler*, 'a case of extracts merely;' the sole subject of complaint there was a reprint, in the defendant's magazine, of an extract from the narrative of Dr. Johnson's ' Prince of Abyssinia.' Another extract the plaintiffs had themselves published in the London ' Chronicle' newspaper. Lord *Eldon* refused an injunction and clearly stated why he did so. He said: ' What I materially rely upon is that it could not tend to prejudice the plaintiffs when they had before published an abstract of the work in the London ' Chronicle.'

(a) See also Lord *Lyndhurst*, C.B. in *D'Almaine* v. *Boosey*, post p. 141

(b) 3 Swanst 681

(c) *Bell* v. *Walker* 1 Bro. C. C. 151

h.

' What constitutes a fair and bonâ fide abridgement in the sense of the law' was said by the American judge *Story* to be one of the most difficult points under particular circumstances which could well arise for judicial discussion. And in *Folsom* v. *Marsh(a)* he observed: 'It is clear that a mere selection or different arrangement of parts of the original work, so as to bring the work into a smaller compass, will not be held to be a fair and bonâ fide abridgement.' He then added: 'There must be real substantial condensation of the material and intellectual labour and judgment bestowed thereon, and not merely the facile use of the scissors or extracts of the essential parts constituting the chief value of the work.' In *Folsom* v. *Marsh* the compositions alleged to be pirated were the writings of Washington, and an injunction issued, because the defendant had selected and imported into his publication (consisting of 866 pages) 353 pages from the plaintiff's, the defendant's work was mainly founded on those selections, which constituted more than one-third of its bulk and imparted to it its essential value, the publication was not therefore an abbreviation or abridgement in the strict sense of that word.

Again, 'To constitute a true and proper abridgement,' said Lord *Apsley*, C. in *Newbery's* case, (b) 'the whole must be preserved in its sense, and then the act of abridgement is an act of understanding employed in carrying a large work into a smaller compass and rendering it less expensive and more convenient, both to the time and ease of the reader, which made an abridgement in the nature of a new and meritorious work.' In reference to the case before him and his colleague (*Blackstone*, J.) he observed, 'that this had been done by Mr. Newbery.' On that occasion he and Mr. Justice *Blackstone* had spent some hours together, and were agreed that an abridgement, where the understanding is employed in retrenching unnecessary and uninteresting circumstances which rather deaden the narration, (*a*) is not an act of plagiarism upon the original work, nor against any property of the author in it, but an allowable and meritorious work.

In a recent suit, (*b*) Sir *W. P. Wood*, V.C. did not agree that an abridger was a benefactor; he regarded him rather as a sort of jackall to the public, to point out the beauties of authors.

Next as to a digest. Upon a special case one question for the opinion of the Court of Common Bench was, whether the publication in the form of an analytical digest of certain head-notes copied by the defendant from a periodical law report, composed by the plaintiff, was a piracy. Judgment was there given for the plaintiff, though the Bench was not unanimous. (*c*) Sir *John Jervis*, L C.J. held that the defendant had been guilty of infringement; he admitted that a digest might be made from published reports without necessarily subjecting the compiler to a charge of piracy, but considered that in the case before him no thought or skill had been brought to bear upon the defendant's work, and that the work in question was a mere mechanical stringing

(*a*) Newbery's publication was an abridgement of Dr Hawkesworth's Voyages.'

(*b*) *Tinsley v Lacy*, 11 W R 877

(*c*) *Sweet v Benning*, 16 C B 185

K 2

together of the notes which the labour and intelligence of the authors had fashioned ready to the compiler's hand, he also thought *Butterworth* v *Robinson*, 5 Ves. 709, (*a*) to be precisely in point. *Maule, J.* did not concur in the opinion of the Chief Justice as to the infringement in question; the grounds of his conclusion appear in the following extract from his judgment: ' In the present case the inclination of my opinion is that the work of the defendant is a different work, having a different object in view, and being totally different in its result from the work published by the plaintiffs; it may be that some persons may dispense with the plaintiff's work and take the defendant's, though a very imperfect substitute for it, though I should very much doubt whether it would enable any person, who really wanted it, to dispense with the plaintiff's publication. The object of a digest is to afford facilities for finding out cases that are inserted in the reports, without buying the reports themselves in extenso The effect may be to induce many persons to abstain from purchasing the reports, relying upon the means of access to public libraries and other institutions for the fuller and more perfect information when they have occasion for it. But that, I think, is no argument in favour of this being a piracy; rather the contrary, because it shows that the defendant's work is useful only for a different purpose from that of the plaintiff's, and is not, and never was,

---

(*a*) *Butterworth* v *Robinson* was an ex parte application for an injunction to restrain the sale of ' An Abridgement of Cases Argued and Determined in the Courts of Law,' &c The application was supported by evidence that the abridgement was not a fair abridgement, but, under colour of a new work, a verbatim copy of reports of which the plaintiff was proprietor An interim injunction was granted The case is very shortly reported

intended as a substitute for it.' Sir *C. Cresswell* concurred with the Chief Justice in his conclusion upon the facts before them; so did Sir *R. Crowder*, J.: but the latter concurred reluctantly. Sir *R. Crowder* said: 'Looking at the language of the statute, I feel very reluctantly bound to express my opinion that it may and does amount to piracy. It falls exactly within the 15th section, taken in connection with the interpretation clause, s. 2. The result of these two sections is this, that a person is guilty of piracy who prints or causes to be printed for sale any book or part of a book in which there is subsisting copyright, without the consent in writing of the author or proprietor; that which the defendants have printed and published without the sanction of the plaintiffs is undoubtedly a part, and a very considerable and important part, of the work.'

16. An unauthorised copy of a translation of a foreign work, though the foreign work be not entitled to copyright here, is a piracy.

16 Piracy by translation

This was decided by Lord *Eldon* in *Wyatt* v. *Barnard*, in the year 1814: (*a*) there the plaintiff was the proprietor of a periodical called 'The Repertory of Arts, Manufacture, and Agriculture,' and the defendants were the publishers of another periodical which contained various articles copied, contracted, or taken from the plaintiff's work without his consent, being translations from the French and German languages, and specifications of patents. Sir Samuel Romilly moved on behalf of the plaintiffs for an injunction against such publication by the defendants. Sir John Leach, on the other side, argued that it had never been decided that a translator

(*a*) 3 V & B 78

had a copyright in his translation. Sir Samuel Romilly in reply insisted that translation was as much the subject of copyright as original composition. Upon an affidavit that the translations were made by a person employed and paid by the plaintiff at considerable expense, Lord *Eldon* pronounced an order for an injunction as to the translations. In delivering judgment, the Chancellor said: 'With respect to the translations of original works, whether made by the plaintiff or given to him, they could not be distinguished from other works. The injunction, therefore, must go restraining the defendants from publishing the translations first published by the plaintiffs'

There is no doubt that the defendant in the case last cited might have himself translated the foreign work, although he was not allowed to copy the plaintiff's translation

The foreign work in *Wyatt* v. *Barnard*, it may be observed, was not entitled to English copyright.

It seems that Lord *Eldon* decided *Wyatt* v. *Barnard* upon a conclusion that every translation was an original composition. If that decision be law the translation of an English copyright work can scarcely be a piracy. That has not, however, been directly decided, although *Yates*, J. in *Miller* v. *Taylor* was clearly of opinion that the purchaser of a published work entitled to statutory copyright might with impunity translate it. (*a*)

Lord *Macclesfield* also seems to support that view of copyright law in *Burnett* v. *Chetwood*. (*b*) And Sir J. L. K. Bruce, V.C. said in *Prince Albert* v. *Strange* 'A work lawfully published in the popular sense of the

(*a*) 1 Burr. 2318   (*b*) 2 Meriv. 441

term stands in this respect, I conceive, differently from a work which has never been in that situation. The former may be liable to be translated, abridged, analysed, exhibited, complimented, (a) and otherwise treated in a manner that the latter is not.' (b) The learned American Judge *Story* is in favour of copyright in a translation. (c)

As the opinion of a great author on the subject of translation, and the talent necessary in a translator, may not be inappropriately quoted here, attention is called to the following words put by the witty Cervantes into the mouth of his hero, when conversing at Barcelona with an author. Don Quixote is made to say: ' Nevertheless, I cannot but think that translation from one language into another, unless it be from the noblest of all languages, Greek and Latin, is like presenting the back of a piece of tapestry where, though the figures are seen, they are obscured by various knots and threads, very different from the smooth and agreeable texture of the proper face of the work, and to translate easy languages of a similar construction requires no more talent than transcribing one paper from another. But I would not hence infer that translating is not a laudable exercise, for a man may be worse and more unprofitably employed Nor can my observation apply to the two celebrated translations of Doctor Christopher de Figueroa in his ' Pastor Fido' and Don John de Xaurigui in his ' Aminta,' who with singular felicity have made it difficult to decide which is the translation and which the original.'

The International Copyright Act hereafter referred to

(a) Qy complemented?

(b) 5 De G & Sm

(c) See *Emerson v Davies*, 3 Story, 780

extends to prevent translations of foreign works which have become by treaty entitled to protection in this country.(a)

Further, it seems that a re-translation without the consent of the author of the original work is open to a charge of piracy whenever that original work is entitled to copyright, for in *Murray* v. *Bogue* (b) Sir *R. Kindersley*, V.C. expressly laid it down that if A had translated B's English book into German, and then C had translated A's book into English, even if C did not know that A's book was a translation of B's, he (the Vice-Chancellor) would not allow B's book to be thus indirectly pirated.

17. No piracy save by multi- plication of copies

17. The intention of the Literary Copyright Act is to secure to an author the benefit of his labours, but his rights are limited to what is given by the Legislature. The privilege of a literary author is confined by the Act 5 & 6 Vict. c. 45, to multiplying copies of his work, any other person may, therefore, make what use he pleases of the work, save that of multiplication of copies. (c)

The public performance on the stage of a play representing the incidents of a published novel is, therefore, no infringement within the meaning of the Act 5 & 6 Vict. c. 45, of any copyright in the novel. This was determined in *Reade* v. *Conquest*. (d) Mr. Reade, the novelist, brought an action against Conquest for dramatising and causing to be acted, at the Grecian Theatre, a novel written by him, the plaintiff; the defendant demurred to the declaration, and the Court of Common Pleas allowed the demurrer. In delivering

(a) 15 & 16 Vict c 12   *Tinsley* v *Lacy*, 11 W R 877
(b) 1 Drew 353   (d) 9 C B n s 755
(c) See Sir H P Wood in

judgment, *Williams*, J. observed: ' It was held in the case of *Coleman* v. *Wathen*, 5 T. R. 245, (a) that representing a published dramatic piece of the plaintiff's upon the stage was not a publication within the meaning of the Act 8 Anne, c. 19, so as to subject the defendant to the penalty imposed by that statute; and the 2nd section 5 & 6 Vict. c. 45, defining copyright to mean the sole and exclusive liberty of printing or otherwise multiplying copies of any subject to which the said word is therein applied, seems to furnish a complete answer to the plaintiff's claim under that statute.' The Court also considered that *Murray* v. *Elliston* (b) was in the defendant's favour.

Neither is the public recitation of a published copyright work a piracy. It was not so when the Act of Queen Anne was in operation, (c) and the decision in *Reade* v. *Conquest* leads to a similar conclusion at the

---

(a) *Coleman* v *Wathen*, being a statutory action for a penalty, of course depended on the statute 1 Anne, c 19, upon which it was founded That statute was repealed by 5 & 6 Vict c 45 A verdict was taken in *Coleman* v *Wathen* for the plaintiff, with nominal damages, in order to raise the question, whether the public representation of a piece called ' The Agreeable Surprise,' upon a stage at Richmond, was a mode of publication which came within the meaning of the Act 8 Anne, c 19 A rule to set aside the verdict was made absolute by the Court of King's Bench, Lord Chief Justice *Kenyon* observing ' There is no evidence to support the action in this case The statute for the

protection of copyright only extends to prohibit the publication of the book itself by any other than the author or his lawful assignees It was so held in the great copyright case (*Millar* v *Taylor*) by the House of Lords But here was no publication' *Buller*, J added 'Reporting anything from memory can never be a publication within the statute Some instances of strength of memory are very surprising, but the mere act of repeating such a performance cannot be left as evidence to the jury that the defendant had pirated the work itself'

(b) See *post*, p 182

(c) See *Buller*, J in *Coleman* v *Wathen*, 5 T R 245

present day in respect to any work, not being a dramatic piece, within the protection of the statute 3 & 4 Will. 4, c. 15, hereafter referred to.

In the recent case of *Tinsley* v. *Lacy*, Sir *W. P. Wood*, V.C. expressly declared that any person might lawfully read out the whole of any copyright novel to a public meeting without any infringement of the right; such person cannot, however, for the purpose of assisting the audience to follow his lecture, distribute copies of the book among them. This multiplication of the work would be a clear violation of literary copyright. (a)

The multiplication of copies of a work in which there is copyright, though not for sale or hire, is an infringement of the right. It was argued for the defendant, in *Novello* v. *Sudlow*, (b) that the Legislature did not intend by the Act 5 & 6 Vict. c. 45, to interfere with persons who were not moved with a desire of profit, but the judgment of the Court, delivered by Sir *T. N. Talfourd*, J. was, that by such multiplication the copyright of the plaintiff was violated, and, therefore, the remedy for the plaintiff by action on the case attached.

The facts of that case were these: there was a Philharmonic Society, established for giving concerts to gratify the members of the Society and to promote music, not for giving concerts which should be a source of profit; the concerts were performed gratuitously by the members, to all these concerts were admitted, besides the members, many other persons at a fixed price; the defendant, a member and manager of the Society, being desirous of performing at one of the

(a) *Tinsley* v. *Lacy*, 11 W. R.   (b) 12 C. B. 177
577

concerts music from the plaintiff's work, had caused portions of the work to be lithographed for the use of the performers; and these he had then supplied to them without the plaintiff's consent.

The Scotch Court of Session had previously held, that to circulate gratuitously, without the consent of the author or his assigns, among the members of the Society of Writers to the Signet, a copy of a collection of legal precedents wherein copyright subsisted, was piracy. (a)

18. As to the simple embellishment of letter-press by the addition of plates, that would not excuse publication of the text. Sir *L. Kenyon*, M.R. (b) observed: 'Suppose it was only adding plates to an edition of " Don Quixote," the mere act of embellishing could not divest the right of the owner in the text.'

18 Embellishment by plates excuses not piracy of letter-press

19. A plaintiff may with propriety claim copyright in a book, and sue in respect of its infringement, although it be only a musical composition, consisting of words and accompaniment, and he be the composer of the words only, the accompaniment having been written for him gratuitously. (c)

19 As to piracy of musical compositions

In any case of alleged piracy of a musical composition the language of Lord *Lyndhurst*, L. C. B. in *D'Almaine* v. *Boosey*, (d) may, perhaps, be usefully referred to There a foreigner composed the music of an opera and duly assigned the right of publishing it in England to the plaintiffs, who were Englishmen; the assignees entered at Stationers' Hall the opera, its overture and airs, and first published here the overture, the airs, and two sets of quadrilles arranged from the opera.

(a) *Alexander* v *M'Kenzie*, Dec in Ct of Sess vol ix n s 718
(b) 2 Bro C C 85
(c) *Leader* v *Purday*, 7 C B 14
(d) 1 Y & Coll 301

The defendant afterwards published in this country several of the airs, with some alterations, in the shape of quadrilles and waltzes, which were all described on the title page as taken from the opera, though arranged by another person. The Lord Chief Baron, in granting an injunction, thus expressed himself 'The other point raised by the defendant is this, " whether his work, from its particular nature, is to be deemed a piracy?" With reference to this question, the facts of the case are as follow The plaintiffs published first the overture and then a number of airs and all the melodies It is admitted that the defendant has published portions of the opera containing the melodious parts of it, that he has also published entire airs, and that in one of his waltzes he has introduced seventeen bars in succession, containing the whole of the original air, although he adds fifteen other bars which are not to be found in it. Now it is said that this is not a piracy, first, because the whole of each air has not been taken, and secondly, because what the plaintiffs purchased was the entire opera, and the opera consists not merely of certain airs and melodies, but of the whole score But in the first place, piracy may be of part of an air as well as of the whole; and in the second place, admitting that the opera consists of the whole score, yet, if the plaintiffs were entitled to the whole, à fortiori they were entitled to publish the melodies which form a part. Again, it is said that the present publication is adapted for dancing only, and that some degree of art is needed for the purpose of so adapting it, and that but a small part of the merit belongs to the original composer That is a nice question. It is a nice question what shall be deemed such a modification of an original work as shall absorb

the merit of the original in the new composition. No
doubt such a modification may be allowed in some
cases, as in that of an abridgement or a digest: such
publications are in their nature original. Their compiler intends to make of them a new use; not that
which the author proposed to make. Digests are of
great use to practical men, though not so comparatively
to students. The same may be said of an abridgement
of any study, but it must be a bonâ fide abridgement;
because, if it contains many chapters of the original
work, or such as made that work most saleable, the
maker of the abridgement commits a piracy. Now it
will be said that one author may treat the same subject
very differently from another who wrote before him.
That observation is true in many cases. A man may
write upon morals in a manner quite distinct from that
of others who preceded him, but the subject of music
is to be regarded upon very different principles. It is
the air or melody which is the invention of the author,
and which may in such case be the subject of piracy;
and you commit a piracy if, by taking not a single bar
but several, you incorporate in the new work that in
which the whole meritorious part of the invention consists. I remember, in a case of copyright at nisi prius,
a question arising as to how many bars were necessary
for the constitution of a subject or phrase. Sir George
Smart, who was a witness in the case, said that a mere
bar did not constitute a phrase, though three or four
bars might do so. Now it appears to me that if you
take from the composition of an author all those bars
consecutively which form the entire air or melody,
without any material alteration, it is a piracy, though
on the other hand you might take them in a different

order, or broken by the intersection of others, like words, in such a manner as should not be a piracy. It must depend on whether the air taken is substantially the same with the original. Now the most unlettered in music can distinguish one song from another; and the mere adaptation of the air, either by changing it to a dance, or by transferring it from one instrument to another, does not even to common apprehensions alter the original subject. The ear tells you that it is the same. The original air requires the aid of genius for its construction, but a mere mechanic in music can make the adaptation or accompaniment. Substantially, the piracy is where the appropriated music, though adapted to a different purpose from that of the original, may still be recognised by the ear. The adding variations makes no difference in the principle.' (a)

20 Intention not necessary to piracy

20. Doubtless an infringement of statutory copyright may be unintentional, nevertheless it is an unlawful invasion of property. (b)

After the expiry of the statutory term of protection in a work, copies lawfully multiplied may be sold. (c)

21 Remedy at law for infringement of the right

21. Legal reparation for an infringement of the copyright is provided by ss. 15 & 16 of the Act 5 & 6 Vict. c. 45. They enact that if any person shall, in any part of the British dominions, after the passing of that Act, print, or cause to be printed, either for sale or exportation, any book in which there shall be subsisting copyright, without the consent in writing of the proprietor

---

(a) See also *Russell v Smith*, 15 Sim 182

(b) Lord *Ellenborough*, C J in *Roworth v Wilkes*, 1 Camp 98 See also Sir R T Kindersley, V C. in *Murray v Bogue*, 1 Drew 353,

Sir H P Wood, V C in *Reade v Lacy*, 1 Jo & H 524, and *Story*, J in *Folsom v Marsh*, 2 Story, 115

(c) See *Howitt v Hall*, ante p 65

thereof; or shall import for sale or hire any such book
so having been unlawfully printed from parts beyond
the sea, or knowing such book to have been so unlawfully printed or imported, shall sell, publish, or expose
to sale or hire, or cause to be sold, published, or exposed
to   or hire, or shall have in his possession for sale
or hire any such book so unlawfully printed or imported,
without such consent as aforesaid, such offender shall be
liable to a special action on the case, at the suit of the
proprietor of such copyright, to be brought in any Court
of Record in that part of the British dominions in which
the offence shall be committed: provided always that
in Scotland such offender shall be liable to an action in
the Court of Session in Scotland, which shall and may
be brought and prosecuted in the same manner in which
any other action of damages to the like amount may be
brought and prosecuted there. Further, that after the
passing of that Act, in any action brought within the British
dominions against any person for printing such book for
sale or exportation, or for importing, selling, publishing,
or exposing for sale or hire, or causing to be imported,
sold, published, or exposed to sale or hire any such book,
the defendant, on pleading thereto, shall give to the
plaintiff a notice in writing of any objections on which
he means to rely on the trial of such action, and if the
nature of his defence be that the plaintiff in such action
was not the author or first publisher of the book in
which he shall by such action claim copyright, or is not
the proprietor of the copyright therein, or that some
other person than the plaintiff was the author, or first
publisher of such book, or is the proprietor of the
copyright therein, then the defendant shall specify in
such notice the name of the person whom he alleges to

have been the author or first publisher of such book, or the proprietor of the copyright therein, together with the title of such book, and the time when, and the place where, such book was first published; otherwise the defendant in such action shall not at the trial or hearing of such action be allowed to give any evidence that the plaintiff in such action was not the author or first publisher of the book in which he claims such copyright as aforesaid, or that he was not the proprietor of the copyright therein; and at such trial or hearing no other objection shall be allowed to be made on behalf of such defendant than the objections stated in such notice, or that any other person was the author or first publisher of such book, or the proprietor of the copyright therein, than the person so specified in such notice, or give in evidence in support of his defence any other book than one substantially corresponding in title, time, and place of publication with the title, time, and place specified in such notice.

In *Leader* v. *Purday* it was accordingly ruled that points not raised in the notice of objections could not be raised upon the plaintiff's evidence on the trial. (*a*)

A general objection will not do. The Act throws on a defendant, if he seek to defend an infringement on the ground that the plaintiff is not the proprietor, the onus of specifying the person whom he alleges to be the proprietor, in order that the plaintiff may not be taken by surprise; at the trial the defendant must also give the title of the book, and the time when (the year is sufficient) and the place where published. (*b*)

(*a*) 7 C B 11   1038 and see *Nelson* v *Harford*,
(*b*) *Boosey* v *Davidson*, 1 D &   8 M & W 806
L 147, *Boosey* v *Purday* 10 Jur

In the action the defendant may plead the general issue, and give the special matter in evidence; and if a verdict shall be given for the defendant, or the plaintiff shall become non-suited, or discontinue his action, then the defendant can recover his full costs, and for them he has the same remedy as a defendant in any case by law has. (a)

All actions, suits, bills, indictments, or informations for any offence committed against and under the Act 5 & 6 Vict. c. 45, except in respect of copies of books to be delivered to the British Museum, &c., must be commenced within twelve calendar months next after the commission of the offence. (b)

Besides the remedy under 5 & 6 Vict. c. 45, s. 15, an infringement is actionable at law. (c) As to books published before that Act an action for damages will lie in respect of a violation of copyright after the expiry of the twelve calendar months: contrary doctrine was urged and repelled in an action brought at the instance of Colonel *Matthew Stewart* (son of Dugald Stewart), against Messrs. *Black*, the Edinburgh booksellers. The action was in respect of an alleged piracy of the Professor's 'Dissertations on the Progress of Philosophy since the Revival of Letters in Europe.' (d)

In an action in England for piracy, the consideration of the two works has been referred to an arbitrator, who would have leisure to compare them. (e) In Scotland, the enquiry has been likewise referred by the Court to an arbitrator, (f) a jury generally, however, determines the question of piracy.

(a) 5 & 6 Vict c 45, s. 26.
(b) Ibid
(c) In *Novello* v *Sudlow*, 12 C B 177, and see *Boozey* v *Tolken*, 5 C B 476
(d) *Stewart* v *Black* 9 Dec of Court of Sess. 2d series, p 1026
(e) *Trusler* v *Murray*, 11 East, 363, n. See present practice in Chancery, *post*, p 164
(f) *Alexander* v *M'Kenzie*, 9 Dec of Court of Sess n s. 751

To make the publisher of a piratical work which
another has printed liable at law for the infringement,
guilty knowledge must be brought home to him.
Although the 15th section of the Act of Victoria pre-
sumes guilty knowledge in some cases, it does not
presume it from the mere fact of selling piratical works
in print. This was ruled by Chief Justice *Wilde*, in the
Court of Common Pleas. (*a*)

If several plaintiffs join in an action for piracy, it
may of course be defeated by showing that one of them
has deprived himself of all right of complaint. In
Sweet v. *Archbold* it was held that the publication
complained of being pursuant to the conditions of a
cognovit given by the defendant to one of the plaintiffs
was a complete answer to the action. (*b*)

The report of a select committee of the House of
Commons, in the year 1836, recommended a cheap
accessible tribunal for the protection of copyright; but
their recommendation has not yet been followed. The
necessity for such a tribunal has been insisted upon by
many writers. (*c*)

22 Relief in equity against infringement of the right

22 A person aggrieved by a threatened infringement
of his copyright under the Act 5 & 6 Vict. c. 45, may
also get relief in a court of equity, (*d*) which, on a
proper application, will restrain a violation of the right.
The principle of granting the injunction is that
damages may not give adequate relief, and that the
sale of copies by the defendant is in each instance not
only taking away the profit upon the individual book,

(*a*) *Leader* v *Strange*, 2 C & K
1010

(*b*) 10 Bingh 133

(*c*) See Blanc on 'Artistic Copy-

right,' p 5.

(*d*) See *Sheriff* v *Coates*, 1 R &
M 159

which the plaintiff probably would have sold, but may injure him to an extent which no enquiry for the purpose of damages can ascertain. (a)

Upon a motion to dissolve an injunction against the infringement of a copyright, Lord *Eldon*, C. remarked that jurisdiction upon subjects of this nature is assumed merely for the purpose of making effectual the legal right, which cannot be made effectual by any action for damages, as if the work is pirated it is impossible to lay before a jury the whole evidence as to all the publications which go out to the world to the plaintiff's prejudice; a court of equity therefore acts with a view to making the legal right effectual by preventing the publication altogether (b) Accordingly, in the exercise of this jurisdiction, where a fair doubt appeared as to the plaintiff's legal right, the Court, before the passing of Rolt's Act, (c) always directed it to be tried, making some provision in the interim, the best that could be for the benefit of both parties. The particular provision was dictated by the circumstances of each case (d)

In another suit Lord *Eldon* said 'The owner of the copyright has a right to bring an action for invading it, and upon that this Court has founded the right to have

(a) See *Hogg* v *Kirby*, 8 Ves 221, and *Geary* v *Norton*, 1 De G & Sm 9

(b) In *Wilkins* v *Aikin*, 17 Ves. 421

(c) 25 & 26 Vict c 42

(d) See Lord *Eldon*, C in *Walcot* v *Walker*, 7 Ves 14, and *Laurence* v *Smith*, Jac 472 See also Lord *Cottenham*, C in *Saunders* v *Smith* 3 M & Cr 728, and Sir *J L. K Bruce*, V C in *M'Neill* v *Williams*, 11 Jur 344, *Chappell* v *Davidson*, 2 Ka & Jo 123, Sir *J. Wigram*, V C in *Cory* v. *Yarmouth Railway Company*, 3 Hare, 600, *Spottiswoode* v *Clarke*, 2 Phill 155, *Jarrold* v *Houston*, 3 Ka & Jo 724, Lord *Langdale*, in *Dalglish* v *Jarvie*, 2 M & Gor 242

an injunction on the ground that if it were necessary to bring action after action the expense of asserting the title might exceed the advantages to be derived from it.' (a)

A court of equity has no jurisdiction to give to a plaintiff a remedy for an alleged piracy, unless he can make out that he is entitled to the equitable inter-position by injunction, and in such case the Court will also give him an account that his remedy in equity may be effectual. If the court of equity do not inter-fere by injunction, then his remedy, as in the case of any other injury to his property, is at law. (b) Unless that primary right to an injunction exist, a court of equity has no jurisdiction with reference to a mere question of damages. (c)

It has very recently been ruled by the Lords Justices in the Court of Chancery that it is now the duty of that Court to decide all questions of law or fact upon the determination of which relief in equity depends. (d) This ruling will probably tend very much to alter the practice of the Court of Chancery in withholding in-junctions pending proceedings at law to establish the fact of piracy.

Distinct invasions of copyright by several persons cannot be restrained in one suit (e)

The minuteness of the injury inflicted by a piracy has weighed with a court of equity in its refusal of an injunction. (f)

(a) In *Rundell* v *Murray*, Jac R 852
311

(b) Sir *J Leach*, M R in *Bailey* v *Taylor* 1 R & M 75

(c) Sir *W P Wood*, V C in *London and South-Western Railway Company* v *Smith*, 1 K & J, 112, and see *Johnson* v *Wyatt* 11 W

(d) Re *Hooper*, 11 W R 130.

(e) *Dilly* v *Doig*, 2 Ves. 486, and see *Hudson* v *Maddison*, 12 Sim 116

(f) *Bell* v *Whitehead*, 3 Jurist, 68, and see Sir *L Shadwell*, V C E in *Saunders* v *Smith*,

Prior to the passing of the statute 25 & 26 Vict. c. 12, an author might have so conducted himself in reference to his copyright as to have lost all title to relief in a court of equity until his title at law had been established. (a)

Where a mode of dealing had been commonly admitted and adopted by writers as no violation of copyright, and plaintiff had himself acquiesced therein, a court of equity would not, it seems, prior to that Act, restrain without a previous trial at law. In *Saunders* v. *Smith*, (b) which was a suit to restrain the publication of the second volume of 'Smith's Leading Cases,' and in which Lord *Cottenham* refused the injunction, he is reported as saying: 'In this case I find the publication complained of to be of a character (c) which, whether it be or be not an infringement of the copyright of the plaintiffs, is a course of proceeding which has been pretty largely admitted, and pretty generally adopted. Several cases occurred to me, and several were mentioned to me at the bar, in which a gentleman at the bar desirous of publishing a work upon a particular subject has collected the cases upon that subject, and has taken those cases, generally speaking, verbatim from reports which are covered by copyright. No instance has been represented to me in which those entitled to the copyright have interfered; no judgment, therefore, has been pronounced upon that subject. I am not stating whether the owner of the copyright is entitled to interfere in such a case, or whether that use of published reports is or is not to be permitted. That

---

(a) *Southey* v *Sherwood, ante*, Cr 711.
p 19

(b) *Saunders* v *Smith*, 3 M &

(c) As to the character of the publication, see *post*, p 151

is a question of legal right upon which I find, at present, no reason for coming to an adjudication. But in considering whether I am to exercise an equitable jurisdiction in such case, before the legal right has been established, it is very important to observe that, for many years, such a course as I have stated has been pretty generally adopted, 'more particularly when I find that these plaintiffs have themselves acquiesced in a similar course of proceeding.' In *Platt* v. *Button*, (a) too, Lord *Eldon* directed the plaintiff to bring his action, and then to apply for an injunction: he observed that the plaintiff had permitted several persons to publish the dances alleged to have been pirated by the defendant, some of them for fifteen years, and that the plaintiff had thus encouraged others to do so. 'That, it is true,' said the learned Judge, 'is no justification; but, under these circumstances, a court of equity will not interfere in the first instance.'

Further, a person cannot call for the interposition of a court of equity to protect copyright from infringement if—aware of the labours of another on the work complained of, of the character of the new work and of the intention to publish it—he makes no remonstrance whatever prior to its publication. *Rundell* v. *Murray* (b) is an authority on this point: there the plaintiff had written a book on domestic cookery, which she had given to the plaintiff for publication at his risk; the book also contained a statement by the plaintiff, that she gave it to the public without prospect of emolument, the defendant published it at his own cost,

(a) 19 Ves 118, Coop 303   *Chapman*, 3 Beav 135.
(b) Jac 311   See also *Lewis* v

and when it had obtained a large sale he sent 150*l.*
to the writer, which sum she acknowledged as a free
gift, at the end of the first statutory term of copyright
in the work under the statute of Queen Anne the
plaintiff obtained an injunction to restrain the defendant against further publication; but, on argument,
Lord *Eldon* declining to state in whom the copyright
was vested, dissolved the injunction: he did so on the
ground of the plaintiff's acquiescence in the defendant's
outlay.

The principle of the last decision was followed in
Saunders v. *Smith.* (a) The defendant in that suit had
published without interference by the plaintiffs the first
volume of his work, and an injunction was asked at
the eleventh hour to restrain his publication of the
second volume. Lord *Cottenham,* C. refused the writ,
saying: ' When I look at this book, I see that it is a
work of very great labour, and I find the principle is
to take, first, the marginal note, sometimes with some
alteration, and then to take the leading case, as a principle, and then, by very voluminous and obviously
laborious notes, to work out the principle. It is clear,
therefore, that the work is one of great labour, and
that this was evident from the first volume; and I find
that the plaintiffs were informed in March 1837 of
an intention to deal with the existing reports in the
manner now complained of. I find the first volume
published, announcing the intention of going on with
the same plan, which necessarily would run over the
period to which the copyrights of the plaintiffs relate,
and that no remonstrance is made to Mr. Smith upon

(a) 3 M. & Cr. 711

the nature of the work, but he is permitted to go on
with this laborious undertaking until the period at
which the first part of the second volume is published.
In the meantime there was a communication between
the plaintiffs and Mr. Maxwell, who was interested in
the publication of the work, and who has as much right
to the protection of the Court as Mr. Smith; and in
the proposal which he makes to the plaintiffs, he deals
with the work as property he is entitled to deal with,
wishing to make it the subject of arrangement between
himself and the plaintiffs, and I do not find that this
leads to any caution or interference on the part of the
plaintiffs as to that course which Mr. Smith had pursued
in part, and which the plaintiffs must have been fully
aware he intended to pursue further. I do not give
any opinion upon the legal question. I am only to
decide that whatever legal right the plaintiffs may have,
the circumstances are such as to make it the duty of a
court of equity to withhold its hand and to abstain
from exercising its equitable jurisdiction, at all events,
until the plaintiffs shall come here with the legal title
established. In doing this, I am only doing what Lord
Eldon did in *Rundell* v. *Murray*, and what is very
generally done upon questions of patent right. The
Court always exercises its discretion as to whether it
shall interfere by injunction before the establishment
of the legal right.'

If an author or proprietor gave permission to several
persons to publish his copyright work, such permission
made it necessary for him to bring an action at law against
others who publish a copy of it. Lord *Eldon*, C. was
of this opinion in *Rundell* v. *Murray*, when he said
'There has often been great difficulty about granting

injunctions where the plaintiff has previously by acquiescing permitted many others to publish the work; where ten have been allowed to publish the Court will not restrain the eleventh. (a)

It is very important for authors and proprietors to assert their rights at the earliest period of infringement. In *Tinsley* v. *Lacy*, (b) a case of an alleged infringement of copyright in the popular novels 'Aurora Floyd' and 'Lady Audley's Secret,' Sir *W. P. Wood*, V.C. remarked that if the plaintiff in that case had hesitated to apply to the Court in respect of what had been pirated, not amounting to more than one-fourth of the contents of the piracy, she would have been estopped from afterwards applying if a much larger proportion had been taken. The one-fourth, it should however be observed, there embraced the chief incidents of the plaintiff's work.

It is not absolutely necessary for the plaintiff in a suit seeking an injunction against the publication of a work partly pirated to state in his bill or in the affidavit in support of it the piratical portion. (c)

A court of equity will not restrain the infringement of a copyright, but will leave the plaintiff to his remedy at law if he be guilty of delay in his application.

When a defendant denies piracy he will do well to produce his MS. notes, or explain their non-production. (d)

An author's delay of several years has been held to

(a) Lord *Eldon*, C in *Rundell* v. *Murray*, Jac 511, also Lord *Brougham* in *Guichard* v *Mort*, 9 L J ch 227, and see *Platt* v *Button*, Coop. Ch Ca 303.

(b) 11 W R 877

(c) *Sweet* v *Maugham*, 11 Sim 51

(d) See *Murray* v *Bogue*, 1 Drev 361

be a sufficient reason for refusing him an injunction. (a)
Five months' delay on the part of the plaintiff, in *Mawman* v. *Tegg*, (b) was accounted for to the satisfaction
of Lord *Eldon*, C. by the necessity of comparing the
whole of the two works (which were bulky) for the
purpose of seeing how much of the earlier work had
been in a substantial sense taken from it and infused
into the later.

An unexplained delay of nine months would probably be fatal. (c) In a suit (d) where it appeared
that the plaintiff and defendant were simultaneously pre-
paring topographical dictionaries for publication; that
the defendant's publication began first; that the plaintiff's attention was drawn to it at its commencement,
and during its progress to complete publication, which
occurred six and a half years before the filing of the
plaintiff's bill; and when it also appeared that the plaintiff had possession for more than one year before the
commencement of the suit of a complete copy of the
defendant's work, with a view to its examination, Lord
Langdale, M R. refused an injunction solely on the
ground of delay: he thought it his duty to impute to
the plaintiff such a knowledge of the contents of the
defendant's work as made it obligatory on the former
to apply for injunction, if at all, at a much earlier
period.

When a piracy was discovered in June, and the bill
to restrain it was filed in the following month, Lord

(a) *Bailey* v. *Taylor*, 1 R &
M 76; S C 1 Tamlyn, 303, and
see *Bacon* v. *Jones*, 4 M & Cr
133, and see *Saunders* v *Smith*,
3 M & Cr 711

(b) 2 Russ 393

(c) *Smith* v *London and S B
Railway Company*, 1 Kay, 412

(d) *Lewis* v *Chapman*, 3 Beav
135, and see *Bridson* v *Benecke*,
12 Beav 3.

Langdale, M.R. considered that there had been no improper or unnecessary delay. (*a*) In the year 1849 the state of the law rendered it doubtful whether a certain work was entitled to copyright. The work was copied, and the copies were sold without the consent of the proprietor of the original work: he did not apply immediately for an injunction, but gave notice of his ownership to the vendor, and threatened him with legal proceedings unless the sale was discontinued and the plates were broken up. No attention was paid to this notice. In March 1851, the proprietor issued a notice to the publishers, which notice contained a claim of his right to the work. On May 20, 1851 a decision at law established the claim of such a work to copyright. In August 1851, the proprietor again warned the vendor. In November 1851, he filed a bill to restrain the sale. Sir *James Parker*, V.C. held that the delay was fully explained, and granted the injunction (*b*)

A court of equity was, prior to the Act 25 & 26 Vict. c. 42, less likely to issue or to continue an injunction against an alleged infringement of a literary work of a transitory nature than of a work permanent in its character. (*c*)

The language of the Court in *Spottiswoode* v. *Clarke* (*d*) (although not a copyright case) shows the difficulties which then beset a court of equity called upon to restrain the publication of an ephemeral work. Lord *Cottenham* there said: ' But the greatest of all objections is that the Court runs the risk of doing the greatest

(*a*) *Lewis* v *Fullarton*, 2 Bear 8

(*b*) *Buxton* v *James*, 5 De G & Sm 84

(*c*) See Lord *Eldon*, C in *Matthewson* v *Stockdale*, 12 Ves

275, see also *Gurney* v *Longman*, 13 Ves 505, and *Sheriff* v *Coates*, 1 R & M 169

(*d*) 2 Phill 154 It was a suit to restrain the sale of an almanack

injustice in case its opinion upon the legal right should turn out to be erroneous. Here is a publication which if not issued this month (a) will lose a great part of its sale for the ensuing year. If you restrain the party from selling immediately, you probably make it impossible for him to sell at all. You take property out of his pocket and give it to nobody. In such a case, if the plaintiff is right, the Court has some means, at least, of indemnifying him, by making the defendant keep an account; whereas, if the defendant be right, and he be restrained, it is utterly impossible to give him compensation for the loss he will have sustained. And the effect of the order in that case will be to commit a great and irremediable injury. Unless, therefore, the Court is quite clear as to what are the legal rights of the parties it is much the safest course to abstain from exercising its jurisdiction till the legal right has been determined.'

A person having a complete equitable title to a copyright may institute a suit in respect thereof.

It was observed by Lord *Mansfield*, in the great case of *Millar* v. *Taylor*, that unless a court of equity saw a legal right in an author it would not interfere; but if by that, said Lord *Lyndhurst*, the Chief Justice meant to say that a court of equity would only interfere when the legal right to sue was in the applicant for interference, then he (Lord *Lyndhurst*) would not go so far, because he thought that a court of equity would assist any party having an equitable right when the legal right intervenes to prevent his obtaining justice, otherwise great fraud would ensue. (b)

(a) December   C 192
(b) *Chappell* v *Purday* 4 Y &

Lord *Eldon*, too, sitting in the Court of Chancery, once (*a*) broadly intimated his opinion that a court of equity could not give equitable relief to any claimant of copyright by assignment not in writing. Afterwards, however, (*b*) in a case of *Mawman* v. *Tegg*, he at least qualified that statement. The work there alleged to be pirated had belonged one-third to Mr. Curtis, one-third to Miss Richardson, one-third to Mr. Fenner. Mr. Curtis had sold, but he had executed no assignment of his share to Mr. Fenner. Mr. Fenner had since become bankrupt. Miss Richardson had duly assigned her share to two of the plaintiffs (those two plaintiffs were the assignees in bankruptcy of Mr. Fenner), and a third person (not a party to the suit), in trust for her creditors. One objection relied on by the defendants was the absence of title in the plaintiffs to the work. To this Lord *Eldon* replied. ' Observations have been made upon the nature of the title of Mr. Mawman and his twenty associates in this work. Whether the title be a good legal title in them or be not is one question; but it appears to me that they have a complete equitable title.' On that title he gave relief.

Again, in allusion to an alleged piracy of Roscoe's ' Illustrations of the Life of Lorenzo de Medici,' Sir *L. Shadwell* declared that the Court of Chancery always took notice of the equitable interest, and if the equitable right to the copyright is complete, that Court would take care that the real question should be tried, notwithstanding there might be a defect in respect of the legal property (*c*)

(*a*) In *Rundell* v *Murray*, Jac 31)

(*b*) 2 Russ 385

(*c*) In *Bohn* v *Bogue*, 10 Jur 120

The person who has the legal title to a copyright invaded should, however, be a party to the suit for an injunction against such infringement.

This point was established by a decision in *Colburn* v. *Sims*. (*a*) That was a suit to restrain an alleged piracy of a diary illustrative of the times of George IV.: the plaintiff claimed under an agreement in writing for an assignment of the copyright in the work. The injunction was granted, but subsequently upon demurrer to the bill, the Vice-Chancellor of England, Sir *L. Shadwell*, considered the suit to be manifestly defective in not having the author of the work a party. Inasmuch, however, as the bill was sufficient in the opinion of the Court to show that the plaintiff had a good title in equity, that Judge gave leave to amend the bill without prejudice to the injunction.

Where it appeared in the Court of Chancery, upon an application to restrain the infringement of copyright in certain published law reports, for the preparation of which the plaintiffs, being law booksellers and publishers, had agreed in writing with several gentlemen at the bar, and the Court thought proper to direct an action to try the fact of piracy, it ordered that the defendants should at law admit the legal copyright in the plaintiffs (*b*)

In a still later case, when an injunction had been granted upon the plaintiff's undertaking to try his right at law, and the legal proprietor of the right, a party to the suit, declined to lend his name in the action to the plaintiff, who was considered in equity his assign,

(*a*) 9 Sim 154   (*b*) *Sweet v. Shaw*, 3 Jur 217

Sir *L. Shadwell*, V.C.E. ordered the defendant to admit at the trial that the plaintiff was the legal proprietor. (a)

Any person associated by the proprietor of a copyright with himself in an entry in the book of registry at Stationers' Hall has primâ facie a title to sue jointly with him in a court of equity in respect of a violation of the right. (b)

By analogy to Patent Law, it seems that the proprietor of a copyright may, during its term of protection, apply for and obtain an injunction against the publication after the term of a piracy prepared during that term. (c)

If a person purchase a stereotype plate of a literary work, upon an undertaking with the vendor that the plate is to be used for the production of that work without any additions, he may, of course, be restrained at the suit of the vendor from publishing by means of the plate that work with additions; (d) because such a publication would be a breach of contract.

Where an injunction against the piratical part of a work would practically restrain the whole work, a court of equity will issue an injunction against the whole work. Where that result would not necessarily follow from an injunction limited to the piratical part, such

(a) *Sweet v Cater*, 11 Sim 581

(b) *Stevens v Wildy*, 19 Law J ch n s 190

(c) *Crossley v Beverley*, 1 R & M 166, n. The defendants there had been manufacturing the patented articles for some time, and keeping it secret from the plaintiff by excluding him from the premises. They had been doing this fraudulently for the purpose of pouring into the market the articles so patented directly the patent should have expired, and see Sir W P Wood, V C in *Smith v London and South-Western Railway Company*, 1 Kay, 112

(d) *Napier v Paterson*, 13 Dec of Court of Session, n s 219

limited injunction will issue. This appears to be settled by *Jarrold* v. *Houlston*: (a) there the learned Judge so ably reviewed the previous decisions on the point, that an extract from his judgment will perhaps best explain the practice. He is reported as having said in that case: 'The next question is what course the Court should adopt where it appears that the piracy complained of extends to about half of the defendant's book. . . . In *Mawman* v. *Tegg* (b) Lord *Eldon* says· "The persons in the employment of the defendant can state exactly how much they copied, and what parts they copied, and can supply the Court with the knowledge of how the fact really stands, without leaving it to be collected from inferences more or less strong." I have already expressed my great regret that Mr. Philp has not taken that course. It is impossible for me now to ask him for an affidavit stating how much he has copied, when he has already filed an affidavit denying that he has taken a single idea from the plaintiff's book. Had he taken a different course in this respect it might possibly have put the case in a different position. The defendant in *Mawman* v. *Tegg* took a different course, and made an affidavit (c) stating that out of 227,000 lines, 2,160 lines, or somewhere about $\frac{1}{100}$th part of the whole had been copied. The Lord Chancellor felt so much difficulty on the case that he ultimately sent a reference to the Master to investigate the matter; but he makes these observations as to what ought to be done about the injunction. He says: "It

---

(a) 3 Ka & Jo 708

(b) 2 Russ 385 This was the case of an encyclopædia, part of which had been copied into another encyclopædia, the suit ended in a compromise

(c) 2 Russ 395

appears to have been Lord *Hardwicke's* opinion (*a*) that an injunction might be granted against the whole, although only part was pirated; and, in the instance of Milton's ' Paradise Lost,' with Newton's notes, although there was nothing new in that book except the notes, he was of opinion that he could grant, and he did grant, an injunction against the whole book. There is a case of an action tried before Lord *Kenyon*, (*b*) in which a motion was afterwards made for a new trial, and there Lord *Kenyon* states that the question whether you could grant an injunction against the whole of a book on account of the piratical quality of a part came before Lord *Bathurst*; and Lord *Bathurst* seems to have held that you could not do so unless the part pirated was such that granting an injunction against that part necessarily destroyed the whole. Lord *Kenyon*, who possessed great information on this subject, states himself to have been perfectly satisfied with the opinion of Lord *Bathurst*, as bearing upon the judgment of Lord *Hardwicke* and the other cases. In the case before Lord *Kenyon*, the declaration at law contained a count for publishing the whole work, and another for publishing a part; and Lord *Kenyon's* direction to the jury seems to have been to find damages for publishing the part only." Then Lord *Eldon* says: " The difficulty here is this, whether I have before me sufficient grounds to authorise me to say how far the matter which is proved (if I may use that word) to have been copied is sufficient to enable me to decide how much I may enjoin against. And if I can be thus authorised to say how much I can enjoin against, then the

(*a*) 4 Burr 2326   o 0, and *Trusler* v *Murray*, 1
(*b*) *Cary* v *Longman*, 1 East. L t 363

M

question is, what will be the effect of that injunction applied to so much of the work in the state of uncertainty in which we now are? Or whether, on the other hand, as the matter cannot be tried by the eye of the judge, I must not pursue a course which has been adopted in cases of a similar nature, namely, refer it to the Master to report to what extent the one book is a copy of the other." In the previous part of the hearing he had said, " There is no doubt, if a man mixes what belongs to him with what belongs to me, and the mixture be forbidden by the law, he must again separate them, and he must bear all the mischief and loss which the separation may occasion." In *Lewis* v. *Fullarton* (a) Lord *Langdale* came to the conclusion that a considerable part of the plaintiff's work had been pirated, and, though he could not say how much had been so, yet he inferred, from what was already in evidence, that the result of further investigation applied to other parts of the work would be similar; he referred also to Lord *Eldon's* observations in *Mawman* v. *Tegg*, that it was the business of a defendant, when a considerable part of a work is shown to have been pirated, to separate and point out all that has been pirated, and he granted an injunction as to the entire work. It seems to me that the present case is one which differs to a considerable extent both from *Mawman* v. *Tegg* and *Lewis* v. *Fullarton*. Here it is as if the book in question had been published in parts. Had the last

(a) 2 Beav 6 The order made in this case by Lord *Langdale* was 'Let the defendant, his agents, servants, and workmen, be restrained from further printing, publishing, selling, or otherwise disposing of any copy or copies of a book called, &c containing any articles or article, passages or passage, copied, taken, or colourably altered from a book called, &c published by the plaintiffs'

part alone been published, there would have been no
ground for interfering at all. In the first lecture, as it
is called, in the defendant's book, there is nothing of
which the plaintiffs complain. The fourth lecture,
and all those subsequent to the twenty-fifth, I have
carefully examined, and though here and there they
contain passages of which the plaintiffs complain, I
find nothing which can be reasonably objected to as
showing that the writer has made an unfair use of the
plaintiffs' book. The second lecture contains piratical
matter, and as to the rest, between that and the twenty-
fifth, some contain passages which appear to me, after
carefully reading through them, to have been evidently
taken from the plaintiffs' book, and the remainder
contain passages which have a resemblance. Although
I should not have been satisfied in dealing with the
latter had they stood alone, it appears to me, therefore, that I shall be doing complete justice if I restrain
the defendants, as I consider that I am bound to do,
from publishing the second lecture, the third lecture,
and the fifth and following lectures down to and
including the twenty-fifth of the defendant's book.
Adopting the words used by Lord *Langdale* in *Lewis*
v. *Fullarton*, the injunction will restrain the defendant
from publishing a book called "The Reason Why," containing the lectures I have mentioned, and then it will
add, "or any passages or passage copied, taken, or
colourably altered from the book called 'The Guide to
Science' in the plaintiffs' bill mentioned."'(a)

In a plain case of infringement of copyright, Sir
L. Shadwell, V.C.E. observed. 'I do not think that I

(a) See also *Motte* v *Faulkner*, Ves 2234, n , *Reade* v. *Lacy*, 1
cited 1 Bl 331 *King* v *Reed*, 8 John & H 428

M 2

am bound to go through the whole book, but I apprehend that the law at present is in conformity with the old Roman law, which is, that if the defendant will take the plaintiff's corn and mix it with his own, the whole should be taken to be the plaintiff's, and after the defendants have taken so much as I see has been taken in this case, I think the injunction ought to be granted.'

Sir W. *Page Wood*, V.C. has lately said (*a*) that, if in a suit to restrain the violation of a copyright the judge arrives at a conclusion of piracy, he ought to grudge no labour that may be requisite to ascertain how far the injunction should extend. An opposite opinion has been attributed to Lord *Cottenham*, C. but on reference to the case before him (*b*) that conclusion seems to be erroneous.

The proprietor of an invaded copyright is entitled to the protection of an injunction, though the pirate promise to desist from his piracy and to pay the proprietor's costs, and if the pirate do not after the injunction offer to pay the proprietor's costs, the proprietor may

(*a*) In *Jarrold* v. *Houlston*, 3 K & Jo 708 In *Gyles* v. *Wilcox*, 2 Atk 141, Lord *Hardwicke*, C said that he should not be able to determine the question of piracy unless both books were read over, and at law the judge would be in his position in that respect, and he advised the parties to fix upon two persons of learning and ability to examine and compare the works, and report thereon to himself This labour was delegated to a Master in Chancery in *Carnan* v. *Bowles*, 1 Cox 283 s c, 2 Bro C C 80 *Hogg* v. *Bowles*, 1 Dick 129, *Nicol* v. *Stockdale* 12 Ves 277

—— v *Leadbitter*, 4 Ves 681 Lord *Eldon* himself compared the books *Matthewson* v *Stockdale*, 12 Ves 277 Sir *Thomas Plumer*, M R in *Whittingham* v *Wooler*, 2 Swanst 160 Lord *Langdale*, M R in *Lewis* v. *Fullarton*, 2 Beav 8 Sir R T *Kindersley*, V C in *Murray* v *Bogue*, 1 Drew, 368, and Sir W P *Wood*, V C in *Spiers* v *Brown*, 6 W R 352, and *Jarrold* v *Houlston*, 3 K & Jo 708, and *Napier* v *Routledge*, unreported (1859), followed his example

(*b*) *Stevens* v *Wildy*, 19 Law J Ch n s 190

bring the suit to a hearing, and will be entitled to the costs of the suit. (a)

An allegation that 'matter contained in a particular edition of a copyright work is spurious' is irrelevant in a suit to restrain a violation of the right, though it may be the subject of an action, as being a libel on or disparagement of the edition. (b)

In stating in a bill for an injunction against infringement of copyright the title of the plaintiff, the assignee of the author, it seems insufficient to allege that he purchased the copyright without adding 'of the author.' (c)

Of course, piracy proved to be such will not itself be protected from invasion. In *Cary* v. *Faden*, (d) the plaintiff's itinerary was a piracy of Paterson's 'Road Book.' The defendants were alleged to have invaded the itinerary. Lord *Eldon*, C. refused to make any order for an injunction, saying.—'What right had the plaintiff to the original work? If I was to do strict justice, I should order the defendants to take out of their book all they have taken from the plaintiff, and reciprocally, the plaintiff to take out of his book all he has taken from Paterson. I think the plaintiff may be contented that a bill is not filed against him.'

When a perpetual injunction is granted, the Court of Chancery can and will now itself decide the amount of any damages sustained by the plaintiff by reason of the invasion of his right. (e) The value of a copyright is

(a) *Geary* v *Norton*, 1 De G & Sma 9, but see *Millington* v *Fox* 3 M & Cr 338, and *Woodman* v *Robinson*, 2 Sim n s 211

(b) *Sadey* v *Fisher*, 11 Sim 583

(c) *Gulliver* v *Snaggs*, 4 Vin Abr 279, 2 Eq Ca Abr 522

(d) 5 Ves 24

(e) *Tinsley* v *Lacy* 11 W R 878

per se immaterial in the view of a court of equity upon an application to it against an infringement. (a)

It must be borne in mind that no action, or suit, or summary proceeding in respect of any infringement of the copyright of a book published since July 1, 1842, is maintainable before the entry of the book in the registry at Stationers' Hall. (b)

23. Infringement of the right by importation

23. Inasmuch as the copyright of a book may be injuriously affected by the introduction into this country of copies printed abroad, statutory provisions have been framed to counteract that mischief.

The evil was not met, however, in any way until the passing of an Act 12 Geo. 2, c. 36.　That Act expired and similar provisions were then introduced into an Act 34 Geo. 3, c. 20.　The 57th section of that Act provided that it should not be lawful for any person to import here any book first published in this country and reprinted abroad, and that if any person should so do, or should knowingly sell, publish, expose to sale, or have in his possession for sale any such book, the book might be seized by any customs or excise officer, the offender was also to forfeit 10l. and double the value of every copy imported.　The enactment was, however, qualified with a proviso that it should not extend to any book that had not been printed or reprinted in this kingdom within twenty years before the importation, nor to any book reprinted abroad and inserted among other books or tracts to be sold therewith in any collection where the greatest part of such collection should have been first composed or written abroad

(a) *Buxton* v *James*, 5 De G & Sm 83
(b) 5 & 6 Vict c 45, s 24 Sn

R Kindersley in *Murray* v *Bogue*, 1 Drew, 364

The above enactment has never been repealed in toto, but the saving as to the importation of books not reprinted within twenty years is now abolished.

The 17th section of the Act 5 & 6 Vict. c. 45, has dealt with this subject of importation; it especially declares that no person not being the proprietor of the copyright, or some person authorised by him, may import into the British dominions, for sale or hire, any printed book first composed, or written, or printed, and published in the United Kingdom, wherein there shall be copyright, and reprinted out of the British dominions. And if any person not being such proprietor, or person authorised as aforesaid, shall so import, or shall knowingly sell, publish, or expose to sale, or let to hire, or have in his possession for sale or hire any such book, then every such book shall be forfeited, and seized, and destroyed by any officer of customs or excise, and every person so offending, being duly convicted thereof before the justices of the peace for the county or place in which such book shall be found, shall also, for every such offence, forfeit 10l. and double the value of every copy of such book so imported, &c., 5l. to the use of such officer, and the remainder of the penalty to the use of the proprietor of the copyright in such book. (a)

The 15th section of the Act of Victoria, already referred to, has provisions as to the importation of books piratically printed in this country.

By a later Act in the same session further provision was made to prevent the importation of piratical works. The Act 5 & 6 Vict. c. 47 [after reciting 'that by a

(a) As to separate penalties upon each separate violation of the Act on the same day, see 12 George 2, c. 36 and Brook v. Middleton 3 T. R. 509.

* M 1

previous Act of Will. 4, books first composed, or written, or printed in the United Kingdom, and printed or reprinted in any other country, and imported for sale (except books not reprinted within the United Kingdom within twenty years, or being parts of collections, the greater parts of which had been composed or written abroad) were absolutely prohibited to be imported into the United Kingdom, and that great abuse had prevailed with respect to the introduction into this country for private use of such works so reprinted abroad, to the great injury of the authors thereof and of others'] enacted, that from and after the 1st day of April 1843, so much of the Act of William 4 as was therein recited should be repealed, and that from and after the 1st day of April 1843, all books wherein the copyright should be subsisting, first composed, or written, or printed in the United Kingdom, and printed, or reprinted, in any other country, should be, and the same were thereby, absolutely prohibited to be imported into the United Kingdom, provided that no such book should be prohibited to be imported unless the proprietor of such copyright, or his agent, should give notice in writing to the Commissioners of Customs that such copyright subsisted, and in such notice should state when such copyright should expire, and the said Commissioners should cause to be made and to be publicly exposed at the several ports of the United Kingdom from time to time printed lists of the works respecting which such notice should have been duly given, and of which such copyright should not have expired.

The Act 5 & 6 Vict c. 47, has been repealed, but under

an Act 16 & 17 Vict. c. 107, the provision still subsists (a) and extends to importation into the British possessions abroad.

In regard to a British colony, however, if the Government of a colony provides, in a manner sufficient in the opinion of Her Majesty, for the protection within that colony of British authors, Her Majesty may, by Order in Council, declare that so long as such protection shall subsist any statutory prohibitions against the importing, selling, letting out to hire, exposing for sale or hire, or possessing foreign reprints of books first composed, written, printed, or published in the United Kingdom, and entitled to copyright therein, shall be suspended so far as regards such colony. (b)

The following colonies have placed themselves within the provisions of 10 & 11 Vict. c. 95, viz.: Canada, St. Vincent, Jamaica, Mauritius, Nevis, Grenada, Newfoundland, New Brunswick, St. Lucia, St. Kitts, British Guiana, Prince Edward's Island, Barbadoes, Bermuda, the Bahamas, Cape of Good Hope, Nova Scotia, Antigua, and Natal.

24. Forfeiture to the registered proprietor of a copyright book (duly entered) of all copies unlawfully printed or imported, without his consent in writing, is another check imposed by the Act 5 & 6 Vict. c. 45, s. 23; on piracy, and on the importation of foreign reprints, the proprietor may, after demand thereof in writing, sue for and recover the same, or damages for the detention thereof, in an action of detinue against

24. Forfeiture of piratical work to proprietor of copyright.

(a) See also 18 & 19 Vict c 96, s 10

(b) The Act 10 & 11 Vict c. 95,

has not escaped strictures See 6 Jurist, pt. II p 45

any party who shall detain the same; or he may sue for and recover damages for the conversion thereof in an action of trover. (a) The latter part of this provision is now in copyright legislation.

Sir *James Wigram*, V.C. in the year 1843, considered that at all events since the decision in *Donaldson v. Beckett* there has been no common law right in the author or proprietor of a pirated work to the possession of the piratical copies. He thought that there would be great difficulty in applying to the subject the principles of the common law, which in certain cases gives to the owners of an original material the right of seizing it in whatever shape it may be found, if he can prove it to be his own, or which relate to what is termed confusion of goods. 'It might be true,' he said, 'that if one writes or prints upon the paper of another, the writing or printing becomes his to whom the paper belongs; but it does not necessarily follow that the converse of that proposition would be true, that one who writes or prints upon his own paper the composition of another has thereby so mixed his property with the property of the author whose work he has copied, that he has lost his original title to the material which he has so employed. (b)

The 23rd section gives to a registered proprietor a right in a court of equity to an account only of the gains and profits made by an infringement of his copyright. (c)

As to the form of the order for the delivery up of pirated copies of a book, Sir *W. P. Wood*, V.C. observed in *Delfe* v. *Delamotte*, (d) that the old form ran thus:

(a) 5 & 6 Vict c 45, s 23
(b) *Colburn* v *Sims*, 2 Hare, 554

(c) *Delfe* v *Delamotte*, 3 Kn & Jo 581
(d) *Ibid.*

'that the defendants deliver up such copies to be destroyed;' but the order he then made was 'order the defendants to deliver to the plaintiff all copies of, &c.' omitting 'to be destroyed.' (a)

The Act 54 Geo. 3, c. 156, which was repealed by the Act 5 & 6 Vict. c. 45, contained a provision somewhat similar to the 23rd section of the latter Act. The 4th section of the Act of Geo. 3 ran thus: 'If any bookseller or printer, or other person whatsoever, in any part of the United Kingdom of Great Britain and Ireland, in the Isle of Man, Jersey or Guernsey, or in any other part of the British dominions shall, from and after the passing of this Act, within the terms and times granted and limited by this Act as aforesaid, print, reprint, or import, or shall cause to be printed, reprinted, or imported, any such book or books, without the consent of the author or authors, or other proprietor or proprietors of the copyright of and in such book or books, first had and obtained in writing, or knowing the same to be so printed, reprinted, or imported, without the consent of the author or authors, or other proprietor or proprietors, shall sell, publish, or expose to sale, or cause to be sold, published, or exposed to sale, or shall have in his or their possession for sale any such book or books, without such consent first had and obtained as aforesaid, then such offender shall be liable to a special action on the case, at the suit of the author or authors, or other proprietor or proprietors of the copyright of such book or books so unlawfully printed, reprinted, or imported, or published, or exposed to sale,

(a) See *Mayall* v. *Higby*, 1 H & C 148, which, however, involved no question of copyright law, but was simply an action for the wrongful use of a published photograph lent for engraving only

or being in the possession of such offender or offenders as aforesaid, for sale as aforesaid, contrary to the true intent and meaning of this Act. . . . And all and every such offender and offenders shall also forfeit such book or books, and all and every sheet being part of such book or books, and shall deliver the same to the author or authors, or other proprietor or proprietors of the copyright of such book or books, upon order of any Court of Record, in which any action or suit in law or equity shall be commenced or prosecuted by such author or authors, or other proprietor or proprietors, to be made on motion or petition to the said Court, and the said author or authors, or other proprietor or proprietors shall forthwith damask or make waste paper of the said book or books, and sheet or sheets, &c.' Under this section it was held in *Colburn* v. *Sims* (a) that where A having agreed with B to write a book, to assign the copyright to B, and not to write and publish any similar book, writes and employs C to publish a similar book, and C publishes it, C is not liable to forfeit the copies in his possession of the later book, unless the earlier was duly entered when he published.

Further, Sir *J. Wigram*, V.C. observed in that case: 'The claim which I have been called upon to consider is the right of the plaintiff to enforce the extreme penalty which the law imposes in the most aggravated case—a right which the absence of precedent shows to have been scarcely ever resorted to, and therefore not to be practically necessary for the protection of literary property.' (b)

(a) 2 Hare, 543, a suit concerning an invasion of Dr Granville's 'Southern Spas of England'

(b) See the reasons for the enactment of the penalty clauses in the Act 8 Anne, c. 19, *Aston*, J in *Millar* v *Taylor*, 4 Burr 2350

25. It was remarked in *Donaldson* v. *Beckett* by Lord *Northington,* (a) 'that it may be dangerous to vest an exclusive property in authors, for, as that would give them the sole right to publish, it would also give them a right to suppress, and then booksellers possessed of the works of the best of our authors might totally suppress.' This remark appears to have been thought worthy of attention by the framers of the Act 5 & 6 Vict. c. 45: reciting 'that it is expedient to provide against the suppression of books of importance to the public,' it enacts ' that it shall be lawful for the Judicial Committee of Her Majesty's Privy Council, on complaint made to them that the proprietor of the copyright in any book, after the death of its author, has refused to republish, or to allow the republication of the same, and that by reason of such refusal such book may be withheld from the public, to grant a license to such complainant to publish such book in such manner and subject to such conditions as they may think fit, and that it shall be lawful for such complainant to publish such book according to such license.' (b)

25 Abuse of the right.

26. Nothing in the Act 5 & 6 Vict. c. 45 contained affects any right subsisting at the time of the passing of that Act, except as therein expressly contained, or any previous contracts or remedies relating thereto. This is an express provision in the Act. (c)

26 Operation of Talfourd's Act as to copyrights then existing.

27. Thus far the law concerning copyright-after-publication in books generally has been considered, but the copyright in encyclopædias, periodicals, serials, reviews, and magazines has not yet been stated : that right stands in some respects on a peculiar footing.

27 The right in encyclopædias, periodicals, serials, reviews, and magazines.

(a) 2 Eden. 328   (c) Sec 28
(b) Sec. 5

The Act 5 & 6 Vict. c. 45, has specially provided, (a) that when any publisher or other person should before or on the 1st day of July 1842, have projected, conducted, and carried on, or shall after that date project, conduct, and carry on, or be the proprietor of any encyclopædia, review, periodical, magazine, or work published in a series of books or parts, or any book whatsoever, and should have employed or should employ any persons to compose the same, or any volume, parts, essays, articles, or portions thereof for publication in or as part of the same, and such work, volumes, parts, essays, articles, or portions should have been, or should thereafter be, composed under such employment, on the terms that the copyright therein should belong to such proprietor, projector, publisher, or conductor, and be paid for by such proprietor, projector, publisher, or conductor, the copyright in every such encyclopædia, review, magazine, periodical work, and work published in a series of books or parts, and in every volume, part, essay, article, and portion so composed and paid for, should be the property of such proprietor, projector, publisher, or other conductor, who should enjoy the same rights as if he were the actual author thereof, and should have the same term of copyright therein as was given to the authors of books by that Act, except only, that in the case of essays, articles, or portions forming part of and first published in reviews, magazines, or other periodical works of a like nature, after the term of 28 years, from the first publication thereof respectively, the right of publishing the same in a separate form should revert to the

(a) Sec. 18.

author for the remainder of the term given by that Act: provided always, that during the term of 28 years the said proprietor, projector, publisher, or conductor, should not publish any such essay, article, or portion separately or singly without the consent previously obtained of the author thereof or his assigns: provided also that nothing in that Act contained should alter or affect the right of any person who should have been or who should be so implied as aforesaid to publish any such his composition in a separate form, who by any contract express or implied might have reserved, or might thereafter reserve to himself such right; but every author reserving, retaining, or having such right, should be entitled to the copyright in such composition, when published in a separate form, according to that Act, without prejudice to the right of such proprietor, projector, publisher, or conductor as aforesaid.

Long prior to this enactment an injunction was obtained by the proprietor of a periodical to restrain the publication of articles extracted from it, and sworn to have been written by a person employed and paid by the plaintiff. As far back as the year 1814 Sir *Samuel Romilly* obtained from Lord *Eldon* an injunction to restrain the publication of translations (taken from a copyright periodical called the 'Repertory of Arts, Manufacture, and Agriculture') upon an affidavit that the originals were made by a person employed and paid by the plaintiff, and from foreign books imported by the plaintiff at considerable expense. (*a*)

When the owner of a weekly gazette sought to restrain the publication of an alleged piracy of his work,

(*a*) *Wyatt* v *Barnard*, 3 V & in *Barfield* v *Nicholson*, 2 S & S. 1 B 77 , and see Sir *J. Leach*, V.C

Sir *L. Shadwell*, V.C.E. (*a*) refused to interfere, and to a certain extent based his judgment on this fact, viz. that the plaintiff had failed to show that the defendants, who were the original composers of the articles in the gazette, had been actually paid by him.

Lord *Cranworth*, V.C. also considered in *Richardson* v. *Gilbert* (*b*) that the Act of Her present Majesty makes actual payment for an article in a review a condition precedent to the vesting of the copyright therein in the proprietors of the work, though he thought that the title of the plaintiffs, the proprietors in that case, did sufficiently appear upon the bill, inasmuch as it was alleged therein, first, that the article was composed for the plaintiffs by a person employed by them to compose the same on the terms that the copyright therein should belong to the plaintiffs, and should be paid for by them (which was an advance towards a good title), and afterwards that the plaintiffs were then entitled to the exclusive property and copyright in the article, which, regard being had to the first averment, implied that the plaintiffs had paid the composer for the article.

If such actual payment be a condition precedent to the vesting of copyright in an article contributed to a daily paper, this construction of the Act may obviously lead to inconvenient results in the business of every-day literary life.

Within the meaning of the Act 5 & 6 Vict. c. 45, (*c*) a person may be the proprietor of the copyright in the separate publication of parts of a periodical simply by reason of his employment of the writers. This was

(*a*) *Brown* v *Cooke*, 11 Jur 77   (*c*) Sec 18
(*b*) 1 Sim n s 336.

decided in *Sweet* v. *Benning*. (a) There the plaintiffs, the registered proprietors of a periodical, had employed persons to report in their work certain legal decisions; the names of the persons so employed appeared in the periodical, and the arrangement between them and the plaintiffs was verbal; it was to the effect that they (the reporters) should furnish to the plaintiffs for publication in the periodical reports of such cases as they (the reporters) thought proper upon the terms of being paid so much per printed sheet; there was no reservation by the reporters of any personal right of publication or copyright, nor was it expressed between the parties that the copyright should belong to the plaintiffs; in fact, nothing passed between them on the subject. The circumstances of *Sweet* v. *Benning*, in the opinion of the judges who decided it, implied an understanding between the plaintiffs and the reporters that the former should acquire a copyright in the reports. Sir *John Jervis*, C.J. remarked: 'Where the proprietors of a periodical employ a gentleman to write a given article, or a series of articles or reports, expressly for the purpose of publication therein, of necessity it is implied that the copyright of the articles so expressly written for such periodical, and paid for by the proprietors and publishers thereof, shall be the property of such proprietors and publishers; otherwise it might be that the author might, the day after his article had been published by the persons for whom he contracted to write it, republish it in a separate form or in another serial, and there would be no correspondent benefit to the original publishers for the payment they had made.

(a) 16 C B 459, and see Sir *J.*   2 L J o s. ch. 102, and *Wyatt*
Leach,V.C in *Barfield* v. *Nicholson*,   v *Barnard*, 3 V & B 77

A Scotch suit bearing on this point may also be looked to. There a shipping list had been prepared and digested from custom-house statistics, to which the publishers of the list had sole access for publication. Lord *Deas* considered that the assistants whom they employed were not authors in the sense of 5 & 6 Vict. c. 45, s. 18, nor in any reasonable sense whatever. 'It might as well be said,' he remarked, 'that if the persons who plan and get up the Edinburgh almanack were to employ a man to make a good index to it, that person would be author of the index in the sense of the statute. There is less reason here for holding the assistants to be authors than in the case of the almanack, for there many of the assistants must often enquire after and procure information, whereas here they merely methodise and arrange matter previously the property of their employers, and which the assistants could in no event have had any right to use or appropriate.'

A publisher having acquired from an author a right to publish a treatise in a particular large and extended work, such as the 'Encyclopædia Britannica,' is not entitled to make the publication in another work not embraced in the contract, nor to publish generally beyond his license, while in truth and reality he is not publishing the treatise of that work, but is taking advantage of the license beyond its terms, and making a general publication of the treatise. (a)

In the case of the *Bishop of Hereford* v. *Griffin*, (b) the defendant was, on an ex-parte application of the

---

(a) *Stewart* v. *Black*, 9 Dec in Court of Session, 2d series, p 1026

(b) 16 Sim. 190, and see *Mayhew*

v. *Maxwell*, 1 Jo. & H 312, and *Murray* v *Maxwell*, 3 L. T n. s 466 ch.

plaintiff, restrained by Sir *L. Shadwell*, V.C.E. from executing his threat to publish in a separate form an article written by the plaintiff at the request of the defendant for insertion in an encyclopædia. A motion to dissolve the injunction was refused on the ground of an uncontradicted affidavit by the plaintiff, that he had given to the defendant nothing beyond the right of publishing the article in the encyclopædia. *Napier* v. *Paterson*, (a) in the Scotch Court of Session, is another authority on this point. There the proprietor of a copyright in certain notes on the Bible sold the stereotype plates of a quarto edition of the notes, together with the privilege of printing from the plates; the purchaser sold the plates to another person at an auction, whereat a leaf of the book was exhibited by way of specimen; a catalogue referring to the specimen was also distributed. The Court granted an interdict against the buyer at the public sale when he proposed to publish a folio Bible with the notes and a commentary. The Lord Justice-Clerk said: 'Though I am unwilling to interfere with the publication of such a work, yet I think that we cannot do otherwise than grant this interdict. I cannot overlook the understanding conveyed by the entry in the catalogue of the sale, and the reference there made to a specimen page. From these it must have been clear to the purchaser that the thing to be produced from these plates was a quarto Bible with notes, but without a commentary. Now, the nature of stereotype plates is to multiply copies of the same work until the plates are worn out. Here the plates sold were those of a particular Bible, and to

(a) *Napier* v *Paterson*, 13 Dec. of Court of Session, 2d series, p 220 and see *post*

show what it was that was to be thrown off from them as well as to show the state of the type, &c. a specimen leaf is shown at the sale. Stereotype plates are intended to throw off just exactly the work they were made for. Mr. Inglis asked, "May we not print the work on cheaper paper or with a larger margin?" to object to this would be a ruinous interference; but if commentaries be added to each page, thus making it a different work, and this to be sold as cheap as the original quarto, it is clear that the value of the latter will be diminished, and that not by multiplication of the same work, but by the production of a different work from these plates.'

The plaintiff's title in such cases to the protection of a court of equity is, it seems, wholly independent of copyright. (a)

For the breach of a contract by A to publish the literary work of B in a particular shape an action for damages will lie, as a different form of publication may be adverse to B's literary reputation. (b)

When a serial consists of criticisms, and extracts from copyright works to serve as a foundation for the criticisms, it might be fair enough to say that an insertion of the criticisms and extracts in separate numbers was a violation of the copyright. (c)

With regard to the registration of encyclopædias, reviews, magazines, periodicals, and serials, the Act 5 & 6 Vict. c. 45, s. 19, provides that the proprietor of the copyright in any encyclopædia, review, magazine, periodical work, or other work published in a series of

(a) *Mayhew* v. *Maxwell*, 1 Jo. & H. 312

(b) *Planché* v. *Colburn*, 8 Bingh

15

(c) Sir *T Plumer* in *Whittingham* v *Wooller*, 2 Swanst. 431

books or parts, shall be entitled to all the benefits of
the registration at Stationers' Hall under that Act, on
entering, in the book of registry the title of such
encyclopædia, &c., the time of the publication of the
first volume, number, or part thereof, or of the number
or volume first published after the passing of that Act,
in any such work which shall have been published
theretofore, and the name and place of abode of
the proprietor thereof, and of the publisher thereof,
when such publisher shall not also be the proprietor
thereof. (*a*)

(*a*) See *British Museum* v.
Payne, 4 Bingh 510. The price
and day of publication should be
printed on periodical publications
60 Geo 3 & 1 Geo 4, c 9, s 6).
As to the course to be adopted
upon the dissolution of a partnership, and the withdrawal of one
partner from a periodical publica-
cation by the firm, see *Bradbury*
v. *Dickens*, 27 Beav. 53.

CHAPTER IV.

COPYRIGHT IN THE REPRESENTATION AND PERFORMANCE OF DRAMAS AND MUSICAL COMPOSITIONS.

1. *Regulation of the Right.*—2. *The Nature, Duration, and Registry of the Right* —3 *To whom the Right may belong.* — 4 *Assignment of the Right* —5. *Infringement of the Right the Remedies.*

1 Regulation
of the right

1. This copyright depends upon two Acts of Parliament, viz. an Act 3 & 4 Will. 4, c. 15 (commonly called Sir Bulwer Lytton's Act), and the Act 5 & 6 Vict. c. 45.

The decision by the Court of King's Bench, in the year 1822, in *Murray* v. *Elliston,* seems to have led to the passing of the earlier Act.

There (*a*) it appeared upon a case sent by Lord *Eldon,* C. for the opinion of the Court of King's Bench, that the defendant was the manager of Drury Lane Theatre; further, that he had adapted to the stage and had publicly represented at his theatre, and for profit, an abridgement of Lord Byron's printed and published tragedy, entitled ' Marino Faliero;' that the plaintiff was the assignee of the copyright in the tragedy, and that he complained of such representation. The Court of King's Bench, after hearing counsel, certified that an action could not be maintained by the plaintiff against the defendant in respect of such representation. The Court gave no reasons for that judgment.

(*a*) 5 B. & Ald 657.

Prior to *Murray* v. *Elliston*, it had been held (*a*) by Lord *Kenyon* that proof of public performance upon the stage, and for profit, of a dramatic piece, in which copyright-after-publication existed, was no evidence of piracy of the piece within the language of the Act 8 Anne, c. 19. The Act of Will. 4 (dealing with the right to represent published dramas) declares that the author of any tragedy, comedy, play, opera, farce, or any other dramatic piece or entertainment, printed and published within ten years before the passing of the Act, by the author thereof or his assignee, or which should thereafter be so printed and published, or the assignee of such author should, for the period therein mentioned (now altered), have as his own property the sole liberty of representing, or causing to be represented, the same at any place of dramatic entertainment in the British dominions, and should be deemed to be the proprietor, subject, however, to any right of representation in any person previously empowered by the author or his assignee. (*b*)

A room may be a place of dramatic entertainment within the language of the Act 3 & 4 Will. 4, c. 15, though ordinarily used for other purposes. (*c*) Wherever a dramatic piece is represented, that place for the time being is a place of dramatic entertainment within the meaning of the Act.

2. The nature and endurance of copyright in the representation of published dramatic pieces, and the extension

2 The nature, duration, and registry of the right.

(*a*) *Coleman* v. *Wathen*, 5 T R. 245.

(*b*) 3 & 4 Will 4, c 15, s 1.

(*c*) *Russell* v *Smith*, 12 Q. B 217 As to what is an entertainment of the stage within the meaning of 10 Geo. 2, c 28, s 3, see the Lord Justice-Clerk in *Alexander* v. *Anderson*, S & D. 1525

of the right to musical compositions, its endurance, its nature, and the provisions for a registration of the several rights, are set forth in section 20 of the Act 5 & 6 Vict. c. 45. That section declares that the Acts 3 & 4 Will. 4, c. 15, and 5 & 6 Vict. c. 45, shall apply to musical compositions, and that the sole liberty of representing, or performing, or causing (a) or permitting to be represented or performed, any published dramatic piece (b) or musical composition, shall endure and be the property of the author thereof and his assigns for the term in the Act 5 & 6 Vict. c. 45, provided for copyright in books (c) [the term has been already stated in a previous chapter of this work], (d) and that the provisions enacted by the Act 5 & 6 Vict. c. 45, in respect of the property of such copyright and of registering the same (e) shall apply to the liberty of representing or performing any dramatic piece or musical composition, as if the same were therein expressly re-enacted and applied thereto; save and except that the first public representation or performance of any dramatic piece or musical composition shall be deemed equivalent, in the construction of the Act of Victoria, to the first publication of any book. (f)

There is, however, this proviso to the declaration, viz. that in the case of any dramatic piece or musical composition in manuscript it shall be sufficient for the

---

(a) See *Parsons* v. *Chapman*, 5 C & P 33

(b) For definition of dramatic piece, see 5 & 6 Vict. c 45, s 2

(c) *Ibid* ss 3, 4

(d) *Ante*, p 52

(e) 5 & 6 Vict c 45, ss. 11, 12, 13, 14.

(f) It was held in *Macklin* v. *Richardson*, Ambl 694, that the public performance of a dramatic piece was no publication of it within 8 Anne, c 19, and see Lord *Lyndhurst*, C.B in *D'Almaine* v *Boosey*, 1 Y & C. 299

person having the sole liberty of representing or performing, or causing to be represented or performed the same, to register only the title thereof, the name and place of abode of the proprietor thereof, and the time and place of its first representation or performance.

3. The right is expressly given by the Act to the author or his assignee. In delivering the judgment of the Court of Common Bench on a question relating to the assignment of a copyright in the representation of a dramatic piece, Sir *J. Jervis*, L.C.J. guardedly observed: 'We do not think it necessary in the present instance to express any opinion whether, under any circumstances, the copyright in a literary work, or the right of representation, can become vested ab initio in an employer other than the person who has actually composed or adapted a literary work.' (*a*)

3 To whom the right may belong

But it would seem that this copyright cannot become vested ab initio in an employer who merely suggests the subject and has no share in the design or execution of the work. (*b*)

Where it appeared in an action at law, in which Mr. Charles Kean was defendant, that he was the actual designer of a dramatic piece, i.e. by adaptation of a play, 'Much Ado about Nothing,' to the stage, and that with respect to the production of a musical composition, a part, an accessory of that piece, he had employed the plaintiff for reward paid to him, the Court of Common Pleas unanimously held that Mr. Kean was the author of the piece, and therefore entitled to represent it without the consent in writing of the plaintiff. (*c*)

(*a*) *Shepherd* v *Conquest*, 17 C. B. 427

(*b*) See 4 Wash. C C 48.

(*c*) *Hatton* v *Kean*, 7 C B. n s 268

There is no reason to doubt that the decision of the House of Lords in *Jeffreys* v. *Boosey* would govern the claim of any alien to this copyright.

4. Assignment of the right

4. In regard to any assignment of this copyright, the Act 5 & 6 Vict. c. 45, s. 22, has a special provision that no assignment of the copyright of any book consisting of or containing a dramatic piece or musical composition shall be held to convey to the assignee the right of representing or performing such dramatic piece or musical composition, unless an entry shall have been made in the registry book (*a*) at Stationers' Hall of the assignment, and that assignment must express the intention of the parties thereto, that the right of representation or performance should pass by the assignment.

It has not been decided that the Act renders a separate assignment of the right of representation or performance inoperative till registry. The language of the 22d section does not appear to touch such a disposition of the right.

A legal assignment of the copyright must be in writing. This point appears to have been put beyond question by *Shepherd* v. *Conquest*. (*b*) That was an action for piracy of a play, and the facts were these. Plaintiffs had employed Conquest to go to Paris at their expense, for the purpose of adapting a French dramatic piece in London, the copyright of which should be in the plaintiffs; the piece had accordingly been adapted by Conquest, had been represented in London by the plaintiff, and afterwards also in London by the defendant, under an assignment in writing from Conquest. The question was, ' whether the plaintiffs, by the transaction

(*a*) 5 & 6 Vict. c 45, s. 11.   (*b*) 17 C. B 427

between them and Conquest, became entitled to the exclusive representation in London?' The Court of Common Bench held that the plaintiffs had no such right; Conquest was the author, and the plaintiffs had no assignment from him of the right.

An assignment need not now be attested; formerly the attestation of two witnesses appears to have been necessary. (a)

In reference to the language of an Act 54 Geo. 3, c. 156 (an old Copyright Act repealed by the Act of Victoria), it was held that a person to whom the literary copyright of a dramatic piece had been assigned within ten years before the passing of the Act 3 & 4 Will. 4, c. 15, was an assignee within the meaning of that Act, having the sole liberty of representing the piece. (b)

5. As to any infringement of this copyright, the Act 3 & 4 Will. 4, c. 15, provides, that if any person shall, during the continuance of the copyright in the representation of any dramatic piece, contrary to the intent of that Act, or the right of the author or his assignee, represent, or cause to be represented without the consent in writing of the author or other proprietor, first had and obtained, at any place of dramatic entertainment within the British dominions, any dramatic piece or any part thereof, every such offender shall be liable for each and every such representation to the payment of an amount not less than 40s., or to the full amount of the benefit or advantage arising from such representation, or the injury or loss sustained by the plaintiff therefrom, whichever shall be the greater

5 Infringement of the right.

(a) 8 Anne, c 19, *Cumberland*   (b) *Ante*, p 63.
v *Copeland*, 7 H. & N 118

damages to the author or other proprietor of such
dramatic piece, to be recovered, together with double
costs of suit, by such author or other proprietor, in any
Court having jurisdiction in such cases, in that part of
the British dominions in which the offence shall be
committed; and in every such proceeding where the
sole liberty of such author or his assignee shall be subject to such right or authority as aforesaid, it shall be
sufficient for the plaintiff to state that he has such sole
liberty without stating the same to be subject to such
right or authority, or otherwise mentioning the same;
nevertheless, all actions or proceedings for any offence
or injury that shall be committed against the Act 3 & 4
Will. 4, c 15, must be brought, sued, and commenced
within twelve calendar months next after such offence
committed.

In *Cumberland* v. *Planché*, already referred to, (*a*) it
was questioned whether the Act 3 & 4 Will. 4, c. 15,
fixed any direct liability on a person pirating for the
purpose of public representation the words of a musical
composer, but abstaining from any use of his music: the
point has not yet been decided in a court of law or equity.

The penalties for piracy given by the Act of Will. 4
are, by the Act 5 & 6 Vict. c. 45, transferred to the
owner of the representation or performance copyright
created thereby. (*b*)

An injunction or interdict may also be obtained to
restrain the representation or performance of any
dramatic piece or music l composition in violation of
the property therein. (*c*)

(*a*) *Cumberland* v *Planché*, 1 A
& E. 581.

(*b*) 5 & 6 Vict c 45, s 21

(*c*) See *Russell* v. *Smith*, 15
Sim 181

The practice in reference to an action for an infringement of the right, and to the granting or refusing an injunction or interdict, may be gathered from what has already been stated as to proceedings of this sort upon the infringement of literary copyright. *(a)*

The author's consent, referred to in the second section of the Act 3 & 4 Will. 4, c 15, must be in writing, but it may either be in the handwriting of the author himself or of some agent authorised by him. *(b)* *Maule*, J. observed that in the Act 3 & 4 Will. 4, c. 15, not a word was said about whose writing the consent should be : the Act ' was merely designed to exclude that kind of doubt and uncertainty which arises from the circumstance of a thing not being evidenced by writing at all.' *(c)* The onus of proving the consent lies on the party setting it up. *(d)* The consent may apply to future compositions. *(e)*

A person ignorant of the piratical nature of a representation may be an offender within the meaning of the 2d section of the Act 3 & 4 Will. 4, c. 15. *(f)*

It was objected in *Lee* v. *Simpson (g)* that a written introduction to what is called in theatrical parlance 'the comic business,' i. e. the tricks of a pantomime, was not a complete work, and therefore that its representation was not within the protection of the Act 5 & 6 Vict. c. 45, but the Court gave a liberal construction to the Act, and overruled the objection.

(a) For proceedings against an infringement of a popular song by assumption of its name and description, see *Chappell* v. *Sheard*, 2 Ka. & Jo 117.

(b) *Morton* v *Copeland*, 16 C B 517.

(c) *Ibid*

(d) *Ibid*

(e) *Ibid.*

(f) See *Lee* v. *Simpson*, 3 C B. 882

(g) 3 C B 882.

The 24th section of the Act 5 & 6 Vict. c. 45, which enacts that no proprietor of copyright shall sue for any infringement before making entry in the book of registry, is carefully qualified by a proviso that nothing therein contained shall prejudice the remedies which the proprietor of the sole liberty of representing any dramatic piece shall have by virtue of the Act 3 & 4 Will. 4, c. 15, or of that Act, although no entry shall be made in the book of registry.

No one can be considered as an offender against the provisions of the 2d section of the Act 3 & 4 Will. 4, c. 15, so as to subject himself to an action for the penalty of an unauthorised representation of a musical composition, unless by himself or his agent he actually directs or takes part in the direction of a representation or performance which is a violation of the copyright. This was laid down in the case of *Russell* v. *Briant.* (a) There the musical composition in the performance of which the plaintiff claimed copyright had been performed at a tavern, of which the defendant was land-lord, and in a room hired of him by a person for a musical entertainment. After notice to the defendant from the plaintiff of the intended violation of his copyright by such entertainment, the defendant had permitted the entertainment, and the performance thereat of the musical composition; he had furnished a platform and lights, had advertised tickets of admission, and had himself sold one ticket. The Court ruled that these facts afforded no evidence that the defendant performed or caused to be performed the composition within the meaning of the Act; for if it were to be held that all

(a) 8 C. B 836.

those who supply some of the means of performance to him who performs are to be regarded as thereby constituting him their agent, and so causing the performance within the meaning of the Act, such a doctrine would include a class of persons not at all intended by the Legislature.

Russell v. *Briant* has been recently followed by the Court of Queen's Bench in *Lyons* v. *Knowles*. (*a*) The facts in evidence in that action were these the defendant was lessee and licensed proprietor of the theatre at which the plaintiff's copyright music had been performed; the defendant found the gas-light, paid for printing, &c. and provided the music, he also received the moneys taken at the door, retaining half of the gross receipts, and handing the other half to one Dillon, who provided the dramatic performers and selected the pieces without any control by the defendant; the director of the band was under Dillon's orders, and took his orders, but the band were paid by the defendant; Dillon acted, in short, as stage-manager, the defendant being lessee and proprietor; there was no partnership between them. Upon these facts a verdict passed for the plaintiff, reserving the question of liability; but a rule to enter a verdict for the defendant was afterwards made absolute, the Court of Queen's Bench being of opinion that the defendant had not violated the copyright of representation in the music simply by his receipt of the rent. If the arrangement between the defendant and Dillon had been only a colourable scheme for joint performance of the copyright music, the result of the action would have been very different.

(*a*) 11 W. R. 266

The word 'represent' in the Act 3 & 4 Will. 4, c. 15, s. 2, means the bringing forward on a stage or place of public representation.

Even if the words of a single song be taken from a piece the performance of which is protected by the Act, and be sung on a stage or any place of theatrical entertainment, that will be a 'representing' within the provisions of the 2d section.

What is a 'representing' is always a fact for the jury. (a)

No person may 'represent,' without the author's consent, the incidents of his published dramatic piece, however indirectly taken; such a proceeding is a clear invasion of the stage copyright in the piece. (b)

Lastly, No contracts or obligations subsisting on July 1, 1842, in relation to this copyright are, it must be remembered, affected by implication by the Act of Her present Majesty. (c)

(a) *Planché* v *Braham*, 8 C. & P. 68.

(b) *Reade* v. *Conquest*, 11 C. B n s. 479

(c) Sec. 28

CHAPTER V.

CROWN COPYRIGHT.

1. *Nature and Extent of the Right* — 2. *As to the Right in State Documents.* — 3 *As to the Right in Law Reports.* — 4 *As to the Right in the Book of Common Prayer.* — 5. *As to the Right in Almanacks* — 6. *As to the Right in Bibles* — 7. *As to the Right in Lilly's 'Latin Grammar,' &c* — 8. *As to the Patent Rights of the Universities of Oxford and Cambridge.*

1. CROWN Copyright is no creature of the statute law: it is a royal prerogative claim to the exclusive publication of certain books and documents. It has certainly been pushed to an extent far greater than can now be sustained; it has been asserted in all Acts of Parliament, in all Orders of the Privy Council, in all State proclamations, in the Book of Common Prayer, in all almanacks, in the English translation of the Bible, in the Yearbooks, and all reports of judicial proceedings in England; also in Lilly's 'Latin Grammar,' and certain other books composed and published by the Sovereign's command at the national cost. Public policy has been put forward as the foundation of the right. (*a*)

1 Nature and extent of the right

2. The claim of the Crown to copyright in Acts of Parliament, (*b*) in Orders of Council, and in proclama-

2 The right in State documents

(*a*) Lord *Eldon* in *Gurney* v *Longman,* 13 Ves 508

(*b*) See *Baskett* v *University of Cambridge,* 1 W Bl 105, *Baskett* v *Cunningham,* 2 Eden 137, *Manners* v *Blair,* 3 Bli 402, *Grierson* v *Jackson,* Ridg 304

O

tions, (a) has usually been rested upon reasons of State, those works being of public concern, and the Sovereign being the head of the political constitution. (b) These documents are printed by the Queen's printer under a patent.

3 As to the
right in law
reports

3. The claim of the Crown to the copyright in all reports of judicial proceedings has been rested upon the same grounds, also upon the payment out of the public moneys of the salaries of the judges whose decisions are there reported, and upon the payment from the same source of the costs of compilation and publication. (c)

'Possibly,' said Lord *Eldon*, 'the King's printer may be entitled to print the annals of courts of justice.' (d) He did not, however, more directly affirm that doctrine.

The validity of a patent from the Crown for the publication of the cases reported in ' Croke's Reports ' was determined in 1705, on the ground that every man could not by the common law have a liberty of printing things that concerned the government of the country. (e) The claim of the House of Lords to publish and to prohibit other publication of the trial of a peer was raised and disputed in Lord Melville's case, but not determined ; the claim was there rested upon the almost uniform practice, and upon the privileges of the House, and Lord *Eldon* granted interim relief upon a precedent of *Bathurst* v. *Kearsley,* but cautiously declared that the

(a) Case of *Stationers' Company,* 2 Ch Ca 76 , *Willes,* J in *Millar* v *Taylor,* 4 Burr. 2329 , *Yates,* J. *ibid.* 2382 , Lord *Mansfield, ibid.* 2104. See also 2 Bl Comm 410 , Anon case cited 2 V & B. 21 , and Lord *Eldon,* C in *Oxford and Cambridge Universities* v *Richardson,* 6 Ves 704

(b) *Ibid*

(c) *Atkins' case,* cited 4 Burr 2316 , Carter 89 , cited 4 Burr 2315 , and Croke's Reports

(d) *Roper* v *Streater,* Skinner, 234

(e) In *University of Oxford and Cambridge* v *Richardson,* 6 Ves 704

question remained open. A compromise ultimately took place. (a) In *Bathurst* v. *Kearsley* such claim had been recognised, but had not, it seems, been discussed. (b)

The courts of justice in this country may, and probably have, the sole power to authenticate the publication of their own proceedings. (c) Authenticity may give credit, and so impart value to a report of legal proceedings; but this does not necessarily involve an exclusive right of publication.

Manley v. *Owen*, cited Burr. 2329, was supposed by Mr. Justice *Willes*, in *Millar* v. *Taylor*, to establish this point, viz. that the Lord Mayor could confer copyright in the publication of trials at the Old Bailey, (d) but no such proposition necessarily flows from that decision. It may be that the copyright there was acquired by the plaintiff by compilation.

A court of justice may also, in order to preserve the purity of the administration of justice in the course of proceedings then pending before it, prohibit any publication which has a tendency to interfere with a fair and impartial decision: this Lord C. J. *Abbott*, sitting at the Old Bailey, did upon the indictment of Thistlewood and others for high treason, in the year 1820, (e) but it does not thence follow that a Court may altogether prohibit publication of a trial after the proceedings therein are concluded.

It was, indeed, formerly considered a contempt to publish law reports without judicial authority, but that practice does not seem to have been founded on any

(a) *Gurney* v *Longman*, 13 Ves 493
(b) Cited *ibid* 494
(c) 4 Burr 2329
(d) 4 Burr 2329
(e) *R.* v. *Clement*, 4 B & Ald 219

notion of copyright in the Court.   Lord *Bacon* said :
' The common law is no text law, but the substance of
it consisted in the series and succession of judicial acts
which from time to time have been set down in the
reports; so that as these reports are more or less perfect,
the law itself is more or less certain, and indeed better
or worse.'   It was therefore considered very important
that the reports should be authenticated by the Courts,
and accordingly they were kept for a very considerable
period of time under the superintendence of the judges
themselves, and great care was taken in sifting and
ascertaining the grounds of the decisions reported. (*a*)

No prerogative claim to the exclusive publication of
judicial proceedings has now been asserted for very
many years, and in *Butterworth* v. *Robinson* (*b*) and
Saunders v. *Smith* (*c*) individuals were treated as
authors and proprietors of copyright in law reports.

4 As to the
right in the
Book of Com-
mon Prayer

4. The claim of the Crown to the copyright in the
Book of Common Prayer has been rested on reasons of
State and on the supremacy of the Sovereign in eccle-
siastical matters. (*d*)   The Queen's printer exercises
this monopoly under a patent which extends to the
Bible.

5 As to the
right in
almanacks

5. The claim of the Crown to the copyright in
almanacks has been based on reasons of State, (*e*) almanacks generally containing calendars for the regulation of Easter, the saints' days, and other observances

(*a*) Some of the old law reports
were published under the names of
eminent persons, to gain thereby a
reputation   See advertisement to
first edition of Leach's Reports.

(*b*) 5 Ves 709.

(*c*) 3 M & Cr 711

(*d*) 2 Bl Comm. 410 , *Eyre* v
Strahan, 5 Bac Abr Prer F p
597 , *Manners* v *Blair*, 3 Bli
102.

(*e*) *Stationers' Company* v *Seymour*, 1 Mod 256 , *Yates*, J in
Millar v *Taylor*, 4 Burr 2382

of the Church; but the Court of Common Bench long ago certified the invalidity of an exclusive grant of this right, (a) and since that certificate it has not, it seems, been formally asserted. (b) The exclusive privilege of printing, publishing, and selling nautical almanacks is, by the Act 9 Geo. 4, c. 66, given to the Lord High Admiral, or the commissioners for executing his office; the same statute secures the privilege by a penalty; the proceeds of the penalty are directed to be paid and applied to the use of the Royal Hospital for Seamen at Greenwich.

The history of the royal pretension to copyright in almanacks is succinctly stated by Lord *Eldon* in *Gurney* v. *Longman* (c) as an instance of the necessity of caution upon similar claims. He is there reported as saying: 'It appears in the case of *Millar* v. *Taylor* that the Crown had been in the constant course of granting the right of printing almanacks; and at last King James II. granted that right by charter to the Stationers' Company and the two Universities, and for a century they kept up that monopoly by the effect of prosecutions. At length, Carnan, an obstinate man, insisted upon printing them. An injunction was applied for in the Court of Exchequer, and was granted to the hearing; but at the hearing that Court directed the question to be put to the Court of Common Pleas, whether the King had a right to grant the publication of almanacks as not falling within the scope of expediency, the foundation of prerogative copies. It was twice argued in the Court of Common Pleas, and the answer returned by that Court to the Court of

(a) *Stationers' Company* v *Carnan*, 2 W Bl 1004, and see 21 Geo 3, c 56, s 10

(b) Lord *Mansfield*, C J in *Millar* v *Taylor*, 4 Burr 2402

(c) 13 Ves. 508

Exchequer was, that the charter was void, and almanacks were not prerogative copies. The injunction was accordingly dissolved, that usurpation having gone on for a century. The House of Commons afterwards threw out a bill (a) brought in for the purpose of vesting the right in the Stationers' Company.'

6. As to the right in Bibles.

6. The claim of the Crown to copyright in English translations of the Bible (b) has been based upon the position of the Sovereign as chief executive officer of the government of this country (c) and head of the Church (d), and upon the employment by the Crown of the translators of the book at the public cost. (e)

The Universities of Oxford and Cambridge, and the Queen's printer, long exercised this monopoly under patents from the Crown, but the claim has not been very rigidly enforced. The patent granted to the Queen's printer lately expired, a committee of the Commons, by the casting vote of its chairman, recommended that the exclusive privilege of publishing the sacred volume should not be renewed; the House, however, took no action on this recommendation, and the Crown renewed the patent during pleasure. The Scotch Bible patent of the Queen's printer expired in the year 1839.

Be it noted that in *Grierson* v. *Jackson*, (f) Lord *Clare* expressed it to be his opinion that the royal copyright was limited to such Bibles as were intended for the public service. (g)

(a) In the year 1799.

(b) *Mayo* v *Hill*, cited 2 Shaw, 260, *King's Printer* v *Bell*, Mor Dict of Dec 19, 20, p 8316

(c) *Manners* v *Blair*, 3 Bli n s 402

(d) *Yates*, J in *Millar* v *Taylor*, 4 Burr 2382

(e) Lord *Mansfield*, C J *ibid*

(f) 2 Ridg 304

(g) See 'Outline of the History of the Cambridge Press,' by Mr R Potts, in Parliamentary papers, vol xxii, p 73, and the copy of the Queen's printer's patent for the Bible and the Book of Common Prayer, Parliamentary papers, vol xl

7. The claim of the Crown to the copyright in Lilly's ' Latin Grammar,' and certain other works, was rested upon the payment by the Crown out of public moneys of the costs of compilation and publication. (a) This was only claimed when prerogative ran high, and has long been abandoned.

8. The Universities of Oxford and Cambridge are by letters patent (b) (first granted in the thirteenth year of the reign of Queen Elizabeth) authorised to print within the limits of their respective jurisdictions, and to sell, so that such sale interferes not with any prior letters patent, (c) all copies of the Bible, New Testament, and Book of Common Prayer, concurrently with the Queen's printer; and no other person besides them and the Queen's printer may print or publish in England any such copies, or sell in England any other copies of the said books than such as have been printed and published by or for the Universities and the Queen's printer, or one of them. (d)

(a) Lord *Hardwicke*, C in *Stationers' Company* v *Partridge*, 4 Burr 2336 , *Willes*, J in *Millar* v *Taylor*, 4 Burr 2329 , Lord *Mansfield*, C J. *ibid* 2405 See, however, *Gibbs* v *Cole*, 3 P. Williams, 255, a case of a book on architecture , and *Nicol* v. *Stockdale*, 3 Swanst 687, a narrative of a voyage of discovery.

(b) Lord *Eldon* was of opinion that no copyright passed by these letters (6 Ves 713). As to the extent of the privilege, see *Hill* v *Oxford University*, 1 Vern 275

(c) *Barrett* v. *University of Cambridge*, 2 Burr. 661

(d) *Universities of Oxford and Cambridge* v *Richardson*, 6 Ves 689

CHAPTER VI.

UNIVERSITY AND COLLEGE COPYRIGHT.

The Universities of Oxford and Cambridge, the Scotch Universities, and the Colleges of Eton, Westminster, and Winchester, possess a special statutory copyright. It depends on an Act 15 Geo. 3, c. 53. (a) The right exists in all such books as had before the year 1775 or have since been given or bequeathed by the authors of the same, or their representatives, to or in trust for those universities, or any college or house of learning within them, or to or in trust for the Colleges of Eton, Westminster, and Winchester, or any of them, for the beneficial purpose of education within them, or any of them. The copies can only be printed by the universities and colleges at their respective presses, and, unless limited by the language of the gift or bequest, the right in every such book continues so long as such book is printed at such presses, and for the sole benefit of the universities and colleges.

The above-mentioned universities and colleges may, in the same manner as any author might do under the Act 8 Anne, c. 19, sell any copy so given or bequeathed to them; but if they delegate, grant, lease, or sell the copyright of any book, or allow any person to print it, then their privilege ceases to exist

(a) In Appendix   As to the 5th section, see 54 Geo 3, c. 156, and 5 & 6 Vict c 45, ss 1 and 27

The Act 15 Geo. 3, c. 53, provides for the registry of such books, and subjects to a pecuniary penalty any person infringing the copyright. The right is expressly saved from the operation of the Act 5 & 6 Vict. c. 45. (*a*)

A similar copyright is possessed by Trinity College, Dublin. It depends upon an Act passed in the forty-first year of the reign of His late Majesty George 3, c. 107. The provisions of that Act, so far as the same are applicable to the above copyright, are set forth in the Appendix to this work. This right also is expressly saved from the operation of the Act 5 & 6 Vict c. 45.

(*a*) Sec 27

CHAPTER VII.

COPYRIGHT IN LECTURES AFTER PUBLIC DELIVERY.

1 Definition and Basis of the Right.—2 Penalty for Infringement of the Right.—3 Certain Lectures excluded from the Right—4. Protection of the Right at Law and in Equity.

1 Definition
of the right

1. IN certain lectures after public delivery there is also a special statutory copyright, which is defined to be 'the sole right and liberty of printing and publishing' such lectures.

The Lecture Copyright Act is the 5 & 6 Will. 4, c. 65. It is entitled, 'An Act for Preventing the Publication of Lectures without Consent,' and it enacts that from and after September 1, 1835, the author of any lecture, or the person to whom he has sold or otherwise conveyed the copy in order to deliver the same in any school, seminary, institution, or other place, or for any other purpose, should have the sole right and liberty of printing and publishing such lecture.

2 Penalty for
infringement of
the right

2. A violation of the copyright is visited by the Act of Parliament with a penalty. The Act declares, that if any person shall, by taking down a lecture in short-hand, or otherwise in writing, or in any other way, obtain a copy, and shall print or lithograph, or otherwise copy and publish it without the leave of the author or his assignee, and every person who knowing the

same to have been printed, or copied and published without such consent, shall sell, publish, or expose to sale any such lecture, shall forfeit such print or copy, together with 1*d.* for every sheet thereof which should be found in his custody, either printed, lithographed, or copied, or printing, lithographing, or copying, or published, or exposed to sale contrary to the Act, one moiety to the Crown, and the other to the prosecutor; and that any printer or publisher of any newspaper who shall without such consent print and publish in such newspaper any lecture or lectures, should be deemed a person printing and publishing without leave within the provisions of that Act, and liable to the aforesaid penalty and forfeiture in respect of such printing and publishing.

No person allowed for certain fee or reward or otherwise to attend and be present at any lecture delivered in any place is deemed to be licensed to have leave to print, copy, and publish such lectures only because of having leave to attend This is expressly enacted by the third section of the Act, and was also decided, but upon the ground of breach of trust only, in *Abernethy* v. *Hutchinson,* cited early in the first chapter of this work.

3 Lectures published by authority, since the publication of which the period of copyright therein given by the Act 8 Anne, c. 19, and 54 Geo. 3, c. 156, has expired, and lectures printed or published before September 9, 1835, are excluded from the protection of the Act 5 & 6 Will. 4, c. 65; also lectures of the delivery of which notice in writing shall not have been given two days previously to two justices living within five miles of the place of delivery; and lectures delivered in any university, or public school, or college, or on any public

3 Certain lectures excluded from the right

foundation, or by any individual in virtue of or according to any gift, endowment, or foundation. (a)

1 Protection
of the right at
law and in
equity

4. The reports furnish no decisions under this Act; but the parliamentary property in lecture copyright would doubtless be protected in a court of law or equity by a judgment for damages, or an injunction, as the case might be, upon the principles applicable to the violation of any other statutory right.

(a) Sec 4.

CHAPTER VIII.

COPYRIGHT IN PUBLISHED ENGRAVINGS.

1. COPYRIGHT in published engravings depends now at least on Acts of Parliament; the decision of the House of Lords in *Donaldson* v. *Beckett*, although founded on the statute of Anne respecting copyright in books, has firmly established a principle which precludes the right of a common law monopoly in published engravings since the passing of the Act 8 Geo. 2, c. 13. (*a*)

1 Foundation of the right.

The object of the Copyright Engraving Acts has been defined by a learned judge to be, 'not to protect the reputations of engravers, but to vest a commercial property in them.' (*b*)

2. The Act 8 Geo. 2, c. 13, sometimes called Hogarth's

2. Definition and extent of

(*a*) See Appendix and *Best*, J in *Newton* v *Cowie*, 4 Bingh 244
(*b*) See *Erle*, C J and *Keating*,
J in *Gambart* v. *Ball*, 11 W R. 699, 700.

Act [that great artist by his exertions obtained it chiefly for his own protection (a)], was the earliest dealing by the Legislature of this country with the subject of copyright in engravings.

The statute of George 3 was framed upon the precedent of the Act 8 Anne, c. 19. After reciting 'that divers persons had by their own genius, industry, pains, and expense invented and engraved, or worked in mezzotinto or chiaroscuro, sets of historical and other prints in hopes to have reaped the sole benefit of their labours, and that printsellers and other persons had of late, without the consent of the inventors, designers, and proprietors of such prints, frequently taken the liberty of copying, engraving, and publishing, or causing to be copied, engraved, and published base copies of such works, designs, and prints, to the very great prejudice and detriment of the inventors, designers, and proprietors thereof: for remedy thereof, and for preventing such practices for the future,' the Act gave to every person who should invent and design, engrave, etch, or work in mezzotinto or chiaroscuro, or from his own works and inventions should cause to be designed and engraved, etched, or worked in mezzotinto or chiaroscuro, any historical or other print or prints, the sole right of printing and reprinting the same for fourteen (b) years from the first publication.

3. The Act directed the name of the proprietor to be put on each plate and print, forfeited base copies, and imposed a penalty on persons violating the copyright in the prints. It, however, exempted from the penalty

---

(a) Nichols' Biogr Anecd of Hogarth, p 39, 3d edition   (b) Now 28 years, see *post*, p 208

purchasers (*a*) printing from plates purchased by them from the original proprietors, and declared that actions and suits for any offence against the Act should be brought within three months after discovery of the offence.

There is a special clause in the Act 8 Geo. 2, c. 13, giving one Pine a copyright in certain historical prints and drawings copied by him from tapestry in the House of Lords, which tapestry had been copied from original drawings; (*b*) being copies of copies, these prints and drawings had, however, little claim to originality.

Under that Act of Geo. 2, Lord *Hardwicke*, C. very properly refused relief to a person complaining of piracy of a drawing or design which he had only procured to be made. The learned Judge observed that such a person was not within the statute, which was made for the encouragement of genius and art; if he was within the Act, any person who employed a printer or engraver would be so too. (*c*)

Hogarth was the designer as well as engraver of his famous works. That fact may account for the omission in the statute of any provision to protect works of which the engraver is not also the designer.

4. The Legislature, however, again interposed on the subject of copyright in published engravings. In the year 1767, by an Act 7 Geo. 3, c. 38, it declared that every person who should invent or design, engrave, etch, or work in mezzotinto or chiaroscuro, or from his own work, design, or invention, cause to be designed,

4 Extension of the right by 7 Geo. 3, c 38

(*a*) For an action by an assignee of such copyright for piracy, see *Thompson* v *Symonds*, 5 T R 41

(*b*) See Lord *Talbot*, C in *Blackwell* v *Harper*, Barn 212.

(*c*) *Jeffreys* v *Baldwin*, Ambl

engraved, etched, or worked in mezzotinto or chiaroscuro, any historical print, or any other print whatsoever, should have the benefit and protection of the Act
8 Geo. 2, c. 13; and that every person who should engrave, etch, or work in mezzotinto or chiaroscuro,
or cause to be engraved, etched, or worked, any print
taken from any picture, drawing, model, or sculpture,
either ancient or modern, should have the benefit and
protection of the Act 8 Geo. 2, c. 13, and of the amending
Act, for the term of twenty-eight years from the first
publication, in like manner as if such print had been
graved or drawn from the original design of such graver,
etcher, or draftsman, and that if any person should engrave, print, and publish, or import for sale any copy of
such print, he should be liable to the penalties of the
Act 8 Geo. 2, c 13.

All the penalties of 8 Geo. 2 were imported into
7 Geo. 3, but the limitation in the former Act of actions
and suits was extended in the latter to six months.

As a provision for the widow of Hogarth, and by way
of an acknowledgement of his great genius, Parliament
admitted a clause into the Act 7 Geo. 3, c. 38, in her
favour. This clause extended to her the sole right of
printing and reprinting some of her h ' ("s works
for a period of twenty years.

5 Provisions
of 17 Geo 3,
c 57, on the
right.
5. The Act 7 Geo. 3 is not, however, the latest legislation on this copyright. To advance the arts of designing, engraving, and etching, another Act was passed ten
years afterwards.

That Act, 17 Geo. 3, c. 57, provides, that if any person
should within the time limited by the previous Acts, or
either of them, engrave, etch, or work in mezzotinto
or chiaroscuro, or otherwise, or in any other manner

copy in the whole or in part by varying, adding to, or diminishing from the main design; or print, reprint, or import for sale, or publish, sell, or otherwise dispose of any copies of any print engraved, etched, drawn, or designed in Great Britain, without the express consent of the proprietor first had and obtained in writing, signed by him with his own hand, in the presence of and attested by two or more credible witnesses: then every such proprietor may in a special action upon the case brought against the offender recover such damages as a jury, on the trial of such action, or on the execution of a writ of inquiry thereon, should give or assess, together with double costs of suit.

This last Act, in short, gave to a proprietor of a print within the protection of either of the previous Acts an action on the case with double costs against (a) any person who should without his consent engrave, or copy, or print, or reprint, &c. or publish, sell, or otherwise dispose of such print, the same having been engraved in Great Britain.

6. Copyright is not expressly given by any of the Acts to the assignee of an engraver; nevertheless, an assignee may maintain an action of piracy under the Act (b) *6. Who may proceed for piracy*

7. Plates illustrating letter-press, although the letter-press be in the same book as the plates, are under the statutory protection. (c) *7 Piracy by plates in a letter-press book*

8. A copy is piratical under these Acts if it comes so near to the engraving as to give to every person seeing *8 Test of piracy*

(a) A full and reasonable indemnity for all costs of suit is now substituted. 5 & 6 Vict. c 99, s 2

(b) *Thompson* v *Symonds*, 5 T R 41, and see 8 Geo 2, c 13, s 12

(c) See *Roworth* v *Wilkes*, 1 Campb 94

it the idea created by the original; (a) the copy need not be exact, it is a piracy if it is substantially a copy. (b)

9 Piracy by
photography

9. A photographic copy of an engraving is an infringement of the right given to engravers by the statutes of Geo. 2 and Geo. 3   This was determined not very long ago. The decision is reported upon a rule obtained in the Court of Common Pleas, in an action brought in the present year by the engraver of Holman Hunt's picture, 'The Light of the World,' and Rosa Bonheur's picture, 'The Horse Fair,' against a person who had taken and sold some photographs of both those pictures. The defendant's counsel strenuously, but in vain, argued that photographic copies were not within the words or within the mischief of the Engraving Copyright Acts.   The Chief Justice (*Erle*) reviewed the Acts and said: 'This statute (17 Geo. 3, c. 57) contains extremely wide words for the protection of the owner of the print. The question is, whether a person taking a photograph of a print does not in a manner copy the print; the common mode of expressing what the defendant has done is that he has made a photographic copy of the print. The object of this statute also was not to prevent an engraver's reputation being lowered, but to give him the monopoly of selling copies of the engraving. If that be the purpose for which the statute was passed, this is entirely an infringement of the plaintiff's copyright; for a photographic copy may represent to the mind exactly the same idea as the original, and so spoil the sale of the engraver's prints. I cannot see why the statute should not apply to any

(a) *West* v *Francis*, 5 B. & Ald   (b) *Moore* v. *Clarke*, J M & W
713, *Roworth* v *Wilkes*, 1 Campb   692
94

kind of copying which mars ingenuity, or the advance of science produces, though unknown at the time when the statute was passed. It does not make any difference whether the photograph be of the same size or of smaller dimensions than the print. Though of smaller size, it gives the same kind of pleasure to the purchaser that the original does, although no doubt not so high a pleasure as the more perfect article would, yet still sufficient to injure the sale of the print, and therefore within the mischief intended to be remedied by the statute.' The Court was unanimous in making the rule absolute.

The language of the Judges in *Gambart* v. *Ball* also tends to the conclusion that the Act 17 Geo. 3, c. 57, is comprehensive enough to include all mechanical or scientific processes of multiplying copies of engravings.

10. It may be here noticed that a work, as in literary copyright, can be piratical, though the copyist may have no actual knowledge of the existence of copyright in the original. (*a*)

10 Piracy may be unintentional.

11. In an action for the penalty, the Court of Common Pleas ordered judgment of nonsuit to be entered against the plaintiff, because he, being the proprietor of the plate and print in question, had not engraved his name on the plate, or printed it on the print; (*b*) but an action for damages was held to lie at common law against a person pirating a print upon which no name had been inscribed. (*c*) A court of equity has also given relief by injunction, where the date of publication was omitted. In *Blackwell* v. *Harper*, (*d*) the plaintiff

11. Decisions and dicta upon the right

(*a*) *Bayley*, J in *Francis* v *West*, 5 B & Ald 737, *Gambart* v *Sumner*, 8 W. R 27, 5 Jur n s 1109

(*b*) *Sayer* v *Dicey*, 3 Wils 60

(*c*) *Roworth* v *Wilkes*, 1 Campb 94

(*d*) 2 Atk 93, S C Barnard, 210

being the owner of prints in chiaroscuro, which represented medicinal plants, filed a bill for an account of profits, and to restrain the defendant from copying and engraving her prints; the defendant objected that the words 'Elizabeth Blackwell, delineavit, sculpsit, et pinxit,' upon each print did not show who was the proprietor, and that the day of publication did not appear on the plate, or on the prints from the plate, and so the defendant knew not the date of the commencement and expiry of the right. Lord *Hardwicke*, C. granted a perpetual injunction, he being of opinion that the Latin words sufficiently showed the proprietorship, but he refused to make the defendant account, because he thought it would be hard to make him do so, as he was ignorant of the existence of the property. At the same time, the Chancellor intimated that the date of the publication was only necessary to recovery of the penalty under the Acts, that the property in a print vested absolutely in an engraver, though the day of publication was not annexed to the print. In a subsequent case, (*a*) Lord *Alvanley*, M.R. was indeed inclined to differ from him upon this point. The inscription of the date is, it seems, necessary to any proceeding under the Act, (*b*) the statutory protection is only extended to that plate and those prints which have thereon the name of the proprietor and the date of publication. (*c*)

In addition to *Blackwell* v *Harper* may be quoted as to a sufficient disclosure of proprietorship *Newton* v.

(*a*) *Harrison* v. *Hogg*, 2 Ves. 327.

(*b*) *Brooks* v *Cocks*, 3 A. & E. 138.

(*c*) *Colnaghi* v *Ward*, 6 Jur 970 The date is important That the public may know the period of the monopoly, the name of the proprietor should appear, in order that those who wish to copy it may know to whom to apply for consent 5 T R 45

Cowie. (*a*) That was an action under the statute 17 Geo. 3, c. 37, and it was there objected that the name of the proprietor did not appear on the prints, the only words thereon being 'Newton, del. 1st May, 1826: Gladwin, sculp.' The Court of Common Bench, after hearing counsel on the objection, followed the decision in *Blackwell* v. *Harper*, and held that the inscription was sufficient, inasmuch as it accomplished the object of the Act.

Authors of paintings, drawings, and photographs had no copyright in their works prior to July 29, 1862, so that the same might have been and frequently were the subjects of copyright engravings. (*b*)

In *Newton* v. *Cowie* (*c*) an objection was taken by the defendant that the plaintiff was not the inventor or designer of the engraving, because he had engraved it from a drawing by his apprentice of a machine in the specification of a patent; but this objection was overruled. The Court found nothing in the Engraving Acts as to the place in which the original was to be found, and *Best*, C.J. observed. 'An engraver is always a copyist, and if engravings from drawings were not to be deemed within the intention of the Legislature, the Engraving Acts would afford no protection to that most useful body of men, the engravers.'

The engraver, although a copyist, produces the resemblance by means very different from those employed by the painter or draftsman from whom he copies— means which require great labour and talent. The engraver produces his effects by the management of

(*a*) 4 Bingh 234, and see *Buller*, J in *Thompson* v. *Symonds*, 5 T R 45

(*b*) See preamble of 25 & 26 Vict. c 68.

(*c*) 4 Bingh 234

light and shade, or, as the term of his art expresses it, the chiaroscuro. The due degrees of light and shade are produced by different lines and dots. He who is the engraver must decide on the choice of the different lines and dots for himself, and on his choice depends the success of the print. If he copies from another engraving, he may see how the person who engraved that has produced the desired effect, and so without skill or attention become a successful rival. The first engraver does not claim the monopoly of the use of the picture from which the engraving is made. He says: ' Take the trouble of going to the picture yourself, but do not avail yourself of my labour, who have been to the picture and have executed the engraving.'

In *Sayre* v. *Moore*, (a) Lord Chief-Justice *Mansfield* also said: ' In the case of prints, no doubt different men may take engravings from the same picture.'

Piracy in an engraving is not established when the latter work materially differs from the original in character. The well-known case of *Martin* v. *Wright* (b) seems a sound decision as to the Act 17 Geo. 3, c. 57, on this point: (c) there the Vice-Chancellor of England, Sir *L. Shadwell*, refused to restrain the exhibition for money of a coloured dioramic copy on a large scale of a small print in which copyright existed.

An observation of Chief Justice *Best* in *Newton* v. *Cowie* (d) is also an authority against the conclusion of piracy whenever the scale of the copy differs materially from that of the original.

(a) 1 East 361, n , and see *De Berenger* v *Wheble*, 2 Stark 548
(b) 6 Sim 297.

(c) See, however, *Clark* v *Freeman*, 11 Beav. 112.
(d) 4 Bingh. 234.

It has also been determined, and upon the reasoning of the decision in *Clementi* v. *Walker*, that the Legislature did not intend to protect any prints except such as should be engraved, etched, drawn, or designed in Great Britain. The Vice-Chancellor Sir *L. Shadwell* so held. he refused to protect by injunction a print first published in this country and entered at Stationers' Hall, but engraved abroad. (*a*)

In *Murray* v. *Heath*, (*b*) where the defendant, an engraver, took a certain number of impressions from a plate engraved by himself, but which he had undertaken to engrave for the use of the plaintiff, the Court of Queen's Bench ruled that no action was maintainable against him under the Act 17 Geo. 3, c. 57. But an action at common law unquestionably lay against him for damages, by reason of the breach of his contract to deliver to the plaintiff all the impressions.

Where there were illustrations and designs forming part of a book in which a person had copyright under the Act 5 & 6 Vict. c. 45, Sir *James Parker*, V.C. was of opinion that such copyright extended beyond the letter-press and to the illustrations and designs, and so construing the Act he granted an injunction (*c*) upon the plaintiff undertaking to bring an action, although the provisions of the Engraving Acts as to the illustrations and designs had not been complied with.

The same learned Judge thought that prints published separately were not within the protection of the Act 5 & 6 Vict. c. 45. (*d*)

(*a*) *Page* v *Townsend*, 5 Sim 395, and see 7 & 8 Vict c 12, s 19

(*b*) 1 B & Ald 804, see also

P. Albert v *Strange, ante,* p 7.

(*c*) *Bogue* v. *Houlston,* 5 De G. & Sm 275

(*d*) *Ibid.*

The question, copy or not, is one of fact, and a direction to a jury to consider whether a certain print is substantially a copy of another is a proper direction. (a)

12. No inventor, designer, or engraver of a print first published since the 10th day of May 1844 out of Her Majesty's dominions can have copyright therein in this country, (b) except under the International Copyright Acts, and the proprietor of a foreign print must comply with the provisions of the Copyright Engraving Act. (c)

The copyright in an engraving can only be assigned by deed attested by two witnesses.

13. There is an Act of Parliament extending to Ireland the protection of copyright in prints and engravings, which right had been previously confined to Great Britain. (d)

14. For the removal of doubts which had been entertained whether the Acts of Geo. 2, Geo. 3, and Will. 4, extended to lithographs, a clause was inserted (e) in a statute, 15 & 16 Vict. c. 12, expressly declaring that the provisions of those Acts were intended to include prints taken by lithography, or any other mechanical process by which prints or impressions of drawings were capable of being multiplied indefinitely.

15. Of course an action does not lie to recover the value of immoral, obscene, (f) or libellous prints. (g) No copyright can exist in an engraving of a criminal

---

(a) *Moore* v *Clarke*, 9 M & W 692

(b) 7 & 8 Vict. c. 12, s 19, and see *Page* v *Townsend*, previous page

(c) *Avanzo* v *Mudie*, 10 Exch 203

(d) 6 & 7 Will 4, c 59.

(e) See 14

(f) For statutes to check the exhibition and sale of indecent prints and pictures, see 4 Geo 4, c 83, s 4; 1 & 2 Vict. c 38, s 2 and 20 & 21 Vict c 83.

(g) *Fores* v *Johnes*, 4 Esp 97

character, it is not a legal subject of property. If any person destroy a libellous picture, he is at the utmost only liable at law to pay the value of the canvas and paint. (*a*)

16. All pecuniary penalties incurred and all copies forfeited by offenders pursuant to any Act for the protection of copyright engravings may be recovered in England and Ireland, either by action against the party offending, or by summary proceeding before any two justices having jurisdiction. Where the offender resides in Scotland, by action before the Court of Session, in ordinary form, or by summary action before the sheriff of the county where the offence may be committed or the offender resides. (*b*)

16. Proceedings for penalties on violation of the right.

(*a*) *Du Bost* v *Beresford*, 2 Campb 511, see also Nichols' Biogr Anecd. of Hogarth, p. 39, 3d edition

(*b*) 25 & 26 Vict c 68, s 8.

CHAPTER IX.

COPYRIGHT-AFTER-PUBLICATION IN PAINTINGS, DRAWINGS, AND PHOTOGRAPHS.

1 *Creation of the Right.*—2. *Definition of the Right, and by whom it may be claimed, and how long* —3. *Non-Existence of the Right in Criminal Works.*—4 *Nature of the Right.*—5 *Assignment of the Right* —6. *License to Use or Copy the Subject of the Right.*— 7 *Registry of the Right and of every Assignment of the Right.*— 8 *Statutory Penalties for Infringement of the Right* —9. *The Remedy for Piracy.*

1 Creation of the right.

1. PRIOR to the 29th day of July 1862, there was no copyright in any painting, drawing, or photograph. (*a*)

In *De Berenger* v. *Wheble*, in the year 1819, *Abbott*, L.C.J. held that it would destroy all competition in the art to extend copyright to painting. (*b*)

Many eminent artists, however, thought differently, and deplored the want of such a copyright; they also insisted that the protection afforded to the public against the purchase of spurious pictures was insufficient. But a spurious and a piratical production, it must be remembered, are things essentially different. (c) the former may deceive the public and injure the general reputation of an author or artist, and so affect his pocket, but it is not like the latter—a direct invasion of his property.

In July 1858 a petition was addressed to the House

(*a*) Preamble of 25 & 26 Vict
c 68.

(*b*) 2 Stark 548
(*c*) *R* v *Closs*, W R 109

of Lords by the Society of Arts, by the Royal Institute of British Architects, and by a number of painters, sculptors, architects, engravers, photographers, and others interested in the production of works of fine art, praying for an amendment and extension of the law of copyright. A committee of the House was named to examine the statements of the petition. Lord *Lyndhurst* presented the petition in doing so, he stated the then law of copyright affecting engravings, and noticed the absence of any copyright in pictures. He said : 'For a long period of years the law has recognised the principle of granting protection to works of the mind where they assume a material and useful form. Ever since the time of Queen Anne copyright has been granted to authors for the protection of their works. If a painter, not being satisfied with the remuneration for his works, should determine to engrave them, that engraving would be protected by the law of copyright. The protection of a copyright was even extended to works of design applied to manufactures, but it is a strange circumstance that to painting, the most delightful of all the arts, no protection by copyright has ever been given, and yet by the same principle it is an invention of the mind assuming a useful and beneficial form. In practice, the effect of the present state of the law is a very extensive circulation of spurious copies of good paintings, which is most injurious to artists of good reputation, and which operates injuriously in many ways. The artist has lost the copyright in his works, and has been injured in reputation in consequence of their being copied by inferior artists. The public has been injured by the frauds committed. The extent of these frauds is most surprising..... Sometimes lawyers are consulted as to the means of remedying this state of things, and they speak with uncertainty about injunctions from Chancery and actions at law, but it is quite out of question to expect that an artist will leave his studio, and involve himself in the meshes of the Court of Chancery.' This committee made a report, and a bill was prepared upon the basis of that report, but the Parliament then sitting was suddenly dissolved before the bill could be considered.

At last, in the year 1862, the petitioners obtained an Act of Parliament. By it, the property is secured to authors of paintings, drawings, and photographs, the same being original and not sold or disposed of before July 29, 1862. The Act (25 & 26 Vict. c. 68) is entitled 'An Act for amending the Law relating to Copyright in Works of the Fine Arts, and for repressing the Commission of Fraud in the Production or Sale of such Works.'

2 Definition of the right, and by whom it may be claimed, and how long

2. The right and the person entitled to the right are defined by the first section of the Act in these words: 'The author, being a British subject or resident within the dominions of the Crown, of every original painting, drawing, or photograph which shall be or shall have been made, either in the British dominions or elsewhere, and which shall not have been sold or disposed of before the commencement of this Act (a), and his assign, shall have the sole and exclusive right of copying, engraving, reproducing, and multiplying such painting or drawing, and the design thereof, or such photograph and the negative thereof, by any means and of any size, for the term of the natural life of such author and seven years after his death.'

(a) July 29, 1862.

To the above enactment there is this proviso, viz. that where any painting or drawing, or the negative of any photograph, shall, for the first time after the passing of the Act, be sold or disposed of, or shall be made or executed, for or on behalf of any other person, for a good or a valuable consideration, the person so selling or disposing of, or making or executing the same, shall not retain the copyright thereof unless it be expressly reserved to him by agreement in writing, at or before the time of such sale or disposition, by the vendee or assignee of such painting or drawing, or of such negative of a photograph, or by the person for or on whose behalf the same shall be so made or executed; but the copyright shall belong to the vendee or assignee of such painting or drawing, or of such negative of a photograph, or to the person for or on whose behalf the same shall have been made and executed; nor shall the vendee or assignee thereof be entitled to any such copyright, unless at or before the time of such sale or disposition an agreement in writing, signed by the person so selling or disposing the same, or by his agent duly authorised, shall have been made to that effect.

The copyright so given is also carefully qualified by the 2d section of the Act to this extent, viz. that nothing in the Act contained prejudices the right of any person to copy or use any work in which there is no such copyright, or to represent any scene or object, notwithstanding that there may be copyright in some representation of such scene or object.

3. Of course there can be no claim to copyright in an indecent or libellous painting, drawing, or photograph. (*a*)

3 Non-existence of the right in criminal works.

(*a*) See 5 Geo 4, c 83, and 1 & 2 Vict c. 38, and 20 & 21 Vict c 83

The decisions in *Du Bost* v. *Beresford* and *Fores* v. *Johnes* (a) would be applicable to such a work.

4. Further, the right is as to its nature personal or moveable estate. (b)

5. It is assignable at law, and every assignment of it must be in writing, signed by the proprietor of the right, or by his agent appointed for that purpose in writing. (c)

6. Every license to use or copy, by any means or process, the design or work, the subject of the work must also be in the form of a written memorandum or note, signed in the same manner as an assignment of the right. (d)

7. No proprietor of the right is entitled to the benefit of the Act 25 & 26 Vict. c. 68, until registration, and no action is sustainable, nor is any penalty recoverable under that Act in respect of any violation of the right, before compliance with the statutory provisions for registration.   In the register which the Act directs to be kept at the Hall of the Stationers' Company is entered a memorandum of every copyright to which any person is entitled under the Act, and also of every assignment of such copyright.   The memorandum should contain a statement of the date of the assignment and of the names of the parties thereto, and of the name and place of abode of the person in whom the right is vested by virtue thereof, and of the name and place of abode of the author of the work, together with a short description of the nature and subject, and, in addition thereto, if the person registering should

(a) *Ante*, pp 216, 217   (c) *Ibid*
(b) 25 & 26 Vict c 68, s 3   (d) *Ibid.*

so desire, a sketch, outline, or photograph of the work. (a)

The enactments of 5 & 6 Vict. c. 45, in relation to the register thereby prescribed, are applicable to the register under 25 & 26 Vict. c. 68, except that the forms of entry prescribed by the earlier Act may be varied under the later to meet the circumstances of any case. One shilling only can be demanded for an entry in the register of this copyright. (b)

8. Any invasion of the property is guarded against by a special provision in the statute which creates the right. By the sixth section of the Act it is enacted, if the author of any painting, drawing, or photograph in which there shall be subsisting copyright, after having sold or disposed of such copyright, or if any other person not being the proprietor for the time being of copyright in any painting, drawing, or photograph, shall, without the consent of such proprietor, repeat, copy, colourably imitate, or otherwise multiply for sale, hire, exhibition, or distribution, or cause or procure to be repeated, copied, colourably imitated, or otherwise multiplied for sale, hire, exhibition, or distribution any such work, or the design thereof, or knowing that any such repetition, copy, or other imitation has been unlawfully made, shall import into any part of the United Kingdom, or sell, publish, let to hire, exhibit, or distribute, or offer for sale, hire, exhibition, or distribution, or cause or procure to be imported, sold, published, let to hire, distributed, or offered for sale, hire, or exhibition, or distribution, any repetition, copy, or imitation of the said work, or of the design thereof, made without such consent as aforesaid, such person for every such offence

8 Statutory penalties for infringement of the right

(a) 25 & 26 Vict. c 68, s 4   (b) 25 & 26 Vict c 68, s 5

shall forfeit to the proprietor of the copyright for the time being a sum not exceeding 10*l*., and all such repetitions, copies, and imitations made without such consent as aforesaid, and all negatives of photographs made for the purpose of obtaining such copies, shall be forfeited to the proprietor of the copyright.

The recovery of pecuniary penalties incurred and of things forfeited under the Act, may be sought in England and Ireland either by action against the offender, or by summary proceeding before any two justices having jurisdiction; and where the offender resides in Scotland, by action before the Court of Session, in ordinary form, or by summary action before the sheriff of the county where the offence has been committed or the offender resides. (*a*)

9 The remedy for piracy.

9. Lord *Lyndhurst's* complaint of the 'inability of artists to leave their studios and involve themselves in the meshes of the Court of Chancery,' seems to have led to the insertion of a clause in the Act which empowers any of the superior courts of record sitting at Westminster or in Dublin to order an injunction, inspection, or account in any action pending there for infringement of the right. If the Court be not sitting, a judge of the Court can make the order. (*b*)

This clause does not exclude relief in the Court of Chancery, if the aggrieved party should still choose to go thither; of course he may, in lieu of either course, bring his action on the case for damages.

(*a*) 25 & 26 Vict. c 68, s 8   (*b*) *Ibid* s 9

CHAPTER X.

COPYRIGHT-AFTER-PUBLICATION IN SCULPTURE.

1. Foundation of the Right —2. Definition of the Right . its Extent and Duration —3. Protection of the Right against Piracy.— 4 Assignment of the Right. — 5 No Modern Decisions on the Right

1. COPYRIGHT-AFTER-PUBLICATION in sculpture is also founded on Acts of Parliament. The earliest Act was 38 Geo. 3, c. 71, of which it was said by Lord *Ellenborough*, C.J. that it seemed to have been framed with a view to defeat its own object. (*a*) That Act was amended by 54 Geo. 3, c. 56, and is now repealed. (*b*)

1 Foundation of the right.

2. Under the earlier Act, the maker of any new and original sculpture, or model, or copy, or cast of the human figure, or of any bust, or of any part of the human figure, clothed in drapery or otherwise, or of any animal, or of any part of any animal, combined with the human figure or otherwise, or of any subject, being matter of invention in sculpture, or of any alto or bassorelievo representing any of the matters or things hereinbefore mentioned, or of any cast from nature of the human figure, or of any part of the human figure, or of any cast from nature of any animal, or of any part of any animal, or of any such subject containing or

2 Definition of the right its extent and duration

(*a*) *Gahagan* v *Cooper*, 3 Campb. 114   (*b*) 24 & 25 Vict. c 101

Q

representing any of the matters and things already mentioned, whether separate or combined, has the sole right and property therein for fourteen years from publication, provided that he put his name thereon with the date before publication; (a) at the expiry of that period, if he be living and have not in express words parted with his right, his property is then prolonged for another fourteen years. (b)

It is important to bear in mind that there is judicial authority for the statement that a work must be considered as published within the meaning of the Sculpture Copyright Act by exhibition at the Royal Academy, (c) and that no article of sculpture first published after the 10th day of May, 1844, out of Her Majesty's dominions, can have any copyright therein, except under the International Copyright Acts, to which attention will hereafter be called. (d)

3 Protection of the right against piracy.

3. A statutory remedy for an infringement of this copyright is given by s. 3 of the Act 54 Geo. 3, c. 56, which provides, that if any person shall within the first fourteen years of the right make or import, or cause to be made or imported, or exposed to sale, or otherwise disposed of, any pirated copy or pirated cast of a subject entitled to the right under the Acts 38 Geo. 3, c. 71, and 54 Geo. 3, c 56 (whether such copy or cast be produced by moulding or copying from, or imitating in any way, such subject, to the detriment of the proprietor of the right), (e) the proprietor may in an action on the

(a) See 54 Geo. 3, c 56, s 1

(b) Ibid s 6, see *Grantham* v. *Hawley*, Hob 178, cited 1 C B 378, and *Carnan* v. *Bowles*, 2 Bro C C 80

(c) See *Turner* v. *Robinson*, 10 Ir Ch R.

(d) 7 & 8 Vict c. 12, s 19

(e) See 2 of 38 Geo 3, c 71, and *Gahagan* v *Cooper*, 3 Campb 111.

case, brought within six months after the discovery of the offence, recover damages, with double costs of suit.

Any work within the protection of the Sculpture Copyright Act may also be registered under the Designs Acts. (a) If any person during the continuance of the right so registered make, import, expose for sale, or otherwise dispose of any pirated copy or pirated cast of the work, in such manner and under such circumstances as would entitle the proprietor to an action on the case under the Sculpture Copyright Acts, such person is under an Act, 13 & 14 Vict. c. 104, s. 7, also liable to a penalty (not less than 5l., not exceeding 30l.) recoverable by the proprietor; the proprietor must, however, have previously marked the work with the word 're- gistered' and with the date of registration. (b)

The violation of this copyright may also, of course, be the subject of an action at common law, and of a suit in a court of equity.

4. An assignment of this copyright should be by deed, signed by the proprietor in the presence of and attested by two or more witnesses. (c)

4. Assignment of the right

5. Writing in the year 1849, Mr. Turner, in a 'Treatise on Copyright in Design,' states that the only approach to a sculpture case of late years had been a complaint of a theft of the model of Madame Vestris' foot by a rival Italian figure-maker, which case went to a police court, and was supposed to have been manu- factured for advertisement sake. The reports published before and since that year appear to be equally barren in respect to decisions on sculpture copyright. One

5 No modern decisions on the right

(a) 13 & 14 Vict c 104, s 6. See Appendix Directions issued by Board of Trade for registering ornamental designs.

(b) *Ibid* s 7

(c) 54 Geo 3, c 56, s 4

cause of this dearth may be that the works of sculpture are most frequently pirated by a class of persons against whom the existing laws afford an insufficient remedy. (a) The instances of piracy are, it is believed, constant; but, according to a report prepared at the request of the Society of Arts, 'sculptors have wisely submitted to the invasion of their rights rather than embark in litigation with men of straw.'

(a) 4 Jur. n s pt 1 p 88.

CHAPTER XI.

COPYRIGHT IN THE APPLICATION OF DESIGNS.

1. *Division of the Right —2 Regulation of the Right in Designs for Ornament —3. Definition of the Right in Designs for Ornament, and Who may Claim it —4 Duration of the Right in Designs for Ornament —5 Registration of the Right in Designs for Ornament —6. Assignment of the Right in Designs for Ornament — 7. Remedies for Piracy of the Right in Designs for Ornament.— 8. Basis of the Right in Designs of Utility —9. Definition of the Right in Designs of Utility Who may Claim the Right, and its Duration —10 The Transfer and Registry of the Right in Designs of Utility, and the Remedies for its Piracy.—11. Provisional Registration of Designs.*

1. COPYRIGHT in the application of designs for ornament and copyright in the application of designs for utility are distinct rights, founded upon different Acts of Parliament. It is therefore necessary to consider them separately.

1 Division of the right.

2. The right in designs for ornament is regulated by an Act 5 & 6 Vict. c. 100,(*a*) amended by Acts 6 & 7 Vict. c. 65, 13 & 14 Vict. c. 104, 21 & 22 Vict. c. 70, and 24 & 25 Vict. c. 73. The Act 5 & 6 Vict. c. 100, was founded upon a report of a Select Committee of the House of Commons appointed in the year 1836 to enquire (among other things) 'into the best means of extending a knowledge of the arts and of the principles

2 Regulation of the right in designs for ornament

(*a*) This Act repealed the 27 34 Geo. 3, c 23 , 2 Vict c 13 , 2 Geo 3, c 38, 29 Geo. 3, c 19, Vict c. 17.

of design among the people (especially the manufacturing population) of this country.' (a)

3 Definition
of the right in
designs for
ornament, and
who may claim
it

3. Under the Acts above mentioned the proprietor of every new and original design, (b) not previously published in the United Kingdom or elsewhere, whether such design be applicable to the ornamenting of any article of manufacture, or of any substance, artificial or natural, or partly artificial and partly natural, and whether such design be so applicable for the pattern, or for the shape, or configuration, or for the ornament thereof, or for any two or more of such purposes, and by whatever means such design may be so applicable, has the sole right of applying the same to any article of manufacture, or to any such substance as aforesaid during a specified period. (c)

The word 'proprietor' is explained by section 5 of the Act to be the author of any such new and original design, unless he have executed the work on behalf of another person for a good or a valuable consideration, in which case such person is considered the proprietor, and is entitled to be registered in the place of the author. Further, every person acquiring for a good or a valuable consideration a new and original design, or the right to apply the same to ornamenting any one or more articles of manufacture, or any one or more

(a) The precedence given by the Parliament of Victoria in its legislation to ornamental over useful designs may fairly enough be explained by the reply of Victor Hugo's Bishop to his thrifty housekeeper, when she hinted that a flower-bed should, for utility sake, be converted into a herbary 'Madame Magloire,' answered the Bishop, 'vous vous trompez, le beau est aussi utile que l'utile,' and after a pause, 'Plus peut-être' (See Les Misérables, vol 1)

(b) Except for things within 54 Geo 3, c 56

(c) See 5 & 6 Vict c 100, s 3, and 24 & 25 Vict c 73

such substances as aforesaid, either exclusively of any other person or otherwise, and also every person upon whom the property in such design, or such right to the application thereof, has devolved, is considered the proprietor of the design in the respect in which the same has been so acquired, and to that extent only.

In *McRae* v. *Holdsworth* an injunction issued on the plaint of proprietors whose title to the copyright in an ornamental design was based on their employment (a) for valuable consideration of the inventor. (b)

A design entitled to copyright may be applied in the United Kingdom or elsewhere, and any person may be the proprietor or inventor of such design, whether he be or be not a subject of Her Majesty. (c)

The public exposure for sale in this country in a bookseller's shop, and the purchase there by several persons of copies of a book describing an invention, disentitles that invention to a patent. (d)

As to the novelty of a design, the application of an old design to an article or substance to which it has not hitherto been applied does not render the design new and original. There must be a new and original idea in the projection of the design itself to bring it within the Acts. (e)

The result of a new combination of old designs may be a new design within the protection of the Copyright Designs Acts, that is to say, if the result be one design, not a multiplicity of old designs. (f) An

(a) A contract to design cannot be specifically enforced *Clarke* v *Price*, 2 Wils C C 157

(b) 2 De G. & Sm 496

(c) 24 & 25 Vict c 73 ss 1, 2

(d) *Lang* v *Gisborne*, 31 Beav.

133

(e) *Harrison* v *Taylor*, 3 H & N 301, but see *De la Branchardière* v *Elvery*, post, p. 241

(f) *Norton* v *Nicholls*, 7 W R. 421

eminent Judge (*Byles*) has said that configuration may constitute a new design, for where there is alteration of the proportions there may be a new design.

4. The duration of the right in the application of designs for ornament varies in different articles of manufacture.

The proprietor has the sole right to apply a design for ornament—

To articles composed wholly or chiefly of any metal or mixed metals. (*a*)

> During five years from the registry of the design (the term of duration was originally three years from the registry).

To articles composed wholly or chiefly of wood. (*b*)

To . articles composed wholly or chiefly of glass. (*c*)

To articles composed wholly or chiefly of earthenware. (*d*)

To articles of ivory, bone, papier-mâché, and other solid substances, not comprised in the articles above specified. (*e*)

To paper-hangings. (*f*)

To carpets. (*g*)

To floor-cloths or oil-cloths. (*h*)

To shawls to which the design is not applied solely by printing, or by any other process by which colours

> During three years from the registry of the design.

(*a*) Class 1, 5 & 6 Vict c 100

(*b*) Class 2, *ibid* , and see *R* v *West*, 17 Law T 83

(*c*) Class 3, *ibid*

(*d*) Class 4, *ibid*

(*e*) Class 4, 13 & 14 Vict c. 104, s 8, and 5 & 6 Vict c 100

(*f*) Class 5, 5 & 6 Vict. c 100

(*g*) Class 6, *ibid*

(*h*) Class 6, 6 & 7 Vict. c. 65, s 5

are or may be produced upon tissue or textile fabrics. (*a*)

To woven fabrics composed of linen, cotton, wool, silk, or hair, or of any two or more of such materials, if the design be applied by printing or any other process by which colours are or may be hereafter produced upon tissue or textile fabrics, such fabrics being or coming within the description technically called furniture, and the repeat of the design whereof is more than 12 inches by 8 inches. (*b*) } During three years from the registry of the design

To shawls, if the design be applied solely by printing or by any other process by which colours are or may hereafter be produced upon tissue or textile fabrics. (*c*)

To yarn thread or warp, if the design be applied by printing or by any other process by which colours are or may hereafter be produced. (*d*) } During nine calendar months from the registry of the design.

To woven fabric (*e*) composed of linen, cotton, wool, silk, or hair, or any two or more of such materials, if the design be applied by } Until Dec 31, in 2nd year after the year in which the design was registered (see 21 & 22 Vict c

(*a*) Class 8, 5 & 6 Vict c. 100
(*b*) Class 11, *ibid*
(*c*) Class 7, *ibid*
(*d*) Class 9, *ibid*
(*e*) Class 10, *ibid*. Ornamental needlework designs to be trans-

ferred on sewed muslin collars by printing or stamping the collars with colour, to be traced with the needle, are within this class *Lowndes* v. *Browne*, 12 Ir L R 293

printing or by any other process by which colours are or may hereafter be produced upon tissue or textile fabrics, excepting the woven fabrics aforesaid.

70, s 3) The proprietor must give the number and date of registration to any applicant by or on behalf of a person producing or vending any marked article in 10th class (see 21 & 22 Vict c 70, s. 6).

To all other woven fabrics. (*a*)

To lace and any article of manufacture or substance not provided for above. (*b*)

During twelve calendar months from the registry of the design.

The term of the duration in the right is prior to its expiration extendible for three years by an order of the Board of Trade, which order must be registered. (*c*)

In a case of *M'Rae v. Holdsworth*, which ended in compromise, it was argued that the copyright in the application of a certain ornamental design was not infringed by the application of the design to a manufacture which was not intended to be sold during the subsistence of the copyright; but Sir *J. L. Knight Bruce*, V.C. did not agree in that view of the Designs Acts. (*d*)

5 Registration of the right in designs for ornament.

5. No person is entitled to the benefit of the Act 5 & 6 Vict. c. 100, with regard to any design, unless such design has. before publication, been registered according to the Act, and unless at the time of registration such design has been registered, in respect of its application to some or one of the articles of manufacture or substances above mentioned, and that by specifying the

(*a*) Class 12, 5 & 6 Vict c 100.
(*b*) Class 13, 5 & 6 Vict c 100
(*c*) 5 & 6 Vict. c 100
(*d*) See *Crossley v Beverly*, 1

R & M 166, n , and *Smith v London and South-Western Railway Company*, 1 Kay, 415

number of the class in respect of which the registration is made, and unless the proprietor's name has been stated in the registry, and unless after publication of the design every article or substance to which the design is applied has certain specified marks on it, or a label to it, denoting a registered design. (a)

Persons proposing to register a design for ornamenting an article of manufacture should take or send to the Designs Office, with the application to register, (b) two exactly similar copies, drawings (or tracings), (c) photographs, or prints thereof, with the proper fees; (d) also the name and address of the proprietor or proprietors, or the title of the firm under which he or they may be trading together, with his or their place of abode, or place of carrying on business, distinctly written or printed. Lastly, the number of the class in respect of which such registration is intended to be made, except it be for sculpture.

Under the Act 5 & 6 Vict. c. 100, it was held, that inasmuch as the article to which a design was applied was not the design, the deposit of a copy of the article was not a sufficient registration of a design, unless such deposit clearly disclosed the claim of the inventor, which

(a) 5 & 6 Vict c 100, s 4

(b) No 1, Whitehall — The office is open every day between 10 A M and 4 P M for searches and enquiries, but for registry between 11 A M and 3 P M only

(c) The copies may consist of portions of the manufactured articles (except carpets, oil cloths, and woollen shawls) when such can conveniently be done (as in the case of paper hangings, calico prints, &c), which, as well as the drawings or tracings (not in pencil) or prints of the design to be furnished, when the article is of such a nature as not to admit of being pasted in a book, must, whether coloured or not, be fac-similes of each other Should paper hangings or furnitures exceed 42 inches in length by 23 inches in breadth drawings will be required, but they must not exceed these dimensions

(d) See table of fees in directions for registration, in Appendix

it might not do, and fully put the Registrar in possession of all information necessary to his performance of the duties imposed on him by law. (a)   But the Act 21 & 22 Vict. c. 70, s. 5, has since declared that the registration of any pattern or portion of an article of manufacture to which a design is applied instead or in lieu of a copy, drawing, print, specification, or description in writing, shall be as valid and effectual to all intents and purposes as if such copy, drawing, print, specification or description in writing had been furnished to the Registrar. (b)

A design, if described in the register, must be accurately described. (c)

The registry may in certain cases be amended or cancelled. (d)

Blank forms (e) of applications to register, and official directions for registering ornamental designs, have been issued by the Board of Trade. (f)   A copy

(a) *Norton* v. *Nicholls*, 7 W. R. 420

(b) See also 13 & 14 Vict. c. 104, s. 11.

(c) See Sir *J. Romilly*, M. R. in *Windover* v. *Smith*, 11 W. R. 323

(d) 5 & 6 Vict. c. 100, s. 10

(f) 13 & 14 Vict. c. 104, s. 10

(e) The form runs thus —

[C. D. Works, March 31, 1852

To the Registrar of Designs, Designs Office, London

You are hereby requested to register (* *provisionally*) the accompanying   ornamental designs in class (* *or for sculpture*) in the name of (*A B of*   ) or of *A B of* and *C D of*   ) *trading under the style or firm of B D & Co of*   ) who claim to be the proprietors thereof, and to return the same (*if sent by post*) directed to   (*if brought by hand*) to the bearer of the official acknowledgement for the same

Signed B D & Co by J F

* Strike out ' provisionally ' and ' sculpture,' if not so to be registered

of those directions is appended to this work. They are couched in very plain terms, and a perusal prior to any application for registry is calculated to save trouble to the applicant as well as to the Registrar.

A design may be registered in respect of one or more of the classes, (a) according as it is intended to be employed in one or more species of manufacture; but a sepa e fee must be paid on account of each separate class, and all such registrations must be simultaneous.

After a design has been registered, one of the two copies, drawings (or tracings), or prints is filed at the Designs Office, and the other is returned, with a certificate annexed, on which will appear a mark, which must thereafter be placed on each article (b) of manufacture to which the design shall have been applied.

If the design is for sculpture, no mark is required to be placed thereon after registration, but merely the word 'registered,' and the date of registration.

The marks or labels are required as a caution to the public (c) that the design is protected, and upon the Act 5 & 6 Vict. c. 100, s. 4, it was held that they must be affixed to an article in the 10th class, (d) as put forth in the ordinary course of trade, and that no limit was fixed to the size of the article; but the Act 21 & 22 Vict. c 70, s. 4, has since enacted that nothing in the 4th section of the Act 5 & 6 Vict. c. 100, shall extend, or be construed to extend, to deprive the proprietor of any new and original design applied to ornamenting any

(a) As to the consequences of registering under a wrong class, see *Moore* and *Perrin*, JJ in *Lowndes* v *Browne*, 12 Ir L R 293, 301, 302, and *R* v. *West*, 17 L T 83

(b) 5 & 6 Vict c 100, s 15
(c) *Sarazin* v *Hamel*, 9 Jur. n s ch 192, S C 1 N R 253
(d) *Heywood* v *Potter*, 1 Ell & Bl 439, and see 14 & 15 Vict c 8

article of manufacture contained in that class of the benefits of the Act 5 & 6 Vict. c. 100, or the Act 21 & 22 Vict. c. 70, provided there shall have been printed on such article, at each end of the original piece thereof, the name and address of such proprietor, and the word 'registered,' together with the years for which such design was registered.

As to publication of the design prior to any application to register, it was doubted in *Dalglish* v. *Jarvie* (a) whether the exhibition prior to registration of a design for a woven fabric, within the copyright term, not for sale, but in order to attract customers, was not a publication of the design. The words in the Act 5 & 6 Vict. c. 100, s. 4, which suggested this doubt, have, however, since been explained by the Act 21 & 22 Vict. c. 70.

There may be a design, the beauty and utility of which are inseparable, and which may be registered under the Useful or under the Ornamental Designs Acts, but when the registration has been effected and the right in the design is questioned in a suit, the Court can look only at the Act under which the design has been registered. (b)

Registration of a design under the Act 5 & 6 Vict. c. 100, must be effected prior to the expiry of any provisional registration (c) of the same design.

The Act 6 & 7 Vict. c. 65, s. 7, provides for the appointment and payment of a registrar of ornamental designs, and of officers, clerks, and servants to assist him, and the Act 5 & 6 Vict. c. 100, s. 15, sets forth his duties and powers. The Act 5 & 6 Vict. c. 100,

(a) 2 M & Gor 234

(b) Sir *J. Romilly*, M R. in *Windover* v. *Smith*, 11 W R 324

(c) As to provisional registration, see *post*, p 247

provides for a certificate of registration and for a limited public inspection of the registered designs. (a) The certificate of registration is primâ-facie evidence of the design and of the name of the proprietor therein mentioned having been duly registered, and of the commencement of the period of registry, and of the proprietorship, and of the originality of the design, and of compliance with the Act. (b) All designs of which the copyright has expired may be inspected at the Designs Office, on the payment of the proper fee; but no design the copyright of which is existing is, in general, open to inspection. Any person, however, may by application at the office and on production of the registration-mark of any particular design be furnished with a certificate of search, stating whether the copyright be in existence, and in respect to what particular article of manufacture it exists; also the term of such copyright, and the date of registration, and the name and address of the registered proprietor thereof. As this mark is not applied to a provisionally-registered design, or to articles registered under Class 10, certificates of search for such designs will be given on production of the design, or a copy or drawing thereof, or other necessary information, with the date of registration. (c)

The Registrar of Designs determines under which of the Designs Acts any design should be registered; the applicant for registration names the class in which he places his design.

The Act 13 & 14 Vict. c. 104, contains provisions for the production of the documents of registration, and makes official copies thereof evidence.

(a) See 5 & 6 Vict c 100, ss 16, 17   (c) Directions issued by Designs
(b) 5 & 6 Vict c 100, s 16   Office See Appendix

An action lies for false representations as to the registry of a design, (a) and a penalty of 5l. is affixed to the offence of putting the registration mark on any design not registered, or after the expiry of the copyright therein.

6 Assignment of the right in designs for ornament

6. A mode of transfer of this right is provided by the 6th section of the Act 5 & 6 Vict. c. 100; a form of transfer is there given. Any writing purporting to be a transfer of a design, and signed by the proprietor, operates, after registry of the name of the transferee, as an effectual transfer. On request and on the production of the writing, or in the case of acquiring such right by any other mode than that of purchase (e. g. by bankruptcy or legal succession), on the production of any evidence satisfactory to him, the Registrar will insert the name of the new proprietor in the register.

7 Remedies for piracy of the right in designs for ornament.

7. No person may without the written consent of its proprietor apply a design protected by the Act 5 & 6 Vict. c. 100, or any fraudulent imitation of such design, for the purpose of sale, to the ornamenting of any article or substance in respect of which the copyright in the design is in force, and no person may publish, sell, or expose for sale any article or substance to which such design, or any fraudulent imitation thereof, has been so applied, after knowledge from any source other than the proprietor of the design that his consent has not been given to such application, or after having a written notice signed by him or his agent to the same effect. (b)

But it is not sufficient for a proprietor simply to notify to a vendor his proprietorship in the design sold and his intention to prosecute for piracy, the notice

(a) *Barley* v *Walford*, 9 Q. B. 197   (b) 5 & 6 Vict c 100, s 7 should state explicitly that he (the proprietor) has not given his consent to the application by others of his design. (a)

The case of *De la Branchardière v. Elvery* (b) throws some light on the sufficiency of the consent which will justify a sale. The plaintiff in that suit was a teacher to ladies of a mode of making for their own amusement crochet collars; she was also the registered proprietor of designs applicable to such collars; she had published and sold copies of a book of the designs, but with the following notice therein: 'Ladies are respectfully informed that these articles cannot be purchased without the registered mark being affixed, and parties wishing to manufacture for the purpose of sale must have the authoress's permission.' The defendant, after receipt of a formal notice from the plaintiff to desist from so doing, had sold crochet collars to which the plaintiff's designs had been applied without the plaintiff's consent: the Court of Exchequer held that such publication of the book did not authorise any purchaser of the book to apply the designs to crochet collars for sale. (b)

The statutory security against a violation of this right is for each (c) act of piracy a penalty not exceeding 30*l.* and not less than 5*l.*, recoverable by an action or by summary proceeding (d) before two justices; the aggregate amount of penalties for offences in respect of any one design committed by any one person may not, however, exceed 100*l*; the penalty and costs may, on conviction by justices, be recovered by distress upon, and

(a) *Norton* v *Nicholls*, 7 W R 420

(b) 4 Exch 380

(c) See *Brooke* v *Milliken*, 3 T R 509

(d) See *Bissell* v *Wilson*, 1 Ell. & Bl 489

sale of, the offender's goods in England. (a) Every action or proceeding for any offence or injury under the Ornamental Designs Act must be brought within twelve calendar months from the commission of the offence. (b)

An action for damages also lies at common law for an injury of the right, and a violation of the right may be restrained in equity. (c) Further, proceedings may be taken in the County Court of the district within which the piracy is alleged to have been committed. (d)

A court of law has itself compared designs on an action for piracy; (e) but the matter of a design being a question of eye-sight is generally left to the jury.

Ignorance of the registration of a design does not excuse a piracy of the right therein. (f)

8. Basis of the right in designs of utility

8. Copyright in the application of designs of utility is dependent on the Acts 6 & 7 Vict. c. 65, 13 & 14 Vict. c. 104, and 21 & 22 Vict. c. 70.

9. Definition of the right in designs of utility who may claim the right, and its duration

9. The Act 6 & 7 Vict. c. 65, came into operation on September 1, 1843. Under it the proprietor of every new and original design for an article of manufacture having reference to some purpose of utility, so far as such design is for the shape or configuration of such article, or any part of such shape or configuration, has the sole right to apply his design to such article, and to make and sell the same according to the design for three years from the registration of the design.

It is expressly provided by this Act that its language shall not include designs embraced by the Acts 5 & 6 Vict. c. 100, or 38 Geo. 3, c. 71, and 54 Geo. 3, c. 56.

(a) 5 & 6 Vict c 100, s 8
(b) Ibid s 12
(c) Ibid s 9
(d) 21 & 22 Vict c 70, ss 8, 9

(e) Sheriff v Coates, 1 R & M 159
(f) M'Rae v Holdsworth 2 De G & Sm 497

A design for utility applied under 6 & 7 Vict. c. 65, might always, it seems, have been applied in any part of Her Majesty's dominions, and yet have been entitled to copyright; prior to the Act 24 & 25 Vict. c. 73, a doubt existed whether a design for ornament must not have been applied within the United Kingdom, if copyright was claimed therein.

Any alien resident abroad may be a proprietor of a design within the Act 6 & 7 Vict. c. 65. (a)

The utility of a design which may be registered under this Act must depend upon its shape and configuration, not upon any combination of old designs (b). A new design for a brick with a semicircular cavity in two sides of it, in order to save duty and material and to secure ventilation, is an example of a design which may be registered under the Useful Designs Act. (c)

Where a design intended to prevent the loss of labels and consisting of a metal eyelet-hole therein had been registered under the Act 6 & 7 Vict. c. 65, and the same was without authority copied, Sir *J. L. K. Bruce*, V.C. entertained grave doubts whether the design was within the Act: he thought that the language of the statute, 'so far as such design shall be for the shape or configuration of such article,' excluded that design from protection. (d)

In *Millingen* v. *Picken* it was doubted by at least one of the common law judges whether a mechanical contrivance within a parasol handle, for the purpose of raising or lowering it with one hand only, was a design

(a) See 24 & 25 Vict. c 73   C B 809
(b) R v. Bissell, 16 Q B 810   (d) Margetson v Wright, 2 De
(c) Rogers v Driver, 16 Q B   G & Sm 125
102 and Millingen v Picken, 1

for the shape or configuration of an article of manufacture within the Act. (*a*)   The Registrar refuses to
register under the Act 6 & 7 Vict. c. 65, any design the
description of a statement respecting which contains
any wording suggestive of the registration being for
any mechanical action, principle, contrivance, application, or adaptation (except so far as these may be
dependent upon and inseparable from the shape or
configuration), or for the material of which the article
may be composed.

Novelty must be combined with utility in a design
registered under this Act, and the novelty must be substantial.   A claim to a design for the shape or configuration of the body of a four-wheel dog-cart was
rejected, because the design consisted only of an arch
in the fore part of the carriage, made a little higher than
that in ordinary use, to permit the convenience of larger
front wheels. (*b*)

In *R.* v. *Bessell, Patteson,* J. said: ' What is the
general meaning of configuration I cannot exactly
define; but the word must, I think, have been used by
the Legislature to denote some relation to shape visible
to the eye'

Judges have inclined to the opinion that a design
might be registered under the Designs Copyright Acts,
although the subject to which the design was applied
could have obtained a patent. (*c*)

The registry of a design for the purpose of this copyright must be before its publication; (*d*) and every

(*a*) *Millingen* v *Picken,* 1 C B
809
   (*b*) *Windover* v. *Smith,* 11 W.
R 323
   (*c*) *Coleridge* and *Erle,* JJ 16
Q B 108
   (*d*) 6 & 7 Vict c 65, s. 3

article made according to the design by its proprietor must have thereon the word 'registered,' also the date of registration. (a) There is a penalty for affixing the mark of registration on any article not duly registered, or in which the design copyright has expired, or advertising the same for sale as registered. (b)

10. The clauses and provisions of the Act 5 & 6 Vict. c. 100, relating to the transfer of designs, to piracy, to the mode of recovering penalties and damages for piracy, to cancelling and amending registrations, to the limitation of actions for piracy, to the awarding of costs, to the certificate of registration, (c) to the fixing and application of fees (d) of registration, and to the penalty for extortion, were incorporated in the Act 6 & 7 Vict. c. 65, (e) and have not since been altered.

The Act also provides for the appointment and payment of a Registrar of Useful Designs, and of subordinate officers, clerks, and servants.

It further enacted that the Registrar should not register any design for the shape or configuration of any article of manufacture, unless he was furnished with two exactly similar drawings or prints of the design, with an intelligible description in writing of it, with the title of the design, the name of the person, or of the style of the firm claiming the proprietorship, and the proprietor's place of abode, business, or address, but the Act 21 & 22 Vict. c. 70, has since declared, s. 5, that the registration of any pattern or portion of an article of manufacture to which a design is applied, instead of or in lieu of a copy, drawing, print, speci-

10 The mode of transfer and registry of the right in designs of utility, and the remedies for its piracy

(a) 6 & 7 Vict c 65, s 3
(b) Ibid , 4
(c) See 6 & 7 Vict c 72, s 3
(d) See Table of Fees, in Appendix
(e) 6 & 7 Vict c 65, s 6

fication, (a) or description in writing, shall be as valid and effectual as if such copy, &c. had been furnished to the Registrar.

The Registrar may refuse to register, save under 6 & 7 Vict. c. 65, a design within its application; further, he may refuse to register any design intended to be applied only to some label, wrapper, or other covering in which an article of manufacture may be exposed for sale, (b) also any design contrary to public morality or order, but an appeal lies from such refusal to the Board of Trade. (c)

Directions for registering useful designs have been issued by the Board of Trade (d): a perusal of them is necessary to all persons proposing to register or search for useful designs.

Any person may, on payment of a trifling fee, inspect and take copies of extracts from an index which the Registrar is required to keep of the titles of useful designs (e), also to take copies of the particulars registered when the same are required as evidence. (f)

The Board of Trade may, laying the same before Parliament, (g) make, alter, and revoke the rules and regulations with respect to the mode of registration and the particulars to be furnished by persons effecting registration.

11 Provisional registration of designs

11. As a preliminary to registration under the Acts 5 & 6 Vict. c. 100, and 6 & 7 Vict. c. 65, a later statute (13 & 14 Vict. c. 104) permits the provisional registra-

(a) See 13 & 14 Vict c 104, s 11

(b) 6 & 7 Vict c 65, s. 9

(c) Ibid

(d) See copy in Appendix

(e) 6 & 7 Vict c 65, s 10

(f) 13 & 14 Vict. c 104, ss 13 & 14

(g) Ibid s 10

tion of designs. The first section of the Act details the mode in which provisional registration may be effected, and sets out the particulars to be furnished to the Registrar. This proceeding involves the payment of a very trifling fee, and secures copyright to the proprietor of the design during one year (a) from its registry.

The penalties and provisions of the Act 5 & 6 Vict. c. 100, for preventing piracy, extend to the application of any provisionally-registered design, or any fraudulent imitation thereof, to any article of manufacture or to any substance; also to the publication, sale, or exposure for sale, of any article of manufacture or substance to which the design has been applied. (b)

During the continuance of its provisional registration the design may, without prejudice to subsequent registration under the other Designs Acts, be exhibited or exposed in any place where articles are not sold, or exposed or exhibited for sale, and to which the public are not admitted gratuitously, or where exhibition under the Act 13 & 14 Vict. c. 104, is licensed by the Board of Trade. Any article also to which the design has been or is proposed to be applied may be dealt with in like manner, if only it has thereon or attached thereto the words 'provisionally registered,' and the date of registration. (c)

A provisionally-registered design may be sold or transferred during its term of protection, but a sale, exposure, or offer for sale of anything to which the design has been applied, *ipso facto* nullifies the registration immediately before such sale, exposure, or offer. (d)

(a) Extendible six months by the Board of Trade.

(b) 13 & 14 Vict c 104, s 5

(c) 13 & 14 Vict c. 104, s 3

(d) Ibid s 4

Complete registration of a design cannot be effected after the expiry of the provisional term of protection therein. (*a*)

The provisions in the Acts 5 & 6 Vict. c. 100, and 6 & 7 Vict. c. 65, relating to the transfer of designs, to cancelling and amending registration, to the refusal of registration in certain cases, to the mode of recovering penalties, to the awarding and recovery of costs, to actions for damages, to the limitation of actions, to the certificate of registration, to penalties for wrongfully using marks, to the fixing and application of fees for registration, and to the penalty for extortion, apply to the registration, provisional registration, and transfer of designs, and to the designs entitled to protection under the Act 13 & 14 Vict. c. 104. (*b*)

(*a*) 13 & 14 Vict c 104, s. 4.   (*b*) *Ibid.* s 15

CHAPTER XII.

INTERNATIONAL COPYRIGHT-AFTER-PUBLICATION.

1 Origin and Regulation of the Right —2. The Right of French Authors in this Country —3. The Right of other Alien Authors in this Country.

1. ONLY within the last twenty years has copyright-after-publication been secured in this country to books and works of art first published by foreigners abroad. (*a*) An Act 7 & 8 Vict. c. 12, explained by an Act 15 & 16 Vict. c. 12, empowers Her Majesty, by Order in Council, to direct that authors, inventors, designers, engravers, and makers of books, prints, articles of sculpture, and other works of art, first published abroad, shall have copyright here, and that authors of dramatic pieces and musical compositions, first publicly represented and performed abroad, shall have the sole liberty of representing or performing the same here; it also provides for the registry and delivery of copies of the books and works, and protects them from piracy by importation. Carefully guarding against injury to works first published in this country from such an Order in Council (where there should be no international reciprocity), the Act further directs (*b*) that no Order in Council under the Act shall have any effect, unless it shall be stated therein as the ground for issuing the same, 'that due protection has

1. Origin and regulation of the right

(*a*) The first International Copyright Act was 1 & 2 Vict. c. 59. It embraced books only, and was repealed by 7 & 8 Vict. c. 12.
(*b*) Sec. 14.

been secured by the foreign power named in the order for the benefit of persons interested in works first published here, and similar to the works mentioned in the order.'

2 The copyright of French authors in this country

2. The Act 7 & 8 Vict. c 12 was followed by a convention between this country and France. (a) The convention was concluded at Paris, November 3, 1851 (by Her Majesty in exercise of her royal prerogative in that behalf and the French Republic), for an extension to each country of a reciprocal copyright in works of literature and art. In view to that extension, the convention also agreed to reduce certain duties levied in this country on books, prints, drawings, and musical works first published in France.

(a) The articles of this convention with France are couched in the following language —

1 'From and after the date on which, according to the provisions of Art. 1, the present convention shall come into operation, the authors of works of literature or of art, to whom the laws of either of the two countries do now or may hereafter give the right of property or copyright, shall be entitled to exercise that right in the territories of the other of such countries for the same term and to the same extent as the authors of works of the same nature if published in such other country would therein be entitled to exercise such right so that the republication or piracy in either country of any work of literature or of art published in the other shall be dealt with in the same manner as the republication or piracy of a work of the same nature first published in such other country, and so that such authors in the one country shall

have the same remedies before the courts of justice in the other country, and shall enjoy in that other country the same protection against piracy and unauthorised republication as the law does or may hereafter grant to authors in that country The terms "works of literature or of art" employed at the beginning of this article shall be understood to comprise publications of books, of dramatic works, of musical compositions, of painting, of sculpture, of engraving, of lithography, and of any other works whatsoever of literature and of the fine arts The lawful representatives or assigns of authors, translators, composers, painters, sculptors, or engravers, shall in all respects enjoy the same rights which by the present convention are granted to the authors, translators, composers, painters, sculptors, or engravers themselves.

2 'The protection granted to original works is extended to translations, it being, however, clearly

The convention was succeeded by an Order in Council, January 10, 1852, (*a*) which was thus expressed:—

'From and after the 17th day of January 1852, the

understood that the intention of the present article is simply to protect a translator in respect of his own translation, and that it is not intended to confer upon the first translator of any work the exclusive right of translating that work, except in the case and to the extent provided for in the following article

3 'The author of any work published in either of the two countries who may choose to reserve the right of translating it, shall, until the expiration of five years from the date of the first publication of the translation thereof authorised by him, be in the following cases entitled to protection from the publication in the other country of any translation of such work not authorised by him —

'Sec 1 If the original work shall have been registered and deposited in the one country within three months after its publication in the other

'Sec 2 If the author has notified on the title-page of his work his intention to reserve the right of translating it.

'Sec 3 Provided always, that at least a part of the authorised translation shall have appeared within a year after the registration and deposit of the original,

and that the whole shall have been published within three years after the date of such deposit.

'Sec 4 And provided that the publication of the translation shall take place within one of the two countries, and that it shall be registered and deposited according to the provisions of Art 8

'With regard to works which are published in parts, it will be sufficient if the declaration of the author, that he reserves the right of translation, shall appear in the first part. But with reference to the period of five years limited by this article for the exercise of the exclusive right of translation, each part shall be treated as a separate work, and each part shall be registered and deposited in the one country within three months after its first publication in the other

4 'The stipulations of the preceding articles shall also be applicable to the representation of dramatic works, and to the performance of musical compositions, in so far as the laws of each of the two countries are or shall be, applicable in this respect to dramatic and musical works first publicly represented or performed therein.

(*a*) There was another Order in Council of the same date as to the reduction of the duties on books, &c published in France

authors, inventors, designers, engravers, and makers of
any of the following works, that is to say, books, prints,

'In order, however, to entitle the author to legal protection in regard to the translation of a dramatic work, such translation must appear within three months after the registration and deposit of the original.

It is understood that the protection stipulated by the present article is not intended to prohibit fair imitations or adaptations of dramatic works to the stage in England and France respectively, but is only meant to prevent piratical translations

'The question whether a work is an imitation or a piracy shall in all cases be decided by the courts of justice of the respective countries, according to the laws in force in each

5 'Notwithstanding the stipulations of Arts 1 & 2 of the present convention, articles extracted from newspapers or periodicals published in either of the two countries, may be republished or translated in the newspapers or periodicals of the other country, provided the source from whence such articles are taken be acknowledged

'Nevertheless, this permission shall not be construed to authorise the republication in one of the two countries of articles from newspapers or periodicals published in the other country, the authors of which shall have notified, in a conspicuous manner, in the journal or periodical in which such articles

have appeared, that they forbid the republication thereof

6. 'The importation into and the sale in either of the two countries of piratical copies of works which are protected from piracy under Arts 1, 2, 3, & 5, of the present convention are prohibited, whether such piratical copies originate in the country where the work was published or in any other country.

7 'In the event of an infraction of the provisions of the foregoing articles, the pirated works or articles shall be seized and destroyed, and the persons who may have committed such infraction shall be liable in each country to the penalties and actions which are or may be prescribed by the laws of that country for such offences committed in respect of a work or production of home origin

8 'Neither authors nor translators, nor their lawful representatives or assigns, shall be entitled in either country to the protection stipulated by the preceding articles, nor shall copyright be claimable in either country, unless the work shall have been registered in the manner following, that is to say —

'If the work be one that has first appeared in France it must be registered at the Hall of the Company of Stationers in London

'If the work be one that has first appeared in the dominions

articles of sculpture, dramatic works, musical compositions, and any other works of literature and the fine

of Her Britannic Majesty it
must be registered at the Bureau
de la Librairie of the Ministry
of the Interior at Paris

'No person shall be entitled
to such protection as aforesaid
unless he shall have duly complied with the laws and regulations of the respective countries
in regard to the work in respect
of which such protection may be
claimed   With regard to books,
maps, prints, or musical publications, no person shall be entitled to such protection unless
he shall have delivered gratuitously at one or other of the
places mentioned above, as the
case may be, one copy of the
best edition, or in the best state,
in order to its being deposited
at the place appointed for that
purpose in each of the two
countries, that is to say   in
Great Britain, at the British
Museum in London, and in
France, at the National Library
at Paris   In every case the
formality of deposit and registration must be fulfilled within
three months after the first publication of the work in the other
country   With regard to works
published in parts, the period of
three months shall not begin to
run until the date of the publication of the last part, unless
the author shall have notified
his intention to preserve the
right of translating it is provided in Art 3, in which case

each part shall be treated as a
separate work

'A certified copy of the entry
in the register book of the Company of Stationers in London
shall confer within the British
dominions the exclusive right
of republication, until a better
right shall have been established
by any other party before a
court of justice

'The certificate given under
the laws of France proving the
registration of any work in that
country shall be held for the
same purpose throughout the
territories of the French Republic   A certificate or certified
copy of the registration of any
work so registered in either
country shall, if required, be
delivered at the time of registration, and such certificate shall
state the exact date at which the
registration was made

'The charge for the registration of a single work under the
stipulations of this article shall
not exceed one shilling in England, nor one franc and twenty-
five centimes in France, and
the further charge for a certificate of such registration shall
not exceed the sum of five
shillings in England, nor six
francs and twenty-five centimes
in France

'The provisions of this article
shall not extend to articles
which may appear in newspapers
or periodicals, which shall be

arts, in which the laws of Great Britain give to British subjects the privilege of copyright, and the executors,

protected from republication or translation simply by a notice from the author as prescribed by Art 5 But if any article or work which has originally appeared in a newspaper or periodical shall afterwards be published in a separate form, it shall then become subject to the stipulations of the present article.

9 'With regard to any article other than books, prints, maps, and musical publications, in respect to which protection may be claimable under Art 1 of the present convention, it is agreed that any other mode of registration than that prescribed in the preceding article, which is or may be applicable by law in one of the two countries to any work or article first published in such country for the purpose of affording protection to copyright in such work or article, shall be extended on equal terms to any similar work or article first published in the other country

10 'During the continuance of this convention the duties now payable upon the lawful importation into the United Kingdom of Great Britain and Ireland of books, prints, drawings, or musical works published throughout the territories of the French Republic shall be reduced to and fixed at the rates hereinafter specified, that is to say

1 'Duties on books and musical works, viz —

'(a) Works originally produced in the United Kingdom, and republished in France, the cwt — £ s d — 2 10 0

'(b) Works not originally produced in the United Kingdom, the cwt — 0 15 0

'2 Prints or drawings—

'(a) Coloured or plain, single, each — 0 0 0½

'(b) Bound or sewn, the dozen — 0 0 1½

But see now 24 & 25 Vict c. 20 Schedule D

'It is agreed that the rates of duty above specified shall not be raised during the continuance of the present convention, and that if hereafter, during the continuance of this convention, any reduction of those rates should be made in favour of books, prints, drawings, or musical works published in any other country, such reduction shall be at the same time extended to similar articles published in France

'It is moreover understood that all works published in France, of which any part may have been originally produced in the United Kingdom, shall be considered as works originally produced in the United Kingdom and republished in France, and as such shall be subject to the duty of fifty shillings per cwt , although the same may contain also original matter not produced in the United Kingdom, unless such original matter shall be at least equal in bulk to the part of the work originally produced in the United Kingdom, in

administrators, and assigns of such authors, inventors, designers, engravers, and makers respectively, shall, as respects works first published within the dominions of

which case the work shall be subject only to the duty of fifteen shillings per cwt

11 In order to facilitate the execution of the present convention, the two high contracting parties engage to communicate to each other the laws and regulations which may hereafter be established in their respective territories with respect to copyright in works or productions protected by the stipulations of the present convention

12. 'The stipulations of the present convention shall in no way affect the right which each of the two high contracting parties expressly reserves to itself of controlling or prohibiting by measures of legislation, or of internal police, the sale, circulation, representation, or exhibition of any work or production in respect to which either country may deem it expedient to exercise that right

13 'Nothing in this convention shall be construed to affect the right of either of the two high contracting parties to prohibit the importation into its own dominions of such books as by its internal law, or under engagements with other states, are or may be declared to be piracies or infringements of copyright

14 'Her Britannic Majesty engages to recommend to Parliament to pass an Act to enable her to carry into execution such of the arrangements contained in the

present convention as require the sanction of the Legislature When such an Act shall have been passed, the convention shall come into operation from and after a day to be then fixed upon by the high contracting parties Due notice shall be given beforehand in each country by the Government of that country of the day which may be so fixed upon, and the stipulations of the convention shall apply only to works or articles published after that day

'The convention shall continue in force for ten years from the day on which it may come into operation, and if neither party shall, twelve months before the expiration of the said period of ten years, give notice of its intention to terminate its operation, the convention shall continue in force for a year longer, and so on from year to year, until the expiration of a year's notice from either party for its termination

'The high contracting parties, however, reserve to themselves the power of making, by common consent, in this convention any modification which may not be inconsistent with its spirit and principles, and which experience of its working may show to be desirable.

15 'The present convention shall be ratified, and the ratification shall be exchanged at Paris as soon as may be within three months from the date of signature'

France after the said 17th day of January 1852, have the privilege of copyright therein for a period equal to the term of copyright which authors, inventors, designers, engravers, and makers of the like works respectively first published in the United Kingdom are by law entitled to, provided such books, dramatic pieces, musical compositions, prints, articles of sculpture, or other works of art have been registered, and copies thereof have been delivered according to the requirements of the said recited Act (7 & 8 Vict. c. 12) within three months after the first publication thereof in any part of the French dominions, or, if such work be published in parts, then within three months after the publication of the last part thereof.   The authors of dramatic pieces and musical compositions which shall after the said 17th day of January 1852, be first publicly represented or performed within the dominions of France, or their assignees, shall have the sole liberty of representing or performing in any part of the British dominions such dramatic pieces or musical compositions during a period equal to the period during which authors of dramatic pieces and musical compositions, first publicly represented or performed in the United Kingdom, or their assignees, are entitled by law to sole liberty of representing or performing the same, provided such dramatic pieces or musical compositions have been registered, and copies thereof have been delivered, according to the requirements of the said recited Act, within three months after the time of their being first represented or performed in any part of the French dominions.'

It seems that a work published in parts and to be continued for an indefinite period, e. g. a newspaper, is not a work published in parts within the meaning of the provision in this order of Council, because it could not have been intended that at any period, however remote, the publisher of such a work might register it and carry back his copyright therein to the earliest period, in 1852, when French authors first had a copyright in this country. (a)

3 In order to confirm the stipulation in the convention as to the reduction of duties, as well as to enable Her Majesty to make similar stipulations in any treaty on the subject of copyright with other foreign powers, Parliament passed another Act (15 & 16 Vict. c. 12). The first nine sections of that Act are incorporated with 7 & 8 Vict. c. 12, and s. 18 of the earlier Act is repealed by the later so far as the same is inconsistent therewith.

3 The copyright of other alien authors in this country

Under that Act the Queen in Council can now direct that the authors of books published after a specified day in any foreign country, their executors, administrators, or assigns, may (subject to the provisions of the Act 15 & 16 Vict. c. 12) prevent the publication in the British dominions of any translations of such books not authorised by them for a period (to be specified by Her Majesty) not exceeding five years from the first publication of an authorised translation, and in the case of books published in parts for a period not exceeding, as to each part, five years from the first publication of an authorised translation of that part. (b)

The Laws which protect British copyright are, by the same Act, conditionally extended to such authorised translations; and Her Majesty in Council can direct that authors of dramatic pieces first publicly represented in a foreign country, their executors, administrators,

(a) Sir W. P. Wood, V. C. in Cassell v. Stiff 2 Ka. and Jo 279   (b) 15 & 16 Vict c 12, s 2

s

and assigns, may (subject to the provisions of the Act) prevent the representation in the British Dominions of any unauthorised translation of such dramatic pieces for a period not exceeding five years from the first publication or representation of authorised translations thereof.

Further, to prevent representations of any such unauthorised translation, the Act 15 & 16 Vict. c. 12 extends thereto the law of England for ensuring to any author of a dramatic piece first publicly represented in the British dominions the sole liberty of representing it.

However, no author, his executors. administrators, or assigns, can have the benefit of the Act just referred to or of any order in Council in respect of any translation of a book or dramatic piece unless within three months of the first publication of the book or dramatic piece he register and deposit a copy in the manner required for original works by the Act 7 & 8 Vict. c. 12, (a) and unless the author notifies on the title page (if any), or on some conspicuous part of the book or piece, that it is his intention to reserve the right of translating it, and unless the authorised translation, or a part thereof, is published either in the foreign country (named in the order by which the translation is protected) or in the British dominions, within one year, and wholly published within three years after the registry and deposit of the original work under the Act, (b) and unless the translation itself be registered and a copy of it deposited within

(a) In the case of books published in parts, each part of the original work must be registered and deposited in the manner required by the Act 7 & 8 Vict c. 12

within three months after its publication in the foreign country

(b) If a dramatic piece, the publication of the authorised translation must be within three months of the registry of the original work

a period (to be named in the order), relating to such translation and in the manner prescribed by the Act 7 & 8 Vict. c. 12, for the registry and deposit of original works. The above requisitions apply to articles originally published in newspapers or periodicals, if the same be afterwards published in a separate form, but they do not apply to such articles as originally published. (a)

To give effect to those stipulations in the convention with the French Republic, which required the sanction of Parliament, the Act 15 and 16 Vict. c. 12 expressly declared that, during the continuance of that convention, the provisions of the Act already detailed should apply to it and to translations of books and dramatic pieces which should, after the passing of the Act, be published or represented in France, in the same manner as if Her Majesty had issued her order in Council, pursuant to the Act, for giving effect to the convention, and had therein directed that such translations should be protected for five years, from the first publication or public representation thereof respectively, and as if a period of three months from the publication of such translation was specified in the order as the period for registering and depositing a copy of the translation. (b)

The Act 15 & 16 Vict. c. 12, expressly declares that nothing therein contained shall be so construed as to prevent fair imitations or adaptations to the English stage of any dramatic piece or musical composition published in any foreign country, and notwithstanding anything in the Acts 7 & 8 Vict. c. 12, or 15 & 16 Vict. c. 12, contained, any article of political discussion which has been published in any newspaper or periodical in

(a) S 8   (b) S 11

s 2

a foreign country may, if the source from which the same is taken be acknowledged, be republished, or translated in any newspaper or periodical in this country. Any article relating to any other subject which has been so published may, if its source be acknowledged, be also republished or translated in like manner, unless the author has signified his intention of reserving the copyright therein and the right of translating the same in some conspicuous part of the newspaper or periodical in which the same was first published, in which case the same will, without the formalities required by section 8 (*a*) of the Act 15 & 16 Vict. c. 12, receive the same protection as is by virtue of the Acts 7 & 8 Vict. c. 12, and 15 & 16 Vict. c. 12, extended to books. (*b*)

On a motion to restrain the infringement of an alleged copyright in a French newspaper, Sir *W. P. Wood*, V.C., intimated grave doubts whether the protection just alluded to did not mean the same protection which the author of any book would obtain under an order of Council. made pursuant to the International Copyright Acts. He, therefore, refused to assist the plaintiff, because the requisitions of the order in Council governing international copyright in French newspapers as to registry had not been complied with, he directed the motion to stand over, with liberty to the plaintiff to bring an action and liberty to all parties to apply. (*c*)

The Act 15 & 16 Vict. c. 12, prohibits the importation into any part of the British dominions without

(*a*) *Ant*, p. 258.
(*b*) 15 & 16 Vict. c. 12 s. 7.
(*c*) *Cassell* v. *Stiff*, 2 Kay and Jo. 279.

the consent of the registered proprietor or his agent, (a) of any copies of any works of literature or art in which there is copyright under the International Copyright Acts, and which have been printed or made in any foreign country except that country in which such work shall have been first published, also all unauthorised translations of it, and extends to such copies and translations, sections 17 and 23 of the Act 5 & 6 Vict. c. 45.

The French law of copyright taken in connection with the French convention, seems to admit the work of any alien holding a French copyright to the benefit of the convention. (b)

International copyright has been arranged by Her Majesty since the year 1852, with Prussia, Saxony, Brunswick, Thuringia, Hanover, Oldenburgh, Anhalt, Hamburgh, Belgium, Spain, Sardinia, and Hesse.

Cassell v Stiff, already cited, and *Avanzo v. Mudie* are the only cases yet reported on the subject of international copyright; in the latter, the Court of Exchequer decided that the proprietor of a foreign print who claims a copyright therein under the International Copyright Acts must, in reference to such print, comply with the provisions of our own Engraving Acts. (c)

(a) The agent must be authorised in writing

(b) See 1 Jur N S, pt 2, p 523

(c) *Avanzo v Mudie*, 10 Exch 203

APPENDIX.

APPENDIX.

———◇———

8 Anne, c. 19.

An Act for the Encouragement of Learning, by vesting the Copies of printed Books in the Authors or Purchasers of such Copies during the Times therein mentioned.

WHEREAS Printers, Booksellers, and other Persons, have of late Preamble frequently taken the liberty of printing, reprinting, and publishing, or causing to be printed, reprinted, and published books, and other writings, without the consent of the authors or proprietors of such books and writings, to their very great detriment, and too often to the ruin of them and their families . for preventing therefore such practices for the future, and for the encouragement of learned men to compose and write useful books, may it please your Majesty that it may be enacted, and be it enacted by the the Queen's most Excellent Majesty, by and with the advice and consent of the Lords Spiritual and Temporal, and Commons in this present Parliament assembled, and by the authority of the same, that from and after the tenth day of April one thousand seven hundred and ten, the author of any book or books already printed, who hath not transferred to any other the copy or copies of such book or books, share or shares thereof, or the bookseller or booksellers, printer or printers, or other person or persons, who hath or have purchased or acquired the copy or copies of any book or books, in order to print or reprint the same, shall have sole right and liberty of printing such book and books for the term of one and twenty years, to commence from the said tenth day of April, and no longer, and that the author of any book or books already composed, and not printed and published, or that shall hereafter be composed, and his assignee or assigns, shall have the sole liberty of printing and reprinting such book and books for the term of fourteen years, to commence from the day of the first publishing the same, and no longer, and that if any other book-seller, printer, or other person whatsoever, from and after the tenth day of April one thousand seven hundred and ten, within the times granted and limited by this Act, as aforesaid, shall print, reprint, or import, or cause to be printed, reprinted, or im-ported, any such book or books, without the consent of the pro-

a

prietor or proprietors thereof first had and obtained in writing, signed in the presence of two or more credible witnesses; or knowing the same to be so printed or reprinted without the consent of the proprietors, shall sell, publish, or expose to sale, or cause to be sold, published, or exposed to sale, any such book or books, without such consent first had and obtained, as aforesaid, then such offender or offenders shall forfeit such book or books, and all and every sheet or sheets, being part of such book or books, to the proprietor or proprietors of the copy thereof, who shall forthwith damask and make waste-paper of them: and further, that every such offender or offenders, shall forfeit one penny for every sheet which shall be found in his, her, or their custody, either printed or printing, published or exposed to sale, contrary to the true intent and meaning of this Act, the one moiety thereof to the Queen's most Excellent Majesty, her heirs and successors, and the other moiety thereof to any person or persons that shall sue for the same; to be recovered in any of her Majesty's courts of record at Westminster, by action of debt, bill, plaint, or information, in which no wager of law, essoin, privilege, or protection, or more than one imparlance, shall be allowed.

And whereas many persons may through ignorance offend against this Act, unless some provision be made whereby the property in every such book, as is intended by this Act to be secured to the proprietor or proprietors thereof, may be ascertained, as likewise the consent of such proprietor or proprietors for the printing or reprinting of such book or books may from time to time be known, be it therefore further enacted by the authority aforesaid, that nothing in this Act contained shall be construed to extend to subject any bookseller, printer, or other person whatsoever, to the forfeitures or penalties therein mentioned, for or by reason of the printing or reprinting of any book or books without such consent, as aforesaid, unless the title to the copy of such book or books hereafter published shall, before such publication, be entered in the register-book of the company of Stationers, in such manner as hath been usual; which register-book shall at all times be kept at the hall of the said company, and unless such consent of the proprietor or proprietors be in like manner entered, as aforesaid; for every of which several entries sixpence shall be paid, and no more which said register-book may, at all seasonable and convenient times, be resorted to, and inspected by any bookseller, printer, or other person, for the purposes before mentioned, without any fee or reward, and the clerk of the said Company of Stationers shall, when and as often as thereunto required, give a certificate under his hand of such entry or entries, and for every such certificate may take a fee not exceeding sixpence

Provided nevertheless, that if the clerk of the said Company of Stationers for the time being shall refuse or neglect to register, or make such entry or entries, or to give such certificate, being thereunto required by the author or proprietor of such copy or copies, in the presence of two or more credible witnesses, that then such person and persons so refusing, notice being first duly given of such refusal, by an advertisement in the

Gazette, shall have the like benefit, as if such entry or entries, certificate or certificates had been duly made and given; and that the clerks so refusing shall, for any such offence, forfeit to the proprietor of such copy or copies the sum of twenty pounds, to be recovered in any of her Majesty's courts of record at Westminster, by action of debt, bill, plaint, or information, in which no wager of law, essoin, privilege, or protection, or more than one imparlance, shall be allowed

Provided nevertheless, and it is hereby further enacted by the authority aforesaid, that if any bookseller or booksellers, printer or printers, shall, after the said five-and-twentieth day of March one thousand seven hundred and ten, set a price upon, or sell or expose to sale any book or books at such a price or rate as shall be co ved by any person or persons to be high and unreasonable; it sha ..d may be lawful for any person or persons to make complaint thereof to the Lord Archbishop of Canterbury for the time being, the Lord Chancellor, or Lord Keeper of the Great Seal of Great Britain for the time being, the Lord Bishop of London for the time being; the Lord Chief Justice of the Court of Queen's Bench, the Lord Chief Justice of the Court of Common Pleas, the Lord Chief Baron of the Court of Exchequer, for the time being; the Vice-Chancellors of the Two Universities for the time being, in that part of Great Britain called England, the Lord President of the Sessions for the time being, the Lord Justice General for the time being; the Lord Chief Baron of the Exchequer for the time being; the Rector of the College of Edinburgh for the time being, in that part of Great Britain called Scotland; who, or any one of them, shall and have hereby full power and authority from time to time to send for, summon, or call before him or them such bookseller or booksellers, printer or printers, and to examine and enquire of the reason of the dearness and inhauncement of the price or value of such book or books by him or them so sold or exposed to sale, and if, upon such enquiry and examination, it shall be found that the price of such book or books is inhaunced, or any wise too high or unreasonable, then, and in such case, the said Archbishop of Canterbury, Lord Chancellor or Lord Keeper, Bishop of London, two Chief Justices, Chief Baron, Vice-Chancellors of the Universities, in that part of Great Britain called England, and the said Lord President of the Sessions, Lord Justice General, Lord Chief Baron, and Rector of the College of Edinburgh, in that part of Great Britain called Scotland, or any one or more of them, so enquiring and examining, have hereby full power and authority to reform and redress the same, and to limit and settle the price of every such printed book and books, from time to time, according to the best of their judgements, and as to them shall seem just and reasonable, and in case of alteration of the rate or price from what was set or demanded by such bookseller or booksellers, printer or printers, to pay all the costs and charges that the person or persons so complaining shall be put unto by reason of such complaint, and of the causing such rate or price to be so limited and settled, all which shall be done by the said Archbishop of Canterbury, Lord Chancellor, or Lord

Keeper, Bishop of London, two Chief Justices, Chief Baron, Vice-Chancellors of the two Universities, in that part of Great Britain called England, and the said Lord President of the Sessions, Lord Justice General, Lord Chief Baron, and Rector of the College of Edinburgh, in that part of Great Britain called Scotland, or any one of them, by writing under their hands and seals, and thereof publick notice shall be forthwith given by the said bookseller or booksellers, printer or printers, by an advertisement in the Gazette; and if any bookseller or booksellers, printer or printers, shall, after such settlement made of the said rate and price, sell or expose to sale any book or books at a higher or greater price than what shall have been so limited and settled as aforesaid, then, and in every such case, such bookseller and booksellers, printer and printers, shall forfeit the sum of five pounds for every such book so by him, her, or them sold or exposed to sale, one moiety thereof to the Queen's most excellent Majesty, her heirs and successors, and the other moiety to any person or persons that shall sue for the same, to be recovered, with costs of suit, in any of her Majesty's courts of record at Westminster, by action of debt, bill, plaint, or information, in which no wager of law, essoin, privilege, or protection, or more than one imparlance, shall be allowed

Provided always, and it is hereby enacted, that nine copies of each book or books, upon the best paper, that from and after the said tenth day of April One thousand seven hundred and ten shall be printed and published, as aforesaid, or reprinted and published with additions, shall, by the printer and printers thereof be delivered to the warehouse-keeper of the said Company of Stationers for the time being, at the hall of the said Company, before such publication made, for the use of the royal library, the libraries of the Universities of Oxford and Cambridge, the libraries of the four universities in Scotland, the library of Sion College in London, and the library commonly called the library belonging to the Faculty of Advocates at Edinburgh, respectively, which said warehouse-keeper is hereby required, within ten days after demand by the keepers of the respective libraries, or any person or persons by them or any of them authorised to demand the said copy, to deliver the same, for the use of the aforesaid libraries, and if any proprietor, bookseller, or printer, or the said warehouse-keeper of the said Company of Stationers, shall not observe the direction of this Act therein, that then he and they, so making default in not delivering the said printed copies as aforesaid, shall forfeit, besides the value of the said printed copies, the sum of five pounds for every copy not so delivered, as also the value of the said printed copy not so delivered, the same to be recovered by the Queen's Majesty, her heirs and successors, and by the chancellor, masters, and scholars of any of the said universities, and by the president and fellows of Sion College, and the said Faculty of Advocates at Edinburgh, with their full costs respectively

Provided always, and be it further enacted, that if any person or persons incur the penalties contained in this Act, in that part of Great Britain called Scotland, they shall be recoverable by any action before the Court of Session there

Provided, that nothing in this Act contained do extend, or shall be construed to extend, to prohibit the importation, vending, or selling of any books in Greek, Latin, or any other foreign language, printed beyond the seas, any thing in this Act contained to the contrary notwithstanding.

And be it further enacted by the authority aforesaid, that if any action or suit shall be commenced or brought against any person or persons whatsoever, for doing, or causing to be done, any thing in pursuance of this Act, the defendants in such action may plead the general issue, and give the special matter in evidence, and if upon such action a verdict be given for the defendant, or the plaintiff become nonsuited, or discontinue his action, then the defendant shall have and recover his full costs, for which he shall have the same remedy as a defendant in any case by law hath.

Provided, that nothing in this Act contained shall extend, or be construed to extend, either to prejudice or confirm any right that the said universities, or any of them, or any person or persons have, or claim to have, to the printing or reprinting any book or copy already printed, or hereafter to be printed.

Provided nevertheless, that all actions, suits, bills, indictments, or informations for any offence that shall be committed against this Act, shall be brought, sued, and commenced within three months next after such offence committed, or else the same shall be void and of none effect.

Provided always, that after the expiration of the said term of fourteen years, the sole right of printing or disposing of copies shall return to the authors thereof, if they are then living, for another term of fourteen years.

---

8 Geo II. c 13.

An Act for the Encouragement of the Arts of Designing, Engraving, and Etching Historical and other Prints, by vesting the Properties thereof in the Inventors and Engravers during the time therein mentioned

WHEREAS divers persons have, by their own genius, industry, pains, and expense, invented and engraved, or worked in mezzo-tinto, or chiaro oscuro, sets of historical and other prints, in hopes to have reaped the sole benefit of their labours and whereas printsellers and other persons have of late, without the consent of the inventors, designers, and proprietors of such prints, frequently taken the liberty of copying, engraving, and publishing, or causing to be copied, engraved, and published, base copies of such works, designs, and prints, to the very great prejudice and detriment of the inventors, designers, and proprietors thereof for remedy thereof, and for preventing such practices for the future, may it please your Majesty that it may be enacted, and be it enacted by the King's most Excellent Majesty, by and with the

advice and consent of the Lords Spiritual and Temporal, and
Commons, in this present Parliament assembled, and by the
authority of the same, that from and after the twenty-fourth day
of June which shall be in the year of our Lord one thousand
seven hundred and thirty-five, every person who shall invent and
design, engrave, etch, or work, in mezzotinto or chiaro oscuro, or
from his own works and invention shall caused to be designed and
engraved, etched, or worked, in mezzotinto or chiaro oscuro, any
historical or other print or prints, shall have the sole right and
liberty of printing and reprinting the same for the term of fourteen years, to commence from the day of the first publishing
thereof, which shall be truly engraved with the name of the proprietor on each plate, and printed on every such print or prints,
and that if any printseller or other person whatsoever, from and
after the said twenty-fourth day of June one thousand seven
hundred and thirty-five, within the time limited by this Act,
shall engrave, etch, or work as aforesaid, or in any other manner
copy and sell, or cause to be engraved, etched, or copied and sold,
in the whole or in part, by varying, adding to, or diminishing from
the main design, or shall print, reprint, or import for sale, or cause
to be printed, reprinted, or imported for sale, any such print or
prints, or any parts thereof, without the consent of the proprietor
or proprietors thereof first had and obtained in writing signed by
him or them respectively in the presence of two or more credible
witnesses, or, knowing the same to be so printed or reprinted
without the consent of the proprietor or proprietors, shall publish,
sell, or expose to sale, or otherwise or in any other manner dispose of, or cause to be published, sold, or exposed to sale, or
otherwise or in any other manner disposed of, any such print or
prints, without such consent first had and obtained as aforesaid,
then such offender or offenders shall forfeit the plate or plates
on which such print or prints are or shall be copied, and all
and every sheet or sheets (being part of or whereon such print or
prints are or shall be so copied or printed), to the proprietor or
proprietors of such original print or prints, who shall forthwith
destroy and damask the same, and further, that every such offender
or offenders shall forfeit five shillings for every print which shall
be found in his, her, or their custody, either printed or published,
and exposed to sale or otherwise disposed of, contrary to the true
intent and meaning of this Act, the one moiety thereof to the
King's most Excellent Majesty, his heirs and successors, and the
other moiety thereof to any person or persons that shall sue for
the same, to be recovered in any of His Majesty's Courts of
Record at Westminster, by action of debt, bill, plaint, or information, in which no wager of law, essoign, privilege, or protection,
or more than one imparlance, shall be allowed

II Provided nevertheless, that it shall and may be lawful for
any person or persons who shall hereafter purchase any plate or
plates for printing from the original proprietors thereof to print
and reprint from the said plates without incurring any of the
penalties in this Act mentioned

III. And be it further enacted by the authority aforesaid, that

if any action or suit shall be commenced or brought against any
person or persons whatsoever for doing or causing to be done anything in pursuance of this Act, the same shall be brought within
the space of three months after so doing, and the defendant and
defendants in such action or suit shall or may plead the general
issue, and give the special matter in evidence; and if upon such
action or suit a verdict shall be given for the defendant or defendants, or if the plaintiff or plaintiffs become nonsuited, or discontinue his, her, or their action or actions, then the defendant or
defendants shall have and recover full costs, for the recovery
whereof he shall have the same remedy as any other defendant or
defendants in any other case hath or have by law.

(margin: actions for anything done in pursuance of Act. General issue.)

IV. Provided always, and be it further enacted by the authority
aforesaid, that if any action or suit shall be commenced or brought
against any person or persons for any offence committed against
this Act, the same shall be brought within the space of three
months after the discovery of every such offence, and not afterwards, anything in this Act contained to the contrary notwithstanding.

(margin: Limitation of actions for offences against this Act.)

V. And whereas John Pine of London, engraver, doth propose
to engrave and publish a set of prints copied from several pieces
of tapestry in the House of Lords, and His Majesty's wardrobe,
and other drawings relating to the Spanish invasion in the year of
our Lord one thousand five hundred and eighty-eight: be it
further enacted by the authority aforesaid, that the said John
Pine shall be entitled to the benefit of this Act, to all intents and
purposes whatsoever, in the same manner as if the said John Pine
had been the inventor and designer of the said prints.

(margin: Clause relating to J Pine.)

VI And be it further enacted by the authority aforesaid, that
this Act shall be deemed, adjudged, and taken to be a public Act,
and be judicially taken notice of as such by all judges, justices,
and other persons, whatsoever, without specially pleading the
same.

(margin: Public Act.)

7 GEO. III. c. 38

*An Act to amend and render more effectual an Act made in the
Eighth Year of the Reign of King George the Second, for En-
couragement of the Arts of Designing, Engraving, and Etching
Historical and other Prints and for vesting in, and securing to
Jane Hogarth, widow, the Property in certain Prints*

WHEREAS an Act of Parliament passed in the eighth year of the
reign of his late Majesty King George the Second, intituled 'An
Act for the Encouragement of the Arts of Designing, Engraving,
and Etching Historical and other Prints, by vesting the properties
thereof in the Inventors and Engravers, during the time therein
mentioned,' has been found ineffectual for the purposes thereby
intended , be it enacted by the King's most excellent Majesty,

(margin: Preamble, reciting Act 8, Geo 2)

by and with the advice and consent of the Lords Spiritual and Temporal, and Commons, in this present Parliament assembled, and by the authority of the same, that from and after the first day of January, one thousand seven hundred and sixty-seven, all and every person and persons who shall invent or design, engrave, etch, or work in mezzotinto or chiaro oscuro, or from his own work, design, or invention, shall cause or procure to be designed, engraved, etched, or worked in mezzotinto or chiaro oscuro, any historical print or prints, or any print or prints of any portrait, conversation, landscape, or architecture, map, chart, or plan, or any other print or prints whatsoever, shall have, and are hereby declared to have, the benefit and protection of the said Act and this Act, under the restrictions and limitations hereinafter mentioned.

And be it further enacted by the authority aforesaid, that from and after the said first day of January, one thousand seven hundred and sixty-seven, all and every person and persons who shall engrave, etch, or work in mezzotinto or chiaro oscuro, or cause to be engraved, etched, or worked, any print, taken from any picture, drawing, model or sculpture, either ancient or modern, shall have, and are hereby declared to have, the benefit and protection of the said Act, and this Act, for the term hereinafter mentioned, in like manner as if such print had been graved or drawn from the original design of such graver, etcher, or draftsman, and if any person shall engrave, print, and publish, or import for sale, any copy of any such print, contrary to the true intent and meaning of this and the said former Act, every such person shall be liable to the penalties contained in the said Act, to be recovered as therein and hereinafter is mentioned

And whereas William Hogarth, late of the City of Westminster, painter and graver, did etch and engrave, and cause to be etched and engraved, several prints from his own invention and design, the property and sole right of vending all such prints being secured to him the said William Hogarth for the term of fourteen years from their first publication, by the said former Act of Parliament; which said property, by his last will, became vested in his widow and executrix : and whereas since the first publication of several of the said prints the term of fourteen years is expired and several base copies of the same have been since printed and published, whereby the sale of the originals has been considerably lessened, to the great detriment of the said widow and executrix and whereas since the publication of others of the said prints, the term of fourteen years is now near expiring, be it enacted by the authority aforesaid, that Jane Hogarth, widow and executrix of the said William Hogarth, shall have the sole right and liberty of printing and reprinting all the said prints, etchings, and engravings of the design and invention of the said William Hogarth, for and during the term of twenty years, to commence from the said first day of January, one thousand seven hundred and sixty-seven, and that all and every person and persons who shall at any time hereafter, before the expiration of the said term of twenty years, engrave, etch, or work in mezzotinto or chiaro oscuro, or otherwise copy, sell, or expose to sale, or cause or procure to be etched, engraved, or worked in mezzotinto or chiaro oscuro, any of the said works of the said William Hogarth, shall be liable to the penalties and forfeitures contained in this and the said former Act of Parliament; to be recovered in like manner as in and by this and the said former Act are given, directed, and appointed.

Provided nevertheless, that the proprietor or proprietors of such of the copies of the said William Hogarth's works, which have been copied and printed, and exposed to sale, after the expiration of the term of fourteen years from the time of their first publication by the said William Hogarth, and before the said first day of January, shall not be liable or subject to any of the penalties contained in this Act; anything herein before contained to the contrary thereof in anywise notwithstanding.

And be it further enacted by the authority aforesaid, that all and every the penalties and penalty inflicted by the said Act, and extended, and meant to be extended, to the several cases comprised in this Act, shall and may be sued for and recovered in like manner, and under the like restrictions and limitations, as in and by the said Act is declared and appointed; and the plaintiff or common informer in every such action (in case such plaintiff or common informer shall recover any of the penalties incurred by this or the said former Act) shall recover the same, together with his full costs of suit.

Provided also, that the party prosecuting shall commence his prosecution within the space of six calendar months after the offence committed.

And be it further enacted by the authority aforesaid, that the sole right and liberty of printing and reprinting intended to be secured and protected by the said former Act and this Act, shall be extended, continued, and be vested in the respective proprietors, for the space of twenty-eight years, to commence from the day of the first publishing of any of the works respectively hereinbefore and in the said former Act mentioned.

And be it further enacted by the authority aforesaid, that if any action or suit shall be commenced or brought against any person or persons whatsoever, for doing, or causing to be done, any thing in pursuance of this Act, the same shall be brought within the space of six calendar months after the fact committed; and the defendant or defendants in any such action or suit shall or may plead the general issue, and give the special matter in evidence, and if, upon such action or suit, a verdict shall be given for the defendant or defendants, or if the plaintiff or plaintiffs become nonsuited, or discontinue his, her, or their action or actions, then the defendant or defendants shall have and recover full costs, for the recovery whereof he shall have the same remedy as any other defendant or defendants, in any other case, hath or have by law.

15 Gᴇo. III. c. 53.

An Act for enabling the Two Universities in England, the Four Universities in Scotland, and the several Colleges of Eton, Westminster, and Winchester, to hold in Perpetuity their Copy Right in Books, given or bequeathed to the said Universities and Colleges for the Advancement of useful Learning and other Purposes of Education, and for amending so much of an Act of the Eighth year of the Reign of Queen Anne, as relates to the Delivery of Books to the Warehouse Keeper of the Stationers' Company, for the Use of the several Libraries therein mentioned.

Preamble

Wʜᴇʀᴇᴀs authors have heretofore bequeathed or given, and may hereafter bequeath or give, the copies of books composed by them, to or in trust for one of the two universities in that part of Great Britain called England, or to or in trust for some of the colleges or houses of learning within the same, or to or in trust for the four universities in Scotland, or to or in trust for the several colleges of Eaton, Westminster, and Winchester, and in and by their several wills or other instruments of donation, have directed or may direct, that the profits arising from the printing and reprinting such books shall be applied or appropriated as a fund for the advancement of learning, and other beneficial purposes of education within the said universities and colleges aforesaid: and whereas such useful purposes will frequently be frustrated, unless the sole printing and reprinting of such books, the copies of which have been or shall be so bequeathed or given as aforesaid, be preserved and secured to the said universities, colleges, and houses of learning respectively in perpetuity; may it therefore please your Majesty that it may be enacted, and be it enacted by the King's most excellent Majesty, by and with the advice and consent of the Lords Spiritual and Temporal, and Commons, in this present Parliament assembled, and by the authority of the same, that the said universities and colleges respectively shall, at their respective presses, have, for ever, the sole liberty of printing and reprinting all such books as shall at any time heretofore have been, or (having not been heretofore published or assigned) shall at any time hereafter be bequeathed, or otherwise given by the author or authors of the same respectively, or the representatives of such author or authors, to or in trust for the said universities, or to or in trust for any college or house of learning within the same, or to or in trust for the said four universities in Scotland, or to or in trust for the said colleges of Eaton, Westminster, and Winchester, or any of them, for the purposes aforesaid, unless the same shall have been bequeathed or given, or shall hereafter be bequeathed or given, for any term of years, or other limited term, any law or usage to the contrary hereof in any wise notwithstanding

And it is hereby further enacted, that if any bookseller, printer, or other person whatsoever, from and after the twenty-fourth day of June, one thousand seven hundred and seventy-five, shall print,

Universities, &c in England and Scotland to have, for ever, the sole right of printing, &c such books as have been, or shall be bequeathed to them,

unless the same have been, or shall be, given for a limited time.
After June 24, 1775, persons printing

reprint, or import, or cause to be printed, reprinted, or imported,
any such book or books; or, knowing the same to be so printed or
reprinted, shall sell, publish, or expose to sale, or cause to be
sold, published, or exposed to sale, any such book or books;
then such offender or offenders shall forfeit such book or books,
and all and every sheet or sheets, being part of such book or
books, to the university, college, or house of learning respectively, to whom the copy of such book or books shall have been
bequeathed or given as aforesaid, who shall forthwith damask and
make waste paper of them; and further, that every such offender
or offenders shall forfeit one penny for every sheet which shall be
found in his, her, or their custody, either printed or printing, published or exposed to sale, contrary to the true intent and meaning
of this Act; the one moiety thereof to the King's most excellent
Majesty, his heirs and successors, and the other moiety thereof to
any person or persons who shall sue for the same; to be recovered
in any of his Majesty's Courts of Record at Westminster, or in the
Court of Session in Scotland, by action of debt, bill, plaint, or information, in which no wager of law, essoin, privilege, or protection, or more than one imparlance, shall be allowed.

Provided nevertheless, that nothing in this Act shall extend to
grant any exclusive right otherwise than so long as the books or
copies belonging to the said universities or colleges are printed
only at their own printing presses within the said universities or
colleges respectively, and for their sole benefit and advantage,
and that if any university or college shall delegate, grant, lease,
or sell their copy rights, or exclusive rights of printing the books
hereby granted, or any part thereof, or shall allow, permit, or
authorise any person or persons, or bodies corporate, to print or
reprint the same, that then the privileges hereby granted are to
become void and of no effect, in the same manner as if this Act
had not been made, but the said universities and colleges, as
aforesaid, shall nevertheless have a right to sell such copies so
bequeathed or given as aforesaid, in like manner as any author or
authors now may do under the provisions of the statute of the
eighth year of Her Majesty Queen Anne

And whereas many persons may through ignorance offend
against this Act, unless some provision be made whereby the
property of every such book as is intended by this Act to be
secured to the said universities, colleges, and houses of learning
within the same, and to the said Universities in Scotland, and to
the respective colleges of Eaton, Westminster, and Winchester,
may be ascertained and known, be it therefore enacted by the
authority aforesaid, that nothing in this Act contained shall be
construed to extend to subject any bookseller, printer, or other
person whatsoever, to the forfeitures or penalties herein mentioned, for or by reason of the printing or reprinting, importing or
exposing to sale, any book or books, unless the title to the copy of
such book or books, which has or have been already bequeathed
or given to any of the said universities or colleges aforesaid, be
entered in the register book of the Company of Stationers kept for
that purpose, in such manner as hath been usual, on or before the

twenty-fourth day of June, one thousand seven hundred and
seventy-five; and of all and every such book or books as may or
shall hereafter be bequeathed or given as aforesaid, be entered in
such register within the space of two months after any such
bequest or gift shall have come to the knowledge of the vice
chancellors of the said universities, or heads of houses and colleges
of learning, or of the principal of any of the said four universities
respectively, for every of which entries so to be made as aforesaid, the sum of sixpence shall be paid, and no more; which said
register book shall and may, at all seasonable and convenient
times, be referred to and inspected by any bookseller, printer, or
other person, without any fee or reward; and the clerk of the said
Company of Stationers shall, when and as often as thereunto
required, give a certificate under his hand of such entry or entries,
and for every such certificate may take a fee not exceeding
sixpence.

And be it further enacted, that if the clerk of the said Company
of Stationers for the time being shall refuse or neglect to register
or make such entry or entries, or to give such certificate, being
thereunto required by the agent of either of the said universities
or colleges aforesaid, lawfully authorised for that purpose, then
either of the said universities or colleges aforesaid, being the pro-

prietor of such copy right or copy rights as aforesaid (notice being
first given of such refusal by an advertisement in the Gazette),
shall have the like benefit as if such entry or entries, certificate or
certificates, had been duly made and given; and the clerk so
refusing shall, for every such offence, forfeit twenty pounds to the
proprietor or proprietors of every such copy right; to be recovered
in any of His Majesty's Courts of Record at Westminster, or in the
Court of Session in Scotland, by action of debt, bill, plaint, or
information, in which no wager of law, essoin, privilege, protection,
or more than one imparlance, shall be allowed.

And whereas in and by an Act of Parliament, made in the
eighth year of the reign of her late majesty Queen Anne, intituled, 'An Act for the Encouragement of Learning, by vesting
the Copies of printed Books in the Authors or Purchasers of such
Copies during the Times therein mentioned,' it is enacted, that
nine copies of each book or books, upon the best paper, that, from
and after the tenth day of April, one thousand seven hundred and
ten, should be printed and published, as therein mentioned, or
reprinted and published with additions, shall, by the printer and
printers thereof, be delivered to the warehouse keeper of the said
Company of Stationers for the time being, at the hall of the said
company, before such publication made, for the use of the Royal
Library, the libraries of the universities of Oxford and Cambridge,
the libraries of the four universities in Scotland, the library of
Sion College in London, and the library commonly called the
library belonging to the Faculty of Advocates in Edinburgh, respectively, which such warehouse keeper was thereby required,
within ten days after demand by the keepers of the respective
libraries, or any person or persons by them, or any of them, authorised to demand the said copy, to deliver the same for the use of

the aforesaid libraries; and if any proprietor, bookseller, or printer, or the said warehouse keeper of the said Company of Stationers, should not observe the direction of the said Act therein, that then he and they so making default, in not delivering the said printed copies as aforesaid, should forfeit as therein mentioned: and whereas the said provision has not proved effectual, but the same hath been eluded by the entry only of the title to a single volume, or of some part of such book or books so printed and published, or reprinted and republished, as aforesaid; be it enacted by the authority aforesaid, that no person or persons whatsoever shall be subject to the penalties in the said Act mentioned, for or by reason of the printing or reprinting, importing or exposing to sale, any book or books, without the consent mentioned in the said Act, unless the title to the copy of the whole of such book, and every volume thereof, be entered, in manner directed by the said Act, in the register book of the Company of Stationers, and unless nine such copies of the whole of such book or books, and every volume thereof printed and published, or reprinted or republished, as therein mentioned, shall be actually delivered to the warehouse keeper of the said company, as therein directed, for the several uses of the several libraries in the said Act mentioned.

No person subject to penalties in the said Act for printing, &c. any book, unless the title to the copy of the whole be entered, &c

And be it further enacted by the authority aforesaid, that if any action or suit shall be commenced or brought against any person or persons whatsoever, for doing, or causing to be done, any thing in pursuance of this Act, the defendants in such action may plead the general issue, and give the special matter in evidence; and if upon such action a verdict, or if the same shall be brought in the court of session in Scotland, a judgement, be given for the defendant, or the plaintiff become nonsuited, and discontinue his action, then the defendant shall have and recover his full costs, for which he shall have the same remedy as a defendant in any case by law hath.

Limitation of actions.

General issue.

And be it further enacted by the authority aforesaid, that this Act shall be adjudged, deemed, and taken to be a public Act, and shall be judicially taken notice of as such, by all judges, justices, and other persons whatsoever, without specially pleading the same.

Public Act

---

17 GEO III. c. 57

An Act for more effectually securing the Property of Prints to Inventors and Engravers, by enabling them to sue for and recover Penalties in certain Cases

WHEREAS an Act of Parliament passed in the eighth year of the reign of his late Majesty King George the Second, intituled 'An Act for the Encouragement of the Arts of Designing, Engraving, and Etching Historical and other Prints, by vesting the properties thereof in the Inventors and Engravers, during the time therein

Recital of Acts 8 Geo 2, and 7 Geo 3.

mentioned·' and whereas by an Act of Parliament passed in the seventh year of the reign of his present Majesty, for amending and rendering more effectual the aforesaid Act, and for other purposes therein mentioned, it was (among other things) enacted, that from and after the first day of January one thousand seven hundred and sixty-seven, all and every person or persons who should engrave, etch, or work in mezzotinto or chiaro oscuro, or cause to be engraved, etched, or worked, any print taken from any picture, drawing, model, or sculpture, either ancient or modern, should have, and were thereby declared to have, the benefit and protection of the said former Act and that Act, for the term thereinafter mentioned, in like manner as if such print had been graved or drawn from the original design of such graver, etcher, or draughtsman and whereas the said Acts have not effectually answered the purposes for which they were intended, and it is necessary, for the encouragement of artists, and for securing to them the property of and in their works, and for the advancement and improvement of the aforesaid arts, that such further provisions should be made as are hereinafter mentioned and contained· may it therefore please your Majesty that it may be enacted; and be it enacted by the King's most excellent Majesty, by and with the advice and consent of the Lords Spiritual and Temporal, and Commons, in this present Parliament assembled, and by the authority of the same, that from and after the twenty-fourth day of June one thousand seven hundred and seventy-seven, if any engraver, etcher, printseller, or other person, shall, within the time limited by the aforesaid Acts, or either of them, engrave, etch, or work, or cause or procure to be engraved, etched, or worked, in mezzotinto or chiaro oscuro, or otherwise, or in any other manner copy in the whole or in part, by varying, adding to, or diminishing from the main design, or shall print, reprint, or import for sale, or cause or procure to be printed, reprinted, or imported for sale, or shall publish, sell, or otherwise dispose of, or cause or procure to be published, sold, or otherwise disposed of, any copy or copies of any historical print or prints, or any print or prints of any portrait, conversation, landscape, or architecture, map, chart, or plan, or any other print or prints whatsoever, which hath or have been, or shall be engraved, etched, drawn, or designed, in any part of Great Britain, without the express consent of the proprietor or proprietors thereof first had and obtained in writing, signed by him, her, or them respectively, with his, her, or their own hand or hands, in the presence of and attested by two or more credible witnesses, then every such proprietor or proprietors shall and may, by and in a special action upon the case, to be brought against the person or persons so offending, recover such damages as a jury on the trial of such action, or on the execution of a writ of enquiry thereon, shall give or assess, together with double costs of suit

After June 24, 1777, if any engraver, &c. shall, within the time limited by the aforesaid Acts, engrave or etch, &c. any print, without the consent of the proprietor, he shall be liable to damages, and double costs

38 GEO. III. c. 71.

An Act for encouraging the Art of making new Models and Casts of Busts, and other Things therein mentioned.

WHEREAS divers persons have, by their own genius, industry, pains, and expense, improved and brought the art of making new models and casts of busts, and of statues of human figures, and of animals, to great perfection, in hopes to have reaped the sole benefit of their labours; but that divers persons have (without the consent of the proprietors thereof) copied and made moulds from the said models and casts, and sold base copies and casts of such new models and casts, to the great prejudice and detriment of the original proprietors, and to the discouragement of the art of making such new models and casts as aforesaid for remedy whereof, and for preventing such practices for the future, may it please your Majesty that it may be enacted , and be it enacted by the King's most excellent Majesty, by and with the advice and consent of the Lords Spiritual and Temporal, and Commons, in this present Parliament assembled, and by the authority of the same, that from and after the passing of this Act, every person who shall make or cause to be made any new model, or copy or cast made from such new model, of any bust, or any part of the human figure, or any statue of the human figure, or the head of any animal, or any part of any animal, or the statue of any animal, or shall make or cause to be made any new model, copy, or cast from such new model, in alto or basso relievo, or any work in which the representation of any human figure or figures, or the representation of any animal or animals shall be introduced, or shall make or cause to be made any new cast from nature of any part or parts of the human figure, or of any part or parts of any animal, shall have the sole right and property in every such new model, copy, or cast, and also in every such new model, copy, or cast in alto or basso relievo, or any work as aforesaid, and also in every such new cast from nature as aforesaid, for and during the term of fourteen years from the time of first publishing the same provided always that every person who shall make or cause to be made any such new model, copy, or cast, or any such new model, copy, or cast in alto or basso relievo, or any work as aforesaid, or any new cast from nature as aforesaid, shall cause his or her name to be put thereon, with the date of the publication, before the same shall be published and exposed to sale

II And be it further enacted, that if any person shall, within the said term of fourteen years, make or cause to be made any copy or cast of any such new model, copy, or cast, or any such model, copy, or cast in alto or basso relievo, or any such work as aforesaid, or any such new cast from nature as aforesaid, either by adding to or diminishing from any such new model, copy, or cast, or adding to or diminishing from any such new model, copy, or cast in alto or basso relievo, or any such work as aforesaid, or

Marginal notes: Preamble | The sole right and property of making models or casts shall be vested in the original proprietor. | Persons making copies of any model or cast, without the consent of the proprietor, may be prosecuted

adding to or diminishing from any such new cast from nature, or shall cause or procure the same to be done, or shall import any copy or cast of such new model, copy, or cast, or copy or cast of such new model, copy, or cast in alto or basso relievo, or any such work as aforesaid, or any copy or cast of any such new cast from nature as aforesaid, for sale, or shall sell or otherwise dispose of, or cause or procure to be sold or exposed to sale, or otherwise disposed of, any copy or cast of any such new model, copy, or cast, or any copy or cast of such new model, copy, or cast in alto or basso relievo, or any such work as aforesaid, or any copy or cast of any such new cast from nature as aforesaid, without the express consent of the proprietor or proprietors thereof first had and obtained, in writing signed by him, her, or them respectively, with his, her, or their hand or hands, in the presence of and attested by two or more credible witnesses, then and in all or any of the cases aforesaid, every proprietor or proprietors of any such original model, copy, or cast, and every proprietor or proprietors of any such original model, or copy or cast in alto or basso relievo, or any such work as aforesaid, or the proprietor or proprietors of any such new cast from nature as aforesaid respectively, shall and may, by and in a special action upon the case, to be brought against the person or persons so offending, recover such damages as a jury on the trial of such action, or on the execution of a writ of enquiry thereon, shall give or assess, together with full costs of suit.

Except such persons who shall purchase the same of the original proprietor.

III. Provided nevertheless, that no person who shall hereafter purchase the right, either in any such model, copy, or cast, or in any such model, copy, or cast in alto or basso relievo, or any such work as aforesaid, or any such new cast from nature, of the original proprietor or proprietors thereof, shall be subject to any action for vending or selling any cast or copy from the same, any thing contained in this Act to the contrary hereof notwithstanding

Limitation of actions.

IV Provided also, that all actions to be brought as aforesaid, against any person or persons for any offence committed against this Act, shall be commenced within six calendar months next after the discovery of every such offence, and not afterwards.

---

41 GEO. III. c. 107.

An Act for the further Encouragement of Learning, in the United Kingdom of Great Britain and Ireland, by securing the Copies and Copyright of printed Books, to the Authors of such Books, or their Assigns, for the time herein mentioned.

Preamble

WHEREAS it is expedient that further protection should be afforded to the authors of books and the purchasers of the copies and copyright of the same, in the United Kingdom of Great Bri-

tain and Ireland; may it therefore please your Majesty that it may
be enacted, and be it enacted by the King's most excellent Majesty, by and with the advice and consent of the Lords Spiritual
and Temporal, and Commons, in this present Parliament assembled, and by the authority of the same, that the author of any book
or books already composed, and not printed or published, and the
author of any book or books which shall hereafter be composed,
and the assignee or assigns of such authors respectively, shall have
the sole liberty of printing and reprinting such book and books,
for the term of fourteen years, to commence from the day of first
publishing the same, and no longer; and that if any other bookseller, printer, or other person whosoever, in any part of the said
United Kingdom, or in any part of the British dominions in Europe,
shall, from and after the passing of this Act, print, reprint, or
import, or shall cause to be printed, reprinted, or imported, any
such book or books, without the consent of the proprietor or proprietors of the copyright of and in such book or books first had
and obtained in writing, signed in the presence of two or more
credible witnesses, or, knowing the same to be so printed, reprinted, or imported, without such consent of such proprietor or
proprietors, shall sell, publish, or expose to sale, or cause to be
sold, published, or exposed to sale, or shall have in his or their
possession for sale, any such book or books, without such consent
first had and obtained as aforesaid, then such offender or offenders
shall be liable to a special action on the case, at the suit of the
proprietor or proprietors of the copyright of such book or books so
unlawfully printed, reprinted, or imported, or published or exposed
to sale, or being in the possession of such offender or offenders for
sale as aforesaid, contrary to the true intent and meaning of this
Act; and every such proprietor and proprietors shall and may, by
and in such special action upon the case to be so brought against
such offender or offenders in any Court of Record in that part of
the said United Kingdom, or of the British dominions in Europe,
in which the offence shall be committed, recover such damages as
the jury on the trial of such action, or on the execution of a writ
of enquiry thereon, shall give or assess, together with double costs
of suit, in which action no wager of law, essoign, privilege, or
protection, nor more than one imparlance, shall be allowed, and
all and every such offender or offenders shall also forfeit such book
or books, and all and every sheet and sheets being part of such
book or books, and shall deliver the same to the proprietor or proprietors of the copyright of such book or books, upon order of any
Court of Record in which any action or suit, in law or equity,
shall be commenced or prosecuted by such proprietor or proprietors, to be made on motion or petition to the said court, and the
said proprietor or proprietors shall forthwith damask or make
waste paper of the said book or books, and sheet or sheets respectively, and all and every such offender or offenders shall also forfeit the sum of threepence for every sheet which shall be found in
his or their custody, either printed or printing, or published or
exposed to sale, contrary to the true intent and meaning of this
Act, the one moiety thereof to the King's most excellent Majesty,

Authors of books already composed, and not printed or published, and of books to be hereafter composed, and their assigns, shall have the sole right of printing them for 14 years: book-sellers, &c. in any part of the United Kingdom, or British European dominions, who shall print, reprint, or import, &c. any such book, without consent of the proprietor, shall be liable to an action for damages, and shall also forfeit the books to the proprietor, and 3d per sheet, half to the king, and half to the informer.

his heirs and successors, and the other moiety thereof to any person or persons who shall sue for the same in any such Court of Record, by action of debt, bill, plaint, or information, in which no wager of law, essoign, privilege, or protection, nor more than one imparlance, shall be allowed: provided always, that after the expiration of the said term of fourteen years, the right of printing or disposing of copies shall return to the authors thereof, if they are then living, for another term of fourteen years.

II. Provided also, and be it further enacted, that nothing in this Act contained shall extend, or be construed to extend, to any book or books heretofore composed, and printed or published in any part of the said United Kingdom, nor to exempt or indemnify any person or persons whomsoever, from or against any penalties or actions, to which he, she, or they shall or may have become, or shall or may hereafter be liable for on account of the unlawfully printing, reprinting, or importing such book or books, or the selling, publishing, or exposing the same to sale, or the having the same in his or their possession for sale, contrary to the laws and statutes in force respecting the same, at the time of the passing an Act in the session of Parliament of the thirty-ninth and fortieth years of the reign of his present Majesty, intituled 'An Act for the Union of Great Britain and Ireland.'

III. And whereas authors have heretofore bequeathed, given, or assigned, and may hereafter bequeath, give, or assign, the copies or copyrights of and in books composed by them, to or in trust for the college of the Holy Trinity of Dublin, and, in and by their several wills or other instruments, have directed or may direct, that the profits arising from the printing or reprinting such books shall be applied or appropriated as a fund for the advancement of learning, and other beneficial purposes of education, within the college aforesaid: and whereas such useful purposes will frequently be frustrated, unless the sole right of printing and reprinting of such books, the copies of which shall have been or shall be so bequeathed, given, or assigned as aforesaid, be preserved and secured to the said college in perpetuity, be it therefore further enacted, that the said college shall, at their own printing press, within the said college, have for ever the sole liberty of printing and reprinting all such books as shall at any time heretofore have been, or (not having been heretofore published or assigned) shall at any time hereafter be bequeathed, or otherwise given or assigned by the author or authors of the same respectively, or the representatives of such author or authors, to or in trust for the said college for the purposes aforesaid, unless the same shall have been bequeathed, given, or assigned, or shall hereafter be bequeathed, given, or assigned for any term of years, or any other limited term, any law or usage to the contrary thereof in anywise notwithstanding; and that if any printer, bookseller, or other person whomsoever, shall, from and after the passing of this Act, unlawfully print, reprint, or import, or cause to be printed, reprinted, or imported, or, knowing the same to be so unlawfully printed, reprinted, or imported, shall sell, publish, or expose to sale, or cause to be sold, published, or exposed to sale, or have in his or their possession for sale, any such lastmentioned book or books, such offender and offenders shall be subject and liable to the like actions, penalties, and forfeitures, as are hereinbefore mentioned and contained with respect to offenders against the copyrights of authors and their assigns; provided nevertheless, that nothing in this Act shall extend to grant any exclusive right to the said college of the Holy Trinity of Dublin, otherwise than so long as the books or copies belonging to the said college are and shall be printed only at the printing press of the said college within the said college, and for the sole benefit and advantage of the said college; and that if the said college shall delegate, grant, lease, or sell the copyrights or exclusive rights of printing the books hereby granted, or any part thereof, or shall allow, permit, or authorise any person or persons, or bodies corporate, to print or reprint the same, then the privilege hereby granted shall become void and of no effect, in the same manner as if this Act had not been made; but the said college shall nevertheless have a right to sell such copies so bequeathed or given as aforesaid, in like manner as any author or authors can or may lawfully do under the provisions of this Act, or any other Act now in force.

To extend only to books printed at the College press.

But the College may sell their copyrights.

IV Provided also, and be it further enacted, that no bookseller, printer, or other person whomsoever, shall be liable to the said penalty of threepence per sheet, for or by reason of the printing, reprinting, importing, or selling of any such book or books, or the having the same in his or their custody for sale, without the consent of the proprietor or proprietors of the copyright thereof as aforesaid, unless before the time of the publication of such book or books by the proprietor or proprietors thereof (other than the said college) the right and title of such proprietor or proprietors shall be duly entered in the register book of the Company of Stationers in London, in such manner as hath been usually heretofore done by the proprietors of copies and copyrights in Great Britain, nor if the consent of such proprietor or proprietors for the printing, reprinting, importing, or selling such book or books, shall be in like manner entered; nor unless the right and title of the said college to the copyright of such book or books as has or have been already bequeathed, given, or assigned to the said college, be entered in the said register book before the twenty-ninth day of September, one thousand eight hundred and one, and of all and every such book or books as may or shall hereafter be bequeathed, given. or assigned as aforesaid, be entered in the said register book within the space of two months after any such bequest, gift, or assignment shall have come to the knowledge of the provost of the said college, for every of which several entries sixpence shall be paid, and no more; which said register book shall at all times be kept at the hall of the said company, and shall and may at all seasonable and convenient times be resorted to and inspected by any bookseller, printer, or other person, for the purposes before mentioned, without any fee or reward, and the clerk of the said Company of Stationers shall, when and as often as thereunto required, give a certificate under his hand of such entry or entries,

Booksellers, &c. shall not be liable to the penalty of 3d. per sheet, unless the title to the copyright be entered by the proprietor, &c at Stationers Hall, London, nor if the consent of the proprietor be so entered

Clerk of the Company shall give certificates

of entries, and make a half-yearly list of the books so entered for the use of Trinity College.

and for every such certificate may take a fee not exceeding sixpence, and the said clerk shall also, without fee or reward, within fifteen days next after the thirty-first day of December, and the thirtieth day of June in each and every year, make, or cause to be made, for the use of the said college, a list of the titles of all such books, the copyright to which shall have been so entered in the course of the half-year immediately preceding the said thirty-first day of December and the thirtieth day of June respectively, and shall upon demand deliver the said lists, or cause the same to be delivered, to any person or persons duly authorised to receive the same for and on behalf of the said college.

If the clerk refuses to make entries, &c parties may give notice in the London Gazette, and the clerk shall forfeit 20l

V. Provided also, and be it further enacted, that if the clerk of the said Company of Stationers for the time being shall refuse or neglect to register or make such entry or entries, or to give such certificate or certificates, being thereunto respectively required by the author or authors, proprietor or proprietors of such copies or copyrights, or by the person or persons to whom such consent shall be given, or by some person on his or their behalf, in the presence of two or more credible witnesses, then such party or parties so refused, notice being first duly given by advertisement in the London Gazette, shall have the like benefit as if such entry or entries, certificate or certificates, had been duly made and given; and the clerk so refusing shall, for any such offence, forfeit to the author or proprietor of such copy or copies, or to the person or persons to whom such consent shall be given, the sum of twenty pounds; or if the said clerk shall refuse or neglect to make the list aforesaid, or to deliver the same to any person duly authorised to demand the same on behalf of the said college, the said clerk shall also forfeit to the said college the like sum of twenty pounds, which said respective penalties shall and may be recovered in any of his Majesty's Courts of Record in the said United Kingdom, by action of debt, bill, plaint, or information, in which no wager of law, essoign, privilege, or protection, nor more than one imparlance, shall be allowed

Two additional copies of books entered at Stationers Hall, shall be delivered there for the use of the libraries of Trinity College, and the King's Inns, Dublin

VI. Provided also, and be it further enacted, that from and after the passing of this Act, in addition to the nine copies now required by law to be delivered to the warehouse-keeper of the said Company of Stationers, of each and every book and books which shall be entered in the register book of the said company, one other copy shall be in like manner delivered for the use of the library of the said college of the Holy Trinity of Dublin, and also one other copy for the use of the library of the Society of the King's Inns, Dublin, by the printer or printers of all and every such book and books as shall hereafter be printed and published, and the title to the copyright whereof shall be entered in the said register book of the said company, and that the said college and the said society shall have the like remedies for enforcing the delivery of the said copies, and that all proprietors, booksellers, and printers, and the warehouse-keeper of the said company, shall be liable to the like penalties for making default in delivering the said copies for the use of the said college and the said society, as are now in force with respect to the delivering or making default in delivering the nine copies now required by law to be delivered in manner aforesaid

VII And be it further enacted, that, from and after the passing of this Act, it shall not be lawful for any person or persons whomsoever to import or bring into any part of the said United Kingdom of Great Britain and Ireland for sale, any printed book or books, first composed, written, or printed, and published in any part of the said United Kingdom, and reprinted in any other country or place whatsoever, and if any person or persons shall import or bring, or cause to be imported or brought for sale, any such printed book or books into any part of the said United Kingdom, contrary to the true intent and meaning of this Act, or shall knowingly sell, publish, or expose to sale, or have in his or their possession for sale, any such book or books, then every such book or books shall be forfeited, and shall and may be seized by any officer or officers of customs or excise, and the same shall be forthwith made waste paper; and all and every person and persons so offending, being duly convicted thereof, shall also, for every such offence, forfeit the sum of ten pounds, and double the value of each and every copy of such book or books which he, she, or they shall so import or bring, or cause to be imported or brought into any part of the said United Kingdom, or shall knowingly sell, publish, or expose to sale, or shall cause to be sold, published, or exposed to sale, or shall have in his or their possession for sale, contrary to the true intent and meaning of this Act; and the commissioners of customs in England, Scotland, and Ireland respectively (in case the same shall be seized by any officer or officers of customs), and the commissioners of excise in England, Scotland, and Ireland respectively (in case the same shall be seized by any officer or officers of excise), shall also reward the officer or officers who shall seize any books which shall be so made waste paper of, with such sum or sums of money as they the said respective commissioners shall think fit, not exceeding the value of such books; such reward respectively to be paid by the said respective commissioners, out of any money in their hands respectively arising from the duties of customs and excise. provided, that no person or persons shall be liable to any of the last-mentioned penalties or forfeitures, for or by reason or means of the importation of any book or books which has not been printed or reprinted in some part of the said United Kingdom, within twenty years next before the same shall be imported, or of any book or books reprinted abroad, and inserted among other books or tracts to be sold therewith in any collection, where the greatest part of such collection shall have been first composed or written abroad

VIII. And be it further enacted, that if any action or suit shall be commenced or brought against any person or persons whomsoever, for doing or causing to be done any thing in pursuance of this Act, the defendants in such action may plead the general issue, and give the special matter in evidence, and if upon such action a verdict shall be given for the defendant, or the plaintiff become nonsuited, or discontinue his action, then the defendant

No person shall import into any part of the United Kingdom, for sale, any book first composed, &c. within the United Kingdom and reprinted elsewhere. Penalty on importing, selling, or keeping for sale, any such books, forfeiture thereof, and also 10l and double the value. Books may be seized by officers of Customs or Excise, who shall be rewarded

Not to extend to books not having been printed in the United Kingdom for 20 years

General issue

Limitation of
actions under
this Act six
months.

shall have and recover his full costs, for which he shall have the
same remedy as a defendant in any case by law hath, and that all
actions, suits, bills, indictments, or informations, for any offence
that shall be committed against this Act, shall be brought, sued,
and commenced within six months next after such offence committed, or else the same shall be void and of none effect.

---

54 Geo. III. c. 156.

*An Act to amend the several Acts for the Encouragement of Learn-
ing, by securing the Copies and Copyright of printed Books to the
Authors of such Books or their Assigns.*

8 Anne, c 19.

WHEREAS by an Act made in the eighth year of the reign of
her late Majesty Queen Anne, intituled 'An Act for the Encouragement of Learning, by vesting the Copies of printed Books in
the Authors or Purchasers of such Copies, during the Times
therein mentioned,' it was among other things provided and enacted, that nine copies of each book or books, upon the best paper,
that from and after the tenth day of April one thousand seven
hundred and ten should be printed and published as in the said
Act mentioned, or reprinted and published with additions, should,
by the printer and printers thereof, be delivered to the warehousekeeper of the Company of Stationers for the time being, at the hall
of the said company, before such publication made, for the use of
the Royal library, the libraries of the Universities of Oxford and
Cambridge, the libraries of the four Universities in Scotland, the
library of Sion College in London, and the library of the Faculty
of Advocates at Edinburgh, which said warehousekeeper is by the
said Act required to deliver such copies for the use of the said
libraries, and that if any proprietor, bookseller, or printer, or the
said warehousekeeper, should not observe the directions of the said
Act therein, that then he or they so making default in not delivering the said printed copies should forfeit, besides the value of
the said printed copies, the sum of five pounds for every copy not
so delivered. and whereas by an Act made in the forty-first year

41 G. 3, c. 107.

of the reign of his present Majesty, intituled 'An Act for the
further Encouragement of Learning in the United Kingdom of
Great Britain and Ireland, by securing the Copies and Copyright
of printed Books to the Authors of such Books, or their Assigns,
for the time herein mentioned,' it is amongst other things provided and enacted, that in addition to the nine copies required by
law to be delivered to the warehousekeeper of the said Company
of Stationers of each and every book and books which shall be
entered in the register books of the said company, two other
copies shall in like manner be delivered for the use of the library
of the College of the Holy Trinity, and the library of the Society
of the King's Inns in Dublin, by the printer and printers of all
and every such book and books as should thereafter be printed

and published, and the title of the copyright whereof should be entered in the said register book of the said company; and whereas it is expedient that copies of books hereafter printed or published should be delivered to the libra   is hereinafter mentioned, with the modifications that shall be provided by this Act: may it therefore please your Majesty that it may be enacted, and be it enacted by the King's most excellent Majesty, by and with the advice and consent of the Lords Spiritual and Temporal, and Commons, in this present Parliament assembled, and by the authority of the same, that so much of the said several recited Acts of the eighth year of Queen Anne and of the forty-first year of his present Majesty as requires that any copy or copies of any book or books which shall be printed or published, or reprinted and published with additions, shall be delivered by the printer or printers thereof to the warehousekeeper of the said Company of Stationers, for the use of any of the libraries in the said Act mentioned, and as requires the delivery of the said copies by the said warehousekeeper for the use of the said libraries, and as imposes any penalty on such printer or warehousekeeper for not delivering the said copies, shall be and the same is hereby repealed.

II And be it further enacted, that eleven printed copies of the whole of every book and of every volume thereof, upon the paper upon which the largest number or impression of such book shall be printed for sale, together with all maps and prints belonging thereto, which, from and after the passing of this Act, shall be printed and published, on demand thereof being made in writing to or left at the place of abode of the publisher or publishers thereof, at any time within twelve months next after the publication thereof, under the hand of the warehousekeeper of the Company of Stationers, or the librarian or other person thereto authorised by the persons, or body politic and corporate, proprietors or managers of the libraries following ; *videlicet*, the British Museum, Sion College, the Bodleian library at Oxford, the public library at Cambridge, the library of the Faculty of Advocates at Edinburgh, the libraries of the four Universities of Scotland, Trinity College library, and the King's Inns library at Dublin, or so many of such eleven copies as shall be respectively demanded on behalf of such libraries respectively, shall be delivered by the publisher or publishers thereof respectively, within one month after demand made thereof in writing as aforesaid, to the warehousekeeper of the said Company of Stationers for the time being; which copies the said warehousekeeper shall and he is hereby required to receive at the hall of the said company, for the use of the library for which such demand shall be made within such twelve months as aforesaid, and the said warehousekeeper is hereby required, within one month after any such book or volume shall be so delivered to him as aforesaid, to deliver the same for the use of such library, and if any publisher, or the warehousekeeper of the said Company of Stationers, shall not observe the directions of this Act therein, that then he and they so making default in not delivering or receiving the said eleven printed copies as aforesaid shall forfeit, besides the value of the said printed copies, the sum of five pounds for each copy not so delivered or received, together with the full costs of suit, the same to be recovered by the person or persons, or body politic or corporate, proprietors or managers of the library for the use whereof such copy or copies ought to have been delivered or received, for which penalties and value such person or persons, body politic or corporate, is or are now hereby authorised to sue by action of debt or other proper action in any Court of Record in the United Kingdom.

No copies of a second or subsequent edition, without addition or alteration, to be demanded

Additions to be printed and delivered separate.

III Provided always, and be it further enacted, that no such printed copy or copies shall be demanded by or delivered to or for the use of any of the libraries hereinbefore mentioned, of the second edition, or of any subsequent edition of any book or books so demanded and delivered as aforesaid, unless the same shall contain additions or alterations, and in case any edition after the first of any book so demanded and delivered as aforesaid shall contain any addition or alteration, no printed copy or copies thereof shall be demanded or delivered as aforesaid if a printed copy of such additions or alterations only, printed in an uniform manner with the former edition of such book, be delivered to each of the libraries aforesaid for whose use a copy of the former edition shall have been demanded and delivered as aforesaid : provided also, that the copy of every book that shall be demanded by the British Museum shall be delivered of the best paper on which such work shall be printed

Instead of copyright for 14 years, and continuously for 14 more, authors and their assigns shall have 28 years copyright in their works, and for the residue of their life

IV And whereas by the said recited Acts of the eighth year of Queen Anne and the forty-first year of his present Majesty's reign it is enacted, that the author of any book or books, and the assignee or assigns of such author respectively, should have the sole liberty of printing and reprinting such book or books for the term of fourteen years, to commence from the day of first publishing the same, and no longer, and it was provided that after the expiration of the said term of fourteen years, the right of printing or disposing of copies should return to the authors thereof, if they were then living, for another term of fourteen years and whereas it will afford further encouragement to literature if the duration of such copyright were extended in manner hereinafter mentioned, be it further enacted, that from and after the passing of this Act the author of any book or books composed and not printed and published, or which shall hereafter be composed, and be printed and published, and his assignee or assigns, shall have the sole liberty of printing and reprinting such book or books for the full term of twenty-eight years, to commence from the day of first publishing the same, and also, if the author shall be living at the end of that period, for the residue of his natural life, and that if any bookseller or printer or other person whatsoever in any part of the United Kingdom of Great Britain and Ireland, in the Isles of Man, Jersey, or Guernsey, or in any other part of the British dominions, shall, from and after the passing of this Act, within the terms and times granted and limited by this Act as aforesaid, print, reprint, or import, or shall cause to be printed, reprinted, or imported, any such book or books, without the consent of the author or authors, or other proprietor or proprietors of the copyright of and in such book and

Booksellers, &c in any part of the United Kingdom, or British dominions, who shall print, reprint, or import, &c any such book, books, first had and obtained in writing, or knowing the same to be so printed, reprinted, or imported, without such consent of such author or authors, or other proprietor or proprietors, shall sell, publish, or expose to sale, or cause to be sold, published, or exposed to sale, or shall have in his or their possession for sale, any such book or books, without such consent first had and obtained as aforesaid, then such offender or offenders shall be liable to a special action on the case, at the suit of the author or authors, or other proprietor or proprietors of the copyright of such book or books so unlawfully printed, reprinted, or imported, or published or exposed to sale, or being in the possession of such offender or offenders for sale as aforesaid, contrary to the true intent and meaning of this Act, and every such author or authors, or other proprietor or proprietors, shall and may, by and in such special action upon the case to be so brought against such offender or offenders in any Court of Record in that part of the said United Kingdom or of the British dominions in which the offence shall be committed, recover such damages as the jury on the trial of such action, or on the execution of a writ of enquiry thereon, shall give or assess, together with double costs of suit, in which action no wager of law, essoign, privilege, or protection, nor more than one imparlance, shall be allowed; and all and every such offender and offenders shall also forfeit such book or books, and all and every sheet being part of such book or books, and shall deliver the same to the author or authors, or other proprietor or proprietors of the copyright of such book or books, upon order of any Court of Record in which any action or suit in law or equity shall be commenced or prosecuted by such author or authors, or other proprietor or proprietors, to be made on motion or petition to the said court; and the said author or authors, or other proprietor or proprietors, shall forthwith damask or make waste paper of the said book or books, and sheet or sheets, and all and every such offender and offenders shall also forfeit the sum of three-pence for every sheet thereof, either printed or printing, or published or exposed to sale, contrary to the true intent and meaning of this Act; the one moiety thereof to the King's most excellent Majesty, his heirs and successors, and the other moiety thereof to any person or persons who shall sue for the same, in any such Court of Record, by action of debt, bill, plaint, or information, in which no wager of law, essoign, privilege, or protection, nor more than one imparlance, shall be allowed provided always, that in Scotland such offender or offenders shall be liable to an action of damages in the Court of Session in Scotland, which shall and may be brought and prosecuted in the same manner in which any other action of damages to the like amount may be brought and prosecuted there; and in any such action where damages shall be awarded, double costs of suit or expenses of process shall be allowed

V And, in order to ascertain what books shall be from time to time published, be it enacted, that the publisher or publishers of any and every book demandable under this Act, which shall be published at any time after the passing of this Act, shall, within one calendar month after the day

Marginal notes:

without consent of the proprietor, shall be liable to an action for damages, and shall also forfeit the books to the proprietor, and 3d. per sheet

Double costs.

The title of all books shall be entered at Stationers Hall within one

on which any such book or books respectively shall be first
sold, published, advertised, or offered for sale, within the bills
of mortality, or within three calendar months if the said book
shall be sold, published, or advertised in any other part of the
United Kingdom, enter the title to the copy of every such book,
and the name or names and place of abode of the publisher or publishers thereof, in the register book of the Company of Stationers in
London, in such manner as hath been used with respect to books
the title whereof hath heretofore been entered in such register
book, and deliver one copy on the best paper, as aforesaid, for the
use of the British Museum; which register book shall at all times
be kept at the hall of the said company; for every of which several
entries the sum of two shillings shall be paid, and no more; which
said register book may at all seasonable and convenient times be
resorted to and inspected by any person; for which inspection the
sum of one shilling shall be paid to the warehousekeeper of the
said Company of Stationers, and such warehousekeeper shall, when
and as often as thereto required, give a certificate under his hand
of every or any such entry, and for every such certificate the sum
of one shilling shall be paid; and in case such entry of the title of
any such book or books shall not be duly made by the publisher
or publishers of any such book or books, within the said calendar
month, or three months, as the case may be, then the publisher or
publishers of such book or books shall forfeit the sum of five
pounds, together with eleven times the price at which such book
shall be sold or advertised, to be recovered, together with full
costs of suit, by the person or persons, body politic or corporate,
authorised to sue, and who shall first sue for the same, in any
Court of Record in the United Kingdom, by action of debt, bill,
plaint, or information, in which no wager of law, essoign, privilege,
or protection, nor more than one imparlance, shall be allowed:
provided always, that in the case of magazines, reviews, or other
periodical publications, it shall be sufficient to make such entry in
the register book of the said company within one month next after
the publication of the first number or volume of such magazine,
review, or other periodical publication provided always, that no
failure in making any such entry shall in any manner affect any
copyright, but shall only subject the person making default to the
penalty aforesaid under this Act.

VI And be it further enacted, that the said warehousekeeper
of the Company of Stationers shall, from time to time and at all
times, without any greater interval than three months, transmit
to the librarian or other person authorised on behalf of the
libraries before mentioned correct lists of all books entered in the
books of the said company, and not contained in former lists; and
that on being required so to do by the said librarians or other
authorised person, or either of them, he shall call on the publisher
or publishers of such books for as many of the said copies as may
have been demanded of them

VII. Provided always, and be it further enacted, that if any
publisher shall be desirous of delivering the copy of such book or
volume as aforesaid as shall be demanded on behalf of any of the

said libraries at such library, it shall and may be lawful for him to deliver the same at such library to the librarian or other person authorised to receive the same (who is hereby required to receive and to give a receipt in writing for the same), and such delivery shall, to all intents and purposes of this Act, be held as equivalent to a delivery to the said warehousekeeper.

VIII. And whereas it is reasonable that authors of books already published, and who are now living, should also have the benefit of the extension of copyright; be it further enacted, that if the author of any book or books which shall not have been published fourteen years at the time of passing this Act shall be living at the said time, and if such author shall afterwards die before the expiration of the said fourteen years, then the personal representative of the said author, and the assignee or assigns of such personal representative, shall have the sole right of printing and publishing the said book or books for the further term of fourteen years after the expiration of the first fourteen years: Provided that nothing in this Act contained shall affect the right of the assignee or assigns of such author to sell any copies of the said book or books which shall have been printed by such assignee or assigns within the first fourteen years, or the terms of any contract between such author and such assignee or assigns.

Authors of books already published, now living, to have the benefit of the extension of copyright ;

IX. And be it also further enacted, that if the author of any book or books which have been already published shall be living at the end of twenty-eight years after the first publication of the said book or books, he or she shall for the remainder of his or her life have the sole right of printing and publishing the same, provided that this shall not affect the right of the assignee or assigns of such author to sell any copies of the said book or books which shall have been printed by such assignee or assigns within the said twenty-eight years, or the terms of any contract between such author and such assignee or assigns

and if living at the end of 28 years the sole right of publication shall be in them during life

X. Provided nevertheless, and be it further enacted, that all actions, suits, bills, indictments, or informations for any offence that shall be committed against this Act shall be brought, sued, and commenced within twelve months next after such offence committed, or else the same shall be void and of no effect.

Limitation of actions.

---

3 & 4 WILL IV. c 15.

An Act to amend the Laws relating to Dramatic Literary Property.

WHEREAS by an Act passed in the fifty-fourth year of the reign of his late Majesty King George the Third, intituled 'An Act to amend the several Acts for the Encouragement of Learning, by securing the Copies and Copyright of printed Books to the Authors of such Books, or their Assigns,' it was amongst other things provided and enacted, that from and after the passing of the said Act the author of any book or books composed and not printed or published, or which should hereafter be composed and printed and

54 G 3, c. 156.

published, and his assignee or assigns, should have the sole liberty of printing and reprinting such book or books for the full term of twenty-eight years, to commence from the day of first publishing the same, and also, if the author should be living at the end of that period, for the residue of his natural life · and whereas it is expedient to extend the provisions of the said Act : be it therefore enacted by the King's most excellent Majesty, by and with the advice and consent of the Lords Spiritual and Temporal, and Commons, in this present Parliament assembled, and by the authority of the same, that from and after the passing of this Act

The author of any dramatic piece shall have as his property the sole liberty of representing it or causing it to be represented at any place of dramatic entertainment

the author of any tragedy, comedy, play, opera, farce, or any other dramatic piece or entertainment, composed, and not printed and published by the author thereof or his assignee, or which hereafter shall be composed, and not printed or published by the author thereof or his assignee, or the assignee of such author, shall have as his own property the sole liberty of representing, or causing to be represented, at any place or places of dramatic entertainment whatsoever, in any part of the United Kingdom of Great Britain and Ireland, in the Isles of Man, Jersey, and Guernsey, or in any part of the British dominions, any such production as aforesaid, not printed and published by the author thereof or his assignee, and shall be deemed and taken to be the proprietor thereof ; and that the author of any such production, printed and published within ten years before the passing of this Act by the author thereof or his assignee, or which shall hereafter be so printed and published, or the assignee of such author, shall, from the time of passing this Act, or from the time of such publication respectively, until the end of twenty-eight years from the day of such first publication of the same, and also, if the author or authors, or the survivor of the authors, shall be living at the end of that period, during the residue of his natural life, have as his own property the sole liberty of representing, or causing to be represented, the same at any such place of dramatic entertainment as aforesaid, and shall be deemed and taken to be the proprietor thereof   provided

Proviso as to cases where previous to the passing of this Act, a consent has been given

nevertheless, that nothing in this Act contained shall prejudice, alter, or affect the right or authority of any person to represent or cause to be represented, at any place or places of dramatic entertainment whatsoever, any such production as aforesaid, in all cases in which the author thereof or his assignee shall, previously to the passing of this Act, have given his consent to or authorised such representation, but that such sole liberty of the author or his assignee shall be subject to such right or authority

Penalty on persons performing pieces contrary to this Act

II. And be it further enacted, that if any person shall, during the continuance of such sole liberty as aforesaid, contrary to the intent of this Act, or right of the author or his assignee, represent, or cause to be represented, without the consent in writing of the author or other proprietor first had and obtained, at any place of dramatic entertainment within the limits aforesaid, any such production as aforesaid, or any part thereof, every such offender shall be liable for each and every such representation to the payment of an amount not less than forty shillings, or to the full amount of the benefit or advantage arising from such representation, or the

injury or loss sustained by the plaintiff therefrom, whichever shall
be the greater damages, to the author or other proprietor of such
production so represented contrary to the true intent and meaning
of this Act, to be recovered, together with double costs of suit, by
such author or other proprietors, in any court having jurisdiction
in such cases in that part of the said United Kingdom or of the
British dominions in which the offence shall be committed; and in
every such proceeding where the sole liberty of such author or his
assignee as aforesaid shall be subject to such right or authority as
aforesaid, it shall be sufficient for the plaintiff to state that he has
such sole liberty, without stating the same to be subject to such
right or authority, or otherwise mentioning the same

III. Provided nevertheless, and be it further enacted, that all
actions or proceedings for any offence or injury that shall be
committed against this Act shall be brought, sued, and commenced
within twelve calendar months next after such offence committed,
or else the same shall be void and of no effect **Limitation of actions.**

IV And be it further enacted, that whenever authors, persons,
offenders, or others are spoken of in this Act in the singular
number or in the masculine gender, the same shall extend to
any number of persons and to either sex. **Explanation of words.**

------

5 & 6 WILL. IV c. 65.

An Act for preventing the Publication of Lectures without Consent.

WHEREAS printers, publishers, and other persons have frequently
taken the liberty of printing and publishing lectures delivered
upon divers subjects, without the consent of the authors of such
lectures, or the persons delivering the same in public, to the great
detriment of such authors and lecturers be it enacted by the
King's most excellent Majesty, by and with the advice and consent of the Lords Spiritual and Temporal, and Commons, in this
present Parliament assembled, and by the authority of the same,
that from and after the first day of September one thousand eight
hundred and thirty-five the author of any lecture or lectures, or
the person to whom he hath sold or otherwise conveyed the copy
thereof, in order to deliver the same in any school, seminary,
institution, or other place, or for any other purpose, shall have
the sole right and liberty of printing and publishing such lecture
or lectures, and that if any person shall, by taking down the
same in short-hand or otherwise in writing, or in any other way,
obtain or make a copy of such lecture or lectures, and shall print
or lithograph or otherwise copy and publish the same, or cause
the same to be printed, lithographed, or otherwise copied and published, without leave of the author thereof, or of the person to
whom the author thereof hath sold or otherwise conveyed the
same, and every person who, knowing the same to have been
printed or copied and published without such consent, shall sell, **Authors of lectures, or their
assigns, to have
the sole right of
publishing them**

**Penalty on other
persons publish-
ing, &c. lectures
without leave**

publish, or expose to sale, or cause to be sold, published, or exposed to sale, any such lecture or lectures, shall forfeit such printed or otherwise copied lecture or lectures, or parts thereof, together with one penny for every sheet thereof which shall be found in his custody, either printed, lithographed, or copied, or printing, lithographing, or copying, published or exposed to sale, contrary to the true intent and meaning of this Act, the one moiety thereof to His Majesty, his heirs or successors, and the other moiety thereof to any person who shall sue for the same, to be recovered in any of his Majesty's courts of record in Westminster, by action of debt, bill, plaint, or information, in which no wager of law, essoign, privilege, or protection, or more than one imparlance, shall be allowed.

Penalty on printers or publishers of newspapers publishing lectures without leave

II And be it further enacted, that any printer or publisher of any newspaper who shall, without such leave as aforesaid, print and publish in such newspaper any lecture or lectures, shall be deemed and taken to be a person printing and publishing without leave within the provisions of this Act, and liable to the aforesaid forfeitures and penalties in respect of such printing and publishing.

Persons having leave to attend lectures not on that account licensed to publish them.

III. And be it further enacted, that no person allowed for certain fee and reward, or otherwise, to attend and be present at any lecture delivered in any place, shall be deemed and taken to be licensed or to have leave to print, copy, and publish such lectures only because of having leave to attend such lecture or lectures

Act not to prohibit the publishing of lectures after expiration of the copyright.

IV Provided always, that nothing in this Act shall extend to prohibit any person from printing, copying, and publishing any lecture or lectures which have or shall have been printed and published with leave of the authors thereof or their assignees, and whereof the time hath or shall have expired within which the sole right to print and publish the same is given by an Act passed

8 Anne, c 19

in the eighth year of the reign of Queen Anne, intituled 'An Act for the Encouragement of Learning, by vesting the Copies of printed Books in the Authors or Purchasers of such Copies during the Times therein mentioned,' and by another Act passed in the

54 G 3, c. 156.

fifty-fourth year of the reign of King George the Third, intituled 'An Act to amend the several Acts for the Encouragement of Learning, by securing the Copies and Copyright of printed Books to the Authors of such Books, or their Assigns,' or to any lectures which have been printed or published before the passing of this Act

Act not to extend to lectures delivered in unlicensed places, &c.

V. Provided further, that nothing in this Act shall extend to any lecture or lectures, or the printing, copying, or publishing any lecture or lectures, or parts thereof, of the delivering of which notice in writing shall not have been given to two justices living within five miles from the place where such lecture or lectures shall be delivered two days at the least before delivering the same, or to any lecture or lectures delivered in any University or public school or college, or on any public foundation, or by any individual in virtue of or according to any gift, endowment, or foundation, and that the law relating thereto shall remain the same as if this Act had not been passed

6 & 7 WILL. IV. c. 59.

An Act to extend the Protection of Copyright in Prints and Engravings to Ireland

WHEREAS an Act was passed in the seventeenth year of the reign of his late Majesty King George the Third, intituled 'An Act for more effectually securing the Property of Prints to Inventors and Engravers, by enabling them to sue for and recover Penalties in certain Cases.' and whereas it is desirable to extend the provisions of the said Act to Ireland; be it therefore enacted by the King's most excellent Majesty, by and with the advice and consent of the Lords Spiritual and Temporal, and Commons, in this present Parliament assembled, and by the authority of the same, that from and after the passing of this Act all the provisions contained in the said recited Act of the seventeenth year of the reign of his late Majesty King George the Third, and of all the other Acts therein recited, shall be and the same are hereby extended to the United Kingdom of Great Britain and Ireland.

17 G 3, c. 57.

Provisions of recited Act extended to Ireland.

II. And be it further enacted, that from and after the passing of this Act, if any engraver, etcher, printseller, or other person shall, within the time limited by the aforesaid recited Acts, engrave, etch, or publish, or cause to be engraved, etched, or published, any engraving or print of any description whatever, either in whole or in part, which may have been or which shall hereafter be published in any part of Great Britain or Ireland, without the express consent of the proprietor or proprietors thereof first had and obtained in writing, signed by him, her, or them respectively, with his, her, or their own hand or hands, in the presence of and attested by two or more credible witnesses, then every such proprietor shall and may, by and in a separate action upon the case, to be brought against the person so offending in any court of law in Great Britain or Ireland, recover such damages as a jury on the trial of such action or on the execution of a writ of enquiry thereon shall give or assess, together with double costs of suit.

Penalty on engraving or publishing any print without consent of proprietor.

---

5 & 6 VICT. c 45.

An Act to amend the Law of Copyright

WHEREAS it is expedient to amend the law relating to copyright, and to afford greater encouragement to the production of literary works of lasting benefit to the world be it enacted by the Queen's most excellent Majesty, by and with the advice and consent of the Lords Spiritual and Temporal, and Commons, in this present Parliament assembled, and by the authority of the same, that from the passing of this Act an Act passed in the eighth year of the

Repeal of former Acts.

reign of her Majesty Queen Anne, intituled 'An Act for the Encouragement of Learning, by vesting the Copies of printed Books in the Authors or Purchasers of such Copies during the Times therein mentioned;' and also an Act passed in the forty-first year of the reign of his Majesty King George the Third, intituled 'An Act for the further Encouragement of Learning in the United Kingdom of Great Britain and Ireland, by securing the Copies and Copyright of printed Books to the Authors of such Books, or their Assigns, for the Time therein mentioned;' and also an Act passed in the fifty-fourth year of the reign of his Majesty King George the Third, intituled 'An Act to amend the several Acts for the Encouragement of Learning, by securing the Copies and Copyright of printed Books to the Authors of such Books, or their Assigns,' be and the same are hereby repealed, except so far as the continuance of either of them may be necessary for carrying on or giving effect to any proceedings at law or in equity pending at the time of passing this Act, or for enforcing any cause of action or suit, or any right or contract, then subsisting.

II. And be it enacted, that in the construction of this Act the word 'book' shall be construed to mean and include every volume, part or division of a volume, pamphlet, sheet of letter-press, sheet of music, map, chart, or plan separately published, that the words 'dramatic piece' shall be construed to mean and include every tragedy, comedy, play, opera, farce, or other scenic, musical, or dramatic entertainment; that the word 'copyright' shall be construed to mean the sole and exclusive liberty of printing or otherwise multiplying copies of any subject to which the said word is herein applied; that the words 'personal representative' shall be construed to mean and include every executor, administrator, and next of kin entitled to administration, that the word 'assigns' shall be construed to mean and include every person in whom the interest of an author in copyright shall be vested, whether derived from such author before or after the publication of any book, and whether acquired by sale, gift, bequest, or by operation of law, or otherwise, that the words 'British dominions' shall be construed to mean and include all parts of the United Kingdom of Great Britain and Ireland, the islands of Jersey and Guernsey, all parts of the East and West Indies, and all the colonies, settlements, and possessions of the Crown which now are or hereafter may be acquired, and that whenever in this Act, in describing any person, matter, or thing, the word importing the singular number or the masculine gender only is used, the same shall be understood to include and to be applied to several persons as well as one person, and females as well as males, and several matters or things as well as one matter or thing, respectively, unless there shall be something in the subject or context repugnant to such construction

III And be it enacted, that the copyright in every book which shall after the passing of this Act be published in the lifetime of its author shall endure for the natural life of such author, and for the further term of seven years, commencing at the time of his death, and shall be the property of such author and his assigns·

prov'led always, that if the said term of seven years shall expire before the end of forty-two years from the first publication of such book, the copyright shall in that case endure for such period of forty-two years; and that the copyright in every book which shall be published after the death of its author shall endure for the term of forty-two years from the first publication thereof, and shall be the property of the proprietor of the author's manuscript from which such book shall be first published, and his assigns.

IV. And whereas it is just to extend the benefits of this Act to authors of books published before the passing thereof, and in which copyright still subsists; be it enacted, that the copyright which at the time of passing this Act shall subsist in any book theretofore published (except as herein-after mentioned) shall be extended and endure for the full term provided by this Act in cases of books thereafter published, and shall be the property of the person who at the time of passing of this Act shall be the proprietor of such copyright: provided always, that in all cases in which such copyright shall belong in whole or in part to a publisher or other person who shall have acquired it for other consideration than that of natural love and affection, such copyright shall not be extended by this Act, but shall endure for the term which shall subsist therein at the time of passing of this Act, and no longer, unless the author of such book, if he shall be living, or the personal representative of such author, if he shall be dead, and the proprietor of such copyright, shall, before the expiration of such term, consent and agree to accept the benefits of this Act in respect of such book, and shall cause a minute of such consent in the form in that behalf given in the schedule to this Act annexed to be entered in the book of registry herein-after directed to be kept, in which case such copyright shall endure for the full term by this Act provided in cases of books to be published after the passing of this Act, and shall be the property of such person or persons as in such minute shall be expressed

V And whereas it is expedient to provide against the suppression of books of importance to the public, be it enacted, that it shall be lawful for the Judicial Committee of her Majesty's Privy Council, on complaint made to them that the proprietor of the copyright in any book after the death of its author has refused to republish or to allow the republication of the same, and that by reason of such refusal such book may be withheld from the public, to grant a licence to such complainant to publish such book, in such manner and subject to such conditions as they may think fit, and that it shall be lawful for such complainant to publish such book according to such licence.

VI. And be it enacted, that a printed copy of the whole of every book which shall be published after the passing of this Act, together with all maps, prints, or other engravings belonging thereto, finished and coloured in the same manner as the best copies of the same shall be published, and also of any second or subsequent edition which shall be so published with any additions or alterations, whether the same shall be in letterpress, or in the maps, prints, or other engravings belonging thereto, and whether the

c

first edition of such book shall have been published before or after the passing of this Act, and also of any second or subsequent edition of every book of which the first or some preceding edition shall not have been delivered for the use of the British Museum, bound, sewed, or stitched together, and upon the best paper on which the same shall be printed, shall, within one calendar month after the day on which any such book shall first be sold, published, or offered for sale within the bills of mortality, or within three calendar months if the same shall first be sold, published, or offered for sale in any other part of the United Kingdom, or within twelve calendar months after the same shall first be sold, published, or offered for sale in any other part of the British dominions, be delivered, on behalf of the publisher thereof, at the British Museum.

VII. And be it enacted, that every copy of any book which under the provisions of this Act ought to be delivered as aforesaid shall be delivered at the British Museum between the hours of ten in the forenoon and four in the afternoon on any day except Sunday, Ash Wednesday, Good Friday, and Christmas Day, to one of the officers of the said Museum, or to some person authorised by the Trustees of the said Museum to receive the same, and such officer or other person receiving such copy is hereby required to give a receipt in writing for the same, and such delivery shall to all intents and purposes be deemed to be good and sufficient delivery under the provisions of this Act

VIII And be it enacted, that a copy of the whole of every book and of any second or subsequent edition of every book containing additions and alterations, together with all maps and prints belonging thereto, which after the passing of this Act shall be published, shall, on demand thereof in writing, left at the place of abode of the publisher thereof at any time within twelve months next after the publication thereof, under the hand of the officer of the Company of Stationers who shall from time to time be appointed by the said Company for the purposes of this Act, or under the hand of any other person thereto authorised by the persons or bodies politic and corporate, proprietors and managers of the libraries following (videlicet), the Bodleian Library at Oxford, the Public Library at Cambridge, the Library of the Faculty of Advocates at Edinburgh, the Library of the College of the Holy and Undivided Trinity of Queen Elizabeth near Dublin, be delivered, upon the paper of which the largest number of copies of such book or edition shall be printed for sale, in the like condition as the copies prepared for sale by the publisher thereof respectively, within one month after demand made thereof in writing as aforesaid, to the said officer of the said Company of Stationers for the time being, which copies the said officer shall and he is hereby required to receive at the Hall of the said Company, for the use of the library for which such demand shall be made within such twelve months as aforesaid, and the said officer is hereby required to give a receipt in writing for the same, and within one month after any such book shall be so delivered to him as aforesaid to deliver the same for the use of such library

IX. Provided also, and be it enacted, that if any publisher shall be desirous of delivering the copy of such book as shall be demanded on behalf of any of the said libraries at such library, it shall be lawful for him to deliver the same at such library, free of expense, to such librarian or other person authorised to receive the same (who is hereby required in such case to receive and give a receipt in writing for the same), and such delivery shall to all intents and purposes of this Act be held as equivalent to a delivery to the said officer of the Stationers Company.

copies to the libraries, instead of at the Stationers Company.

X. And be it enacted, that if any publisher of any such book, or of any second or subsequent edition of any such book, shall neglect to deliver the same, pursuant to this Act, he shall for every such default forfeit, besides the value of such copy of such book or edition which he ought to have delivered, a sum not exceeding five pounds, to be recovered by the librarian or other officer (properly authorised) of the library for the use whereof such copy should have been delivered in a summary way, on conviction before two Justices of the Peace for the county or place where the publisher making default shall reside, or by action of debt or other proceeding of the like nature, at the suit of such librarian or other officer, in any Court of Record in the United Kingdom, in which action, if the plaintiff shall obtain a verdict, he shall recover his costs reasonably incurred, to be taxed as between attorney and client.

Penalty for default in delivering copies for the use of the libraries.

XI. And be it enacted, that a book of registry, wherein may be registered, as herein-after enacted, the proprietorship in the copyright of books and assignments thereof, and in dramatic and musical pieces, whether in manuscript or otherwise, and licences affecting such copyright, shall be kept at the Hall of the Stationers Company, by the officer appointed by the said Company for the purposes of this Act, and shall at all convenient times be open to the inspection of any person, on payment of one shilling for every entry which shall be searched for or inspected in the said book, and that such officer shall, whenever thereunto reasonably required, give a copy of any entry in such book, certified under his hand, and impressed with the stamp of the said Company, to be provided by them for that purpose, and which they are hereby required to provide, to any person requiring the same, on payment to him of the sum of five shillings, and such copies so certified and impressed shall be received in evidence in all courts, and in all summary proceedings, and shall be *primâ facie* proof of the proprietorship or assignment of copyright or licence as therein expressed, but subject to be rebutted by other evidence, and in the case of dramatic or musical pieces shall be *primâ facie* proof of the right of representation or performance, subject to be rebutted as aforesaid

Book of registry to be kept at Stationers Hall.

XII And be it enacted, that if any person shall wilfully make or cause to be made any false entry in the registry book of the Stationers Company, or shall wilfully produce or cause to be tendered in evidence any paper falsely purporting to be a copy of any entry in the said book, he shall be guilty of an indictable misdemeanor, and shall be punished accordingly.

Making a false entry in the book of registry, a misdemeanor.

XIII. And be it enacted, that after the passing of this Act it shall be lawful for the proprietor of copyright in any book hereto-

Entries of copyright may be

made in the book
of registry

fore published, or in any book hereafter to be published, to make
entry in the registry book of the Stationers Company of the title
of such book, the time of the first publication thereof, the name
and place of abode of the publisher thereof, and the name and
place of abode of the proprietor of the copyright of the said book,
or of any portion of such copyright, in the form in that behalf
given in the schedule to this Act annexed, upon payment of the
sum of five shillings to the officer of the said Company, and that
it shall be lawful for every such registered proprietor to assign his
interest, or any portion of his interest therein, by making entry in
the said book of registry of such assignment, and of the name
and place of abode of the assignee thereof, in the form given in
that behalf in the said schedule, on payment of the like sum, and
such assignment so entered shall be effectual in law to all intents
and purposes whatsoever, without being subject to any stamp or
duty, and shall be of the same force and effect as if such assignment had been made by deed.

Persons aggriev-
ed by any entry
in the book of
registry may
apply to a court
of law in term,
or judge in vaca-
tion, who may
order such entry
to be varied or
expunged.

XIV. And be it enacted, that if any person shall deem himself
aggrieved by any entry made under colour of this Act in the said
book of registry, it shall be lawful for such person to apply by
motion to the Court of Queen's Bench, Court of Common Pleas,
or Court of Exchequer, in term time, or to apply by summons to
any judge of either of such courts in vacation, for an order that
such entry may be expunged or varied; and that upon any such
application by motion or summons to either of the said courts, or
to a judge as aforesaid, such court or judge shall make such order
for expunging, varying, or confirming such entry, either with or
without costs, as to such court or judge shall seem just, and the
officer appointed by the Stationers Company for the purposes of
this Act shall, on the production to him of any such order for
expunging or varying any such entry, expunge or vary the same
according to the requisitions of such order

Remedy for the
piracy of books
by action on
the case

XV And be it enacted, that if any person shall, in any part of
the British dominions, after the passing of this Act, print or cause
to be printed, either for sale or exportation, any book in which
there shall be subsisting copyright, without the consent in writing
of the proprietor thereof, or shall import for sale or hire any such
book so having been unlawfully printed from parts beyond the
sea, or, knowing such book to have been so unlawfully printed or
imported, shall sell, publish, or expose to sale or hire, or cause to
be sold, published, or exposed to sale or hire, or shall have in his
possession, for sale or hire, any such book so unlawfully printed or
imported, without such consent as aforesaid, such offender shall be
liable to a special action on the case at the suit of the proprietor
of such copyright, to be brought in any Court of Record in that
part of the British dominions in which the offence shall be committed · provided always, that in Scotland such offender shall be
liable to an action in the Court of Session in Scotland, which shall
and may be brought and prosecuted in the same manner in which
any other action of damages to the like amount may be brought
and prosecuted there.

In actions for

XVI. And be it enacted, that after the passing of this Act, in any action brought within the British dominions against any person for printing any such book for sale, hire, or exportation, or for importing, selling, publishing, or exposing to sale or hire, or causing to be imported, sold, published, or exposed to sale or hire, any such book, the defendant, on pleading thereto, shall give to the plaintiff a notice in writing of any objections on which he means to rely on the trial of such action; and if the nature of his defence be, that the plaintiff in such action was not the author or first publisher of the book in which he shall by such action claim copyright, or is not the proprietor of the copyright therein, or that some other person than the plaintiff was the author or first publisher of such book, or is the proprietor of the copyright therein, then the defendant shall specify in such notice the name of the person whom he alleges to have been the author or first publisher of such book, or the proprietor of the copyright therein, together with the title of such book, and the time when and the place where such book was first published, otherwise the defendant in such action shall not at the trial or hearing of such action be allowed to give any evidence that the plaintiff in such action was not the author or first publisher of the book in which he claims such copyright as aforesaid, or that he was not the proprietor of the copyright therein, and at such trial or hearing no other objection shall be allowed to be made on behalf of such defendant than the objections stated in such notice, or that any other person was the author or first publisher of such book, or the proprietor of the copyright therein, than the person specified in such notice, or give in evidence in support of his defence any other book than one substantially corresponding in title, time, and place of publication with the title, time, and place specified in such notice

piracy the defendant to give notice of the objections to the plaintiff's title on which he means to rely.

XVII And be it enacted, that after the passing of this Act it shall not be lawful for any person, not being the proprietor of the copyright, or some person authorised by him, to import into any part of the United Kingdom, or into any other part of the British dominions, for sale or hire, any printed book first composed or written or printed and published in any part of the said United Kingdom, wherein there shall be copyright, and reprinted in any country or place whatsoever out of the British dominions, and if any person, not being such proprietor or person authorised as aforesaid, shall import or bring, or cause to be imported or brought, for sale or hire, any such printed book, into any part of the British dominions, contrary to the true intent and meaning of this Act, or shall knowingly sell, publish, or expose to sale or let to hire, or have in his possession for sale or hire, any such book, then every such book shall be forfeited, and shall be seized by any officer of Customs or Excise, and the same shall be destroyed by such officer, and every person so offending, being duly convicted thereof before two Justices of the Peace for the county or place in which such book shall be found, shall also for every such offence forfeit the sum of ten pounds, and double the value of every copy of such book which he shall so import or cause to be imported into any part of the British dominions, or shall knowingly sell, publish, or expose to sale or let to hire, or shall cause to be sold, published, or

No person, except the proprietor, &c. shall import into the British dominions for sale or hire any book first composed, &c. within the United Kingdom, and reprinted elsewhere, under penalty of forfeiture thereof, and also of 10*l* and double the value Books may be seized by officers of Customs or Excise.

exposed to sale or let to hire, or shall have in his possession for sale or hire, contrary to the true intent and meaning of this Act, five pounds to the use of such officer of Customs or Excise, and the remainder of the penalty to the use of the proprietor of the copyright in such book.

XVIII And be it enacted, that when any publisher or other person shall, before or at the time of the passing of this Act, have projected, conducted, and carried on, or shall hereafter project, conduct, and carry on, or be the proprietor of any encyclopædia, review, magazine, periodical work, or work published in a series of books or parts, or any book whatsoever, and shall have employed or shall employ any person to compose the same, or any volumes, parts, essays, articles, or portions thereof, for publication in or as part of the same, and such work, volumes, parts, essays, articles, or portions shall have been or shall hereafter be composed under such employment, on the terms that the copyright therein shall belong to such proprietor, projector, publisher, or conductor, and paid for by such proprietor, projector, publisher, or conductor, the copyright in every such encyclopædia, review, magazine, periodical work, and work published in a series of books or parts, and in every volume, part, essay, article, and portion so composed and paid for, shall be the property of such proprietor, projector, publisher, or other conductor, who shall enjoy the same rights as if he were the actual author thereof, and shall have such term of copyright therein as is given to the authors of books by this Act; except only that in the case of essays, articles, or portions forming part of and first published in reviews, magazines, or other periodical works of a like nature, after the term of twenty-eight years from the first publication thereof respectively the right of publishing the same in a separate form shall revert to the author for the remainder of the term given by this Act. provided always, that during the term of twenty-eight years the said proprietor, projector, publisher, or conductor shall not publish any such essay, article, or portion separately or singly without the consent previously obtained of the author thereof, or his assigns provided also, that nothing herein contained shall alter or affect the right of any person who shall have been or who shall be so employed as aforesaid to publish any such his composition in a separate form, who by any contract, express or implied, may have reserved or may hereafter reserve to himself such right; but every author reserving, retaining, or having such right shall be entitled to the copyright in such composition when published in a separate form, according to this Act, without prejudice to the right of such proprietor, projector, publisher, or conductor as aforesaid.

XIX. And be it enacted, that the proprietor of the copyright in any encyclopædia, review, magazine, periodical work, or other work published in a series of books or parts, shall be entitled to all the benefits of the registration at Stationers Hall under this Act, on entering in the said book of registry the title of such encyclopædia, review, periodical work, or other work published in a series of books or parts, the time of the first publication of the first volume, number, or part thereof, or of the first number or volume first published after the passing of this Act in any such work which shall have been published heretofore, and the name and place of abode of the proprietor thereof, and of the publisher thereof, when such publisher shall not also be the proprietor thereof

registration of the whole

XX. And whereas an Act was passed in the third year of the reign of his late Majesty, to amend the law relating to dramatic literary property, and it is expedient to extend the term of the sole liberty of representing dramatic pieces given by that Act to the full time by this Act provided for the continuance of copyright: and whereas it is expedient to extend to musical compositions the benefits of that Act, and also of this Act; be it therefore enacted, that the provisions of the said Act of his late Majesty, and of this Act, shall apply to musical compositions, and that the sole liberty of representing or performing, or causing or permitting to be represented or performed, any dramatic piece or musical composition, shall endure and be the property of the author thereof, and his assigns, for the term in this Act provided for the duration of copyright in books, and the provisions herein-before enacted in respect of the property of such copyright, and of registering the same, shall apply to the liberty of representing or performing any dramatic piece or musical composition, as if the same were herein expressly re-enacted and applied thereto, save and except that the first public representation or performance of any dramatic piece or musical composition shall be deemed equivalent, in the construction of this Act, to the first publication of any book. provided always, that in case of any dramatic piece or musical composition in manuscript, it shall be sufficient for the person having the sole liberty of representing or performing, or causing to be represented or performed the same, to register only the title thereof, the name and place of abode of the author or composer thereof, the name and place of abode of the proprietor thereof, and the time and place of its first representation or performance.

The provisions of 3 & 4 W 4, c 15, extended to musical compositions, and the term of copyright, as provided by this Act, applied to the liberty of representing dramatic pieces and musical compositions.

XXI. And be it enacted, that the person who shall at any time have the sole liberty of representing such dramatic piece or musical composition shall have and enjoy the remedies given and provided in the said Act of the third and fourth years of the reign of his late Majesty King William the Fourth, passed to amend the laws relating to dramatic literary property, during the whole of his interest therein, as fully as if the same were re-enacted in this Act

Proprietors of right of dramatic representations shall have all the remedies given by 3 & 4 W. 4, c 15

XXII. And be it enacted, that no assignment of the copyright of any book consisting of or containing a dramatic piece or musical composition shall be holden to convey to the assignee the right of representing or performing such dramatic piece or musical composition, unless an entry in the said registry book shall be made of such assignment, wherein shall be expressed the intention of the parties that such right should pass by such assignment.

Assignment of copyright of a dramatic piece not to convey the right of representation.

XXIII And be it enacted, that all copies of any book wherein there shall be copyright, and of which entry shall have been made in the said registry book, and which shall have been unlawfully printed or imported without the consent of the registered pro-

Books pirated shall become the property of the proprietor of the copyright, and may be recovered by action

prietor of such copyright, in writing under his hand first obtained, shall be deemed to be the property of the proprietor of such copyright, and who shall be registered as such, and such registered proprietor shall, after demand thereof in writing, be entitled to sue for and recover the same, or damages for the detention thereof, in an action of detinue, from any party who shall detain the same, or to sue for and recover damages for the conversion thereof in an action of trover.

No proprietor of copyright commencing after this Act shall sue or proceed for any infringement before making entry in the book of registry

Proviso for dramatic pieces.

XXIV. And be it enacted, that no proprietor of copyright in any book which shall be first published after the passing of this Act shall maintain any action or suit, at law or in equity, or any summary proceeding, in respect of any infringement of such copyright, unless he shall, before commencing such action, suit, or proceeding, have caused an entry to be made, in the book of registry of the Stationers Company, of such book, pursuant to this Act provided always, that the omission to make such entry shall not affect the copyright in any book, but only the right to sue or proceed in respect of the infringement thereof as aforesaid· provided also, that nothing herein contained shall prejudice the remedies which the proprietor of the sole liberty of representing any dramatic piece shall have by virtue of the Act passed in the third year of the reign of his late Majesty king William the Fourth, to amend the laws relating to dramatic literary property, or of this Act, although no entry shall be made in the book of registry aforesaid.

Copyright shall be personal property

XXV And be it enacted, that all copyright shall be deemed personal property, and shall be transmissible by bequest, or, in case of intestacy, shall be subject to the same law of distribution as other personal property, and in Scotland shall be deemed to be personal and moveable estate

General issue.

Limitation of actions,

not to extend to actions, &c in respect of the delivery of books.

XXVI. And be it enacted, that if any action or suit shall be commenced or brought against any person or persons whomsoever for doing or causing to be done anything in pursuance of this Act, the defendant or defendants in such action may plead the general issue, and give the special matter in evidence, and if upon such action a verdict shall be given for the defendant, or the plaintiff shall become nonsuited, or discontinue his action, then the defendant shall have and recover his full costs, for which he shall have the same remedy as a defendant in any case by law hath, and that all actions, suits, bills, indictments, or informations, for any offence that shall be committed against this Act shall be brought, sued, and commenced within twelve calendar months next after such offence committed, or else the same shall be void and of none effect provided that such limitation of time shall not extend or be construed to extend to any actions, suits, or other proceedings which under the authority of this Act shall or may be brought, sued, or commenced for or in respect of any copies of books to be delivered for the use of the British Museum, or of any one of the four libraries herein-before mentioned.

Saving the rights of the universities, and the

XXVII. Provided always, and be it enacted, that nothing in this Act contained shall affect or alter the rights of the two universities of Oxford and Cambridge, the colleges or houses of learning within the same, the four universities in Scotland, the College of colleges of Eton, the Holy and Undivided Trinity of Queen Elizabeth, near Dublin, Westminster, and and the several colleges of Eton, Westminster, and Winchester, in Winchester. any copyrights heretofore and now vested or hereafter to be vested in such universities and colleges respectively, any thing to the contrary herein contained notwithstanding.

XXVIII. Provided also, and be it enacted, that nothing in this Saving all sub-
Act contained shall affect, alter, or vary any right subsisting at sisting rights,
the time of passing of this Act, except as herein expressly enacted; contracts, and
and all contracts, agreements, and obligations made and entered engagements.
into before the passing of this Act, and all remedies relating
thereto, shall remain in full force, any thing herein contained to
the contrary notwithstanding.

XXIX. And be it enacted, that this Act shall extend to the Extent of the
United Kingdom of Great Britain and Ireland, and to every part Act
of the British dominions

XXX And be it enacted, that this Act may be amended or Act may be
repealed by any Act to be passed in the present session of amended this
Parliament. session.

---

5 & 6 VICT. c 100

An Act to consolidate and amend the Laws relating to the Copyright
of Designs for ornamenting Articles of Manufacture.

WHEREAS by the several Acts mentioned in the Schedule (A) to this Act annexed there was granted, in respect of the woven fabrics therein mentioned, the sole right to use any new and original pattern for printing the same during the period of three calendar months. and whereas by the Act mentioned in the Schedule (B) to this Act annexed there was granted, in respect of all articles except lace, and except the articles within the meaning of the Acts herein-before referred to, the sole right of using any new and original design, for certain purposes, during the respective periods therein mentioned, but forasmuch as the pro-tection afforded by the said Acts in respect of the application of designs to certain articles of manufacture is insufficient it is ex-pedient to extend the same, but upon the conditions hereinafter expressed now for that purpose, and for the purpose of consoli-dating the provisions of the said Acts, be it enacted by the Queen's most Excellent Majesty, by and with the advice and consent of the Lords Spiritual and Temporal, and Commons, in this present Parliament assembled, and by the authority of the same, that this Act shall come into operation on the First day of September One Commencement thousand eight hundred and forty-two, and that thereupon all the of Act and said Acts mentioned in the said Schedules (A) and (B) to this repeal of former Act annexed shall be and they are hereby repealed Acts

II Provided always, and be it enacted, that notwithstanding Proviso as to such repeal of the said Acts every copyright in force under the existing copyrights

same shall continue in force till the expiration of such copyright; and with regard to all offences or injuries committed against any such copyright before this Act shall come into operation, every penalty imposed and every remedy given by the said Acts, in relation to any such offence or injury, shall be applicable as if such Acts had not been repealed; but with regard to such offences or injuries committed against any such copyright after this Act shall come into operation, every penalty imposed and every remedy given by this Act in relation to any such offence or injury shall be applicable as if such copyright had been conferred by this Act

Grant of
copyright.

III And with regard to any new and original design (except for sculpture and other things within the provisions of the several Acts mentioned in the Schedule (C) to this Act annexed), whether such design be applicable to the ornamenting of any article of manufacture, or of any substance, artificial or natural, or partly artificial and partly natural, and that whether such design be so applicable for the pattern, or for the shape or configuration, or for the ornament thereof, or for any two or more of such purposes, and by whatever means such design may be so applicable, whether by printing, or by painting, or by embroidery, or by weaving, or by sewing, or by modelling, or by casting, or by embossing, or by engraving, or by staining, or by any other means whatsoever, manual, mechanical, or chemical, separate or combined. be it enacted, that the proprietor of every such design, not previously published, either within the United Kingdom of Great Britain and Ireland or elsewhere, shall have the sole right to apply the same to any articles of manufacture, or to any such substances as aforesaid, provided the same be done within the United Kingdom of Great Britain and Ireland, for the respective terms hereinafter mentioned, such respective terms to be computed from the time of such design being registered according to this Act, (that is to say,)

In respect of the application of any such design to ornamenting any article of manufacture contained in the first, second, third, fourth, fifth, sixth, eighth, or eleventh of the classes following, for the term of three years·

In respect of the application of any such design to ornamenting any article of manufacture contained in the seventh, ninth, or tenth of the classes following, for the term of nine calendar months

In respect of the application of any such design to ornamenting any article of manufacture or substance contained in the twelfth or thirteenth of the classes following, for the term of twelve calendar months.

Class 1.—Articles of manufacture composed wholly or chiefly of any metal or mixed metals.

Class 2—Articles of manufacture composed wholly or chiefly of wood.

Class 3—Articles of manufacture composed wholly or chiefly of glass

Class 4—Articles of manufacture composed wholly or chiefly of earthenware

Class 5—Paper hangings.

Class 6.—Carpets:

Class 7.—Shawls, if the design be applied solely by printing, or by any other process by which colours are or may hereafter be produced upon tissue or textile fabrics:

Class 8.—Shawls not comprised in Class 7 ·

Class 9.—Yarn, thread or warp, if the design be applied by printing, or by any other process by which colours are or may hereafter be produced :

Class 10.—Woven fabrics composed of linen, cotton, wool, silk, or hair, or of any two or more of such materials, if the design be applied by printing, or by any other process by which colours are or may hereafter be produced upon tissue or textile fabrics, excepting the articles included in Class 11 ·

Class 11.—Woven fabrics composed of linen, cotton, wool, silk, or hair, or of any two or more of such materials, if the design be applied by printing, or by any other process by which colours are or may hereafter be produced upon tissue or textile fabrics, such woven fabrics being or coming within the description technically called furnitures, and the repeat of the design whereof shall be more than twelve inches by eight inches

Class 12.—Woven fabrics not comprised in any preceding class ·

Class 13.—Lace, and any article of manufacture or substance not comprised in any preceding class.

IV. Provided always, and be it enacted, that no person shall be entitled to the benefit of this Act, with regard to any design in respect of the application thereof to ornamenting any article of manufacture, or any such substance, unless such design have before publication thereof been registered according to this Act, and unless at the time of such registration such design have been registered in respect of the application thereof to some or one of the articles of manufacture or substances comprised in the above-mentioned classes, by specifying the number of the class in respect of which such registration is made, and unless the name of such person shall be registered according to this Act as a proprietor of such design, and unless after publication of such design every such article of manufacture, or such substance to which the same shall be so applied, published by him, hath thereon, if the article of manufacture be a woven fabric for printing, at one end thereof, or if of any other kind or such substance as aforesaid, at the end or edge thereof, or other convenient place thereon, the letters 'R^d,' together with such number or letter, or number and letter, and in such form as shall correspond with the date of the registration of such design according to the registry of designs in that behalf, and such marks may be put on any such article of manufacture or such substance, either by making the same in or on the material itself of which such article or such substance shall consist, or by attaching thereto a lable containing such marks

V. And be it enacted, that the author of any such new and original design shall be considered the proprietor thereof, unless he

(marginal notes:) Conditions of copyright

Registration

Marks denoting a registered design.

The term
'proprietor'
explained

have executed the work on behalf of another person for a good or a valuable consideration, in which case such person shall be considered the proprietor, and shall be entitled to be registered in the place of the author, and every person acquiring for a good or a valuable consideration a new and original design, or the right to apply the same to ornamenting any one or more articles of manufacture, or any one or more such substances as aforesaid, either exclusively of any other person or otherwise, and also every person upon whom the property in such design or such right to the application thereof shall devolve, shall be considered the proprietor of the design in the respect in which the same may have been so acquired, and to that extent, but not otherwise

Transfer of
copyright and
register thereof.

VI And be it enacted, that every person purchasing or otherwise acquiring the right to the entire or partial use of any such design may enter his title in the register hereby provided, and any writing purporting to be a transfer of such design, and signed by the proprietor thereof, shall operate as an effectual transfer, and the registrar shall, on request, and the production of such writing, or, in the case of acquiring such right by any other mode than that of purchase, on the production of any evidence to the satisfaction of the registrar, insert the name of the new proprietor in the register, and the following may be the form of such transfer, and of such request to the registrar:

Form of Transfer, and Authority to register.

'I A.B., author [or proprietor] of design No   having transferred my right thereto, [or, if such transfer be partial,] so far as regards the ornamenting of   [describe the articles of manufacture or substances, or the locality, with respect to which the right is transferred,] to B.C. of   do hereby authorise you to insert his name on the register of designs accordingly'

Form of Request to register.

'I B C, the person mentioned in the above transfer, do request you to register my name and property in the said design as entitled [if to the entire use] to the entire use of such design, [or, if to the partial use,] to the partial use of such design, so far as regards the application thereof [describe the articles of manufacture, or the locality, in relation to which the right is transferred].'

But if such request to register be made by any person to whom any such design shall devolve otherwise than by transfer, such request may be in the following form ·

'I C.D, in whom is vested by [state bankruptcy or otherwise] the design, No.   [or, if such devolution be of a partial right, so far as regards the application thereof] to [describe the articles of manufacture or substance, or the locality, in relation to which the right has devolved]'

Piracy of
designs

VII And for preventing the piracy of registered designs, be it enacted, that during the existence of any such right to the entire or partial use of any such design no person shall either do or cause to be done any of the following acts with regard to any articles of manufacture or substances in respect of which the copyright of such design shall be in force, without the licence or consent in writing of the registered proprietor thereof, (that is to say,)

No person shall apply any such design, or any fraudulent imitation thereof, for the purpose of sale, to the ornamenting of any article of manufacture, or any substance artificial or natural, or partly artificial and partly natural ·

No person shall publish, sell, or expose for sale any article of manufacture, or any substance, to which such design, or any fraudulent imitation thereof, shall have been so applied, after having received, either verbally or in writing, or otherwise, from any source other than the proprietor of such design, knowledge that his consent has not been given to such application, or after having been served with or had left at his premises a written notice signed by such proprietor or his agent to the same effect.

VIII. And be it enacted, that if any person commit any such act he shall for every offence forfeit a sum not less than five pounds and not exceeding thirty pounds to the proprietor of the design in respect of whose right such offence has been committed; and such proprietor may recover such penalty as follows:

Recovery of penalties for piracy.

In England, either by an action of debt or on the case against the party offending, or by summary proceeding before two justices having jurisdiction where the party offending resides; and if such proprietor proceed by such summary proceeding, any justice of the peace acting for the county, riding, division, city, or borough where the party offending resides, and not being concerned either in the sale or manufacture of the article of manufacture, or in the design, to which such summary proceeding relates, may issue a summons requiring such party to appear on a day and at a time and place to be named in such summons, such time not being less than eight days from the date thereof, and every such summons shall be served on the party offending, either in person or at his usual place of abode, and either upon the appearance or upon the default to appear of the party offending, any two or more of such justices may proceed to the hearing of the complaint, and upon proof of the offence, either by the confession of the party offending, or upon the oath or affirmation of one or more credible witnesses, which such justices are hereby authorised to administer, may convict the offender in a penalty of not less than five pounds or more than thirty pounds, as aforesaid, for each offence, as to such justices doth seem fit, but the aggregate amount of penalties for offences in respect of any one design committed by any one person, up to the time at which any of the proceedings herein mentioned shall be instituted, shall not exceed the sum of one hundred pounds, and if the amount of such penalty or of such penalties and the costs attending the conviction, so assessed by such justices, be not forthwith paid, the amount of the penalty or of the penalties, and of the costs, together with the costs of the distress and sale, shall be levied by distress and sale of the goods and chattels of the offender, wherever the same happen to be in England; and the justices before whom the party has been convicted, or, on proof of the conviction, any two justices acting for any county, riding, division, city, or borough in England, where goods and chattels of the person offending happen to be, may grant a warrant for such distress and sale; and the overplus, if any, shall be returned to the owner of the goods and chattels, on demand; and every information and conviction which shall be respectively laid or made in such summary proceeding before two Justices under this Act may be drawn or made out in the following forms respectively, or to the effect thereof, *mutatis mutandis*, as the case may require:

Form of Information.

'BE it remembered, that on the   at   in the county of   A.B of   in the county of   [or C D of   in the county of   at the instance and on the behalf of A B of   in the county of   ] cometh before us   and   two of her Majesty's Justices of the Peace in and for the county of   , and giveth us to understand that the said A B before and at the time when the offence herein-after mentioned was committed, was the proprietor of a new and original design for [*here describe the design*], and that within twelve calendar months last past, to wit, on the   at   in the county of   E.F of   in the county of   did [*here describe the offence*], contrary to the form of the Act passed in the   year of the reign of her present Majesty, intituled "An Act to consolidate and amend the Laws relating to the Copyright of Designs for ornamenting Articles of Manufacture "'

Form of Conviction.

'BE it remembered, that on the   day of   in the year of our Lord   at   in the county of   E F of   in the county aforesaid is convicted before us   and   two of her Majesty's Justices of the Peace for the said county, for that he the said E F on the   day of   in the year   at   in the county of   did [*here describe the offence*] contrary to the form of the statute in that case made and provided, and we the said justices do adjudge that the said E F for his offence aforesaid hath forfeited the sum of   to the said A.B.'

In Scotland, by action before the Court of Session in ordinary form, or by summary action before the sheriff of the county where the offence may be committed or the offender resides, who, upon proof of the offence or offences, either by confession of the party offending or by the oath or affirmation of one or more credible witnesses, shall convict the offender and find him liable in the penalty or penalties aforesaid, as also in expenses; and it shall be lawful for the sheriff, in pronouncing such judgment for the penalty or penalties and costs, to insert in such judgment a warrant, in the event of such penalty or penalties and costs not being paid, to levy and recover the amount of the same by poinding: provided always, that it shall be lawful to the sheriff, in the event of his dismissing the action, and assoilzieing the defender, to find the complainer liable in expenses, and any judgment so to be pronounced by the sheriff in such summary application shall be final and conclusive, and not subject to review by advocation, suspension, reduction, or otherwise.

In Ireland, either by action in a superior court of law at Dublin, or by civil bill in the Civil Bill Court of the county or place where the offence was committed.

IX. Provided always, and be it enacted, that, notwithstanding the remedies hereby given for the recovery of any such penalty as aforesaid, it shall be lawful for the proprietor in respect of whose right such penalty shall have been incurred (if he shall elect to do so) to bring such action as he may be entitled to for the recovery of any damages which he shall have sustained, either by the application of any such design or of a fraudulent imitation thereof, for the purpose of sale, to any articles of manufacture or substances, or by the publication, sale or exposure to sale, as aforesaid, by any person, of any article or substance to which such design or any fraudulent imitation thereof shall have been so applied, such person knowing that the proprietor of such design had not given his consent to such application

Proviso as to action for damages.

X. And be it enacted, that in any suit in equity which may be instituted by the proprietor of any design or the person lawfully entitled thereto, relative to such design, if it shall appear to the satisfaction of the judge having cognisance of such suit that the design has been registered in the name of a person not being the proprietor or lawfully entitled thereto, it shall be competent for such judge, in his discretion, by a decree or order in such suit to direct either that such registration be cancelled (in which case the same shall thenceforth be wholly void), or that the name of the proprietor of such design, or other person lawfully entitled thereto, be substituted in the register for the name of such wrongful proprietor or claimant, in like manner as is herein-before directed in case of the transfer of a design, and to make such order respecting the costs of such cancellation or substitution, and of all proceedings to procure and effect the same, as he shall think fit, and the registrar is hereby authorised and required, upon being served with an official copy of such decree or order, and upon payment of the proper fee, to comply with the tenor of such decree or order, and either cancel such registration or substitute such new name, as the case may be

Registration may in some cases be cancelled or amended.

Penalty for wrongfully using marks denoting a registered design.

XI And be it enacted, that unless a design applied to ornamenting any article of manufacture or any such substance as aforesaid be so registered as aforesaid, and unless such design so registered shall have been applied to the ornamenting such article or substance within the United Kingdom of Great Britain and Ireland, and also after the copyright of such design in relation to such article or substance shall have expired, it shall be unlawful to put on any such article or such substance, in the manner herein-before required with respect to articles or substances whereto shall be applied a registered design, the marks herein-before required to be so applied, or any marks corresponding therewith or similar thereto, and if any person shall so unlawfully apply any such marks, or shall publish, sell, or expose for sale any article of manufacture, or any substance with any such marks so unlawfully applied, knowing that any such marks have been unlawfully applied, he shall forfeit for every such offence a sum not exceeding five pounds, which may be recovered by any person proceeding for the same by any of the ways herein-before directed with respect to penalties for pirating any such design.

Limitation of actions

Costs

XII And be it enacted, that no action or other proceeding for any offence or injury under this Act shall be brought after the expiration of twelve calendar months from the commission of the offence; and in every such action or other proceeding the party who shall prevail shall recover his full costs of suit or of such other proceeding

Justices may order payment of costs in cases of summary proceeding

XIII And be it enacted, that in the case of any summary proceeding before any two justices in England such justices are hereby authorised to award payment of costs to the party prevailing, and to grant a warrant for enforcing payment thereof against the summoning party, if unsuccessful, in the like manner as is herein-before provided for recovering any penalty with costs against any offender under this Act

Registrar, &c of designs to be appointed

XIV And for the purpose of registering designs for articles of manufacture, in order to obtain the protection of this Act, be it enacted, that the Lords of the Committee of Privy Council for the consideration of all matters of trade and plantations may appoint a person to be a registrar of designs for ornamenting articles of manufacture, and, if the Lords of the said Committee see fit, a deputy registrar, clerks, and other necessary officers and servants, and such registrar, deputy registrar, clerks, officers, and servants, shall hold their offices during the pleasure of the Lords of the said Committee, and the Commissioners of the Treasury may from time to time fix the salary or remuneration of such registrar, deputy registrar, clerks, officers, and servants, and, subject to the provisions of this Act, the Lords of the said Committee may make rules for regulating the execution of the duties of the office of the said registrar; and such registrar shall have a seal of office

Registrar's duties

XV And be it enacted, that the said registrar shall not register any design in respect of any application thereof to ornamenting any articles of manufacture or substances, unless he be furnished, in respect of each such application, with two copies, drawings, or prints of such design, accompanied with the name of every person who shall claim to be proprietor, or of the style or title of the firm under which such proprietor may be trading, with his place of abode or place of carrying on his business, or other place of address, and the number of the class in respect of which such registration is made, and the registrar shall register all such copies, drawings, or prints, from time to time successively as they are received by him for that purpose; and on every such copy, drawing, or print he shall affix a number corresponding to such succession, and he shall retain one copy, drawing, or print, which he shall file in his office, and the other he shall return to the person by whom the same has been forwarded to him; and in order to give ready access to the copies of designs so registered, he shall class such copies of designs, and keep a proper index of each class

XVI. And be it enacted, that upon every copy, drawing, or print of an original design so returned to the person registering as aforesaid, or attached thereto, and upon every copy, drawing, or print thereof received for the purpose of such registration, or of the transfer of such design being certified thereon or attached thereto, the registrar shall certify under his hand that the design has been so registered, the date of such registration, and the name of the registered proprietor, or the style or title of the firm under which such proprietor may be trading, with his place of abode or place of carrying on his business, or other place of address, and also the number of such design, together with such number or letter, or number and letter, and in such form as shall be employed by him to denote or correspond with the date of such registration; and such certificate made on every such original design, or on such copy thereof, and purporting to be signed by the registrar or deputy registrar, and purporting to have the seal of office of such registrar affixed thereto, shall, in the absence of evidence to the contrary, be sufficient proof, as follows, *Certificate of registration of design.*

Of the design, and of the name of the proprietor therein mentioned, having been duly registered, and

Of the commencement of the period of registry, and

Of the person named therein as proprietor being the proprietor, and

Of the originality of the design, and

Of the provisions of this Act, and of any rule under which the certificate appears to be made, having been complied with ·

And any such writing purporting to be such certificate shall, in the absence of evidence to the contrary, be received as evidence, without proof of the handwriting of the signature thereto, or of the seal of office affixed thereto, or of the person signing the same being the registrar or deputy registrar

XVII And be it enacted, that every person shall be at liberty to inspect any design whereof the copyright shall have expired, paying only such fee as shall be appointed by virtue of this Act in that behalf, but with regard to designs whereof the copyright shall not have expired, no such design shall be open to inspection, except by a proprietor of such design, or by any person authorised *Inspection of registered designs* by him in writing, or by any person specially authorised by the registrar, and then only in the presence of such registrar or in the presence of some person holding an appointment under this Act, and not so as to take a copy of any such design or of any part thereof, nor without paying for every such inspection such fee as aforesaid · provided always, that it shall be lawful for the said registrar to give to any person applying to him, and producing a particular design, together with the registration mark thereof, or producing such registration mark only, a certificate stating whether of such design there be any copyright existing, and if there be, in respect to what particular article of manufacture or substance such copyright exists, and the term of such copyright, and the date of registration, and also the name and address of the registered proprietor thereof

Application of fees of registration

XVIII And be it enacted, that the Commissioners of the Treasury shall from time to time fix fees to be paid for the services to be performed by the registrar, as they shall deem requisite, to defray the expenses of the said office, and the salaries or other remuneration of the said registrar, and of any other persons employed under him, with the sanction of the Commissioners of the Treasury, in the execution of this Act, and the balance, if any, shall be carried to the consolidated fund of the United Kingdom, and be paid accordingly into the receipt of her Majesty's Exchequer at Westminster, and the Commissioners of the Treasury may regulate the manner in which such fees are to be received, and in which they are to be kept, and in which they are to be accounted for, and they may also remit or dispense with the payment of such fees in any cases where they may think it expedient so to do provided always, that the fee for registering a design to be applied to any woven fabric mentioned or comprised in classes 7, 9, or 10, shall not exceed the sum of one shilling, that the fee for registering a design to be applied to a paper hanging shall not exceed the sum of ten shillings, and that the fee to be received by the registrar for giving a certificate relative to the existence or expiration of any copyright in any design printed on any woven fabric, yarn, thread, or warp, or printed, embossed, or worked on any paper hanging, to any person exhibiting a piece end of a registered pattern, with the registration mark thereon, shall not exceed the sum of two shillings and sixpence

Penalty for extortion

XIX. And be it enacted, that if either the registrar or any person employed under him either demand or receive any gratuity or reward, whether in money or otherwise, except the salary or remuneration authorised by the Commissioners of the Treasury, he shall forfeit for every such offence fifty pounds to any person suing for the same by action of debt in the Court of Exchequer at Westminster, and he shall also be liable to be either suspended or dismissed from his office, and rendered incapable of holding any situation in the said office, as the Commissioners of the Treasury see fit

Interpretation of Act.

XX. And for the interpretation of this Act, be it enacted, that the following terms and expressions, so far as they are not repugnant to the context of this Act, shall be construed as follows;

(that is to say,) the expression 'Commissioners of the Treasury' shall mean the Lord High Treasurer for the time being, or the Commissioners of her Majesty's Treasury for the time being, or any three or more of them; and the singular number shall include the plural as well as the singular number; and the masculine gender shall include the feminine gender as well as the masculine gender.

XXI. And be it enacted, that this Act may be amended or re- Alteration of pealed by any Act to be passed in the present session of Parliament. Act

---

SCHEDULES referred to by the foregoing Act.

SCHEDULE (A)

DATE OF ACTS.	TITLE
27 Geo. 3, c. 38 (1787)	An Act for the Encouragement of the Arts of designing and printing Linens, Cottons, Calicoes, and Muslins, by vesting the Properties thereof in the Designers, Printers, and Proprietors for a limited Time
29 Geo 3, c 19. (1789)	An Act for continuing an Act for the Encouragement of the Arts of designing and printing Linens, Cottons, Calicoes, and Muslins, by vesting the Properties thereof in the Designers, Printers, and Proprietors for a limited Time
34 Geo 3, c 23 (1794)	An Act for amending and making perpetual an Act for the Encouragement of the Arts of designing and printing Linens, Cottons, Calicoes, and Muslins, by vesting the Properties thereof in the Designers, Printers, and Proprietors for a limited Time
2 Vict c. 13 (1839)	An Act for extending the Copyright of Designs for Calico Printing to Designs for printing other woven Fabrics.

SCHEDULE (B)

DATE OF ACT	TITLE
2 Vict c 17. (1839)	An Act to secure to Proprietors of Designs for Articles of Manufacture the Copyright of such Designs for a limited Time.

SCHEDULE (C.)

DATE OF ACTS.	TITLE
38 Geo. 3, c. 71. (1798)	An Act for encouraging the Art of making new Models and Casts of Busts and other Things therein mentioned.
54 Geo. 3, c. 56. (1814)	An Act to amend and render more effectual an Act for encouraging the Art of making new Models and Casts of Busts and other Things therein mentioned, and for giving further Encouragement to such Arts.

6 & 7 Vict. c. 65.

An Act to amend the Laws relating to the Copyright of Designs.

5 & 6 Vict. c 100

WHEREAS by an Act passed in the fifth and sixth years of the reign of her present Majesty, intituled 'An Act to consolidate and amend the Laws relating to the Copyright of Designs for ornamenting Articles of Manufacture,' there was granted to the proprietor of any new and original design, with the exceptions therein mentioned, the sole right to apply the same to the ornamenting of any article of manufacture or any such substance as therein described during the respective periods therein mentioned. and whereas it is expedient to extend the protection afforded by the said Act to such designs herein-after mentioned, not being of an ornamental character, as are not included therein be it therefore enacted by the Queen's most Excellent Majesty, by and with the advice and consent of the Lords Spiritual and Temporal, and Commons, in this present Parliament assembled, and by the authority of the same, that this Act shall come into operation on the First day of September One thousand eight hundred and forty-three

Commencement of Act
Grant of copyright

II And with regard to any new or original design for any article of manufacture having reference to some purpose of utility, so far as such design shall be for the shape or configuration of such article, and that whether it be for the whole of such shape or configuration or only for a part thereof, be it enacted, that the proprietor of such design not previously published within the United Kingdom of Great Britain and Ireland or elsewhere shall have the sole right to apply such design to any article, or make or sell any article according to such design, for the term of three years, to be computed from the time of such design being registered according to this Act · provided always, that this enactment shall not extend to such designs as are within the provisions of the said Act, or of two other Acts passed respectively in the thirty-eighth and fifty-fourth years of the reign of his late Majesty King George the Third, and intituled respectively 'An Act for encouraging the Art of making new Models and Casts of Busts, and other Things therein mentioned,' and 'An Act to amend and render more effectual an Act for encouraging the Art of making new Models and Casts of Busts, and other Things therein mentioned '

III. Provided always, and be it enacted, that no person shall be entitled to the benefit of this Act unless such design have before publication thereof been registered according to this Act, and unless the name of such person shall be registered according to this Act as a proprietor of such design, and unless after publication of such design every article of manufacture made by him according to such design or on which such design is used, hath thereon the word 'registered,' with the date of registration.

IV And be it enacted, that unless a design applied to any article of manufacture be registered either as aforesaid or according to the provisions of the said first-mentioned Act, and also after the copyright of such design shall have expired, it shall be unlawful to put on any such article the word 'registered,' or to advertise the same for sale as a registered article, and if any person shall so unlawfully publish, sell, or expose or advertise for sale any such article of manufacture, he shall forfeit for every such offence a sum not exceeding five pounds nor less than one pound, which may be recovered by any person proceeding for the same by any of the remedies hereby given for the recovery of penalties for pirating any such design

V And be it enacted, that all such articles of manufacture as are commonly known by the name of floor cloths or oil cloths shall henceforth be considered as included in Class Six in the said first-mentioned Act in that behalf mentioned, and be registered accordingly

VI And be it enacted, that all and every the clauses and provisions contained in the said first-mentioned Act, so far as they are not repugnant to the provisions contained in this Act, relating respectively to the explanation of the term proprietor, to the transfer of designs, to the piracy of designs, to the mode of recovering penalties, to actions for damages, to cancelling and amending registrations, to the limitation of actions, to the awarding of costs, to the certificate of registration, to the fixing and application of fees of registration, and to the penalty for extortion, shall be applied and extended to this present Act as fully and effectually, and to all intents and purposes, as if the said several clauses and provisoes had been particularly repeated and re-enacted in the body of this Act

VII And be it enacted, that so much of the said first-mentioned Act as relates to the appointment of a registrar of designs for ornamenting articles of manufacture, and other officers, as well as to the fixing of the salaries for the payment of the same, shall be

Proviso.

38 G 3, c. 71

54 G. 3, c 56.

Conditions of copyright.

Penalty for wrongfully using marks denoting a registered design

Floor or oil cloths included in Class Six

Certain provisions of 5 & 6 Vict. c 100, to apply to this Act

Appointment of registrar, &c.

and the same is hereby repealed, and for the purpose of carrying into effect the provisions as well of this Act as of the said first-mentioned Act, the Lords of the Committee of the Privy Council for the consideration of all matters of trade and plantations may appoint a person to be registrar of designs for articles of manufacture, and, if the Lords of the said Committee see fit, an assistant registrar and other necessary officers and servants; and such registrar, assistant registrar, officers, and servants shall hold their offices during the pleasure of the Lords of the said Committee; and such registrar shall have a seal of office, and the Commissioners of Her Majesty's Treasury may from time to time fix the salary or other remuneration of such registrar, assistant registrar, and other officers and servants; and all the provisions contained in the said first-mentioned Act, and not hereby repealed, relating to the registrar, deputy registrar, clerks, and other officers and servants thereby appointed and therein named, shall be construed and held to apply respectively to the registrar, assistant registrar, and other officers and servants to be appointed under this Act

Registrar's duties.

VIII. And be it enacted, that the said registrar shall not register any design for the shape or configuration of any article of manufacture as aforesaid unless he be furnished with two exactly similar drawings or prints of such design, with such description in writing as may be necessary to render the same intelligible according to the judgment of the said registrar, together with the title of the said design and the name of every person who shall claim to be proprietor, or of the style or title of the firm under which such proprietor may be trading, with his place of abode, or place of carrying on business, or other place of address, and

Drawings

every such drawing or print, together with the title and description of such design, and the name and address of the proprietor aforesaid, shall be on one sheet of paper or parchment, and on the same side thereof, and the size of the said sheet shall not exceed twenty-four inches by fifteen inches, and there shall be left on one of the said sheets a blank space on the same side on which are the said drawings, title, description, name, and address, of the size of six inches by four inches, for the certificate herein mentioned, and the said drawings or prints shall be made on a proper geometric scale, and the said description shall set forth such part or parts of the said design (if any) as shall not be new or original, and the said registrar shall register all such drawings or prints from time to time as they are received by him for that purpose, and on every such drawing or print he shall affix a number corresponding to the order of succession in the register, and he shall retain one drawing or print which he shall file at his office, and the other he shall return to the person by whom the same has been forwarded to him, and in order to give a ready access to the designs so registered he shall keep a proper index of the titles thereof

Discretionary power as to registry vested

IX And be it enacted, that if any design be brought to the said registrar to be registered under the said first-mentioned Act, and it shall appear to him that the same ought to be registered

under this present Act, it shall be lawful for the said registrar to
refuse to register such design otherwise than under the present
Act and in the manner hereby provided; and if it shall appear to
the said registrar that the design brought to be registered under
the said first-mentioned Act or this Act is not intended to be
applied to any article of manufacture, but only to some label,
wrapper, or other covering in which such article might be exposed
for sale, or that such design is contrary to public morality or order,
it shall be lawful for the said registrar in his discretion wholly to
refuse to register such design: provided always, that the Lords of
the said Committee of Privy Council may, on representation made
to them by the proprietor of any design so wholly refused to be
registered as aforesaid, if they shall see fit, direct the said registrar
to register such design, whereupon and in such case the said
registrar shall be and is hereby required to register the same
accordingly.

In the registrar

Proviso.

X. And be it enacted, that every person shall be at liberty to
inspect the index of the titles of the designs, not being ornamental
designs registered under this Act, and to take copies from the
same, paying only such fees as shall be appointed by virtue of this
Act in that behalf; and every person shall be at liberty to inspect
any such design, and to take copies thereof, paying such fee as
aforesaid, but no design whereof the copyright shall not have
expired shall be open to inspection except in the presence of such
registrar, or in the presence of some person holding an appointment under this Act, and not so as to take a copy of such design,
nor without paying such fee as aforesaid

Inspection of Index of Titles of Designs, &c

XI And, for the interpretation of this Act, be it enacted, that
the following terms and expressions, so far as they are not repugnant to the context of this Act, shall be construed as follows;
(that is to say,) the expression 'Commissioners of the Treasury'
shall mean the Lord High Treasurer for the time being, or the
Commissioners of her Majesty's Treasury of the United Kingdom
of Great Britain and Ireland for the time being, or any three or
more of them, and the singular number shall include the plural
as well as the singular number, and the masculine gender shall
include the feminine gender as well as the masculine gender

Interpretation of Act.

XII And be it enacted, that this Act may be amended or
repealed by any Act to be passed in the present session of
Parliament.

Alteration of Act.

---

7 VICT c 12

An Act to amend the Law relating to International Copyright

WHEREAS by an Act passed in the session of Parliament held in
the first and second years of the reign of her present Majesty,
intituled 'An Act for securing to Authors in certain Cases the
Benefit of international Copyright' (and which Act is hereinafter,

1 & 2 Vict.
c 59

for the sake of perspicuity, designated as 'The International Copyright Act'), her Majesty was empowered by order in Council to direct that the authors of books which should after a future time, to be specified in such order in Council, be published in any foreign country, to be specified in such order in Council, and their executors, administrators, and assigns, should have the sole liberty of printing and reprinting such books within the British dominions for such term as her Majesty should by such order in Council direct, not exceeding the term which authors, being British subjects, were then (that is to say), at the time of passing the said Act, entitled to in respect of books first published in the United Kingdom; and the said Act contains divers enactments securing to authors and their representatives the copyright in the books to which any such order in Council should extend. And whereas an Act was passed in the session of Parliament held in 5 & 6 Vict. c. 45 the fifth and sixth years of the reign of her present Majesty, intituled 'An Act to amend the Law of Copyright' (and which Act is hereinafter, for the sake of perspicuity, designated as 'The Copyright Amendment Act'), repealing various Acts therein mentioned relating to the copyright of printed books, and extending, defining, and securing to authors and their representatives the copyright of books. And whereas an Act was passed in the session of Parliament held in the third and fourth years of the reign of his late 3 & 4 W 4, c 15 Majesty King William the Fourth, intituled 'An Act to amend the Laws relating to Dramatic Literary Property' (and which Act is hereinafter, for the sake of perspicuity, designated as 'The Dramatic Literary Property Act'), whereby the sole liberty of representing or causing to be represented any dramatic piece in any place of dramatic entertainment in any part of the British dominions, which should be composed and not printed or published by the author thereof or his assignee, was secured to such author or his assignee; and by the said Act it was enacted, that the author of any such production which should thereafter be printed and published, or his assignee, should have the like sole liberty of representation until the end of twenty-eight years from the first publication thereof. And whereas by the said Copyright Amendment Act the provisions of the said Dramatic Literary Property Act and of the said Copyright Amendment Act were made applicable to musical compositions, and it was thereby also enacted, that the sole liberty of representing or performing, or causing or permitting to be represented or performed, in any part of the British dominions, any dramatic piece or musical composition, should endure and be the property of the author thereof and his assigns for the term in the said Copyright Amendment Act provided for the duration of the copyright in books, and that the provisions therein enacted in respect of the property of such copyright should apply to the liberty of representing or performing any dramatic piece or musical composition. And whereas under or by virtue of the four several Acts next hereinafter mentioned, (that is to say,) an Act passed in the eighth year of the reign of 8 G 2 c 13 his late Majesty King George the Second, intituled 'An Act for the Encouragement of the Arts of designing, engraving, and

etching historical and other Prints, by vesting the Properties
thereof in the Inventors or Engravers during the Time therein
mentioned;' an Act passed in the seventh year of his late 7 G 3, c. 38.
Majesty King George the Third, intituled 'An Act to amend
and render more effectual an Act made in the Eighth Year of the
Reign of King George the Second, for Encouragement of the Arts
of designing, engraving, and etching historical and other Prints,
and for vesting in and securing to Jane Hogarth, Widow, the
Property in certain Prints;' an Act passed in the seventeenth 17 G 3, c 57
year of the reign of his late Majesty King George the Third,
intituled 'An Act for more effectually securing the Property of
Prints to Inventors and Engravers, by enabling them to sue for
and recover Penalties in certain Cases;' and an Act passed in the
session of Parliament held in the sixth and seventh years of the 6 & 7 W 4,
reign of his late Majesty King William the Fourth, intituled 'An c 59
Act to extend the Protection of Copyright in Prints and Engravings to Ireland,' (and which said four several Acts are hereinafter,
for the sake of perspicuity, designated as the Engraving Copyright
Acts,) every person who invents or designs, engraves, etches, or
works in mezzotinto or chiaro-oscuro, or from his own work,
design, or invention causes or procures to be designed, engraved,
etched, or worked in mezzotinto or chiaro-oscuro any historical
print or prints, or any print or prints of any portrait, conversation,
landscape, or architecture, map, chart, or plan, or any other print
or prints whatsoever, and every person who engraves, etches, or
works in mezzotinto or chiaro-oscuro, or causes to be engraved,
etched, or worked, any print taken from any picture, drawing,
model, or sculpture, either ancient or modern, notwithstanding
such print shall not have been graven or drawn from the original
design of such graver, etcher, or draughtsman, is entitled to the
copyright of such print for the term of twenty-eight years from
the first publishing thereof, and by the said several Engraving
Copyright Acts it is provided that the name of the proprietor
shall be truly engraved on each plate, and printed on every such
print, and remedies are provided for the infringement of such
copyright And whereas under and by virtue of an Act passed in
the thirty-eighth year of the reign of his late Majesty King George 38 G 3, c 71.
the Third, intituled 'An Act for encouraging the Art of making
new Models and Casts of Busts and other Things therein men-
tioned,' and of an Act passed in the fifty-fourth year of the reign 54 G 3, c 56.
of his late Majesty King George the Third, intituled 'An Act to
amend and render more effectual an Act of his present Majesty,
for encouraging the Art of making new Models and Casts of Busts
and other Things therein mentioned, and for giving further Encouragement to such Arts' (and which said Acts are, for the sake
of perspicuity, hereinafter designated as the Sculpture Copyright
Acts), every person who makes or causes to be made any new
and original sculpture, or model or copy or cast of the human
figure, any bust or part of the human figure clothed in drapery or
otherwise, any animal or part of any animal combined with the
human figure or otherwise, any subject, being matter of invention
in sculpture, any alto or basso relievo, representing any of the

matters aforesaid, or any cast from nature of the human figure or part thereof, or of any animal or part thereof, or of any such subject representing any of the matters aforesaid, whether separate or combined, is entitled to the copyright in such new and original sculpture, model, copy, and cast, for fourteen years from first putting forth and publishing the same, and for an additional period of fourteen years in case the original maker is living at the end of the first period; and by the said Acts it is provided that the name of the proprietor, with the date of the publication thereof, is to be put on all such sculptures, models, copies, and casts, and remedies are provided for the infringement of such copyright· And whereas the powers vested in her Majesty by the said International Copyright Act are insufficient to enable her Majesty to confer upon authors of books first published in foreign countries copyright of the like duration, and with the like remedies for the infringement thereof, which are conferred and provided by the said Copyright Amendment Act with respect to authors of books first published in the British dominions; and the said International Copyright Act does not empower her Majesty to confer any exclusive right of representing or performing dramatic pieces or musical compositions first published in foreign countries upon the authors thereof, nor to extend the privilege of copyright to prints and sculpture first published abroad, and it is expedient to vest increased powers in her Majesty in this respect, and for that purpose to repeal the said International Copyright Act, and to give such other powers to her Majesty, and to make such further provisions, as are hereinafter contained. Be it therefore enacted by the Queen's most excellent Majesty, by and with the advice and consent of the Lords Spiritual and Temporal, and Commons, in this present Parliament assembled, and by the authority of the same, that the said recited Act herein designated as the International Copyright Act shall be and the same is hereby repealed.

Repeal of International Copyright Act

II And be it enacted, That it shall be lawful for her Majesty, by any order of her Majesty in Council, to direct that, as respects all or any particular class or classes of the following works (namely), books, prints, articles of sculpture, and other works of art, to be defined in such order, which shall after a future time, to be specified in such order, be first published in any foreign country to be named in such order, the authors, inventors, designers, engravers, and makers thereof respectively, their respective executors, administrators, and assigns, shall have the privilege of copyright therein during such period or respective periods as shall be defined in such order, not exceeding, however, as to any of the above-mentioned works, the term of copyright which authors, inventors, designers, engravers, and makers of the like works respectively first published in the United Kingdom may be then entitled to under the hereinbefore recited Acts respectively, or under any Acts which may hereafter be passed in that behalf

Her Majesty, by order in Council, may direct that authors, &c of works first published in foreign countries shall have copyright therein within her Majesty's dominions

III. And be it enacted, that in case any such order shall apply to books, all and singular the enactments of the said Copyright Amendment Act, and of any other Act for the time being in force

If the order applies to books, the copyright

with relation to the copyright in books first published in this country, shall, from and after the time so to be specified in that behalf in such order, and subject to such limitation as to the duration of the copyright as shall be therein contained, apply to and be in force in respect of the books to which such order shall extend, and which shall have been registered as hereinafter is provided, in such and the same manner as if such books were first published in the United Kingdom, save and except such of the said enactments, or such parts thereof, as shall be excepted in such order, and save and except such of the said enactments as relate to the delivery of copies of books at the British Museum, and to or for the use of the other libraries mentioned in the said Copyright Amendment Act. law as to books first published in this country shall apply to the books to which the order relates, with certain exceptions.

IV. And be it enacted, that in case any such order shall apply to prints, articles of sculpture, or to any such other works of art as aforesaid, all and singular the enactments of the said Engraving Copyright Acts and the said Sculpture Copyright Acts, or of any other Act for the time being in force with relation to the copyright in prints or articles of sculpture first published in this country, and of any Act for the time being in force with relation to the copyright in any similar works of art first published in this country, shall, from and after the time so to be specified in that behalf in such order, and subject to such limitation as to the duration of the copyright as shall be therein contained respectively, apply to and be in force in respect of the prints, articles of sculpture, and other works of art to which such order shall extend, and which shall have been registered as hereinafter is provided, in such and the same manner as if such articles and other works of art were first published in the United Kingdom, save and except such of the said enactments or such parts thereof as shall be excepted in such order. If the order applies to prints, sculptures, &c., the copyright law as to prints or sculptures first published in this country shall apply to the prints, sculptures, &c. to which such order relates.

V. And be it enacted, that it shall be lawful for her Majesty, by any order of her Majesty in Council, to direct that the authors of dramatic pieces and musical compositions which shall after a future time, to be specified in such order, be first publicly represented or performed in any foreign country to be named in such order, shall have the sole liberty of representing or performing in any part of the British dominions such dramatic pieces or musical compositions during such period as shall be defined in such order, not exceeding the period during which authors of dramatic pieces and musical compositions first publicly represented or performed in the United Kingdom may for the time be entitled by law to the sole liberty of representing and performing the same, and from and after the time so specified in any such last-mentioned order the enactments of the said Dramatic Literary Property Act and of the said Copyright Amendment Act, and of any other Act for the time being in force with relation to the liberty of publicly representing and performing dramatic pieces or musical compositions, shall, subject to such limitation as to the duration of the right conferred by any such order as shall be therein contained, apply to and be in force in respect of the dramatic pieces and musical compositions to which such order shall extend, and which Her Majesty may, by order in Council, direct that authors and composers of dramatic pieces and musical compositions first publicly represented and performed in foreign countries shall have similar rights in the British dominions

shall have been registered as herein-after is provided, in such and the same manner as if such dramatic pieces and musical compositions had been first publicly represented and performed in the British dominions, save and except such of the said enactments or such parts thereof as shall be excepted in such order

VI Provided always, and be it enacted, that no author of any book, dramatic piece or musical composition, or his executors, administrators, or assigns, and no inventor, designer, or engraver of any print, or maker of any article of sculpture, or other work of art, his executors, administrators, or assigns, shall be entitled to the benefit of this Act, or of any order in Council to be issued in pursuance thereof, unless within a time or times to be in that behalf prescribed in each such order in Council, such book, dramatic piece, musical composition, print, article of sculpture, or other work of art, shall have been so registered, and such copy thereof shall have been so delivered as herein-after is mentioned , (that is to say,) as regards such book, and also such dramatic piece or musical composition, (in the event of the same having been printed,) the title to the copy thereof, the name and place of abode of the author or composer thereof, the name and place of abode of the proprietor of the copyright thereof, the time and place of the first publication, representation, or performance thereof, as the case may be, in the foreign country named in the order in Council under which the benefits of this Act shall be claimed, shall be entered in the register book of the Company of Stationers in London, and one printed copy of the whole of such book, and of such dramatic piece or musical composition, in the event of the same having been printed, and of every volume thereof, upon the best paper upon which the largest number or impression of the book, dramatic piece, or musical composition shall have been printed for sale, together with all maps and prints relating thereto, shall be delivered to the officer of the Company of Stationers at the Hall of the said Company , and as regards dramatic pieces and musical compositions in manuscript, the title to the same, the name and place of abode of the author or composer thereof, the name and place of abode of the proprietor of the right of representing or performing the same, and the time and place of the first representation or performance thereof in the country named in the order in Council under which the benefit of the Act shall be claimed, shall be entered in the said register book of the said Company of Stationers in London ; and as regards prints, the title thereof, the name and place of abode of the inventor, designer, or engraver thereof, the name of the proprietor of the copyright therein, and the time and place of the first publication thereof in the foreign country named in the order in Council under which the benefits of the Act shall be claimed, shall be entered in the said register book of the said Company of Stationers in London, and a copy of such print, upon the best paper upon which the largest number or impressions of the print shall have been printed for sale, shall be delivered to the officer of the Company of Stationers at the Hall of the said Company , and as regards any such article of sculpture, or any such other work of art as aforesaid, a descriptive title thereof,

the name and place of abode of the maker thereof, the name of
the proprietor of the copyright therein, and the time and place of
its first publication in the foreign country named in the order in
Council under which the benefit of this Act shall be claimed, shall
be entered in the said register book of the said Company of Stationers in London; and the officer of the said Company of Stationers
receiving such copies so to be delivered as aforesaid shall give a
receipt in writing for the same, and such delivery shall to all
intents and purposes be a sufficient delivery under the provisions
of this Act

VII. Provided always, and be it enacted, that if a book be
published anonymously it shall be sufficient to insert in the entry
thereof in such register book the name and place of abode of the
first publisher thereof, instead of the name and place of abode of
the author thereof, together with a declaration that such entry is
made either on behalf of the author or on behalf of such first
publisher, as the case may require

In case of books
published anony-
mously, the
name of the
publisher to be
sufficient.

VIII. And be it enacted, that the several enactments in the said
Copyright Amendment Act contained with relation to keeping the
said register book, and the inspection thereof, the searches therein,
and the delivery of certified and stamped copies thereof, the reception of such copies in evidence, the making of false entries in the
said book, and the production in evidence of papers falsely purporting to be copies of entries in the said book, the applications to
the courts and judges by persons aggrieved by entries in the said
book, and the expunging and varying such entries, shall apply to
the books, dramatic pieces, and musical compositions, prints,
articles of sculpture, and other works of art, to which any order
in Council issued in pursuance of this Act shall extend, and to the
entries and assignments of copyright and proprietorship therein,
in such and the same manner as if such enactments were here
expressly enacted in relation thereto, save and except that the
forms of entry prescribed by the said Copyright Amendment Act
may be varied to meet the circumstances of the case, and that the
sum to be demanded by the officer of the said Company of Stationers
for making any entry required by this Act shall be one shilling
only.

The provisions
of the Copy-
right Amend-
ment Act as
regards entries
in the register
book of the
Company of
Stationers, &c.
to apply to
entries under
this Act

IX. And be it enacted, that every entry made in pursuance of
this Act of a first publication shall be *primâ facie* proof of a rightful
first publication, but if there be a wrongful first publication, and
any party have availed himself thereof to obtain an entry of a
spurious work, no order for expunging or varying such entry shall
be made unless it be proved to the satisfaction of the Court or of
the judge taking cognisance of the application for expunging or
varying such entry, first, with respect to a wrongful publication in
a country to which the author or first publisher does not belong,
and in regard to which there does not subsist with this country
any treaty of international copyright, that the party making the
application was the author or first publisher, as the case requires,
second, with respect to a wrongful first publication either in the
country where a rightful first publication has taken place, or in
regard to which there subsists with this country a treaty of inter-

As to expunging
or varying entry
grounded in
wrongful first
publication

national copyright, that a court of competent jurisdiction in any such country where such wrongful first publication has taken place has given judgment in favour of the right of the party claiming to be the author or first publisher.

Copies of books wherein copyright is subsisting under this Act printed in foreign countries other than those wherein the book was first published prohibited to be imported

X. And be it enacted, that all copies of books wherein there shall be any subsisting copyright under or by virtue of this Act, or of any order in Council made in pursuance thereof, printed or reprinted in any foreign country except that in which such books were first published, shall be and the same are hereby absolutely prohibited to be imported into any part of the British dominions, except by or with the consent of the registered proprietor of the copyright thereof, or his agent authorised in writing, and if imported contrary to this prohibition the same and the importers thereof shall be subject to the enactments in force relating to goods prohibited to be imported by any Act relating to the customs, and as respects any such copies so prohibited to be imported, and also as respects any copies unlawfully printed in any place whatsoever of any books wherein there shall be any such subsisting copyright as aforesaid, any person who shall in any part of the British dominions import such prohibited or unlawfully printed copies, or who, knowing such copies to be so unlawfully imported or unlawfully printed, shall sell, publish, or expose to sale or hire, or shall cause to be sold, published, or exposed to sale or hire, or have in his possession for sale or hire, any such copies so unlawfully imported or unlawfully printed, such offender shall be liable to a special action on the case at the suit of the proprietor of such copyright, to be brought and prosecuted in the same courts and in the same manner, and with the like restrictions upon the proceedings of the defendant, as are respectively prescribed in the said Copyright Amendment Act with relation to actions thereby authorised to be brought by proprietors of copyright against persons importing or selling books unlawfully printed in the British dominions

Officer of Stationers Company to deposit books, &c in the British Museum

XI And be it enacted, that the said officer of the said Company of Stationers shall receive at the Hall of the said Company every book, volume, or print so to be delivered as aforesaid, and within one calendar month after receiving such book, volume, or print shall deposit the same in the library of the British Museum

Second or subsequent editions

XII Provided always, and be it enacted, that it shall not be requisite to deliver to the said officer of the said Stationers Company any printed copy of the second or of any subsequent edition of any book or books so delivered as aforesaid, unless the same shall contain additions or alterations.

Orders in Council may specify different periods for different foreign countries and for different classes of works

XIII. And be it enacted, that the respective terms to be specified by such orders in Council respectively for the continuance of the privilege to be granted in respect of works to be first published in foreign countries may be different for works first published in different foreign countries and for different classes of such works; and that the times to be prescribed for the entries to be made in the register book of the Stationers Company, and for the deliveries of the books and other articles to the said officer of the Stationers Company, as herein-before is mentioned, may be different for different foreign countries and for different classes of books or other articles.

XIV. Provided always, and be it enacted, that no such order in Council shall have any effect unless it shall be therein stated, as the ground for issuing the same, that due protection has been secured by the foreign power so named in such order in Council for the benefit of parties interested in works first published in the dominions of her Majesty similar to those comprised in such order.

XV. And be it enacted, that every order in Council to be made under the authority of this Act shall as soon as may be after the making thereof by her Majesty in Council be published in the 'London Gazette,' and from the time of such publication shall have the same effect as if every part thereof were included in this Act

XVI. And be it enacted, that a copy of every order of her Majesty in Council made under this Act shall be laid before both Houses of Parliament within six weeks after issuing the same, if Parliament be then sitting, and if not, then within six weeks after the commencement of the then next session of Parliament

XVII. And be it enacted, that it shall be lawful for her Majesty by an order in Council from time to time to revoke or alter any order in Council previously made under the authority of this Act, but nevertheless without prejudice to any rights acquired previously to such revocation or alteration.

XVIII. Provided always, and be it enacted, that nothing in this Act contained shall be construed to prevent the printing, publication, or sale of any translation of any book, the author whereof and his assigns may be entitled to the benefit of this Act.

XIX And be it enacted, that neither the author of any book, nor the author or composer of any dramatic piece or musical composition, nor the inventor, designer, or engraver of any print, nor the maker of any article of sculpture, or of such other work of art as aforesaid, which shall after the passing of this Act be first published out of her Majesty's dominions, shall have any copyright therein respectively, or any exclusive right to the public representation or performance thereof, otherwise than such (if any) as he may become entitled to under this Act.

XX And be it enacted, that in the construction of this Act the word 'book' shall be construed to include 'volume,' 'pamphlet,' 'sheet of letter-press,' 'sheet of music,' 'map,' 'chart,' or 'plan,' and the expression 'articles of sculpture' shall mean all such sculptures, models, copies, and casts as are described in the said Sculpture Copyright Acts, and in respect of which the privileges of copyright are thereby conferred; and the words 'printing' and 're-printing' shall include engraving and any other method of multiplying copies, and the expression 'Her Majesty' shall include the heirs and successors of her Majesty; and the expressions 'Order of her Majesty in Council,' 'Order in Council,' and 'Order,' shall respectively mean order of her Majesty acting by and with the advice of her Majesty's most Honourable Privy Council, and the expression 'Officer of the Company of Stationers' shall mean the officer appointed by the said Company of Stationers for the purposes of the said Copyright Amendment Act ; and in describing any persons or things any word importing the plural number shall mean also one person or thing, and any word importing the singular number shall include several persons or things, and any word importing the masculine shall include also the feminine gender, unless in any of such cases there shall be something in the subject or context repugnant to such construction

Act may be repealed this session. XXI. And be it enacted, that this Act may be amended or repealed by any Act to be passed in this present session of Parliament.

---

7 & 8 VICT. c. 79.

An Act to reduce, under certain Circumstances, the Duties payable upon Books and Engravings

WHEREAS by an Act passed in the session of Parliament held in the fifth and sixth years of her present Majesty, intituled 'An Act to amend the Laws relating to the Customs,' certain duties of Customs were granted and made payable upon books and prints of or from foreign countries and whereas by an Act passed in the present session of Parliament, intituled 'An Act to amend the Law relating to International Copyright,' it is amongst other things enacted, that it shall be lawful for her Majesty, by any order in Council, to grant unto the authors, inventors, designers, engravers, or makers of any books, prints, or other works of art first published in any foreign country specified in such order, the privilege of copyright therein for certain periods, and under certain conditions, in the said last-mentioned Act defined and contained: and whereas it is expedient that provision should be made in the manner hereinafter mentioned for reducing, in cases where her Majesty shall have issued any such order in Council as aforesaid, the duties of customs now payable on the importation of books and prints be it therefore enacted by the Queen's most Excellent Majesty, by and with the advice and consent of the Lords Spiritual and Temporal, and Commons, in this present Parliament assembled, and by the authority of the same, that whenever and so often as her Majesty shall by virtue of the said recited power, by any order or orders in Council, declare that the authors, inventors, designers, engravers, or makers of any books, prints, or other works of art first published in any foreign country, shall have the privilege of copyright therein, then and in every such case it shall be lawful for her Majesty, by any order or orders in Council, to declare that in respect of books and prints, or either of them, published in and imported from such foreign country, the duties of customs now payable on the importation of books and prints respectively shall, from and after a time to be named in such order or orders,

5 & 6 Vict c 47

7 & 8 Vict. c. 12

Her Majesty, by order in Council, may reduce the duties on foreign books and prints in cases in which copyright is allowed to the country of export under 7 & 8 Vict. c. 12,

altogether cease and determine; and that in lieu thereof there shall be payable on such books or prints respectively, from and after such time as aforesaid, only such duties of Customs as are set forth in the Schedule to this Act annexed.

II And be it enacted, that with regard to books and prints published in and imported from any foreign country, between which country and her Majesty there is now subsisting, and shall at the time of the making of any such order in Council as is hereinafter described subsist, any treaty or convention binding her Majesty to admit the books and prints of such country, either conditionally or unconditionally, into the United Kingdom, on the same terms as those of the most favoured nation, it shall be lawful for her Majesty, by any order or orders in Council, to declare that in respect of books and prints, or either of them, published in and imported from such foreign country, the duties of Customs now payable on the importation of books and prints respectively shall, from and after a time to be named therein, altogether cease and determine, and that in lieu thereof there shall be payable on the importation of such books or prints respectively, from and after such time as aforesaid, only such duties of Customs as are set forth in the Schedule to this Act annexed. provided always, that in case the privileges granted by any treaty to any foreign country, in respect of which any such order or orders in Council as last aforesaid shall by virtue of this enactment be issued, shall have been granted conditionally, such order shall expressly declare that such foreign country hath duly fulfilled the conditions required in return for such privileges, and that it is entitled thereto

and may reduce the duties on books and prints in favour of countries with which her Majesty has treaties of reciprocity.

If any treaty be conditional, order to state the fulfilment of the condition.

III. And be it enacted, that it shall be lawful for her Majesty, by any further order or orders in Council, from time to time to revoke the whole or any part of any order or orders issued by her Majesty in Council under the authority of this Act, and that from and after a day to be named in such Order or Orders of Revocation, such order or orders issued under the authority of this Act, or such part thereof as shall be specified in such Order or Orders of Revocation, shall cease and determine, and that the duties of Customs now payable upon books and prints respectively shall be payable in like manner as if such order or orders, or such part or parts thereof respectively, had not been made

Power to her Majesty in Council to revoke any orders

IV And be it enacted, that every order or orders in Council issued under the authority of this Act shall, within fourteen days after the issuing thereof, be twice published in the 'London Gazette'

Orders to be published in the Gazette,

V. And be it enacted, that a copy of every order or orders in Council issued under the authority of this Act shall be laid before both Houses of Parliament within six weeks after issuing the same, if Parliament be then sitting, and if not, then within six weeks after the commencement of the then next session of Parliament

and to be laid before Parliament

VI And be it enacted, that this Act may be amended or repealed by any Act to be passed in the present session of Parliament

Act may be amended this session

SCHEDULE to which the foregoing Act refers.

Books, viz.

	s.	d.
Works in the language or languages of the country of export, originally produced therein, or original works of that country in the dead languages, or other works in the dead languages with original commentaries produced in that country - the cwt.	15	0
All other works published in the country of export, if printed prior to the year 1801 - - the cwt.	20	0
If printed in or since the year 1801 - the cwt	50	0
Prints and drawings, plain or coloured single - each	0	0¼
Ditto - bound or sewn - the dozen	0	1½

---

10 & 11 Vict. c. 95.

An Act to amend the Law relating to the Protection in the Colonies of Works entitled to Copyright in the United Kingdom

WHEREAS by an Act passed in the session of Parliament holden in the fifth and sixth years of her present Majesty, intituled 'An Act to amend the Law of Copyright,' it is amongst other things enacted, that it shall not be lawful for any person not being the proprietor of the copyright, or some person authorised by him, to import into any part of the United Kingdom, or into any other part of the British dominions, for sale or hire, any printed book first composed or written or printed or published in any part of the United Kingdom wherein there shall be copyright, and reprinted in any country or place whatsoever out of the British dominions and whereas by an Act passed in the session of Parliament holden in the eighth and ninth years of the reign of her present Majesty, intituled 'An Act to regulate the Trade of the British Possessions abroad,' books wherein the copyright is subsisting, first composed or written or printed in the United Kingdom, and printed or reprinted in any other country, are absolutely prohibited to be imported into the British possessions abroad and whereas by the said last-recited Act it is enacted, that all laws, bye laws, usages, or customs in practice, or endeavoured or pretended to be in force or practice in any of the British possessions in America, which are in anywise repugnant to the said Act or to any Act of Parliament made or to be made in the United Kingdom, so far as such Act shall relate to and mention the said possessions, are and shall be null and void to all intents and purposes whatsoever. now be it enacted, by the Queen's most Excellent Majesty, by and with the advice and consent of the Lords Spiritual and Temporal, and Commons, in this present Parliament assembled, and by the authority of the same, that in case the Legislature or proper legislative authorities in any British possession shall be disposed to make due provision for securing or protecting the rights

Margin notes:

& 6 Vict. c 45.

8 & 9 Vict c 93

Her Majesty may suspend in certain cases

of British authors in such possession, and shall pass an Act or
make an ordinance for that purpose, and shall transmit the same
in the proper manner to the Secretary of State, in order that it
may be submitted to her Majesty, and in case her Majesty shall
be of opinion that such Act or ordinance is sufficient for the purpose
of securing to British authors reasonable protection within such
possession, it shall be lawful for her Majesty, if she think fit so
to do, to express her royal approval of such Act or ordinance, and
thereupon to issue an order in Council declaring that so long as
the provisions of such Act or ordinance continue in force within
such colony the prohibitions contained in the aforesaid Acts, and
herein-before recited, and any prohibitions contained in the said
Acts or in any other Acts against the importing, selling, letting
out to hire, exposing for sale or hire, or possessing foreign reprints
of books first composed, written, printed, or published in the
United Kingdom, and entitled to copyright therein, shall be suspended as far as regards such colony, and thereupon such Act or
ordinance shall come into operation, except so far as may be otherwise provided therein, or as may be otherwise directed by such
order in Council, any thing in the said last-recited Act or in any
other Act to the contrary notwithstanding.

the prohibitions
against the
admission of
pirated books
into the colonies
in certain cases.

II And be it enacted, that every such order in Council shall,
within one week after the issuing thereof, be published in the
'London Gazette,' and that a copy thereof, and of every such Colonial Act or ordinance so approved as aforesaid by her Majesty,
shall be laid before both Houses of Parliament within six weeks
after the issuing of such order, if Parliament be then sitting, or if
Parliament be not then sitting, then within six weeks after the
opening of the next session of Parliament

Orders in
Council to be
published in
Gazette
Orders in
Council and the
colonial acts or
ordinances to
be laid before
Parliament

III And be it enacted, this Act may be amended or repealed by
any Act to be passed in the present session of Parliament

Act may be
amended, &c.

---

13 & 14 VICT c 104.

*An Act to extend and amend the Acts relating to the Copyright of
Designs*

WHEREAS it is expedient to extend and amend the Acts relating
to the copyright of designs be it therefore enacted by the Queen's
most excellent Majesty, by and with the advice and consent of
the Lords Spiritual and Temporal, and Commons, in this present
Parliament assembled, and by the authority of the same

I. That the registrar of designs, upon application by or on
behalf of the proprietor of any design not previously published
within the United Kingdom of Great Britain and Ireland or elsewhere, and which may be registered under the Designs Act, 1842,
or under the Designs Act, 1843, for the provisional registration of
such design, under this Act, and upon being furnished with such
copy, drawing, print, or description in writing or in print as in the

Certain designs
may be registered
provisionally
for one year

judgment of the said registrar shall be sufficient to identify the particular design in respect of which such registration is desired, and the name of the person claiming to be proprietor, together with his place of abode or business, or other place of address, or the style or title of the firm under which he may be trading, shall register such design in such manner and form as shall from time to time be prescribed or approved by the Board of Trade; and any design so registered shall be deemed 'provisionally registered,' and the registration thereof shall continue in force for the term of one year from the time of the same being registered as aforesaid; and the said registrar shall certify, under his hand and seal of office, in such form as the said board shall direct or approve, that the design has been provisionally registered, the date of such registration, and the name of the registered proprietor, together with his place of abode or business, or other place of address.

Benefits conferred by provisional registration.

II. That the proprietor of any design which shall have been provisionally registered shall, during the continuance of such registration, have the sole right and property in such design; and the penalties and provisions of the said Designs Act, 1842, for preventing the piracy of designs, shall extend to the acts, matters, and things next hereinafter enumerated, as fully as if those penalties and provisions had been re-enacted in this Act, and expressly extended to such acts, matters, and things respectively, that is to say,

1. To the application of any provisionally registered design, or any fraudulent imitation thereof, to any article of manufacture or to any substance ·

2. To the publication, sale, or exposure for sale of any article of manufacture or any substance to which any provisionally registered design shall have been applied

The exhibition of provisionally registered designs in certain places not to defeat copyright, &c

III That during the continuance of such provisional registration neither such registration nor the exhibition or exposure of any design provisionally registered, or of any article to which any such design may have been or be intended to be applied, in any place, whether public or private, in which articles are not sold or exposed or exhibited for sale, and to which the public are not admitted gratuitously, or in any place which shall have been previously certified by the Board of Trade to be a place of public exhibition within the meaning of this Act, nor the publication of any account or description of any provisionally registered design exhibited or exposed or intended to be exhibited or exposed in any such place of exhibition or exposure in any catalogue, paper, newspaper, periodical, or otherwise, shall prevent the proprietor thereof from registering any such design under the said Designs Acts at any time during the continuance of the provisional registration, in the same manner and as fully and effectually as if no such registration, exhibition, exposure, or publication had been made provided that every article to which any such design shall be applied, and which shall be exhibited or exposed by or with the licence or consent of the proprietor of such design, shall have thereon or attached thereto the words 'provisionally registered,' with the date of registration

IV. That if during the continuance of such provisional registration the proprietor of any design provisionally registered shall sell, expose, or offer for sale any article, substance, or thing to which any such design has been applied, such provisional registration shall be deemed to have been null and void immediately before any such sale, offer, or exposure shall have been first made; but nothing herein contained shall be construed to hinder or prevent such proprietor from selling or transferring the right and property in any such design

V That the Board of Trade may by order in writing with respect to any particular class of designs, or any particular design, extend the period for which any design may be provisionally registered under this Act, for such term not exceeding the additional term of six months as to the said board may seem fit, and whenever any such order shall be made, the same shall be registered in the office for the registration of designs, and during the extended term the protection and benefits conferred by this Act in case of provisional registration shall continue as fully as if the original term of one year had not expired.

VI That the registrar of designs, upon application by or on behalf of the proprietor of any sculpture, model, copy, or cast within the protection of the Sculpture Copyright Acts, and upon being furnished with such copy, drawing, print, or description, in writing or in print, as in the judgment of the said registrar shall be sufficient to identify the particular sculpture, model, copy, or cast in respect of which registration is desired, and the name of the person claiming to be proprietor, together with his place of abode or business or other place of address, or the name, style, or title of the firm under which he may be trading, shall register such sculpture, model, copy, or cast in such manner and form as shall from time to time be prescribed or approved by the Board of Trade for the whole or any part of the term during which copyright in such sculpture, model, copy, or cast may or shall exist under the Sculpture Copyright Acts, and whenever any such registration shall be made, the said registrar shall certify under his hand and seal of office, in such form as the said board shall direct or approve, the fact of such registration, and the date of the same, and the name of the registered proprietor, or the style or title of the firm under which such proprietor may be trading, together with his place of abode or business or other place of address

VII That if any person shall, during the continuance of the copyright in any sculpture, model, copy, or cast which shall have been so registered as aforesaid, make, import, or cause to be made, imported, exposed for sale, or otherwise disposed of, any pirated copy or pirated cast of any such sculpture, model, copy, or cast, in such manner and under such circumstances as would entitle the proprietor to a special action on the case under the Sculpture Copyright Acts, the person so offending shall forfeit for every such offence a sum not less than five pounds and not exceeding thirty pounds to the proprietor of the sculpture, model, copy, or cast whereof the copyright shall have been infringed, and for the recovery of any such penalty the proprietor of the sculpture, model, copy, or cast which shall have been so pirated shall have and be entitled to the same remedies as are provided for the recovery of penalties incurred under the Designs Act, 1842; provided always, that the proprietor of any sculpture, model, copy, or cast which shall be registered under this Act shall not be entitled to the benefit of this Act, unless every copy or cast of such sculpture, model, copy, or cast which shall be published by him after such registration shall be marked with the word 'registered,' and with the date of registration.

VIII. That designs for the ornamenting of ivory, bone, papier maché, and other solid substances not already comprised in the classes numbered 1, 2, or 3 in the Designs Act, 1842, shall be deemed and taken to be comprised within the class numbered 4 in that Act, and such designs shall be so registered accordingly.

IX. That the Board of Trade may from time to time order that the copyright of any class of designs or any particular design registered or which may be registered under the Designs Act, 1842, may be extended for such term, not exceeding the additional term of three years, as the said board may think fit, and the said board shall have power to revoke or alter any such order as may from time to time appear necessary; and whenever any order shall be made by the said board under this provision, the same shall be registered in the office for the registration of designs, and during the extended term the protection and benefits conferred by the said Designs Acts shall continue as fully as if the original term had not expired.

X. That the Board of Trade may from time to time make, alter, and revoke rules and regulations with respect to the mode of registration, and the documents and other matters and particulars to be furnished by persons effecting registration and provisional registration under the said Acts and this Act; provided always, that all such rules and regulations shall be published in the 'London Gazette,' and shall forthwith upon the issuing thereof be laid before Parliament, if Parliament be sitting, and if Parliament be not sitting, then within fourteen days after the commencement of the then next session, and such rules and regulations, or any of them, shall be published or notified by the registrar of designs in such other manner as the Board of Trade shall think fit to direct.

XI. That if in any case in which the registration of a design is required to be made under either of the said Designs Acts it shall appear to the registrar that copies, drawings, or prints, as required by those Acts cannot be furnished, or that it is unreasonable or unnecessary to require the same, the said registrar may dispense with such copies, drawings, or prints, and may allow in lieu thereof such specification or description in writing or in print as may be sufficient to identify and render intelligible the design in respect of which registration is desired, and whenever registration shall be so made in the absence of such copies, drawings, or prints, the registration shall be as valid and effectual to all intents and purposes as if such copies, drawings, or prints, had been furnished.

XII That in order to prevent the frequent and unnecessary removal of the public books and documents in the office for the registration of designs, no book or document in the said office shall be removed for the purpose of being produced in any court or before any justice of the peace, without a special order of a judge of the Court of Chancery, or of one of her Majesty's superior courts of law, first had and obtained by the party who shall desire the production of the same.

XIII That if application shall be made to a judge of any of her Majesty's Courts of Law at Westminster by any person desiring to obtain a copy of any registration, entry, drawing, print, or document, of which such person is not entitled as of right to have a copy, for the purpose of being used in evidence in any cause, or otherwise howsoever, and if such judge shall be satisfied that such copy is *bonâ fide* intended for such purpose as aforesaid, such judge shall order the registrar of designs to deliver such copy to the party applying, and the registrar of designs shall, upon payment for the same of such fee or fees as may be fixed according to the provisions of the said Designs Act in this behalf, deliver such copy accordingly

XIV That every copy of any registration, entry, drawing, print, or document delivered by the registrar of designs to any person requiring the same shall be signed by the said registrar, and sealed with his seal of office, and every document sealed with the said seal purporting to be a copy of any registration, entry, drawing, print, or document, shall be deemed to be a true copy of such registration, entry, drawing, print, or document, and shall, without further proof, be received in evidence before all courts in like manner and to the same extent and effect as the original book, registration, entry, drawing, print, or document would or might be received if tendered in evidence, as well for the purpose of proving the contents, purport, and effect of such book, registration, entry, drawing, print, or document, as also proving the same to be a book, registration, entry, drawing, print, or document of or belonging to the said office, and in the custody of the registrar of designs

XV That the several provisions contained in the said Designs Acts (so far as they are not repugnant to the provisions of this Act) relating to the transfer of designs, to cancelling and amending registration, to the refusal of registration in certain cases, to the mode of recovering penalties, to the awarding and recovery of costs, to actions for damages, to the limitation of actions, to the certificate of registration, to penalties for wrongfully using marks, to the fixing and application of fees for registration, and to the penalty for extortion, shall apply to the registration, provisional registration, and transfer of designs, sculptures, models, copies, and casts, and to the designs, sculptures, models, copies, and casts entitled to protection under this Act, and to matters under this Act, as fully and effectually as if those provisions had been re-enacted in this Act with respect to designs, sculptures, models, copies, and casts registered and provisionally registered under this Act, and the forms contained in the Designs Act, 1842, may for the purposes of this Act be varied so as to meet the circumstances of the case.

Interpretation of terms

XVI That in the interpretation of this Act the following terms and expressions shall have the meanings hereinafter assigned to them, unless such meanings shall be repugnant to or inconsistent with the context or subject matter, that is to say,

The expression 'Designs Act, 1842,' shall mean an Act passed in the sixth year of the reign of her present Majesty, intituled 'An Act to consolidate and amend the Laws relating to the Copyright of Designs for ornamenting Articles of Manufacture:'

The expression 'Designs Act, 1843,' shall mean an Act passed in the seventh year of her present Majesty, intituled 'An Act to amend the Laws relating to the Copyright of Designs.'

The expression 'Sculpture Copyright Acts' shall mean two Acts passed respectively in the thirty-eighth and fifty-fourth years of the reign of King George the Third, and intituled respectively, 'An Act for encouraging the Art of making new Models and Casts of Busts and other Things herein mentioned,' and 'An Act to amend and render more effectual an Act for encouraging the Art of making new Models and Casts of Busts and other Things therein mentioned.'

The expression 'The Board of Trade,' shall mean the Lords of the Committee of Privy Council for the consideration of all matters of Trade and Plantations:

The expression 'Registrar of Designs,' shall mean the Registrar or Assistant Registrar of Designs for Articles of Manufacture.

The expression 'Proprietor' shall be construed according to the interpretation of that word in the said Designs Act, 1842.

And words in the singular number shall include the plural, and words applicable to males shall include females.

Short title

XVII That in citing this Act in other Acts of Parliament, and in any instrument, document, or proceeding, it shall be sufficient to use the words and figures following, that is to say, 'The Designs Act, 1850.'

---

15 VICT c 12.

An Act to enable her Majesty to carry into effect a Convention with France on the Subject of Copyright, to extend and explain the International Copyright Acts; and to explain the Acts relating to Copyright in Engravings

7 & 8 Vict c 12

WHEREAS an Act was passed in the seventh year of the reign of her present Majesty, intituled 'An Act to amend the Law relating to International Copyright,' hereinafter called 'The International Copyright Act:' and whereas a convention has lately been concluded between her Majesty and the French Republic, for extending in each country the enjoyment of copyright in works of literature and the fine arts first published in the other, and for certain reductions of duties now levied on books, prints, and musical works published in France: and whereas certain of the stipulations on the part of her Majesty contained in the said treaty require the authority of Parliament. and whereas it is expedient that such authority should be given, and that her Majesty should be enabled to make similar stipulations in any treaty on the subject of copyright which may hereafter be concluded with any foreign power: be it enacted by the Queen's most Excellent Majesty, by and with the advice and consent of the Lords Spiritual and Temporal, and Commons, in this present Parliament assembled, and by the authority of the same, as follows.

I The eighteenth section of the said Act of the seventh year of her present Majesty, chapter twelve shall be repealed, so far as the same is inconsistent with the provisions hereinafter contained

II Her Majesty may, by order in Council, direct that the authors of books which are, after a future time, to be specified in such order, published in any foreign country, to be named in such order, their executors, administrators, and assigns, shall, subject to the provisions hereinafter contained or referred to, be empowered to prevent the publication in the British dominions of any translations of such books not authorised by them, for such time as may be specified in such order, not extending beyond the expiration of five years from the time at which the authorised translations of such books hereinafter mentioned are respectively first published, and in the case of books published in parts, not extending as to each part beyond the expiration of five years from the time at which the authorised translation of such part is first published.

III Subject to any provisions or qualifications contained in such order, and to the provisions herein contained or referred to, the laws and enactments for the time being in force for the purpose of preventing the infringement of copyright in books published in the British dominions shall be applied for the purpose of preventing the publication of translations of the books to which such order extends which are not sanctioned by the authors of such books, except only such parts of the said enactments as relate to the delivery of copies of books for the use of the British Museum, and for the use of the other libraries therein referred to

IV Her Majesty may, by order in Council, direct that authors of dramatic pieces which are, after a future time, to be specified in such order, first publicly represented in any foreign country, to be named in such order, their executors, administrators, and assigns, shall, subject to the provisions hereinafter mentioned or referred to, be empowered to prevent the representation in the British dominions of any translation of such dramatic pieces not authorised by them, for such time as may be specified in such order, not extending beyond the expiration of five years from the time at which the authorised translations of such dramatic pieces hereinafter mentioned are first published or publicly represented

V. Subject to any provisions or qualifications contained in such

law for pro-
tecting the
representation
of such pieces
shall extend
to prevent
unauthorised
translations

last-mentioned order, and to the provisions hereinafter contained
or referred to, the laws and enactments for the time being in force
for ensuring to the author of any dramatic piece first publicly
represented in the British dominions the sole liberty of representing
the same shall be applied for the purpose of preventing the representation of any translations of the dramatic pieces to which such
last-mentioned order extends, which are not sanctioned by the
authors thereof.

Adaptations,
&c of dramatic
pieces to the
English stage
not prevented
All articles in
newspapers, &c
relating to
politics may be
republished or
translated ; and
also all similar
articles on any
subject, unless
the author has
notified his
intention to
reserve the right.

VI. Nothing herein contained shall be so construed as to prevent
fair imitations or adaptations to the English stage of any dramatic
piece or musical composition published in any foreign country.

VII Notwithstanding anything in the said International Copyright Act or in this Act contained, any article of political discussion
which has been published in any newspaper or periodical in a
foreign country may, if the source from which the same is taken
be acknowledged, be republished or translated in any newspaper
or periodical in this country ; and any article relating to any other
subject which has been so published as aforesaid may, if the source
from which the same is taken be acknowledged, be republished or
translated in like manner, unless the author has signified his intention of preserving the copyright therein, and the right of translating
the same, in some conspicuous part of the newspaper or periodical
in which the same was first published, in which case the same
shall, without the formalities required by the next following
section, receive the same protection as is by virtue of the International Copyright Act or this Act extended to books

No author to be
entitled to benefit
of this Act
without com-
plying with the
requisitions
herein specified.

VIII. No author, or his executors, administrators, or assigns,
shall be entitled to the benefit of this Act, or of any order in
Council issued in pursuance thereof, in respect of the translation
of any book or dramatic piece, if the following requisitions are not
complied with (that is to say) —

1 The original work from which the translation is to be made
    must be registered and a copy thereof deposited in the
    United Kingdom in the manner required for original works
    by the said International Copyright Act, within three
    calendar months of its first publication in the foreign
    country ·

2 The author must notify on the title-page of the original
    work, or if it is published in parts on the title-page of the
    first part, or if there is no title-page on some conspicuous
    part of the work, that it is his intention to reserve the right
    of translating it

3 The translation sanctioned by the author, or a part thereof,
    must be published either in the country mentioned in the
    order in Council by virtue of which it is to be protected or
    in the British dominions, not later than one year after the
    registration and deposit in the United Kingdom of the
    original work, and the whole of such translation must be
    published within three years of such registration and
    deposit

4 Such translation must be registered and a copy thereof
    deposited in the United Kingdom within a time to be

mentioned in that behalf in the order by which it is protected, and in the manner provided by the said International Copyright Act for the registration and deposit of original works.

5. In the case of books published in parts, each part of the original work must be registered and deposited in this country in the manner required by the said international copyright within three months after the first publication thereof in the foreign country:

6 In the case of dramatic pieces, the translation sanctioned by the author must be published within three calendar months of the registration of the original work.

7 The above requisitions shall apply to articles originally published in newspapers or periodicals, if the same be afterwards published in a separate form, but shall not apply to such articles as originally published.

IX. All copies of any works of literature or art wherein there is any subsisting copyright by virtue of the International Copyright Act and this Act, or of any order in Council made in pursuance of such Acts or either of them, and which are printed, reprinted, or made in any foreign country except that in which such work shall be first published, and all unauthorised translations of any book or dramatic piece the publication or public representation in the British dominions of translations whereof not authorised as in this Act mentioned shall for the time being be prevented under any order in Council made in pursuance of this Act, are hereby absolutely prohibited to be imported into any part of the British dominions, except by or with the consent of the registered proprietor of the copyright of such work or of such book or piece, or his agent authorised in writing; and the provision of the Act of the sixth year of her Majesty, 'to amend the Law of Copyright,' for the forfeiture, seizure, and destruction of any printed book first published in the United Kingdom wherein there shall be copyright, and reprinted in any country out of the British dominions, and imported into any part of the British dominions by any person not being the proprietor of the copyright or a person authorised by such proprietor, shall extend and be applicable to all copies of any works of literature and art, and to all translations the importation whereof into any part of the British dominions is prohibited under this Act

Pirated copies prohibited to be imported, except with consent of proprietor.

Provisions of 5 & 6 Vict c 45, as to forfeiture, &c of pirated works, &c to extend to works prohibited to be imported under this Act.

X. The provisions hereinbefore contained shall be incorporated with the International Copyright Act, and shall be read and construed therewith as one Act

XI And whereas her Majesty has already, by order in Council under the said International Copyright Act, given effect to certain stipulations contained in the said convention with the French Republic, and it is expedient that the remainder of the stipulations on the part of her Majesty in the said convention contained should take effect from the passing of this Act without any further order in Council during the continuance of the said convention, and so long as the order in Council already made under the said International Copyright Act remains in force, the provisions

Foregoing provisions and 7 & 8 Vict c 12, to be read as one Act French translations to be protected as hereinbefore mentioned, without further order in Council.

hereinbefore contained shall apply to the said convention, and to translations of books and dramatic pieces which are, after the passing of this Act, published or represented in France, in the same manner as if her Majesty had issued her order in Council in pursuance of this Act for giving effect to such convention, and had therein directed that such translations should be protected as hereinbefore mentioned for a period of five years from the date of the first publication or public representation thereof respectively, and as if a period of three months from the publication of such translation were the time mentioned in such order as the time within which the same must be registered and a copy thereof deposited in the United Kingdom.

Reduction of Duties

Recital of 9 & 10 Vict. c 58

XII. And whereas an Act was passed in the tenth year of her present Majesty, intituled 'An Act to amend an Act of the Seventh and Eighth Years of her present Majesty, for reducing, under certain Circumstances, the Duties payable upon Books and Engravings,' and whereas by the said convention with the French Republic it was stipulated that the duties on books, prints, and drawings published in the territories of the French Republic should be reduced to the amounts specified in the Schedule to the said Act of the tenth year of her present Majesty, chapter fifty-eight and whereas her Majesty has, in pursuance of the said convention, and in exercise of the powers given by the said Act, by order in Council declared that such duties shall be reduced accordingly and whereas by the said convention it was further stipulated that the said rates of duty should not be raised during the continuance of the said convention, and that if during the continuance of the said convention any reduction of those rates should be made in favour of books, prints, or drawings published in any other country, such reduction should be at the same time extended to similar articles published in France · and whereas doubts are entertained whether such last-mentioned stipulations can be carried into effect

Rates of duty not to be raised during continuance of treaty, and if further reduction is made for other countries it may be extended to France

without the authority of Parliament be it enacted, that the said rates of duty so reduced as aforesaid shall not be raised during the continuance of the said convention, and that if during the continuance of the said convention any further reduction of such rates is made in favour of books, prints, or drawings published in any other foreign country, her Majesty may, by order in Council, declare that such reduction shall be extended to similar articles published in France, such order to be made and published in the same manner and to be subject to the same provisions as orders made in pursuance of the said Act of the tenth year of her present Majesty, chapter fifty-eight.

XIII And whereas doubts have arisen as to the construction of the Schedule of the Act of the tenth year of her present Majesty, chapter fifty-eight

For removal of doubts is to construction of schedule to 9 & 10 Vict c 58

It is hereby declared, that for the purposes of the said Act every work published in the country of export, of which part has been originally produced in the United Kingdom, shall be deemed to be and be subject to the duty payable on 'works originally produced in the United Kingdom, and republished in the country of export,' although it contains also original matter not produced

In the United Kingdom, unless it shall be proved to the satisfaction of the Commissioners of her Majesty's Customs by the importer, consignee, or other person entering the same, that such original matter is at least equal to the part of the work produced in the United Kingdom, in which case the work shall be subject only to the duty on 'works not originally produced in the United Kingdom.'

XIV. And whereas by the four several Acts of Parliament following, (that is to say,) an Act of the eighth year of the reign of King George the Second, chapter thirteen, an Act of the seventh year of the reign of King George the Third, chapter thirty-eight, an Act of the seventeenth year of the reign of King George the Third, chapter fifty-seven, and an Act of the seventh year of King William the Fourth, chapter fifty-nine, provision is made for securing to every person who invents, or designs, engraves, etches, or works in mezzotinto or chiaro-oscuro, or, from his own work, design, or invention, causes or procures to be designed, engraved, etched, or worked in mezzotinto or chiaro-oscuro, any historical print or prints, or any print or prints of any portrait, conversation, landscape, or architecture, map, chart, or plan, or any other print or prints whatsoever, and to every person who engraves, etches, or works in mezzotinto or chiaro-oscuro, or causes to be engraved, etched, or worked any print taken from any picture, drawing, model, or sculpture, notwithstanding such print has not been graven or drawn from his own original design, certain copyrights therein defined, and whereas doubts are entertained whether the provisions of the said Acts extend to lithographs and certain other impressions, and it is expedient to remove such doubts.

Lithographs, &c

Recital of 8 G. 2, c. 13. 7 G. 3, c. 38. 17 G. 3, c. 57. 6 & 7 W. 4, c. 59.

It is hereby declared, that the provisions of the said Acts are intended to include prints taken by lithography, or any other mechanical process by which prints or impressions of drawings or designs are capable of being multiplied indefinitely, and the said Acts shall be construed accordingly.

For removal of doubts as to the provisions of the said Acts including lithographs, prints, &c.

---

21 & 22 VICT. c 70.

An Act to amend the Act of the Fifth and Sixth Years of her present Majesty, to consolidate and amend the Laws relating to the Copyright of Designs for ornamenting Articles of Manufacture.

WHEREAS by an Act passed in the fifth and sixth years of the reign of her present Majesty, intituled 'An Act to consolidate and amend the Laws relating to the Copyright of Designs for ornamenting Articles of Manufacture,' herein-after called 'The Copyright of Designs Act, 1842,' there was granted to the proprietor of any new and original design in respect of the application of any such design to ornamenting any article of manufacture

5 & 6 Vict c. 100.

contained in the tenth class therein mentioned, with the exceptions therein mentioned, the sole right to apply the same to any articles of manufacture, or any such substances as therein mentioned, for the term of nine calendar months, to be computed from the time of such design being registered according to the said Act, and whereas it is expedient that the term of copyright, in respect of the application of designs to the ornamenting of articles of manufacture comprised in the said tenth class, should be extended, and that some of the provisions of the said Act should be altered, and that further provision should be made for the prevention of piracy, and for the protection of copyright in designs under the Acts in the schedule hereto annexed, and herein-after called 'The Copyright of Designs Acts,' be it therefore enacted, by the Queen's most Excellent Majesty, by and with the advice and consent of the Lords Spiritual and Temporal, and Commons, in this present Parliament assembled, and by the authority of the same, as follows, that is to say,

Short title.

I In citing this Act for any purpose whatsoever it shall be sufficient to use the expression 'The Copyright of Designs Act, 1858'

Copyright of Designs Acts and this Act to be as one.

II. The said Copyright of Designs Acts and this Act shall be construed together as one Act

Extension of term of copyright as to the tenth class mentioned in 5 & 6 Vict c 100

III. In respect of the application of any new and original design for ornamenting any article of manufacture contained in the tenth class mentioned in 'The Copyright of Designs Act, 1842,' the term of copyright shall be three years, to be computed from the time of such design being registered, in pursuance of the provisions of 'The Copyright of Designs Acts,' and of this Act provided nevertheless, that the term of such copyright shall expire on the thirty-first of December in the second year after the year in which such design was registered, whatever may be the day of such registration

Copyright not to be prejudiced if articles marked

IV. Nothing in the fourth section of 'The Copyright of Designs Act, 1842,' shall extend or be construed to extend to deprive the proprietor of any new and original design applied to ornamenting any article of manufacture contained in the said tenth class of the benefits of 'The Copyright of Designs Acts,' or of this Act provided there shall have been printed on such articles at each end of the original piece thereof the name and address of such proprietor, and the word 'registered,' together with the years for which such design was registered

Pattern may be registered

V. And be it declared, that the registration of any pattern or portion of an article of manufacture to which a design is applied, instead or in lieu of a copy, drawing, print, specification, or description in writing, shall be as valid and effectual to all intents and purposes as if such copy, drawing, print, specification, or description in writing had been furnished to the registrar under 'The Copyright of Designs Acts.'

Proprietor to give the number and date of registration

VI The proprietor of such extended copyright shall, on application by or on behalf of any person producing or vending any article of manufacture so marked, give the number and the date of the registration of any article of manufacture so marked, and any proprietor so applied to who shall not give the number and date of such registration shall be subject to a penalty of ten pounds, to be recovered by the applicant, with full costs of suit, in any court of competent jurisdiction.

VII. Any person who shall wilfully apply any mark of registration to any article of manufacture in respect whereof the application of the design thereto shall not have been registered, or after the term of copyright shall have expired, or who shall, during the term of copyright, without the authority of the proprietor of any registered design, wilfully apply the mark printed on the piece of any article of manufacture, or who shall knowingly sell or issue any article of manufacture to which such mark has been wilfully and without due authority applied, shall be subject to a penalty of ten pounds, to be recovered by the proprietor of such design, with full costs of suit, in any court of competent jurisdiction.

Penalty on issuing articles not so marked.

VIII. Notwithstanding anything in 'The Copyright of Designs Acts,' it shall be lawful for the proprietor of copyright in any design under 'The Copyright of Designs Acts,' or this Act, to institute proceedings in the county court of the district within which the piracy is alleged to have been committed, for the recovery of damages which he may have sustained by reason of such piracy: provided always, that in any such proceedings the plaintiff shall deliver with his plaint a statement of particulars as to the date and title or other description of the registration whereof the copyright is alleged to be pirated, and as to the alleged piracy, and the defendant, if he intends at the trial to rely as a defence on any objection to such copyright, or to the title of the proprietor therein, shall give notice in the manner provided in the seventy-sixth section of the Act of the ninth and tenth Victoria, chapter ninety-five, of his intention to rely on such special defence, and shall state in such notice the date of publication and other particulars of any designs whereof prior publication is alleged, or of any objection to such copyright, or to the title of the proprietor to such copyright, and it shall be lawful for the judge of the county court, at the instance of the defendant or plaintiff respectively, to require any statement or notice so delivered by the plaintiff or of the defendant respectively to be amended in such manner as the said judge may think fit.

Proceedings for prevention of piracy may be instituted in the county courts.

IX. The provisions of an Act of the ninth and tenth Victoria, chapter ninety-five, and of the twelfth and thirteenth Victoria, chapter one hundred, as to proceedings in any plaint, and as to appeal, and as to writs of prohibition, shall, so far as they are not inconsistent with or repugnant to the provisions of this Act, be applicable to any proceedings for piracy of copyright of designs under the said Copyright of Designs Acts or this Act.

The provisions of County Courts Acts applicable to proceedings for piracy of designs.

SCHEDULE referred to in the foregoing Act.

5 & 6 Vict c 100 [10 Aug 1842]	An Act to consolidate and amend the Laws relating to the Copyright of Designs for ornamenting Articles of Manufacture
6 & 7 Vict c 65. [22 Aug 1843]	An Act to amend the Laws relating to the Copyright of Designs
13 & 14 Vict c 104 [11 Aug 1850]	An Act to extend and amend the Acts relating to the Copyright of Designs.
14 Vict c 8 [11 April, 1851]	An Act to extend the Provisions of the Designs Act, 1850, and to give Protection from Piracy to Persons exhibiting new Inventions in the Exhibition of the Works of Industry of all Nations in One thousand eight hundred and fifty-one.

---

21 & 25 VICT c 73

An Act to amend the Law relating to the Copyright of Designs

5 & 6 Vict. c. 100

WHEREAS by an Act passed in the session holden in the fifth and sixth years of the reign of her present Majesty, chapter one hundred, intituled 'An Act to consolidate and amend the Laws relating to the Copyright of Designs for ornamenting Articles of Manufacture,' it was enacted, that the proprietor of every such design as therein mentioned, not previously published either within the United Kingdom of Great Britain and Ireland or elsewhere, should have the sole right to apply the same to any articles of manufacture, or to any such substances as therein mentioned, provided the same were done within the United Kingdom of Great Britain and Ireland, for the respective terms therein mentioned, and should have such copyright in such designs as therein provided and whereas divers Acts have since been passed extending or amending the said recited Acts and whereas it is expedient that the provisions of the said recited Act, and of all Acts extending or amending the same, should apply to designs, and to the application of such designs, within the meaning of the said Acts, whether such application be effected within the United Kingdom or elsewhere · be it enacted by the Queen's most Excellent Majesty, by and with the advice and consent of the Lords Spiritual and Temporal, and Commons, in this present Parliament assembled, and by the authority of the same, as follows.

5 & 6 Vict c. 100, and other Acts relating to copyright of de-

I That the said recited Act, and all Acts extending or amending the same, shall be construed as if the words 'provided the same be done within the United Kingdom of Great Britain and Ireland' had not been contained in the said recited Act, and the

said recited Act, and all Acts extending or amending the same, signs, extended
shall apply to every such design as therein referred to, whether
the application thereof be done within the United Kingdom or
elsewhere, and whether the inventor or proprietor of such design
be or be not a subject of her Majesty

II That the said several Acts shall not be construed to apply to Application of
the subjects of her Majesty only Act.

---

25 & 26 VICT. c. 68

An Act for amending the Law relating to Copyright in Works of the
Fine Arts, and for repressing the Commission of Fraud in the
Production and Sale of such Works

WHEREAS by law, as now established, the authors of paintings,
drawings, and photographs have no copyright in such their works,
and it is expedient that the law should in that respect be amended
Be it therefore enacted by the Queen's most excellent Majesty, by
and with the advice and consent of the Lords Spiritual and
Temporal, and Commons, in this present Parliament assembled,
and by the authority of the same, as follows

I The author, being a British subject or resident within the
dominions of the Crown, of every original painting, drawing, and
photograph which shall be or shall have been made either in the
British dominions or elsewhere, and which shall not have been
sold or disposed of before the commencement of this Act, and his
assigns shall have the sole and exclusive right of copying,
engraving, reproducing, and multiplying such painting or drawing,
and the design thereof, or such photograph, and the negative
thereof, by any means and of any size, for the term of the natural
life of such author, and seven years after his death, provided
that when any painting or drawing, or the negative of any photograph, shall for the first time after the passing of this Act be sold
or disposed of, or shall be made or executed for or on behalf of
any other person for a good or a valuable consideration, the person
so selling or disposing of or making or executing the same shall
not retain the copyright thereof, unless it be expressly reserved to
him by agreement in writing, signed, at or before the time of such
sale or disposition, by the vendee or assignee of such painting or
drawing, or of such negative of a photograph, or by the person for
or on whose behalf the same shall be so made or executed, but the
copyright shall belong to the vendee or assignee of such painting or
drawing, or of such negative of a photograph, or to the person for
or on whose behalf the same shall have been made or executed,
nor shall the vendee or assignee thereof be entitled to any such
copyright, unless, at or before the time of such sale or disposition,
an agreement in writing, signed by the person so selling or disposing of the same or by his agent duly authorised, shall have
been made to that effect

Copyright in
works hereafter
made or sold to
vest in the author
for his life and
for seven years
after his death.

1

II. Nothing herein contained shall prejudice the right of any person to copy or use any work in which there shall be no copyright, or to represent any scene or object, notwithstanding that there may be copyright in some representation of such scene or object.

III. All copyright under this Act shall be deemed personal or moveable estate, and shall be assignable at law, and every assignment thereof, and every licence to use or copy by any means or process the design or work which shall be the subject of such copyright, shall be made by some note or memorandum in writing, to be signed by the proprietor of the copyright, or by his agent appointed for that purpose in writing.

IV There shall be kept at the Hall of the Stationers Company, by the officer appointed by the said Company for the purposes of the Act passed in the sixth year of her present Majesty, intituled 'An Act to amend the Law of Copyright,' a book or books, entitled 'The Register of Proprietors of Copyright in Paintings, Drawings, and Photographs,' wherein shall be entered a memorandum of every copyright to which any person shall be entitled under this Act, and also of every subsequent assignment of any such copyright, and such memorandum shall contain a statement of the date of such agreement or assignment, and of the names of the parties thereto, and of the name and place of abode of the person in whom such copyright shall be vested by virtue thereof, and of the name and place of abode of the author of the work in which there shall be such copyright, together with a short description of the nature and subject of such work, and in addition thereto, if the person registering shall so desire, a sketch, outline, or photograph of the said work, and no proprietor of any such copyright shall be entitled to the benefit of this Act until such registration, and no action shall be sustainable nor any penalty be recoverable in respect of anything done before registration.

V. The several enactments in the said Act of the sixth year of her present Majesty contained, with relation to keeping the register book thereby required, and the inspection thereof, the searches therein, and the delivery of certified and stamped copies thereof, the reception of such copies in evidence, the making of false entries in the said book, and the production in evidence of papers falsely purporting to be copies of entries in the said book, the application to the courts and judges by persons aggrieved by entries in the said book, and the expunging and varying such entries, shall apply to the book or books to be kept by virtue of this Act, and to the entries and assignments of copyright and proprietorship therein under this Act, in such and the same manner as if such enactments were here expressly enacted in relation thereto, save and except that the forms of entry prescribed by the said Act of the sixth year of her present Majesty may be varied to meet the circumstances of the case, and that the sum to be demanded by the officer of the said Company of Stationers for making any entry required by this Act shall be one shilling only

VI If the author of any painting, drawing, or photograph in which there shall be subsisting copyright, after having sold or disposed of such copyright, or if any other person, not being the proprietor for the time being of copyright in any painting, drawing, or photograph, shall, without the consent of such proprietor, repeat, copy, colourably imitate, or otherwise multiply for sale, hire, exhibition, or distribution, or cause or procure to be repeated, copied, colourably imitated, or otherwise multiplied for sale, hire, exhibition, or distribution, any such work or the design thereof, or, knowing that any such repetition, copy, or other imitation has been unlawfully made, shall import into any part of the United Kingdom, or sell, publish, let to hire, exhibit, or distribute, or offer for sale, hire, exhibition, or distribution, or cause or procure to be imported, sold, published, let to hire, distributed, or offered for sale, hire, exhibition, or distribution, any repetition, copy, or imitation of the said work, or of the design thereof, made without such consent as aforesaid, such person for every such offence shall forfeit to the proprietor of the copyright for the time being a sum not exceeding ten pounds, and all such repetitions, copies, and imitations made without such consent as aforesaid, and all negatives of photographs made for the purpose of obtaining such copies, shall be forfeited to the proprietor of the copyright.

VII. No person shall do or cause to be done any or either of the following acts; that is to say, Penalties on fraudulent productions and sales

First, no person shall fraudulently sign or otherwise affix, or fraudulently cause to be signed or otherwise affixed, to or upon any painting, drawing, or photograph, or the negative thereof, any name, initials, or monogram ·

Secondly, no person shall fraudulently sell, publish, exhibit, or dispose of, or offer for sale, exhibition, or distribution, any painting, drawing, or photograph, or negative of a photograph, having thereon the name, initials, or monogram of a person who did not execute or make such work

Thirdly, no person shall fraudulently utter, dispose of, or put off, or cause to be uttered or disposed of, any copy or colourable imitation of any painting, drawing, or photograph, or negative of a photograph, whether there shall be subsisting copyright therein or not, as having been made or executed by the author or maker of the original work from which such copy or imitation shall have been taken ·

Fourthly, where the author or maker of any painting, drawing, or photograph, or negative of a photograph, made either before or after the passing of this Act, shall have sold or otherwise parted with the possession of such work, if any alteration shall afterwards be made therein by any other person, by addition or otherwise, no person shall be at liberty during the life of the author or maker of such work, without his consent, to make or knowingly to sell or publish, or offer for sale, such work or any copies of such work so altered as aforesaid, or of any part thereof, as or for the unaltered work of such author or maker.

Every offender under this section shall upon conviction, forfeit to the person aggrieved a sum not exceeding ten pounds, or not exceeding double the full price, if any, at which all such copies, engravings, imitations, or altered works shall have been sold or Penalties offered for sale, and all such copies, engravings, imitations, or altered works shall be forfeited to the person, or the assigns or legal representatives of the person, whose name, initials, or monogram shall be so fraudulently signed or affixed thereto, or to whom such spurious or altered work shall be so fraudulently or falsely ascribed as aforesaid: provided always, that the penalties imposed by this section shall not be incurred unless the person whose name, initials, or monogram shall be so fraudulently signed or affixed, or to whom such spurious or altered work shall be so fraudulently or falsely ascribed as aforesaid, shall have been living at or within twenty years next before the time when the offence may have been committed

Recovery of pecuniary penalties

VIII All pecuniary penalties which shall be incurred, and all such unlawful copies, imitations, and all other effects and things as shall have been forfeited by offenders, pursuant to this Act, and pursuant to any Act for the protection of copyright engravings, may be recovered by the person hereinbefore and in any such Act as aforesaid empowered to recover the same respectively, and hereinafter called the complainant or the complainer, as follows —

In England and Ireland

In England and Ireland, either by action against the party offending, or by summary proceeding before any two justices having jurisdiction where the party offending resides

In Scotland

In Scotland by action before the Court of Session in ordinary form, or by summary action before the sheriff of the county where the offence may be committed or the offender resides, who, upon proof of the offence or offences, either by confession of the party offending, or by the oath or affirmation of one or more credible witnesses, shall convict the offender, and find him liable to the penalty or penalties aforesaid, as also in expenses, and it shall be lawful for the sheriff, in pronouncing such judgment for the penalty or penalties and costs, to insert in such judgment a warrant, in the event of such penalty or penalties and costs not being paid, to levy and recover the amount of the same by poinding provided always, that it shall be lawful to the sheriff, in the event of his dismissing the action and assoilzieing the defender, to find the complainer liable in expenses, and any judgment so to be pronounced by the sheriff in such summary application shall be final and conclusive, and not subject to review by advocation, suspension, reduction, or otherwise

Superior courts of record in which any action is pending may make an order for an injunction, inspection, or account

IX In any action in any of her Majesty's superior courts of record at Westminster and in Dublin, for the infringement of any such copyright as aforesaid, it shall be lawful for the court in which such action is pending, if the court be then sitting, or if the court be not sitting then for a judge of such court, on the application of the plaintiff or defendant respectively, to make such order for an injunction, inspection, or account, and to give such direction respecting such action, injunction, inspection, and account, and the proceedings therein respectively, as to such court or judge may seem fit

Importation of pirated works prohibited

X All repetitions, copies, or imitations of paintings, drawings, or photographs, wherein or in the design whereof there shall be subsisting copyright under this Act, and all repetitions, copies, and imitations of the design of any such painting or drawing, or of the negative of any such photograph, which, contrary to the provisions of this Act, shall have been made in any foreign state, or in any part of the British dominions, are hereby absolutely prohibited to be imported into any part of the United Kingdom, except by or with the consent of the proprietor of the copyright thereof, or his agent authorised in writing; and if the proprietor of any such copyright, or his agent, shall declare that any goods imported are repetitions, copies, or imitations of any such painting, drawing, or photograph, or of the negative of any such photograph, and so prohibited as aforesaid, then such goods may be detained by the officers of her Majesty's Customs

Application in such cases of Customs Acts

XI If the author of any painting, drawing, or photograph, in which there shall be subsisting copyright, after having sold or otherwise disposed of such copyright, or if any other person, not being the proprietor for the time being of such copyright, shall, without the consent of such proprietor, repeat, copy, colourably imitate, or otherwise multiply, or cause or procure to be repeated, copied, colourably imitated, or otherwise multiplied, for sale, hire, exhibition, or distribution, any such work or the design thereof, or the negative of any such photograph, or shall import or cause to be imported into any part of the United Kingdom, or sell, publish, let to hire, exhibit, or distribute, or offer for sale, hire, exhibition, or distribution, or cause or procure to be sold, published, let to hire, exhibited, or distributed, or offered for sale, hire, exhibition, or distribution, any repetition, copy, or imitation of such work, or the design thereof, or the negative of any such photograph, made without such consent as aforesaid, then every such proprietor, in addition to the remedies hereby given for the recovery of any such penalties, and forfeiture of any such things as aforesaid, may recover damages by and in a special action on the case, to be brought against the person so offending, and may in such action recover and enforce the delivery to him of all unlawful repetitions, copies, and imitations, and negatives of photographs, or may recover damages for the retention or conversion thereof provided that nothing herein contained, nor any proceeding, conviction, or judgment, for any act hereby forbidden, shall affect any remedy which any person aggrieved by such act may be entitled to either at law or in equity

Saving of right to bring action for damages

XII This Act shall be considered as including the provisions of the Act passed in the session of Parliament held in the seventh and eighth years of her present Majesty, intituled 'An Act to amend the Law relating to International Copyright,' in the same manner as if such provisions were part of this Act

Provisions of 7 & 8 Vict c. 12, to be considered as included in this Act

DIRECTIONS

ISSUED BY

BOARD OF TRADE FOR REGISTRATION OF DESIGNS.

—◦◦◦—

ORNAMENTAL DESIGNS

DIRECTIONS FOR REGISTERING AND SEARCHING.

PERSONS proposing to Register a Design for Ornamenting an Article of Manufacture, must bring or send to the Designs Office —

1. TWO EXACTLY SIMILAR *copies, drawings* (or *tracings*), *photographs,* or *prints* thereof, with the proper fees

2. THE NAME AND ADDRESS of the Proprietor or Proprietors, or the Title of the Firm under which he or they may be trading, together with their Place of Abode, or Place of carrying on business, *distinctly written or printed*

3. THE NUMBER of the Class in respect of which such Registration is intended to be made, except it be for Sculpture.

The aforesaid *Copies* may consist of portions of the manufactured articles (*except Carpets, Oil-Cloths, and Woollen Shawls*), when such can conveniently be done (as in the case of *Paper Hangings, Calico Prints, &c*), which, as well as the *Drawings* or *Tracings* (not in Pencil) or *Prints* of the Design, to be furnished when the article is of such a nature as not to admit of being pasted in a book, *must,* whether coloured or not, *be facsimiles of each other*

Should *Paper Hangings or Furnitures* exceed 42 inches in length, by 23 inches in breadth, drawings will be required, but they must not exceed these dimensions

Applications for Registering may be made in the following form.—

APPLICATION TO REGISTER.

(Blank Forms may be obtained at the Office.)

C. D. Works, March 31st, 1852.

You are hereby requested to Register, Provisionally,* the accompanying——Ornamental Designs (in Class 1, [2, 3, 4, &c.]) (or for Sculpture)† in the name of (‡A B of ——, of——,) or, (A B of ——, and C D. of——, &c., trading under the style or firm of B D & Co, of——, of——, of——,) who claim to be the Proprietors thereof, and to return the same (if sent by Post), directed to——, (if brought by hand,) to the bearer of the official acknowledgment for the same.

To the Registrar of Designs,   (Signed)   B D. & Co.,
       Designs Office, London   by J. F.

The person bringing a Design must take an acknowledgment for it, which will be delivered to him on payment of the proper fees   This acknowledgment must be produced on application for the Certified Copy, which will be returned in exchange for the same.

* If not Provisionally strike out the word ' Provisionally.'
† Here insert ' for Sculpture,' if for Sculpture, or the Class or Classes
‡ Insert here the name and address of the Proprietor, in the form in which it is to be entered on the Certificate

A Design may be registered in respect of one or more of the above Classes, according as it is intended to be employed in one or more species of manufacture, but a separate fee must be paid on account of each separate Class, and all such Registrations must be made at the same time.

After the Design has been registered, one of the two copies, drawings (or tracings), or prints, will be filed at the Office, and the other returned to the Proprietor, with a Certificate annexed, on which will appear the *Mark to be placed* on each article of manufacture to which the Design shall have been applied

If the Design is for an Article Registered under Class 10, no Mark is required, but there must be printed on such Article, at each end of the original piece thereof, the Name and Address of the Proprietor, and the word ' Registered,' together with the years for which the Design is registered

If the Design is for Sculpture, no Mark is required to be placed thereon after Registration, but merely the word ' Registered,' and the date of Registration

If the Design is for Provisional Registration, no Mark is required to be placed thereon after Registration, but merely the words ' Provisionally Registered ' and the date of Registration

Any Person who shall put the Registration Mark on any Design not registered, or after the Copyright thereof has expired, or when the Design has not been applied within the United Kingdom, *is liable to forfeit for every such Offence* 5l.

TRANSFERS.

In case of the transfer of a Design, registered, whether Provisionally or completely, a copy or the certified copy thereof must be transmitted to the Registrar, together with the Forms of Application (which may be procured at the Office), properly filled up and signed. The transfer will then be registered and the certified copy returned.

EXTENSION OF COPYRIGHT.

The Copyright may be extended in certain cases in Provisional Registration, for a term not exceeding the additional term of Six Months, and in Complete Registration for a term not exceeding the additional term of Three Years, as the Board of Trade may think fit.

In case of extension, the certified copy, together with the proper fee, should be transmitted to the Designs Office for Registration, *prior to the expiration of the existing copyright.*

SEARCHES.

All Designs of which the Copyright has expired may be inspected at the Designs Office, on the payment of the proper fee; but no Design, the Copyright of which is existing, is in general open to inspection. Any person, however, may, by application at the Office, and on production of the Registration Mark of any Particular Design, be furnished with a Certificate of Search, stating whether the Copyright be in existence and in respect to what particular article of manufacture it exists also, the term of such Copyright and the date of Registration, and the name and address of the Registered Proprietor thereof.

Any party may also, on the production of a piece of the manufactured article with the pattern thereon, together with the Registration Mark, be informed whether such pattern, supposed to be registered, is really so or not.

As this mark is not applied to a Provisionally Registered Design, or to articles Registered under Class 10, Certificates of Search for such Designs will be given on production of the Design, or a copy or drawing thereof, or other necessary information, with the date of Registration.

Persons bringing Designs to be registered, on delivering them, must compare such Designs together, count them, and see that the Name and Address and Number of Class is correctly given, and examine their Certificates previous to leaving the Office, to see that the Name, &c., is correctly entered, as no error can afterwards be rectified.

An acknowledgment of its receipt will be delivered, on payment of the fees, to the person bringing a Design, and no certified copy of a Design will be returned, except to the bearer of this acknowledgment, which must be produced on application at the Office for the certified copy, and given in exchange for the same.

All communications for the Registration of Designs may be made either through the General Post Office, directed to 'The Registrar of Designs, Designs Office, London,' or by any other mode of conveyance, and provided the carriage be paid, and the proper fees, or a Post Office Order for the amount, PAYABLE AT THE POST OFFICE, CHARING CROSS, to J. H. BOWEN, Esq., be enclosed, the Designs will be duly registered, and the Certified Copies returned to the Proprietors free of expense. *Postage Stamps, Orders upon Bankers or other Persons, Country and Scotch Bank Notes, and light gold cannot be received in payment of fees.*

The DESIGNS OFFICE, No. 1, WHITEHALL, S.W., is open every day, between the hours of 10 in the Morning and 4 in the Afternoon, during which time enquiries and searches may be made. Designs and Transfers are registered from 11 until 3, after which latter hour *no money can be received for the same.*

Directions for Registering Designs for Articles of Utility may be procured at the Office.

By Order of the Registrar,

J. H. BOWEN, *Chief Clerk.*

ORNAMENTAL.

COPYRIGHT OF DESIGNS FOR ORNAMENTING ARTICLES OF MANUFACTURE

By PROVISIONAL REGISTRATION under the Designs Act, 1850 (13 & 14 Vict. c. 104) a Copyright of One Year (which may be further extended for six months by order of the Board of Trade) is given to the Author or Proprietor of Original Designs for Ornamenting an Article of Manufacture or Substance. During such terms the Proprietor of the Design may sell the right to apply the same to an article of manufacture, but must not, under the penalty of nullifying the Copyright, sell any article with the Design applied thereto, until after Complete Registration, *which must be effected prior to the expiration of the Provisional Registration.*

By COMPLETE REGISTRATION under the Designs Act, 1842 (5 & 6 Vict. c. 100), a Copyright or Property is given to the Author or Proprietor of any New or Original Design for Ornamenting any Article of Manufacture or Substance for the various Terms specified in the following Classes, which Terms may be extended under special circumstances.

Under the Designs Act, 1858 (21 & 22 Vict. c. 70), a Copyright is given for Articles in CLASS 10, for a term of 3 *years*, subject to the Proviso therein contained.

Class	Article	Copyright	Regis tration Fees £ s d
1.	Articles composed wholly or chiefly of Metal	5 years	1 0
2.	Ditto do. Wood	3 „	1 0
3.	Ditto do. Glass	3 „	1 0
4	Ditto do. Earthenware, Bone, Papier Maché, or other solid substances not comprised in Classes 1, 2, and 3	3 „	1 0
5.	Paper Hangings	3 „	1 0
6	Carpets, Floor Cloths, and Oil Cloths	3 „	0 10
7.	Shawls (patterns printed, &c., &c)	3 „	1 0
	Ditto do. extended term of 9 months	9 months	0 1
	Shawls (patterns printed, &c , &c) for the whole term of 18 months		0 6
8.	Shawls (not comprised in Class 7)		0 7
9	Yarn, Thread or Warp (printed, &c, &c)	3 years	1 0
10.	Woven Fabrics (patterns printed, &c , &c), except those included in Class 11	9 months	0 1
11.	Woven Fabrics, technically called Furnitures (patterns printed, &c , &c), the repeat of the pattern exceeding 12 inches by 8 inches	3 years	0 1
12.	Woven Fabrics (not comprised in any preceding Class)	3 „	0 5
	Woven Fabrics (not comprised in any preceding Class), Damasks and Figured Quilts	12 months	0 5
	Woven Fabrics (not comprised in any preceding Class), Damasks and Figured Quilts extended term of	12 „	0 5
	Woven Fabrics (not comprised in any preceding Class), Damasks and Figured Quilts whole term of	2 years	0 16
13.	Lace and other articles (not comprised in any preceding Class)	3 „	1 0
		12 months	0 5

TABLE OF FEES

PROVISIONAL REGISTRATION.

Registration in all Classes, One Year	1s. each Design.	
Transfer	5	„
Certifying former Registration (*to Proprietor of Design*)	1	„
Cancellation or Substitution (*according to Decree or Order in Chancery*)	5	„

COMPLETE REGISTRATION.

Registering Designs	Copyright	Fee £ s
Class 1 . . .	5 years each Design	1 0
„ 2	3 ditto „	1 0
„ 3 . . .	ditto „	1 0
„ 4	ditto „	1 0
„ 5	ditto „	0 10
„ 6	ditto „	1 0
„ 7	9 months „	0 1
„ „ extended term of .	ditto „	0 6
„ „ whole term of .	18 months „	0 7
„ 8 . . .	3 years „	1 0
„ 9 . . .	9 months „	0 1
„ 10	3 years „	0 1
„ 11	ditto „	0 5
„ 12	12 months „	0 5
Damasks and Figured Quilts .	ditto „	0 5
Ditto do extended term of	2 years „	0 10
Ditto do whole term of .	3 years „	1 0
„ 13 . . .	12 months „	0 5
In all the 13 Classes (Copyright not extended)	„	7 0
In Classes 1, 2, 3, and 4, inclusive, do	„	5 0
In Classes 5 to 13, inclusive, do.	„	3 0

REGISTRATION OF SCULPTURE :—

	Fee £ s
Each Design	5 0

COMPLETE REGISTRATION AND REGISTRATION OF SCULPTURE —

Transfer	Same as Registration Fee, but for Sculpture each Design . .	1 0
Certifying former Registration (*to Proprietor*) .		
Cancellation or Substitution (*according to decree, or order in Chancery*) .		

INSPECTIONS, &c , OF PROVISIONAL AND COMPLETE REGISTRATIONS AND SCULPTURE.—

	£ s
Search	0 2
Inspection of all the Designs of which the Copyright has expired, each quarter or part of quarter of an hour, each Class	0 1
Taking Copies of Expired Designs, for each hour or part of an hour, each Copy .	0 1
Taking Copies of Unexpired Designs (*according to Judge's order*), for each hour or part of an hour, each Copy	0 2

Office Copies of a Design will be charged for according to the nature of the Design

By the Designs Act of 1850, a protection of a nature similar to that granted for Designs for Ornamenting Articles of Manufacture by the Act of 1842, is granted to Sculptures, Models, Copies, or Casts of the whole or part of the human figure, or of animals, for the term or unexpired part of the term, during which Copyright in such Sculpture, Models, Copies, or Casts may or shall exist under the Sculpture Copyright Acts, and the Fee for Registering the same is 5*l*

To obtain this protection it is necessary—

    1st. That the Design *should not have been published*, either within the United Kingdom of Great Britain and Ireland, or elsewhere, previous to its Registration

    2nd. That after PROVISIONAL REGISTRATION, every Copy of the Design *should have thereon, or attached thereto*, the words 'Provisionally Registered,' and the Date of Registration.

    3rd. That after COMPLETE REGISTRATION, every Article of Manufacture published by the Proprietor thereof, to which such Design shall have been applied, *should have thereon, or attached thereto*, a particular MARK, which will be exhibited on the Certificate of Registration.

    4th. That after Registration of SCULPTURE every copy thereof *should have thereon, or attached thereto*, the word 'Registered,' and the Date of Registration.

These Conditions being observed, the right of the Proprietor is protected from piracy by a penalty of from 5*l* to 30*l* for each offence, each individual illegal publication or sale of a Design constituting a separate offence This Penalty may be recovered by the aggrieved party either by action in the superior or County Courts, or by a summary proceeding before two Magistrates

If a Design be executed by the Author on behalf of another Person, for a valuable consideration, the latter is entitled to be registered as the Proprietor thereof, and any person purchasing either the exclusive or partial right to use the Design, is in the same way equally entitled to be registered, and for the purpose of facilitating the transfer thereof a short form (copies of which may be procured at the Designs Office) is given in the Act.

USEFUL.

COPYRIGHT OF DESIGNS FOR ARTICLES OF UTILITY.

By PROVISIONAL Registration under the Designs Act, 1850 (13 & 14 Vict. c 104), a Copyright for One Year (which may be further extended for Six Months by order of the Board of Trade),

FOLLOWING
PAGE(S)
MUTILATED

is given to the Author or Proprietor of any New or Original Design *for the* SHAPE *or* CONFIGURATION *either of the whole or of part of any Article of Manufacture, such* SHAPE *or* CONFIGURATION *having reference to some* PURPOSE *of* UTILITY, whether such Article be made in Metal or any other Substance During such terms the Proprietor of the Design may sell the right to apply the same to an article of manufacture, *but must not, under the penalty of nullifying the Copyright, sell any article with the Design applied thereto, until after Complete Registration, which must be effected prior to the expiration of the Provisional Registration*

By COMPLETE Registration under the Designs Act, 1843 (6 & 7 Vict c 65), a Copyright of THREE YEARS is given to the Author or Proprietor of any new or original design *for the* SHAPE *or* CONFIGURATION *either of the whole or of part of any Article of Manufacture, such* SHAPE *or* CONFIGURATION *having reference to some* PURPOSE *of* UTILITY, whether such Article be made in Metal or any other Substance.

To obtain this protection it is necessary—

    1st That the Design should *not have been published* either within the United Kingdom of Great Britain and Ireland, or elsewhere, previous to its Registration

    2nd That after Registration, or Provisional Registration, every Article of Manufacture made according to such Design, or to which such Design is applied, should have upon it the word ' REGISTERED,' or ' PROVISIONALLY REGISTERED,' *with the Date of Registration*

In case of Piracy of a Design so Registered, the same remedies are given, and the same penalties imposed (from 5*l* to 30*l* for each offence), as under the Ornamental Designs Act, 1842 (5 & 6 Vict c. 100), and all the provisions contained in the latter Act relating to the Transfer of *Ornamental* Designs, in case of purchase or devolution of a Copyright, are made applicable to those *Useful* Designs registered under these Acts

In addition to this, a *Penalty of not more than 5l nor less than 1l is imposed* upon all persons marking, selling, or advertising for sale any article as ' Registered,' unless the Design for such Article has been registered under one of the *above-mentioned Acts.*

DIRECTIONS FOR REGISTERING.

PERSONS proposing to Register a Design for purposes of utility must bring or send to the Designs Office TWO EXACTLY SIMILAR Drawings or Prints thereof, made on a proper geometric scale, marked with letters, figures, or colours, to be referred to as hereinafter mentioned, together with the following

PARTICULARS.

    1st. THE TITLE of the Design
    2nd THE NAME AND ADDRESS of the Proprietor or Proprietors, or the Title of the Firm under which he

or they may be trading, together with their Place of abode, or Place of carrying on business, distinctly written or printed.

3rd A STATEMENT in the following Form, viz. ' The Purpose of Utility to which the Shape or Configuration of (the New Parts of) this Design has reference is' &c., &c.

4th A DESCRIPTION to render the same intelligible, distinguishing the several parts of the Design by reference to letters, figures, or colours.

Note.—No description of the parts of the drawings which are old will be admitted, except such as may be absolutely necessary to render the purpose of utility of the shape of the new parts intelligible.

5th. A SHORT AND DISTINCT STATEMENT of such part or parts (if any) as shall not be new or original, as regards the shape or configuration thereof, which must be in the following form, viz '—(if the whole Design is New, state)—' The whole of this Design is new in so far as regards the shape or configuration thereof.' (If there are any Old Parts, state)—' The Parts of this Design which are not new or original, as regards the shape or configuration thereof, are those marked (A B C, &c), or coloured (blue, green, &c)'

Note.—The above particulars must be given in the aforesaid order under their several heads, and in distinct and separate paragraphs, which must be strictly confined to what is here required to be contained in each.

Each drawing or print, together with the whole of the above particulars, must be drawn, written, or printed on one side of a sheet of paper or parchment, not exceeding in size 24 inches by 15 inches, and on one of the said sheets, on the same side on which are the said drawings and particulars, there must be left two blank spaces each of the size of 6 inches by 4 inches, for the Certificates of Registration.

The above Regulations, which have been made by the Board of Trade, must be strictly complied with

NOTICE.

Parties are strongly recommended to read the Act before determining to register their Designs, in order that they may be satisfied as to the nature, extent, and comprehensiveness of the protection afforded by it, and further, that they come within the meaning and scope of the Acts, of which facts the Registration will not constitute any guarantee.

Specimen Form.

(Title of the Design)

....

(Name of the Proprietor.)

....

(Address of the Proprietor)

....

(The Drawing to be inserted here)

(Statement of Utility)

The purpose of Utility to which the Shape or Configuration of (the New Parts of) this Design has reference is ....

(Description)

(If the whole Design is New, state—)

The whole of this Design is New in so far as regards the Shape or Configuration thereof

(If there are any Old Parts, state—)

The Parts of this Design which are not New or original as regards the Shape or Configuration thereof, are those marked, &c &c

24 inches

6 in
4 in

6 in
4 in

15 inches

TABLES OF FEES.

PROVISIONAL REGISTRATION.

	Fee s
Registering Design	10
Certifying former Registration (*to Proprietor of Design*) .	5
Registering and Certifying Transfer	10
Cancellation or Substitution (*according to decree or order in Chancery*)	5
Extension of Copyright	10

COMPLETE REGISTRATION.

	Stamp £	Fee £	Total £
Registering Design	5	5	10
Certifying former Registration (*to Proprietor of Design*)	5	1	6
Registering and Certifying Transfer . . .	5	1	6
Cancellation or Substitution (*according to decree or order in Chancery*) . . . . —	—	1	1

INSPECTIONS, ETC., OF PROVISIONAL AND COMPLETE REGISTRATIONS.

	Fee s.
Inspecting Register, Index of Titles and Names, for each quarter or part of quarter of an hour . .	1
Inspecting Designs, unexpired Copyright, each Design, ditto, ditto	2
Inspecting Designs, expired Copyright, each volume, ditto, ditto	1
Inspecting the Register of Inventions, under the 'Protection of Inventions Act, 1851,' ditto, ditto .	1
Taking Copies of Designs, unexpired Copyright (*according to Judge's order*), for each hour or part of an hour, each Copy	2
Taking Copies of Designs, expired Copyright, for each hour or part of an hour, each Copy	1

Office Copies of a Design will be charged for according to the nature of the Design.

As the Designs Acts, 1843 (6 & 7 Vict c 65), and 1850 (13 & 14 Vict c. 104), give protection only to the *shape or configuration* of articles of utility (and not to any *mechanical action, principle, contrivance, application, or adaptation* (except in so far as these may be dependent upon, and inseparable from, the shape or configuration), *or to the material of which the article may be com-*

posed), no Design will be registered, the Description of, or State-ment respecting which, shall contain any wording suggestive of the Registration being for any such mechanical action, principle, contrivance, application, or adaptation, or for the material of which the article may be composed.

With this exception and those mentioned in the Act, 1843, Clause IX., *all* Designs, the drawings and descriptions of which are properly prepared and made out, will, on payment of the proper fee, be registered *without reference to the nature or extent of the Copyright sought to be thereby acquired*; as Proprietors of Designs must use their own discretion in judging whether or not the Design proposed for Registration be for the shape or configuration of an article of utility coming within the meaning and scope of the Acts above mentioned

After the Design has been registered, one of the drawings will be filed at the Office, and the other returned to the Proprietor duly stamped and certified.

Parties bringing Designs to this Office before half-past 12 o'clock, will be informed after 3 o'clock the same day whether they are approved of; and if so, they will be registered the following day, and, provided the fee has been paid before half-past 1 o'clock on such day, the certified copies will be ready for delivery after 3 o'clock on that subsequent.

An acknowledgment of its receipt will be delivered, on pay-ment of the fees, to the person bringing a Design, and NO certified copy of a Design will be returned, except to the bearer of this acknowledgment, which must be produced on application at the Office for the certified copy, and given in exchange for the same.

TRANSFERS.

In case of the *transfer* of a COMPLETELY REGISTERED DESIGN, a copy thereof [or the certified copy, provided there is space sufficient thereon for the Certificate], made on one sheet of paper, with a blank space left for the Certificate, must be transmitted to the Registrar, together with the *forms* of application (which may be procured at the Office), properly filled up and signed, the transfer will then be registered, and the certified copy returned

For the Transfer of a Design Provisionally Registered, the new copy will not be required, but the certified copy must be trans-mitted to the Registrar with the above-mentioned *forms*.

EXTENSION OF COPYRIGHT.

The Copyright may be extended in certain cases in Provisional Registration, for a term not exceeding the additional term of Six Months as the Board of Trade may think fit

In case of extension, the certified copy, together with the proper fee, should be transmitted to the Designs Office for Registration, *prior to the expiration of the existing Copyright*

Persons bringing Designs to be registered, on delivering them

g

designs, and ON examining their Certificates, previous to leaving the Office, *must see that the Titles, Names, &c., are correct, as no error can afterwards be rectified.*

SEARCHES.

An Index of the Titles and Names of the Proprietors of all the registered Designs for Articles of Utility is kept at the Designs Office, and may be inspected by any person, and extracts made from it.

Designs, the Copyright of which is *expired*, may be inspected and copied at the Office.

Designs, the Copyright of which is *unexpired*, may also be inspected, *but not copied*, except according to a Judge's order.

ALL COMMUNICATIONS FOR THE REGISTRATION OF DESIGNS, either for ornamental or useful purposes, may be made either through the General Post, directed to 'The Registrar of Designs, Designs Office, London,' or by any other mode of conveyance, and provided the carriage be paid, and the proper fees, or a Post Office Order for the amount, PAYABLE AT THE POST OFFICE, CHARING CROSS, to J. H BOWEN, ESQ., be enclosed, the Designs will be duly registered, and the Certified Copies returned to the Proprietor, free of expense.

Postage Stamps, Orders upon Bankers or other Persons, Scotch and Country Bank Notes, and light gold, cannot be received in payment of fees.

The DESIGNS OFFICE, No 1, WHITEHALL, is open every day, between the hours of 10 in the Morning and 4 in the Afternoon, during which time enquiries and searches may be made   Designs and Transfers are registered from 11 until 3.

Directions for Registering Ornamental Designs may also be procured at the Office.

By Order of the Registrar,

J. H. BOWEN, *Chief Clerk*

INDEX.

—◆—

A

M

MAGAZINE (*See* ENCYCLOPÆDIA.)

MANUSCRIPT. (*See* COPYRIGHT-BEFORE-PUBLICATION.)
    mutilation of, 16

MAP (*See* BOOK)
    is 'book' within 5 & 6 Vict. c. 45, 40

MARK
    on registered design, 237

MISTAKES,
    identity of, on question of piracy, 120

MUSICAL COMPOSITION (*See* BOOK)
    copyright in, 48—181
    piracy of, 130

MUSICAL PERFORMANCE,
    copyright in, 182
        regulation of, 182
        nature of, 183
        duration of, 184
        registry of, 184
        to whom it may belong, 185
        assignment of, 186
        infringement of, 187

N

NAME
    on copyright engraving, 211
NOTICE
    to desist from piracy of design, 240
NOVELTY
    of design, 231

O

OBJECTIONS
    in action under 5 & 6 Vict. c. 45, ss. 15, 16, 144
OBSCENE WORK. (*See* CRIMINAL WORKS.)

V

W

LONDON
PRINTED BY SPOTTISWOODE AND CO
NEW STREET SQUARE

h

VALUABLE LAW WORKS

PUBLISHED BY

V. & R. STEVENS, SONS, & HAYNES,

Law Booksellers and Publishers,

26 BELL YARD, LINCOLN'S INN.

——∘∘⁚∘⁚∘∘——

PHILLIPS ON THE LAW OF COPYRIGHT.

Comprising the Statutes and Reported Decisions of the Courts of Law and Equity relating to Copyright in its various branches. 1 vol. 8vo (*Now ready*)

LEVI'S PRINCIPLES OF BRITISH COMMERCIAL LAW.—SECOND EDITION.

With Commentaries, comprising Illustrations from the Codes and Laws of Commerce of the Principal Mercantile Countries By LEONE LEVI, of Lincoln's Inn, Barrister at Law, and Professor of Commercial Law in King's College, London. 2 vols royal 8vo (*Nearly ready*)

COOKE ON INCLOSURE OF COMMONS, 1864.

The Acts for facilitating the Inclosure of Commons in England and Wales, with a Treatise on the Law of Rights of Commons, in reference to these Acts, &c. &c With Forms as settled by the Inclosure Commissioners. By G WINGROVE COOKE, Esq, Barrister-at-Law Fourth Edition 12mo. (*Nearly ready*)

COOKE ON COPYHOLD ENFRANCHISEMENT, 1864.

With the Forms authorised by the Copyhold Commission and all the Statutes By G WINGROVE COOKE, Esq, Barrister-at-Law Third Edition. By FRANCIS HOUSMAN, Esq, Barrister-at-Law. 12mo. (*In the press*)

WHARTON'S LAW LEXICON. THIRD EDITION, 1864

Or, Dictionary of Jurisprudence, explaining all the Technical Words and Phrases employed in the several Departments of English Law, including also the various Legal Terms used in Commercial Transactions, together with an Explanatory as well as Literal Translation of the Latin Maxims contained in the Writings of the Ancient and Modern Commentators Second Edition Royal 8vo greatly improved and enlarged (*Nearly ready*)

WHARTON'S ARTICLED CLERKS' MANUAL, 1864.

Ninth Edition By C H. ANDERSON, Esq, Solicitor. (*In the press*)

PRIDEAUX'S PRECEDENTS IN CONVEYANCING. FOURTH EDITION.

With Dissertations on its Law and Practice By FREDERICK PRIDEAUX, Esq, Barrister-at Law The Fourth Edition, considerably enlarged and improved, by FREDERICK PRIDEAUX and J WHITCOMBE, Esqs, Barristers at Law In 2 vols royal 8vo. (*Nearly ready.*)

SMITH'S (JOHN W.) MERCANTILE LAW.

A Compendium of Mercantile Law By the late JOHN WILLIAM SMITH, Esq. Seventh Edition By G. M. DOWDESWELL, Esq, Barrister-at Law 1 vol royal 8vo. (*Nearly ready*)

MORGAN'S CHANCERY ACTS AND ORDERS. THIRD EDIT. 1862.

The Statutes, General Orders, and Regulations relating to the Practice, Pleading, and Jurisdiction of the Court of Chancery, with copious Notes, containing a Summary of every reported Decision thereon By GEORGE OSBORNE MORGAN, M A, of Lincoln's Inn, Barrister at-Law. Third Edition, considerably enlarged. 1 vol 8vo, cloth Price 28s.

'No labour has been spared to make the work as complete and accurate as possible With its elaborate index and marginal references, it is impossible to over-estimate its value as a manual of general practice '—LAW MAGAZINE, May 1862.

SHELFORD'S REAL PROPERTY STATUTES

Passed in the Reigns of William IV. and Victoria, with copious Notes of decided Cases, and Forms of Deeds. By LEONARD SHELFORD, Esq   Seventh Edition, 1863, in 8vo   Price 30s. cloth.

CHITTY'S ARCHBOLD'S PRACTICE. ELEVENTH EDIT. 1862.

Practice of the Court of Queen's Bench in Personal Actions and Ejectments   By THOMAS CHITTY, Esq   Including the Practice of the Courts of the Common Pleas and Exchequer. The Eleventh Edition   By SAMUEL PRENTICE, Esq , Barrister-at-Law.   In 2 vols. royal 12mo   Price £2 12s. 6d. cloth.

CHITTY'S FORMS. NINTH EDITION, 1862.

Forms of Practical Proceedings in the Courts of Queen's Bench, Common Pleas, and Exchequer of Pleas. With Notes and Observations thereon. Ninth Edition   By THOMAS CHITTY, Esq. In royal 12mo   Price £1 11s 6d cloth

ROSCOE'S CRIMINAL EVIDENCE, 1862. ·

Roscoe's Digest of the Law of Evidence in Criminal Cases. Sixth Edition, with considerable Additions   By D POWER, Esq , Barrister-at Law.   In royal 12mo. Price 30s. cloth.

ROSCOE'S NISI PRIUS EVIDENCE, 1861.

Roscoe's Digest of the Law of Evidence on the Trial of Actions at Nisi Prius   Tenth Edition   Revised and enlarged by EDWARD SMIRKE, Esq , Barrister at-Law. 1 vol thick royal 12mo. Price 31s 6d cloth.

GREENHOW'S SHIPPING LAW MANUAL, 1863.

A Concise Treatise on the Law governing the Interests of Ship Owners, Merchants, Masters, Seamen, and other persons connected with British Ships, together with the Acts of Parliament, Forms, and Precedents relative to the subject, being specially intended for popular use in Seaport Towns   By WILLIAM THOMAS GREENHOW, of the Middle Temple, Esq , Barrister at-Law. 8vo   Price 20s cloth.

GOUGH'S LAND REGISTRY AND DECLARATION OF TITLES ACTS, 1862.

The Acts to Facilitate the Proof of Title to, and the Conveyance of Real Estates, and for Obtaining a Declaration of Title (25 & 26 Vict cc. 53 and 67). Together with the General Orders, Table of Costs, and Forms for carrying the first-named Act into effect; also an Introduction, Practical Notes, and a full Index. By HENRY GOUGH, Esq , Barrister-at-Law   1 vol 12mo   Price 5s. 6d cloth

SHELFORD'S LAW OF HIGHWAYS, 1862.

The Law of Highways ; including the General Highway Acts for England and Wales, and other Statutes, with copious Notes of the Decisions thereon ; with Forms   The Third Edition, corrected and enlarged   By LEONARD SHELFORD, Esq , of the Middle Temple, Barrister-at-Law. 1 vol 12mo   Price 13s cloth.

WOODFALL'S LAW OF LANDLORD AND TENANT, 1863.

A Practical Treatise on the Law of Landlord and Tenant, with a Full Collection of Precedents and Forms of Procedure   By S. B HARRISON, Esq. Eighth Edition   By W. R. COLE, Esq , Barrister-at-Law. In 1 thick vol. royal 8vo. Price £1 15s. cloth.

STONE'S PETTY SESSIONS PRACTICE, 1863.

With the Statutes, a List of Summary Convictions, and an Appendix of Forms. Seventh Edition, with a Supplement incorporating the Changes made by the Criminal Law Consolidation Acts   By THOMAS BELL, and LEWIS W CAVE, of the Inner Temple, Esqrs Barristers-at-Law   12mo   Price 18s. cloth

⁎ The Supplement may be had separately, price 3s. boards

' It is remarkable for a rare combination of conciseness and clearness in the composition, which have recommended it to magistrates who have not been educated as lawyers, and to whom therefore the books written for the use of lawyers are often obscure by reason of their technicalities   The present editors have preserved this characteristic of Mr Stone's volume in their own abundant additions to it.'—LAW TIMES.

GREENWOOD'S MANUAL OF CONVEYANCING.

A Manual of the Practice of Conveyancing, showing the present Practice relating to the daily routine of Conveyancing in Solicitors' Offices. To which are added, Concise Common Forms and Precedents in Conveyancing ; Conditions of Sales, Conveyances, and all other Assurances in constant use   By G. W. GREENWOOD   Second Edition, enlarged. In 12mo   Price 10s. 6d. cloth   1858.